TRANSLATIONS OF AUTHORITY IN MEDIEVAL ENGLISH LITERATURE

In *Translations of Authority in Medieval English Literature*, leading critic Alastair Minnis presents the fruits of a long-term engagement with the ways in which crucial ideological issues were deployed in vernacular texts. The concept of the vernacular is seen as possessing a value far beyond the category of language – as encompassing popular beliefs and practices which could either confirm or contest those authorized by church and state institutions.

Minnis addresses the crisis for vernacular translation precipitated by the Lollard heresy; the minimal engagement with Nominalism in late fourteenth-century poetry; Langland's views on indulgences; the heretical theology of Walter Brut; Margery Kempe's self-promoting Biblical exegesis; and Chaucer's tales of suspicious saints and risible relics. These discussions disclose different aspects of 'vernacularity', enabling a fuller understanding of its complexity and potency.

ALASTAIR MINNIS is the Douglas Tracy Smith Professor of English at Yale University. Recent authored works include *Magister Amoris: The 'Roman de la Rose' and Vernacular Hermeneutics* (2001), and *Fallible Authors: Chaucer's Pardoner and Wife of Bath* (2007). In addition, he has edited or co-edited fourteen other books, including (with Ian Johnson) *The Cambridge History of Literary Criticism*, II: *The Middle Ages* (2005). He is also the General Editor of Cambridge Studies in Medieval Literature.

TRANSLATIONS OF AUTHORITY IN MEDIEVAL ENGLISH LITERATURE

Valuing the Vernacular

ALASTAIR MINNIS

CAMBRIDGE UNIVERSITY PRESS
Cambridge, New York, Melbourne, Madrid, Cape Town, Singapore, São Paulo, Delhi

Cambridge University Press
The Edinburgh Building, Cambridge, CB2 8RU, UK

Published in the United States of America by Cambridge University Press, New York

www.cambridge.org
Information on this title: www.cambridge.org/9780521515948

First published 2009

Printed in the United Kingdom at the University Press, Cambridge

A catalogue record for this publication is available from the British Library

Library of Congress Cataloguing in Publication data
Minnis, A. J. (Alastair J.)
Translations of authority in medieval English literature : valuing the vernacular / Alastair Minnis.
p.   cm.
Includes bibliographical references and index.
ISBN 978-0-521-51594-8 (hardback)
1. English literature – Middle English, 1100–1500 – Criticism, Textual.   2. English literature –
Middle English, 1100–1500 – History and criticism.   3. Transmission of texts – England – History –
To 1500.   4. Authority in literature.   5. Translating and interpreting – Political aspects – England –
History – To 1500.   6. Latin language – Translating into English – History – To 1500.   7. Politics
and literature – England – History – To 1500.   I. Title.

PR275.T45M56   2009
820.9'001 – dc22   2008039996

ISBN 978-0-521-51594-8 hardback

To Jacques, with affection and admiration

Contents

vii

Preface

I thought of three things in writing an extensive introduction and a
series of notes. It was a literary joke – hence I referred twice in *Slave
Song* to T. S. Eliot, because Eliot had also joked and provided a kind
of spoof gloss to *The Waste Land*. On another level, we had been
arguing for a long time that Creole was a distinctive language. We
made a lot of politics out of that. It was part of the nationalism in
the 60s. We had our own airline, environment, landscape, and fruits,
so we should have our own language. If we were going to take that
seriously we should provide translations to our poems. But the third
reason is the most serious . . . I wanted to question the relationship
between the work of art and the critical industry that arises because
of that work of art.[1]

Here the Guyanan British poet David Dabydeen is explaining why, in *Slave
Song* (1984), he provided his Creole poems with translations and a commentary (comprising an introduction and notes) in Standard English. His
intentions would have been utterly comprehensible to those fourteenth-
century Italian writers who sought to establish an illustrious vernacular in
face of the hegemony of Latin, which in their day enjoyed the prestigious
position occupied by Standard English in Dabydeen's Britain. I am thinking not only of Dante (who managed to praise the vernacular in Latin and
Latin in the vernacular) but also of Francesco da Barberino (1264–1348),
lawyer and lover of Provençal poetry. Francesco's *Documenti d'Amore* is,
like Dabydeen's *Slave Song*, a tripartite work, wherein the central text, an
Italian poem, is accompanied by a literal Latin translation and a substantial
Latin commentary.[2] Thus Dabydeen's *confrères*, in part fired by the Italian
city-state version of 'nationalism', exploited the interpretive conventions
of the 'critical industry' to aggrandize their mother language. Thereby the
vernacular was valued.

In late medieval England, however, there appear to have been no formal hermeneutic enterprises of that kind, or any extensive 'commentated

translations' of authoritative works, whether secular and sacred, on the model of those patronized by King Charles V of France. Such Middle English hermeneutic activity as did exist, and has survived, was largely of Lollard origin, or at least susceptible of infiltration by Lollardy. Perhaps it was fears of association with the 'English heresy' that inhibited the development of a substantial orthodox commentary-tradition in Middle English. Despite such fears, however, Middle English hermeneutics flourished by other means and in other forms – witness William Langland's attempts to find *sensus spiritualis* in the system of issuing indulgences or 'pardons', as demotically understood and practised, and Margery Kempe's allegorical constructions of female authority from quite unpromising materials, Biblical texts which threatened to keep women confined and contained within material marriage. In confronting such issues, along with those relating to the salvation of 'virtuous heathen' who lacked the benefit of conventional baptism, Middle English carried on the business of Latin intellectual culture. Here is a veritable *translatio auctoritatis* – a translation of authoritative discourse and methodology into the 'vulgar' tongue.

However, the relationship between Latin and vernacular posited in this book is more elaborate than that. It includes the notion of vernacular (in the sense of unofficial, non-institutional, disordered) theology being pursued in Latin, as professional theologians – taking their cue from the Lollard layman Walter Brut, who himself could write Latin – engaged in non-orthodox exegesis in the service of orthodoxy. Further, it allows for a concept of vernacular culture which transcends language to encompass acts of cultural transfer, negotiation, appropriation, and indeed resistance – within which wider context language-transfer could play a major role, but not necessarily. David Dabydeen declared himself attracted by the powerful, visceral 'vulgarity' of the Creole language as used by Caribbean canecutters, which was the linguistic inspiration of *Slave Song*, but he looked beyond language to 'the vulgarity of the people, the vulgarity of their way of life'.[3] And that is what I attempt to do in my final chapter, where, in respect of the cult of saints, 'the informal, colloquial or distinctive' religiosity of the so-called 'common people' is investigated, though the caveat must be entered that the clergy often participated in, promoted, and/or sought to control the vernacular practices which are my subject. Here, taking my point of departure from Chaucer's Pardoner, I try to access demotic activities and attitudes through medieval humour, and seek means of understanding medieval humour in demotic activities and attitudes.

In sum, *Translations of Authority* addresses the value and status of 'the vernacular' in the translation of, and engagement with, authoritative

Latin learning. Further, it challenges the appropriateness of the distinction between Latin and vernacular (can Medieval Latin itself not be deemed a vernacular or a group of vernaculars?), and proposes that the very term 'vernacular' has a value which goes far beyond the category of language, to encompass popular cultural beliefs and practices which engaged in complex relationships with those authorized by church and state institutions. This book comprises a series of essays which address those interconnecting topics, four which have been published before – though in rather different (and shorter) versions, for I have substantially revised them for inclusion in this volume. I am grateful to the following presses for allowing me to re-use the relevant materials.

'Absent Glosses; A Crisis of Vernacular Commentary in Late-Medieval England?', in William Fahrenbach (ed.), *Essays in Medieval Studies, 20: Texts and Commentaries. The 2003 Proceedings of the Illinois Medieval Association* (published by the West Virginia University Press for the Illinois Medieval Association, 2004), pp. 1–17.

'Looking for a Sign: The Quest for Nominalism in Chaucer and Langland', in Alastair Minnis, C. C. Morse and T. Turville-Petre (eds.), *Essays on Ricardian Literature in Honour of J. A. Burrow* (Oxford: Clarendon Press, 1997), pp. 142–78.

'Piers' Protean Pardon: The Letter and Spirit of Langland's Theology of Indulgences', in Anne Marie D'Arcy and Alan J. Fletcher (eds.), *Studies in Late Medieval and Early Renaissance Texts in Honour of John Scattergood* (Dublin: Four Courts, 2005), pp. 218–40.

'Making Bodies: Confection and Conception in Walter Brut's Vernacular Theology', *The Medieval Translator*, 8 (2003), 1–16. Edited by R. Voaden, René Tixier, Teresa Sanchez Roura, and Jenny Rebecca Rytting.

The present compilation would have been impossible without the good offices of Cambridge University Press. I owe a special debt to Dr Linda Bree, with whom I have had the pleasure of working, mainly on Cambridge Studies in Medieval Literature, for around nine years. Warm thanks are also due to the following scholars who advised and inspired me as I mulled over the fascinating, and sometimes bizarre, medieval problems and puzzles which are presented below: David Aers, J. W. Binns, Sarah Blick, J. A. Burrow, Rita Copeland, William J. Courtenay, Mary Dove, W. G. East, George Ferzoco, Vincent Gillespie, Richard Firth Green, Ralph Hanna III, Anne Hudson, Ian Johnson, Richard Kieckhefer, Gary Macy, Robyn Malo, Derek Pearsall, Stephen Penn, Jim Rhodes, Robert Shaffern, James Simpson, Robert N. Swanson, Michael Vandussen, David Wallace, Nicholas Watson, and Roger Wright. When I was writing Chapter 6,

Sharon Collingwood helped me untangle some knotty French passages, and Dr Sarah Minnis explained the medical complexities of the urogenital tract. Katherine Minnis made me aware of the self-exegesis of David Dabydeen with which this Preface began. During my time as a Lilly Fellow in Religion and the Humanities at the National Humanities Center (January – May 2006) much progress was made on essential revision and fresh research. The incomparable library resources and research support provided by Yale University provided ideal conditions in which to complete the project.

I dedicate this book, with affection and admiration, to Jacques Berthoud, who was head of the Department of English and Related Literature at the University of York when I was appointed Professor of Medieval Literature there in 1987. (Indeed, Jacques chaired the Department for some seventeen years – no small feat.) It was during my time at York that I first got interested in many of the issues which are discussed below. And I want to pay tribute to Jacques for all he did to make its university a place wherein creative thought and teaching were possible. While not suffering foolish things gladly, Jacques ensured that the English Department thrived within the enervating audit culture which was a consequence of Thatcherism. Yet he retained and affirmed his humanist vision of the importance of literature within the cultural life of the nation – and indeed of all nations, for here is an ardent internationalist. Thank you, Jacques, for everything you taught me.

Abbreviations

Alberti opera	St Albert the Great, *Opera omnia*, ed. A. Borgnet (Paris, 1890–9)
Aquinas, *Summa theologiae*	St Thomas Aquinas, *Summa theologiae,* Blackfriars edn (London and New York, 1964–81)
Aquinatis opera	St Thomas Aquinas, *Opera omnia* (Parma, 1852–72)
Biblia glossata	*Biblia sacra cum Glossa ordinaria et Postilla Nicolai Lyrani* (Antwerp, 1617)
BMK	*The Book of Margery Kempe*, ed. Barry Windeatt (Cambridge, 2004); book and chapter numbers are followed by Windeatt's page-numbering
Bonaventurae opera	St Bonaventure, *Opera omnia* (Quaracchi, 1882–1902)
Brepols Database of Latin Dictionaries	Brepols Database of Latin Dictionaries, consulted online at http://clt.brepolis.net/dld/start.asp?sOwner=menu
Bynum, *Wonderful Blood*	Caroline Walker Bynum, *Wonderful Blood: Theology and Practice in Late Medieval Northern Germany and Beyond* (Philadelphia, 2007)
CCCM	Corpus Christianorum continuatio medievalis

CHLCMA	Alastair Minnis and Ian Johnson (eds.), *The Cambridge History of Literary Criticism*, II: *The Middle Ages* (Cambridge, 2005)
ChR	*The Chaucer Review*
EETS OS	Early English Text Society, Original Series
EETS ES	Early English Text Society, Extra Series
Hudson, *Lollards and their Books*	Anne Hudson, *Lollards and their Books* (London and Ronceverte, 1985)
Hudson, *Premature Reformation*	Anne Hudson, *The Premature Reformation: Wycliffite Texts and Lollard History* (Oxford, 1988)
Kerby-Fulton, *Books under Suspicion*	Kathryn Kerby-Fulton, *Books under Suspicion: Censorship and Tolerance of Revelatory Writing in Late-Medieval England* (Notre Dame, IN, 2006)
Levy (ed.), *Companion to Wyclif*	Ian Christopher Levy (ed.), *A Companion to John Wyclif, Late Medieval Theologian* (Leiden and Boston, 2006)
MED	*Middle English Dictionary*, ed. Hans Kurath, Sherman M. Kuhn *et al.*, in *Middle English Compendium* (Ann Arbor, MI, 1998–), online edition, http://ets.umdl.umich.edu/m/med/
Migne, *PL*	*Patrologia Latina*, ed. J. P. Migne (Paris, 1841–61)
Minnis, *Fallible Authors*	Alastair Minnis, *Fallible Authors: Chaucer's Pardoner and Wife of Bath* (Philadelphia, 2007)
Netter, *Doctrinale*	Thomas Netter, *Doctrinale antiquitatum fidei catholicae ecclesiae* (Venice, 1757–59; repr. Farnborough, Hants., 1967)
OLD	*Oxford Latin Dictionary*, combined edn, repr. with corrections, ed. P. G. W. Glare (Oxford, 1996)

Oxford Reference Online	Oxford Reference Online, consulted at http://www.oxfordreference.com/views/GLOBAL.html
Registrum Johannis Trefnant, ed. Capes	*Registrum Johannis Trefnant*, ed. W. W. Capes, Canterbury and York Series, 20 (London, 1916)
SAC	*Studies in the Age of Chaucer*
Vincent, *The Holy Blood*	Nicholas Vincent, *The Holy Blood: King Henry III and the Westminster Blood Relic* (Cambridge, 2001)

All Chaucer references are to *The Riverside Chaucer*, general ed. Larry D. Benson (Oxford, 1988). For the B-text of *Piers Plowman* I have used the edition of A. V. C. Schmidt (London and Vermont, 1995); for the C-text, Derek Pearsall's edition (Exeter, 1994). References to the *Gawain/Pearl*-poet are to *The Poems of the 'Pearl' Manuscript*, ed. Malcolm Andrew and Ronald Waldron (Exeter, 1987). My translations of Biblical quotations by medieval authors generally follow Challoner's revision of the Douay Bible, as being close to the Latin Vulgate, but where a quotation differs markedly from the accepted Vulgate text, or where I am using a modern translation of the medieval text in question, I have followed the variant.

Introduction: valuing the vernacular

Vulgo – ablativus ponitur adverbialiter – .i. ubique *partout* .i. *quemu-nement, publiquement* vel per vulgum .i. inordinate, incondite, vulgar-iter. Vulgaris et hoc .gare – .i. popularis, publicus, communis, mani-festus .i. *publiques, quemuns*. Vulgariter – adverbium – *populairement, publiquement*. Vulgaritas .tatis – .i. popularitas, communitas vel pub-licatio, manifestatio . . . Vulgo .gas .gatum – .i. publicare, manifestare .i. *publier, manifester*. Vulgatus .a .um – .i. publicatus, manifestatus.[1]

These definitions of terms relating to 'vulgarity' and the 'vulgar' are taken from the learned Latin–French dictionary which Firmin Le Ver compiled at the Carthusian house of St Honoré at Thuison, near Abbeville, in the first half of the fifteenth century. Public, popular, common, manifest . . . such are the concepts deemed crucial here. *Publicus* should be understood as appertaining to people in general (*ad omnes generaliter*),[2] while *popularis* has the sense of 'belonging to or fit for the common people', 'available to, directed towards the whole community, public'.[3] *Publicatio* has the pre-print culture sense of the transmission of information into 'a public sphere of discussion, debate, news, gossip, and rumour, in which things were generally spoken of and generally known'.[4] The various ways in which these ideas were negotiated in different medieval European languages (in official, learned Latin and in demotic 'vulgars' or vernaculars)[5] and in both 'high' and 'low' cultural situations, are the subject of this book. That is to say, 'vernacular' will be deployed in its fullest, richest sense, to encompass acts of cultural transmission and negotiation (in which translation from one language to another may play a major part, but not inevitably). By such a procedure I hope to access some of the ways in which authority was 'translated', appropriated, disposed, exploited, and indeed challenged by Middle English literature. Each of the following chapters is an essay in the politics of *translatio auctoritatis*.

'Le latin n'est si entendible ne si commun que le language maternel', remarks Jacques Bauchant, commissioned by King Charles V to translate

Elisabeth of Schönau's treatises into French. These works will help Charles, Jacques assures him, 'vostre peuple gouverner et entroduire en science et en bonns meurs par exemple de bonne et ordenee vie'.[6] Jacques was one among many scholarly translators who served the pedagogic and political ambitions of Charles V. The king commanded the production of over thirty translations of authoritative texts, as a crucial 'part of a conscious policy to legitimate the new Valois dynasty',[7] most notable being Nicole Oresme's 'commentated translations' – i.e. vernacular renderings which include scholarly *explication de texte*, largely drawn from Latin commentary tradition but sometimes adding fresh exegesis.[8] Here, then, are 'translations of authority' in several senses of that phrase: renderings in the mother tongue of authoritative Latin *originalia*, writings which had been authorized by no less a personage than King Charles 'the wise', and repositories of authoritative 'scientific' knowledge and ethical doctrine which, having been made common, will enable the populace to live well and be governed well. This vital information is supposedly for the public good and the good of the state – and it certainly does the image of the king much good, since Charles is frequently credited with having initiated the process of *translatio* (here using the term to designate cultural transfer in general, which in this case involved language-transfer in particular). For example, Nicole Oresme praises him for having Aristotle's 'moral books', the *Ethics* and *Politics*, translated into French 'pour le bien commun'.[9] Discourse concerning what Geoffrey Chaucer once termed 'commune profit'[10] is a major feature of many of the translations associated with Charles V. And here 'common' functions as a prestige term, which marks the coherence of a nation, united under God and its king.

Furthermore, that nation has its own language, and French imperial success guarantees the authority of French. 'French is a noble language, used by people of great intelligence, ability and prudence', Nicole Oresme remarks in the introduction to his *Livre de éthiques d'Aristote*.[11] Admittedly, 'Latin is at present (*a present*)' the more perfect and richer language (*plus parfait et plus habondant*). But this state of affairs need not continue. French is the 'younger language', the clear implication being that it can, and will, mature, become the latest beneficiary of the *translatio studii*. A comparable vision informs Dante's *Convivio*, wherein an attack is launched on those who believe that a long passage of time is necessary for the creation of nobility.[12] On the contrary, Dante argues, the potential for *gentilezza* is present in each and every one of us, whether aristocrat or churl, but we ourselves have to actualize that potential by behaving nobly. *É gentilezza dovunqu'è vertute*.[13] Because mankind has a common origin or root, any human being can cultivate the virtues and thus attain the true nobility, which is nobility of soul. This sort of argument can, very easily, be appropriated in an affirmation of the worthiness of the Italian language. A language does not have to be ancient (like Latin) to be noble; through careful cultivation it can fulfil its great potential. Thereby the *prezioso volgare* can achieve perfect literary nobility – and also authority, which stems from reason (whether divine or human) rather than from age.

Dante does not spell all of that out, but it is, I believe, quite implicit in what he actually does say.[14] After all, the *Convivio* is a spectacular example of vernacular hermeneutics, whereby several of Dante's own *canzone* are authorized even as they are treated through techniques of exegesis which for generations had been reserved for the Latin *auctores*. It could well be titled *De vulgari auctoritate* – to bring out the parallelism with Dante's *De vulgari eloquentia*, wherein the potential of eloquence in the vernacular is justified. *Nobilior est vulgaris?* Contrasting Latin with the vernacular, Dante argues that the vernacular is indeed the more noble language, giving three reasons. It was the first to be used by mankind (the language spoken in Eden was a vernacular), the whole world makes use of it (all the world's different vernaculars here being understood collectively), and it is natural for us to use (i.e. it is that language 'which infants acquire from those around them when they first begin to distinguish sounds'), as opposed to Latin, which can only be acquired 'through dedication to a lengthy course of study'.[15] Here, in *De vulgari eloquentia*, the vernacular is valued at Latin's expense.[16] Vulgarization rarely gets more prestigious than this.

However, there is nothing in the corpus of Middle English texts which corresponds to either of Dante's literary-theoretical treatises or Oresme's commentated translations, and neither King Richard II of England nor his Lancastrian successors attempted to emulate the 'state hermeneutics' cultivated by the Valois dynasty. Richard II was evidently impressed by the ceremonial practices of the French court, and took as his second wife (or child-bride, to be more exact) the daughter of Charles VI.[17] But he failed to act on the model (exemplified to perfection by Charles V) of the wise, bookish king, whose good governance and nation-building involved the cultivation of the national language and the provision therein of authoritative books which engendered 'affeccion et amour au bien publique', to borrow another phrase from Nicole Oresme.[18] Why was this? Answers are sought in Chapter 1. The basic hypothesis offered there is that vernacular hermeneutics (being practised outside the schools and written *in vulgari*) needed high-level sponsorship to thrive, but the prospect for that happening in Britain was remote at a time when books in English were generally coming under suspicion, due to fears prompted by the Wycliffite heresy. Indeed, there was good reason for that suspicion since the formal exegetical treatises that were produced were Wycliffite in origin or at least open to infiltration by Wycliffite ideas.

The following chapters complicate this picture considerably. Orthodox Middle English hermeneutics flourished in contexts other than those of the formal exegetical treatise (on texts both sacred and secular) or the commentated translation: witness, for example, William Langland's *Piers Plowman* (cf. Chapters 2 and 3) and *The Book of Margery Kempe* (cf. Chapter 5). And while the differences between the textual cultures of Britain and continental Europe highlighted in Chapter 1 are highly significant, it should not be concluded that Britain was mired in its own, solipsistic 'English heresy' to the exclusion of influence from across the Channel, that it lacked awareness of continental heresies, or that it failed to participate in theological disputes which were current in continental schools and universities. Chapter 2 investigates how issues of international concern relating to unusual forms of baptism and the possibility of salvation outside the Christian Church are handled in the poetry of Chaucer and Langland, with the emphasis on the presentation of the pagan emperor Trajan in *Piers Plowman*, which has provoked considerable controversy in recent criticism.

Those are not the only Ricardian poets whose works have been searched for signs of 'Nominalist' influence or 'Pelagian' infiltration; the *Gawain*-poet has received much attention of this kind. Some of the interpretations seem heavily overdetermined, as when certain theological positions and depictions which, arguably, are quite commonplace in medieval theology, or at least explicable with reference to uncontentious traditions, become identified as distinctively 'Nominalist'. For example, the remoteness of God 'from the narrator's world' in *Pearl* has been deemed 'similar to the God of the *Pelagiani moderni*', the assumption being that 'the thinking of men like Ockham, Buckingham, and Holcot implied a God who is distant from His creation'.[19] But one need not turn to 'Neopelagian' theology in quest of a God realized in terms of distance and remoteness – *The Cloud of Unknowing*, and the entire Dionysian tradition in which it participates, afford ample precedent. And anyway, it is highly dubious if the medieval schoolmen who deployed the dialectic of God's two powers would have seen the *potentia absoluta* as being segregated from the *potentia ordinaria* to the extent required for the postulation of a God 'distant from His creation'. I believe they would have been horrified by the suggestion that the divine power was divided and divisive: they saw themselves as dealing with two perceptions (from the human viewpoint) of one and the same power.[20] In any case, several writers on *Pearl* have been sensitive to the presence in the poem of a grace-imbued theology of God as a 'frende ful fyin' (1204), 'a divinity more consistent with the Augustinian tradition'.[21] So, if any Neopelagianism does indeed lurk in the poem, it definitely does not constitute the work's entire theological meaning and message. Either the poem affords credibility to two conflicting positions, one which emphasizes human merit and the other which emphasizes divine grace[22] (a harsher judgement might claim it is irreconcilably divided against itself), or there is one law for the unreliable narrator and another for the better-informed author. Or, maybe we are simply barking up the wrong tree. At any rate, I see no reason to leap to the conclusion that the *Gawain*-poet 'knew the works of Robert Holcot well enough for his imagination to be deeply formed by them',[23] and to postulate further that the poet was the friar's 'student (perhaps informally), whether in one of the universities, or more probably at Northampton or in the household of the bishop of Durham, either in that city or in London'.[24] That is to move beyond historically informed literary criticism to enter the realm of the historical novel.

My own reaction to the possibility of a Ricardian poetics of sceptical fideism is one of total scepticism.[25] There was indeed a well-established 'virtuous heathen scene' in Middle English literature, as Frank Grady has recently argued, but its scope was by no means determined by the doctrines attributed to the *Pelagiani moderni*. Furthermore, 'righteous heathen stories take on lives of their own once the topic escapes into the vernacular realm', and considerable 'weight' must be given to the 'curious and paradoxical rhetorical form[s]' in which they are couched.[26] In Chapter 2 I note that Chaucer engages in elaborate rhetorical convolutions to avoid explicit comment on the fate of the souls of his virtuous heathen, while expressing admiration for their philosophical insight and moral virtues. Langland's position is (typically) more shifting, elusive, maybe even evasive: but there is no reason to doubt its fundamental orthodoxy. On my reading, he stands as a 'radical conservative' thinker who brings out certain complexities and profundities of late medieval orthodox Christianity as never before – hence the epithet 'radical' is utterly appropriate. In Langland's handling of virtuous heathen in general and Trajan in particular, the business of Latin theology is being continued in the vernacular, with exceptional intellectual – and, I would add, emotional – sensitivity. And, by being made the repository of such compelling analysis, the vernacular is highly valued. Here is a veritable *translatio auctoritatis*.

But that certainly does not mean that Langland is valuing the vernacular more highly than he does Latin, that he believes English can afford value, bestow significance, offer resolution, in ways or to extents that Latin, the official theological language, cannot. Hence I must quibble with a reading of Langland's 'Tearing of the Pardon' episode (the subject of Chapter 3) which has been offered by Nicholas Watson, a scholar who has done more than anyone else in recent years to focus attention on the challenges of 'vernacular theology'.[27] In *Piers Plowman* B VII, Watson suggests, the priest figure devotes 'much energy' to proving that 'Piers's merciful vernacular Pardon is truer than the priest's harsh quotation from the Athanasian creed'. But that quotation from the Athanasian Creed *is* the sum total of the original Latin text of the 'Pardon' which Piers has received from Saint Truth. The priest has provided an English translation for the unlettered Plowman and his companions – and this translation is accurate, even though the priest's patronizing, scoffing attitude is highly unfortunate, to say the least. But that is a different matter. The status of vernacular discourse is simply not an issue here. By the same token, when Trajan exclaims 'Baw for bokes!' (B XI. 140) he doesn't care what language they're written in.

What *is* a major issue, as we attempt to understand B VII, is present-day suspicion of the late medieval theory and practice of indulgences (called 'pardons' *vulgariter*),[28] this being the literal base on which Langland constructs his allegorical superstructure. Wyclif had complained that in issuing indulgences the pope arrogates an extraordinary amount of power to himself, acting as the judge of all souls, including those in purgatory, heaven and hell. But that power is God's alone. The Almighty is perfectly capable of dispensing reward Himself, without the help of any pope – and besides, the pope cannot judge who is worthy in God's sight. Then again, if the pope's power in such matters is infinite, why does he not use it to save all the souls he could?[29] Martin Luther went much farther than that, finding in indulgences an easy target for his reformist rage. But one did not have to be a Lollard or a Lutheran to feel concern about how the system of pardoning was being justified and what was being done in the Church's name. Controversy was rife, with a surprising range of opinions and activities being accommodated within an orthodoxy which was far more capacious than sometimes has been claimed.

In Chapter 3 I try to bring out something of that capaciousness, and present Langland as a passionate yet utterly orthodox participant in a debate which had been carried on in Latin for generations, and which was to continue to trouble theologians for a long time to come (a 'radical conservative' approach indeed). I draw particularly on the justifications of indulgences offered by Sts Thomas Aquinas and Bonaventure. Aquinas's views are of special interest inasmuch as they are copiously quoted in a Latin treatise written shortly after the fifth Canterbury jubilee (1420), perhaps by Richard Godmersham (who was appointed head of Canterbury College by Archbishop Arundel in 1403), which stridently defends the authenticity of a generous plenary indulgence allegedly granted by Pope Honorius III on the occasion of the translation on 7 July 1220 of the martyr Thomas à Becket. Anyone who attacks this indulgence, declares Richard (assuming he is indeed the author) is sinning against the Holy Spirit – specific mention being made of those who are 'infected with the execrable dogma of the carping Lollards'.[30] Furthermore, the relevant discussions of Aquinas and Bonaventure are cited at some length in Wyclif's attack on indulgences in *De ecclesia*;[31] here, it would seem, are the views he knew he had to beat. Challenging a current tendency to make such proto-protestant ideology the basis of literary-critical (and indeed moral) judgements concerning the artistic representation of late medieval religiosity, my reading affords all due respect to the power of a doctrine which – offering hope, reassurance, and communality – captured the Catholic imagination for several centuries, yet which was also a source of anxiety and unease, feelings which Langland conveys brilliantly.

What makes Langland's treatment particularly radical is the extent to which he seems willing to acquiesce in aspects of pardoning which were deemed dubious in his day. Professional theologians complained that the vulgar herd did not understand that an indulgence could not liberate from both punishment and guilt, *a pena et a culpa*: only priestly absolution could effect release from the latter. In fact, this comprehension was by no means limited to the ill-educated. Hence in Chapter 3 I speak of a vernacular theology of indulgences *a pena et a culpa*, which was shared by learned and lewd, clerical and lay, and cut across the boundaries of language. Another cause for professional concern was the practice of remaining at home yet claiming the benefit of an indulgence which, in normal circumstances, required much physical effort and travel. The experts found this custom difficult to justify, and it was deemed a fit subject for satire. However, Langland took these slices of life as he knew it, accepted them as historical/literal sense, without explicit questioning; rather he seeks answers in their *sensus spiritualis*. The ultimate solution to the problems posed by *Piers Plowman* B VII seems to lie in the doctrine of the Atonement, the reconciliation of mankind to God through the death of His Son, this being the best pardon of all. But, in the 'Tearing of the Pardon' episode, Langland merely gestures towards that doctrine, aspects of which will be clarified later in the poem.

We must wait for those future steps. For now, the Pardon (i.e. a passage from the Athanasian Creed) is torn apart, the elaborate allegorical edifice in which it featured disowned – and this restless, relentless poem begins its quest afresh.

For her part, Margery Kempe elicits *sensus spiritualis* in two Biblical texts which were of crucial importance for her sense of religious calling, Genesis 1:28 and Luke 11:27–8. The former *auctoritas*, 'be fruitful and multiply', could be used in criticizing women who refused to be contained by their reproductive function, while the latter, beginning 'Blessed is the womb that bore thee', apparently denigrated the material motherhood of the Virgin Mary in particular and womankind in general, in face of the higher calling intimated by Christ's words, 'blessed are they who hear the word of God and keep it'. For a woman to engage in vernacular hermeneutic activity of any kind, let alone of Biblical texts which went to the very heart of the matter of women's roles in Christian society, was a quite daring thing to do in the early 1400s. And inevitably, male interrogators sought to discover if Margery fitted some supposed heretical template or other. In Chapter 5 I explore the possibility that Wycliffite theology affords reasons why Margery's questioners should have been interested in those two specific passages, concluding that a sufficient, perhaps even a satisfying, explanation may indeed be found there. But, going beyond those parameters, I wish to place vernacular English conundrums within the wider European context in which they belong, an ambition which permeates Chapter 2 also.

This sort of enterprise has recently been supported by Kathryn Kerby-Fulton's *Books under Suspicion*, which offers a vision of 'a far less insular England than we are used to seeing – an England swept by fierce, invigorating, often stormy theological winds from across the Channel'.[32] Hence I ask if the 'gret clerke' who asked Margery what she thought of Genesis 1:28 could have been prompted by fears concerning either Catharism or the Heresy of the Free Spirit. Of course, modern scholars are convinced that the former never took root in English soil, and that the latter did not exist as a heresy at all. But Margery's interrogators, lacking the resources of modern academe, did not know that. Medieval English clerics had read about those supposed heresies; so, in that sense such subversive thought-systems (or what were perceived as such) had indeed entered England. They existed in the minds of certain English clerics – and perhaps the English clerics who quizzed Margery may be included among that number.

I conclude, however, that no obvious frisson of those fierce continental winds is evident in Margery's response. And, indeed, the 'gret clerke' may not have been seeking out heresy (whether Lollard, Cathar, Free Spirit, or whatever) at all. A more mundane explanation is possible. Margery did not wish to subvert orthodox constructions of marriage; she was quite willing to see other women endure in that state, while wanting something better for herself. Hence her desire to 'spiritualize' her own social situation as a married woman, to interpret potentially troublesome Scriptural passages in 'gostly' terms which endorsed her talking about the things of God.[33] But, for some contemporaries, her chosen mission posed a threat to the social order and the security of marriage; hence Margery was seen as a sort of female Pied Piper who would give men's wives fancy ideas about their religious potential and lead them away with her on her wanderings. Perhaps that was the threat she was suspected of posing in the episode under discussion.

'Perhaps' is a crucial word in that sentence because throughout Chapter 5 I am seeking to explore possibilities rather than claiming interpretive certainty – which is impossible to achieve, I believe, since *The Book of Margery Kempe* has given us so little to go on. Whatever the facts of Margery's fascinating encounter with the 'gret clerke' may be, this general proposition may be ventured: disruptive Margery certainly was, but heretical she was not. However, the charge of heresy came quickly to the lips of those who wanted her to live the life that other women do; it was all too easy to perceive and present her 'public vernacular ecclesiopolitical discourse'[34] as a form of heterodoxy. In response Margery offered self-authorizing exegesis in her 'vulgar' tongue. Once again, we see the business of Latin hermeneutics being continued in the vernacular, English being the only language of which Margery had full command, as a woman with little, if any, Latin.[35] Her attempt at *translatio auctoritatis* is motivated by desire to rise above and beyond the 'common state of women', and join the company of those who had been specially elected and privileged by God.

What Margery was up against is made abundantly clear in Chapter 4, which discusses views concerning 'women priests' attributed to the Welsh Lollard Walter Brut, who was tried by John Trefnant, bishop of Hereford, during the period 1391–3. Only a mere two pages (approximately) of the 173 pages devoted to Brut's excursus in Capes's edition concern female ministry. But they are the centre of attention in four *quaestiones* preserved in London, British Library, MS 31, presumably the work of members of the team that Trefnant assembled for Brut's trial. My discussion focuses on two of them, *Utrum mulieres sunt ministri ydonei ad conficiendum eukaristie sacramentum* (fols. 196v–205r) and *Utrum mulieres conficiunt vel conficere possunt* (fols. 218r–223r).[36] It cannot be emphasized enough that these texts are not the work of Brut himself but rather the writings of orthodox theologians

who have expanded the heretic's own views (for which Trefnant's Register is
our only reliable source) in order to refute them the more effectively. I find
this 'expansionist' explanation of the *quaestiones* more convincing than the
rival hypothesis, viz. that their authors worked with a substantial body of
material (no longer extant) produced by Brut himself, which they closely
followed before proceeding to refute. The additional materials which bulk
out the *quaestiones* are more comprehensible as *amplificatio* by professional
theologians, with substantial academic resources at their disposal,[37] of what
Brut himself had said, as represented in those brief documents of his own
authorship which have survived in the Register.

This raises fascinating issues concerning professionalism versus (relative)
amateurism, élite versus 'popular' culture (i.e. culture 'of the people'),[38]
official versus unofficial intellectualism, non-institutional versus non- (or
even anti-) institutional theology. In short, the issue of what may justly
be deemed 'vernacular', and how that vernacular may be valued, is here to
the fore. Focusing for the moment on linguistic matters, it is important
to consider the implications of the fact that Walter Brut himself wrote in
Latin: that is the language in which, responding to Trefnant's demand, he
recorded his views, and that is the form in which they have been preserved
in the bishop's Register. Here is no parish-pump philosopher, but a literate
(i.e. Latinate) layman who participated in the authoritative, and authority-
conferring, methodologies of learned discourse.[39] Furthermore, and leaving
linguistic matters aside for the moment, his views on women priests can
hardly be termed 'demotic', inasmuch as they never became major tenets
of Lollard doctrine. (It is one of the deep ironies of the history of Lollardy
that Brut's opponents probably generated far more heretical doctrine on
women priests than their opponent had done.)

What is abundantly clear is that Lollardy cannot be regarded simply
and exclusively as the 'English Heresy'.[40] And the arch-heresiarch himself,
John Wyclif, made no attempt to champion his 'vulgar' tongue (to the
best of our knowledge). No justification of the translation of that most
authoritative of all books, 'The Book of Life', may be found anywhere
in Wyclif's voluminous theological writings, though for centuries he has
been lauded as the *fons et origio* of the first English Bible. Furthermore,
not a scrap of Middle English survives which can with any confidence be
attributed to him, despite the fact that his followers generated a vast corpus
of vernacular theology. It seems quite clear, then, that positioning Latin
and vernacular theology in a relationship of sharp opposition travesties the
complexity of the situation. Thinking back to the terms of reference of
Firmin le Ver's definition of *vulgaritas* and related words, we may recall the

crucial notions of popularity, community, publication, making manifest. All of those notions fit the profile of Medieval Latin exceedingly well. Here is a language which, over and above any other in medieval Europe, caused vast amounts of information 'Foorth to go among the peple' (to borrow a phrase from Thomas Hoccleve).[41] Hence I offer the thought that Medieval Latin could be deemed the great medieval European vernacular. Of course, Jacques Bauchant was quite right to claim that, as far as France was concerned, 'Le latin n'est si entendible ne si commun que le language maternel' (cf. p. 1 above); a medieval Italian or Englishman could have made (and did make) a similar comment about the status of his mother tongue in his own country.[42] But if medieval Europe is considered as a whole, one could easily conclude that Latin was the more 'entendible' and 'commun' language, given its ability to cross national boundaries.[43]

Wyclif's dismissive, perhaps even insulting, remarks in *De veritate sacrae scripturae* (1378) about the skills needed for the making of material Bibles are very much his own – and evidently consistent with what Anne Hudson has termed his 'amazingly nonchalant' attitude to language-transference.[44] Yet behind this may be detected the commonplace medieval belief in the universality of grammar. '*Grammatica* is the same for all men and for all languages', confidently asserts the Parisian *artista* Jean le Danois in his *Summa grammatica* (1280).[45] As Alfonso Manierù has well explained, grammar was sometimes seen as being 'like a genus shared by all species'.[46] Theoretically speaking then, each species had its own share of, or purchase on, *grammatica*; consequently every vernacular should (or at least could) be valued. And the distinction between Latin as master-language and the vernaculars as mere subalterns could hardly be maintained. Wyclif never drew those conclusions (at least, not in any of his extant writings); all we have is evidence of that 'amazingly nonchalant' attitude. But others did, including Dante in *Il convivio* and several of Charles V's translators, who found therein a means of justifying their promotion of French as the current victor in the *translatio studii*. If French had the same fundamental grammar as Latin, it could become the 'new Latin'.

That said, it is inaccurate and misleading to think of vernacular texts as having displaced Latin ones, in respect of prestige – as if *auctoritas* was a finite commodity, whose increment in one area meant its diminution in another. Rather, textual authority in general, like authoritative textual meaning in particular (*sensus*, *sententia*, whatever the term), was regarded as well-nigh inexhaustible, there to be discovered, inscribed, transmitted. This explains the logic of Dante's application of techniques of *divisio textus* (a process of increasingly minute division and subdivision of the text under analysis), which for generations had been practised in the exegesis of authoritative Latin texts,[47] to the vernacular poems included in his *Vita nuova*. Commenting on 'Donne ch'avete intelletto d'amore', Dante remarks, 'to uncover still more meaning (*intendimento*) in this *canzone* it would be necessary to divide it more minutely (*usare di più minute divisioni*)'.[48] The more a text is divided the more meaning emerges. The deeper one digs in search of the treasures of authoritative doctrine, the more one finds – and even more is there for the taking. In this grand scheme of things, whichever language hides that treasure is hardly important.

The hermeneutic manoeuvres of Dante and of Charles V's team of translators represent particularly striking (though quite symptomatic) high-cultural appropriations of vernacular culture – the term 'vernacular' here being used in its widest and most inclusive sense, denoting acts of cultural transfer, negotiation, and appropriation – within which wider context language-transfer could play a major role, as it did in the cases here cited, but certainly not in all cases (as the present book demonstrates). Here are instances of how 'clerical culture', working in the service of the secular élite, 'did not so much replace as restructure'[49] what I am calling vernacular culture, conferring social prestige upon it – in short, authorizing it. However, we should not think simply and exclusively in terms of high culture appropriating only what it wanted and needed. The pressures worked both ways. Hence Aron Gurevich's crucial qualification of Jacques le Goff's account of 'the birth of purgatory': far from being the exclusive invention of twelfth-century theologians, claims Gurevich, this involved the imposition of 'a "conceptual structure" on popular ideas'.[50] According to his analysis, the 'concept' of purgatory went back a long way, and was already a force in early-medieval vision literature; subsequently it 'acquired distinctive outlines from the scholastics, acquired a name, and received an official right to exist'.[51] The voice – or rather the competing, dissonant voices – of vernacular culture could not be ignored.

'The vulgar mob is very fickle and bends like a reed whatever way the wind blows.'[52] In fact, the ecclesiastical authorities themselves often bent in face of public opinion – which is hardly surprising, given that 'cultural adaptation to the common people' was 'necessary for the clergy to achieve its mission'.[53] As André Vauchez says, 'During the last centuries of the Middle Ages, with only rare exceptions, the ecclesiastical authorities did not seek violent confrontation with popular beliefs and practices in the sphere of the cult of saints. Even when they disapproved of them, they preferred to act flexibly.'[54] That flexibility may copiously be illustrated with reference to the gulf between vernacular belief about the power of 'pardons' and the official theological doctrine on indulgences (here I return to the concerns of Chapter 3). In Simon of Cremona's *Disputationes de indulgentiis* (*c.* 1380) the authenticity of two particularly generous indulgences is questioned, one allegedly bestowed upon St Francis's Portiuncula church and the other upon the church of St John of the Desert in Cremona.[55] In their defence, it is argued that the pope knows full well what is going on in those churches, and therefore he condones their devotional practices. Simon's response is that the Church tolerates certain things which, were they subjected to strict legal examination, would not be countenanced. 'Patient tolerance' is deemed better than official condemnation – presumably because of the scandal[56] which would ensue if pilgrims thought that their trust had been betrayed. Indeed, the wish to avoid scandal justified a *laissez-faire* attitude to many practices which could never have received the approval of high-ranking churchmen or the validation of scholastic theology.

To take another instance: it was commonly supposed that each and every person who visited a given shrine received the same indulgence, and hence gained the same amount of release from *pena*. But the legal truth of the matter was that indulgences could be received only by (or, more accurately, were valid only for) the subjects of those bishops who had granted them. Addressing this problem, John of Dambach OP (1288–1372) argues that other people, from different jurisdictions, should be allowed to receive those indulgences, and their validity should be upheld. This is better, it would seem, than burdening people with anxiety-inducing knowledge, or disrupting their simple and sincere beliefs. As Robert Shaffern puts it in his commentary on John's *De quantitate indulgenciarum*, this schoolman's attitude was that 'rights to grant payments from the treasury of merit should be interpreted liberally, lest the church be unreceptive to the piety of the people'.[57]

That same 'piety of the people' produced the conviction that plenary indulgences could effect release *a pena et a culpa* (from punishment *and* guilt), a conviction which Langland afforded high seriousness in *Piers Plowman*, B VII, as already noted. To see this as establishment exploitation of populist gullibility (as Reformation chroniclers of the errors of Rome inevitably did) would be grossly to oversimplify a complex relationship between élite and vernacular cultures. For the *vulgus* wanted indulgences – bigger and better ones, available at each and every shrine. Very few wished or dared to question the authenticity of, say, the generous plenary pardons which were believed (on very shaky grounds) to have been awarded to Becket's shrine at Canterbury in 1220, or to St Francis's Portiuncula church at Assisi during the saint's lifetime. (Wyclif's followers were, of course, among the gainsayers – but old habits died hard.)[58] Official culture could not keep pace; popes and bishops were put under considerable pressure to up the ante (and, admittedly, the more unscrupulous among them tried to turn this populist piety to their own advantage), while scholastic theologians struggled to keep their rationalizations and criticisms up to speed with what was happening on the ground.

There were, of course, clerics aplenty who were willing to defend, support, and even initiate populist practices. Richard Godmersham's zealous defence of the Canterbury plenary indulgence allegedly granted by Honorius III has already been mentioned. Thomas of Chobham, who worked as sub-dean of Salisbury Cathedral in the early 1200s, felt obliged to defend that most bizarre relic of all, the foreskin of Christ (on which more later, in Chapter 6). And no less a personage than Robert Grosseteste – *lector* to the Oxford Franciscans, commentator on Aristotle, expert on astronomical and computational science, and bishop of Lincoln – produced a tract in support of the Westminster Blood Relic around 1247. Grosseteste may have written at the request of King Henry III, who was eager to promote this relic, supposed to be a quantity of the blood shed by Christ during His passion.[59] Another Latin defence appeared in the late 1380s or 1390s, dedicated to King Richard II; this was the work of a Westminster monk, William Sudbury.[60] Vested interests notwithstanding, the generalization may be ventured that vernacular religious culture encompassed and motivated (in one way or another) people from many walks of medieval life. It would be a mistake to assume that an insurmountable gap always existed between the intellectual and social élite and those they denigrated as the *vulgus*. But the *vulgus* was quite capable of resisting the wishes of kings and eminent clerics. The failure of layfolk to warm to the cult of the Westminster Blood Relic meant that Henry III's great hopes for it came to nothing.[61] In contrast, 'the blood of Crist that is in Hayles' (as Chaucer's Pardoner termed it) had many visitors.[62] This cult flourished, with much popular support, until 1538, when the shrine was destroyed,[63] and its precious contents pronounced a fake by the Reformers.

For their part, the eminent clerics often stood on their dignity, distancing themselves from populist practices. Describing a marvellous shrine dedicated to 'St Valery', where urogenital disorders are allegedly cured, Sir/St Thomas More remarks that it is up to the 'vnyuersyte of Parys' to 'defende' or justify what goes on there.[64] The point being that Parisian schoolmen regard such issues as unworthy of their attention. Obviously, More is joking – at least partly. The 'matters of saynt wallery' are described as 'mery', and laughter bubbles up frequently in the course of the text I have been quoting here, the *Dialogue concerning Heresies* (published in 1529). Yet this treatise is a defence of the faith, a critique of Protestant polemic against false relics and inappropriate expectations of saints and their shrines – which nevertheless manages to admit that certain demotic Catholic religious practices look ridiculous to orthodox intellectuals. And herein lies much of the complexity of the *Dialogue*. More dextrously manages to hold together the sublime and the ridiculous, the serious and the silly. Elsewhere they pull apart. What was a good joke in the eyes of a believing Catholic became a risible superstition, the fair target of righteous ridicule, in the eyes of a Protestant reformer. And yet, underlying these 'mery' or offensively superstitious matters (depending on one's viewpoint) was a staunch faith in the healing functions of certain shrines and the efficacy of invocations of saints with special power over life's many ailments and mishaps. Chapter 6 attempts to uncover such vernacular culture, through investigation of Catholic jests and Protestant slurs. It begins and ends with Chaucer's Pardoner, who profits from his large collection of false relics, and ends up being the butt of a particularly cutting joke involving relics and reliquaries. I attempt to find in Chaucer's humour evidence of and comment on vernacular religious practice, and to find in vernacular religious practice the key to understanding Chaucer's humour.

In sum, the subject of my final chapter is the relics of vernacular religion – the term 'relics' being understood on the one hand as sacred body parts together with the materials that had been rendered sacred through contact with them, and on the other as the 'relicts' or remains of vernacular practices that, for the most part, remained under the radar of official literature. Indeed, according to Jonathan Sumption (a writer who brings a quite exceptional degree of imaginative empathy to the study of demotic religious practices), the excesses of saints' cults and relic veneration 'were largely a popular phenomenon', beyond the scope of 'the official doctrines' which the Church sought to disseminate.[65] 'The initiative for the proclamation of miracles almost invariably came from the laity'; 'the combination of a pilgrim who had convinced himself that he had experienced a miracle, and a public which was overwhelmingly anxious to believe him, was impossible for the clergy to resist, even if they wished to'.[66] Gurevich builds on these insights by noting how certain hagiographic texts present people as being 'in close contact and mutual interaction with the saints, and the saints actively [participate] in and [influence] human life and [guard] their own interests'; for example, healing the sick and helping supplicants avoid physical and financial disasters are all in a day's work for 'the saint, the people's protector and defender'.[67] I offer several instances of such 'close contact and mutual interaction', trying to glimpse vernacular religious practices beyond and behind the attempted normalizations of official hagiography. This broad sweep is necessary because some of the practices in question could be, and were, presented as 'vulgar' in the derogatory sense of that term (and as obscene, idolatrous and pagan, to list but a few of the other unflattering epithets). Here we confront not only medieval textual occlusion but also a taste-barrier formed by differences between medieval and modern sensibilities.

Such waters are murky indeed. Gurevich has argued that their depths may be explored 'in terms that are perhaps closest to [those of] social anthropology'.[68] Taking my cue from this, I draw on the research of social anthropologists and folklorists in seeking information about vestiges of medieval religiosity that may throw some light on late medieval practices. Furthermore, in investigating the attitudes to sexuality implied by my exhibits (both written and material – the latter category including the puzzling genital badges which survive in large numbers from the late Middle Ages), I test the merits of the Gurevichian proposition that 'the transition from paganism to Christianity involved a reorganization of existing beliefs rather than a clean sweep'.[69] And in the process discover, *inter alia*, means of further complicating the controversial matter of the Pardoner's sexuality. This return to a relatively well-charted region of Chaucer criticism brings to a close my series of meditations on the scope and significance of 'the vernacular'.

The term 'vernacular' is far too potent to be strait-jacketed within the narrow sphere of language-transfer. Rather it can, and I believe should, be recognized as encompassing a vast array of acts of cultural transmission and negotiation, deviation and/or synthesis, confrontation and/or reconciliation. 'Native to a given community' which may, or may not, be confined within national boundaries; lacking standardization or at least comprising non-standard versions of words and deeds which *are* standardized; constituted by practices or 'forms used locally or characteristic of non-dominant groups or classes',[70] though susceptible to appropriation, authorization, and exploitation by dominant groups or classes: those are a few of the elements of meaning which such terms as *vulgo, vulgum, vulgariter, vulgaritas*, and *vulgatus* carried in the later Middle Ages, and which I wish to recuperate in this book. Only when it is understood in its fullest, richest sense may the true value of 'vernacularity'[71] be realized.

CHAPTER I

Absent glosses: the trouble with Middle English hermeneutics

During the period 1479–82 the massive *Cancionero da Barrantes* was produced, containing works by three of the greatest Spanish poets of the fifteenth century, Santillana, Juan de Mena, and Pérez de Guzmán, accompanied by extensive commentary in Castilian and Latin.[1] Modern scholars of Middle English literature would give much for an English counterpart. Why does such a thing not exist; where have all the English (or indeed Latin) glosses on English texts gone? To be more precise, why were they not written?

Admittedly, occasional glosses may be found in certain manuscripts of Geoffrey Chaucer's works, particularly the *Canterbury Tales*,[2] and the sporadic Latin commentary which John Gower himself seems to have provided for his English *Confessio amantis* has received at least some of the attention which it deserves.[3] 'An elaborate Latin commentary' on the single most popular poem in Middle English, *The Pricke of Conscience* (which survives in well over a hundred manuscripts), has been reported.[4] However, this turns out to comprise nothing more than interpolated passages of Latin; we are dealing with *amplificatio* and re-compilation rather than formal commentary on a 'hermeneutically sealed' textual unit. The mid-fifteenth-century *Court of Sapience* does include an extensive apparatus of Latin source-references (unfortunately omitted in the latest edition of the work),[5] but there is none of the *explication de texte* which medieval commentary characteristically provides.[6]

Things seemed to have been a little better in Scotland, to judge by Gavin Douglas's plan to write a commentary to accompany his translation of the *Aeneid* (1553):

> I haue allso a schort comment compylyt
> To expoun strange histouris and termys wild . . .
> (conclusion, 'Heir the translatar . . . ', 141–2)[7]

17

In his text and gloss Douglas refers to, and draws on, the commentaries of Servius, Cristoforo Landino, Lorenzo Valla, and Josse Badius Ascensius in the 1507 version. Either all of these accompanied the original text in the printed edition of Virgil that he used – printed editions containing as many as five commentaries had been published – or Douglas is bringing together materials which he found in separate copies of the *Aeneid*. Yet he was not content to rely on the commentaries of others; it is evident that scholarly sources were consulted at first hand, such as Augustine's *De civitate Dei*, Boccaccio's *Genealogia Deorum Gentilium*, and Livy's *Ab urbe condita*. Unfortunately, as we have it (and presumably as far as Douglas wrote it) the commentary ends halfway through the translation of Book 1. However, it may be noted that Douglas regarded his entire translation project as, in some measure, a work of academic commentary. This comes out, for example, in his remark that one 'proffit' of his book will be its usefulness to those who 'Virgill to childryn expone': 'Thank me tharfor, masteris of grammar sculys' (conclusion, 'Heir the translatar . . .', 41–8).

But thereafter, little of relevance seemed to occur in either Scotland or England until 'E. K.' produced his glosses on Edmund Spenser's *Shepheardes Calender* (1579). In particular, the contrast between the situation in England under Richard II and his Lancastrian successors and those appertaining in other European countries at roughly the same time is quite marked. In endeavouring to gauge the dimensions of the problem, first I shall offer some evidence to establish just how substantial the cultural discrepancy actually was,[8] and then attempt to identify the causes of the trouble with Middle English hermeneutics.

Within twenty years of Dante's death in 1321 at least eight commentaries on the *Divine Comedy* (some written in Latin, others in Italian) had been produced, including expositions by Dante's two sons Iacopo and Pietro and by Giovanni Boccaccio.[9] The commentaries on the *Comedy* constitute the single most important corpus of contemporary criticism on any medieval vernacular writer. There is considerable debate over the relative datings, but there is no question of the volume of commentary or of its hermeneutic sophistication. Much of the credit for the institution of Dante-commentary must go to Dante himself, who (among so many other things) is one of the most important figures in the history of vernacular hermeneutics. His confidence as self-commentator – in the *Vita nuova* and, more formally, in the *Convivio* – provided a powerful precedent for lesser mortals. The *Convivio* deserves special mention as a work in which the emphases and techniques of academic exegesis are applied to three Italian lyrics, and at the beginning of this work Dante discusses with remarkable cultural awareness the politics of writing a vernacular commentary on vernacular texts (as opposed to writing a Latin commentary on vernacular texts). Following in his master's footsteps, Boccaccio equipped his own *Teseida* (1339–41?) with a vernacular commentary, which in style and scope imitates the Latin commentaries on such classical epics as Virgil's *Aeneid* and Lucan's *Pharsalia*. Moreover, it could be argued that he saw himself as writing within a tradition of vernacular criticism. For, in the *chiose* on the seventh book of the *Teseida*, Boccaccio cites Dino del Garbo's (Latin) commentary on *Donna mi prega*, the *canzone d'amore* of Guido Cavalcanti (*c.*1259–1300). (Indeed, we owe the survival of Dino's commentary to Boccaccio's copy, made by his own hand.) Functioning together, the *Teseida*'s text and gloss make the case that epic poetry may be composed in 'the illustrious vernacular'.

Furthermore, honourable mention may be made of the Latin commentary which Francesco da Barberino, lawyer and episcopal notary, wrote to accompany his Italian *Documenti d'amore* (apparently produced during the period 1309–13). Here Barberino set out to do for 'the laws of love' what Justinian and Gratian had done for Roman law and canon law respectively, i.e. the collection and harmonizing of diverse and discordant documents.[10] The programme of glosses is similarly ambitious. Around the vernacular text is written a Latin translation, and around that is written a Latin commentary, all Barberino's own work.

Moving on to late medieval France, here we encounter the first extensive literary debate over the meaning and morality of a vernacular text. In the *querelle de la Rose*, Jean de Meun's poetry was attacked by Christine de Pizan and Jean Gerson (chancellor of the University of Paris), and eloquently defended by the Col brothers and Jean de Montreuil.[11] Both Gontier and Pierre Col are titled in the debate as 'secretaries of the King our Lord', while Jean de Montreuil served as a secretary to the dukes of Berry, Burgundy, and Orléans, and to King Charles VI himself. Attackers and defenders alike drew on literary-theoretical concepts which had been disseminated in the *accessus ad auctores*, and the Latin commentaries on Ovid are, quite obviously, a major influence.[12] Also from Charles VI's reign dates the first extensive French commentary to have been written on any original French poem, namely the exposition of the anonymous *Echecs amoureux* (i.e. the 'Chess of Love') which Evrart de Conty (*c.* 1330–1405), who had been Charles V's physician, produced in the 1390s.[13] Evrart, like Boccaccio in his *chiose* on the *Teseida*, does have some sense of vernacular literary history, and both writers also seem to share a sense of involvement in the creation of a corpus of criticism on vernacular poetry. Evrart refers to the *Esopet* (the French translation of Aesop), the *Renart*, and Jean Acart's *Prise amoureuse*. He recognizes the *Roman de la Rose* as the major model for the *Echecs amoureux*, and feels free to compare the dream form of the earlier French poem with that of the august *Somnium Scipionis*, and (more generally) to draw on Macrobius's commentary for his own critical discourse.

Apparently antedating Evrart's *Echecs amoureux* commentary is his *Livre des problèmes d'Aristote*, a French translation (which incorporates commentary materials) of the Pseudo-Aristotelian *Problemata*, a rather haphazard compilation of medical lore.[14] Although not completed in the lifetime of Charles V, this treatise bears all the hallmarks of that ruler's extraordinarily ambitious programme of literary patronage.[15] Charles 'le sage' commissioned translations of Bartholomew the Englishman's *De proprietatibus rerum* (by Jean Corbechon, 1372), Valerius Maximus (a translation of the first four books, by Simon de Hesdin, is extant; 1375), Augustine's *De civitate Dei*, portions of the Bible (by Raoul de Presles, between 1371 and 1375), Giles of Rome's *De regimine principum* (by Jean Golein, 1379), and of course the Aristotle translations by Nicole Oresme, who provided scrupulous renderings of the *Politics*, *Nicomachean Ethics*, and *On the Heavens* (*De caelo*) along with the Pseudo-Aristotelian *Economics*. *Le livre des problèmes d'Aristote* was Evrart de Conty's contribution to the French Aristotelian corpus.

Some of these translations incorporate materials from, and carry on the hermeneutic business of, the relevant Latin commentaries. Hence A. D. Menut can refer to Oresme's *Livre de éthiques*, *Livre de politiques*, *Livre de yconomiques*, and *Livre du ciel et du monde* as 'commentated translations' of Aristotle's works.[16] It is 'difficult to determine' what Oresme has taken from Latin commentaries and what he has provided himself,[17] though some sources are evident. For his *Livre de politiques* he consulted the *Politics* commentaries of Albert the Great and Walter Burley, along with the *De potestate regia et papali* of John of Paris and the highly controversial *Defensor pacis* of Marsilius of Padua.[18] And Oresme was acutely aware of the procedures and status of commentary itself. Manuscripts of his Aristotle translations attempt, in various ways, to distinguish between text and gloss, and we need not doubt that this reflects Oresme's own wishes.[19] In preparing his translation of *De civitate Dei*, Raoul de Presles consulted the commentaries on that text by Nicholas Trevet and Thomas Waleys.[20] For his part, Evrart de Conty equipped his rendering of the *Problemata* (the text used being Bartholomew of Messina's Latin version) with extensive vernacular glosses which draw substantially on the Latin commentary by

Peter of Abano.[21] Like Oresme before him, Evrart was not content to pass on uncritically what he found in his Latin commentary; he is quite prepared to discount or even criticize the views of Abano, and generally seeks to improve upon them – after all, he himself was a practising physician.

Spain comes next, and last, in this brief tour of European 'vernacular commentary traditions'.[22] Enrique de Villena (1384–1434) made a complete translation of Virgil's *Aeneid* and produced a vernacular commentary on its first three books. Villena prefaces his commentary with an epistle to Juan de Aragon, who had commissioned it soon after ascending the throne of Navarre. It seems clear that Villena had intended to cover the entire poem, since he knows precisely where material would be placed later; the reasons for its incompletion are unclear. Villena's translation of the *Rhetorica ad Herennium* has been lost, but a version of his translation of Dante's *Comedy* has survived, fitted around a glossed copy (the glosses being in Latin and Castilian) of the original Italian text. This manuscript was owned by his friend Íñigo López de Mendoza, first marquis of Santillana (1398–1458); indeed, many of the Castilian glosses are in Santillana's own hand. The marquis also possessed translations of two Latin commentaries on Dante, an anonymous translation of Pietro Alighieri's commentary, and, commissioned from his physician, Martín González de Lucena, a translation of parts of Benvenuto da Imola's commentary. His library also included a Spanish translation of Pierre Bersuire's *Ovidius moralizatus* and, almost certainly, the *Biblia de osuna* (a Spanish *Bible moralisé*) and the Spanish translation of Old Testament prophetic and wisdom literature (Madrid, Biblioteca Nacional, MS 10288), along with two Latin Bibles and a concordance of the Latin text. Accompanying them was a full translation of portions of Nicholas of Lyre's *Postilla* on the Old Testament, which was made by the Franciscan Alfonso de Algezira at the behest of Alfonso de Guzmàn, son of the first Count of Niebla; the bulk of the work was done between 1420 and 1422.

Now, we should be aware of the dangers of exaggerating and decontextualizing the cultural significance of even the most substantial instances of vernacular commentary-tradition. Consider the curious case of Villena, for instance. His vernacular *Aeneid* commentary was a work of extraordinary density and erudition, yet it seems to have attracted little attention in its own day, is extant in only two manuscripts, and was never printed. There are several possible reasons for this, one of the most likely being the writer's own dubious reputation: accused of sorcery, he had his possessions confiscated, and after his death King Juan II ordered his library to be burnt (which goes some way towards explaining why so much of Villena's work has not survived.) Then again, in the case of the Dante commentaries we should not imagine a smooth transition from medieval to Renaissance, with an early flowering of criticism on vernacular poetry anticipating a spring full of burgeoning varieties of vernacular poetry and prose. Dante was vociferously criticized by humanists who believed that he should have written in Latin, and they came to hold the whip hand. The fourteenth century was the peak period for production of Dante commentary. We have one early fifteenth-century offering, by the Franciscan John of Serraville (1416). And then there is a major gap, of some sixty-five years, until 1481 when Cristoforo Landino produced his heavily allegorizing commentary. He was followed by three sixteenth-century commentators, Alessandro Vellutello (1544), Bernardino Daniello (1568), and Lodovico Castelvetro (1570).[23] These are rather slim pickings, in contrast with the scholarship on classical poetry fostered in Italy at that time. However, the picture is complicated by the fact that the decline of Dante's critical fortunes coincided with the rise of Petrarch's. Ten major commentaries on the latter's works were published between 1476 and 1582.[24] However, even Petrarch commentary was put in the shade by the extraordinary body of sixteenth-century exposition of Ariosto's *Orlando furioso*, which 'quickly became the most widely read work of modern Italian poetry in the sixteenth century' and even joined the *syllabi* of Venetian schools – the only vernacular text to win such approval.[25]

The above remarks are certainly not intended to undermine or undervalue the significance of such vernacular commentary-traditions as we do possess; I simply am seeking to point out their relative fragility, and counter any notion that in the later Middle Ages there was a large-scale displacement of Latin originals by vernacular translations in respect of textual authority and prestige. And here may be found an appropriate basis for consideration of the question: why, compared with several other European countries in the fourteenth and fifteenth centuries, is the level of vernacular hermeneutics so low in England?

The issue of patronage is, of course, crucial. Once commentaries go beyond the schools (where their production is essential as part of the pedagogic process and a means to academic honours), once the discourses move from Latin into the vernaculars, other interpretive communities have to want them and pay for them. And it seems that the English kings were reticent. Certain French and Aragonese courts, as described briefly above, appear to have been far more conducive to literary activity and hermeneutics than the English court of Richard II; and in Italy civic funding of public lectures on poetry was possible in a way that was unimaginable in England.

(For example, the Florentine civic authorities sponsored Boccaccio's lectures on the *Comedy* which commenced on 23 October 1373; one member of Boccaccio's audience, Benvenuto da Imola, was inspired to organize and deliver another series of Dante lectures, at Bologna in 1375).[26] There has been considerable debate about the extent and significance of the literary patronage dispensed by Richard and his familiars, and I do not want to open up those questions here; let me just quickly identify myself as one of those who believe it to have more substance than has sometimes been claimed. But it can only seem small in comparison with the cases I have been citing from Italy, France, and Spain. Moreover, all the blame cannot be laid at the door of Richard II. Henry V's literary patronage marks only a modest increase, and – more significantly for the present argument – in fifteenth-century England there was no significant attempt to promote vernacular hermeneutics. So, perhaps certain other factors were in play, and we should now attempt to seek them out.

We may start by tracking certain texts – albeit not commentaries – which were deemed to be fit for kings and princes. The age of Philippe le Bel (reigned 1285–1314) saw translations of Boethius and Vegetius (the work of Jean de Meun); Giles of Rome's Latin treatise *De regimine principum* was actually written for Philippe, around 1285, and a few years later was translated into French by Henri de Gauchy. Jean de Vignai produced another translation of Vegetius during the reign of King John the Good, whose son, Charles V, patronized an exceptionally ambitious translation programme (as already noted), which included a new French rendering of the *De regimine principum*, by Jean Golein. Giles taught the theory of governance, Vegetius the art of chivalry (for so *De re militari* was regarded). Boethius's secular philosophy was also popular, particularly since the *Consolation* was enlivened not only by rich mythography but also by narratives of kings *versus* philosophers. Then again, Bartholomew the Englishman's *De proprietatibus rerum* (translated for Charles V by by Jean Corbechon) could provide a king with all he needed to know, and more besides, about the properties of natural things. In Ricardian England, however, these texts were associated not with a king, but rather with one magnate and his daughter: Sir Thomas Berkeley (1352–1417) and Elizabeth Berkeley (d. 1422), who married Richard de Beauchamp, earl of Warwick.

It was for Thomas Berkeley that John Trevisa produced English translations of *De proprietatibus rerum* and *De regimine principum* along with Ralph Higden's 'universal history', the *Polychronicon*.[27] An anonymous translation of Vegetius (maybe by one William Clifton) followed in 1408, after Trevisa's death. And the Boethius translation of John Walton (1410) was almost certainly made for Elizabeth Berkeley.[28] The evidence for this claim is found in the first printed edition (1525) of this work, by Thomas Richard, a Benedictine monk of the abbey of Tavistock in Devonshire. The text is followed with verses which in acrostics spell out the names of the dedicatee and the translator; moreover its preface lavishly compliments the 'Madame' at whose 'instance' Walton has done 'seruyce and plesance'. The printed edition also contains an English commentary, being translated extracts and summaries from Nicholas Trevet's long and learned Latin commentary on the original text. Mark Science, the EETS editor of Walton's Boethius, declares that the prose glosses 'are peculiar to the printed text itself and can be found in no manuscripts'.[29] He could say that because there was one crucial manuscript which he did not examine personally, Copenhagen, Kongelige Bibliotek, Thott 304 fol.[30] This contains the English commentary. Unfortunately, the Copenhagen manuscript is defective at both beginning and end, but – since this seems to be the very manuscript which was used in preparing the 1525 edition[31] – it may be assumed that the material relating to Elizabeth Berkeley was once there. From the Copenhagen manuscript and the Richard edition we can, I would argue, imagine Elizabeth Berkeley's presentation copy of Walton's Boethius, wherein commentary was combined with identification and praise of the dedicatee. On this argument, in addition to employing Trevet in the actual process of translation,[32] Walton provided a Middle English commentary based on the same learned Latin commentator in the version of his translation which he addressed to Elizabeth. It represents the most substantial piece of (non-religious) commentary on any Middle English text.

As the closest English counterparts of the French kings and princes, then, we can do no better than nominate the Berkeley family: of course their patronage was on a far more modest scale, but there are unmistakable features in common. In particular, it is possible to find similar ideas concerning the objectives and techniques of translation in statements made by the French translators and by Thomas Berkeley's main translator John Trevisa, as found in the two original prefaces on translation which he prefixed to his *Polychronicon* translation. But there are major differences, which constitute a particularly English slant or savour. The longest preface takes the form of a dialogue between a secular lord and a clerk in which the lord argues convincingly in favour of translation. Here Trevisa gives to the lord – who surely may be taken as a spokesman for views not dissimilar to those held by Thomas Berkeley – certain ideas deriving from, or at least reminiscent of, Oxford debates on Bible translation.[33] This is, as Ralph Hanna III emphasizes and as I would reiterate, not necessarily to attribute Lollard sympathies (yet again) to Trevisa. Anne Hudson notes that 'in

Oxford in 1401 it was still possible for men to urge the desirability of vernacular translations of the Bible without being suspected as heretics'.[34] My point is simply that arguments of a kind which were bandied around by scholars like William Butler, Thomas Palmer, and Richard Ullerston found their way into Trevisa's dialogue on translation. And there are crucial differences of tone and tenor which set them apart from their French counterparts.

One of the most striking differences is the way in which secular interests are vigorously defined as being, to some extent at least, in opposition to those of the clerics; this may be due to the dialogue form, but a note of aggression does seem to be present (or can be read as being present). In Trevisa's dialogue on translation, and in his translation of the Pseudo-Ockham *Dialogus inter militem et clericum*, secular lords set clerics right on matters relating to textual and temporal sovereignty respectively. Secular readers should have access to material hitherto confined within Latin, and secular leaders should take property away from churchmen who are unworthy to hold them; in other words, literate laymen seem to be trespassing on to territory traditionally occupied by the clerics.[35] After Archbishop Thomas Arundel's *Constitutions* of 1407 and 1409, Berkeley and his translators would not have been able to express views like that with such confidence.

The *Constitutions* sought to suppress any unapproved vernacular activities in preaching and in translation, along with debate on supposedly dangerous subjects in the schools. The culture of control and repression fostered by these prohibitions inhibited the development not only of what Nicholas Watson has called 'vernacular theology' but also of vernacular commentary-tradition in general, by which I mean commentary, both in Latin and *in vulgari*, on texts of all kinds – secular and religious – which were composed in English. This point is given more force by the fact that much Middle English Biblical exegesis produced in the late fourteenth and early fifteenth centuries was of Wycliffite origin, including the 'Glossed Gospels' – produced before 1407 in (to simplify the situation somewhat) three versions[36] – and the prefatory and commentary materials included in the various versions of the Lollard Bible, particularly the so-called 'General Prologue'.[37] Morever, the Lollard heresy soon infiltrated and infected quite orthodox hermeneutics. Thomas Berkeley owned a copy of Rolle's glossed Prose Psalter (Oxford, Bodleian Library, MS Bodley 953);[38] Wycliffite ideas are found in interpolated versions of that text,[39] and it has been suggested (although the evidence is inconclusive) that at least one of the two Middle English Apocalypse commentaries adds a Lollard colouring to the Anglo-Norman work on which both are based.[40] An anonymous

Lollard extracted and translated into English certain arguments in favour
of Bible translation which Richard Ullerston had included in his determination, ignoring Ullerston's balancing arguments against translation.[41] In
the Oxford translation debate of *c.* 1401 scholars had clinically debated if
knowledge of God should hierarchically proceed from the Latinate clergy
to the laity, if layfolk could cope with a text so stylistically difficult as the
Bible, and if the barbarous English language was capable of serving as a
vehicle for the communication of divine truth.[42] When issues of social
control impinged on the consciousness of the church authorities, however,
the situation acquired a new urgency. They 'came to see that the vernacular
lay at the root of the trouble', 'that the substitution [of English for Latin]
threw open to all the possibility of discussing the subtleties of the Eucharist,
of clerical claims, of civil dominion, and so on'.[43] The extraordinarily large
number of copies of the Lollard Bible (whole or in part) which survive –
over 250 [44] – give some indication of the scale of the problem, as envisaged
by the ecclesiastical establishment.

   All English writings, no matter how much or how little theology they
contained, no matter how defensible their orthodoxy may have been, could
therefore fall under suspicion. In the later fifteenth century a copy of the
Canterbury Tales was produced for the prosecution during a heresy trial.
As Anne Hudson says, if this manuscript 'had included, for instance, the
Pardoner's Tale, or, even more, the Parson's Tale, it could on a rigorous
interpretation' of the relevant Constitution have been 'regarded as indicative of heresy'.[45] A similar point could be made about *The Wife of Bath's
Prologue and Tale*, which features a woman who is very competent in the
academic discipline of *disputatio* and adept at deploying authorities from
the Bible and the writings of the Church Fathers – one may recall the arguments of the heretics Walter Brut and John Purvey in favour of women
priests and preachers.[46] And, it may be added, Chaucer's creation tells a
tale in which the social order is challenged to the extent that a poor woman
of low birth manifests moral dominion over a churlish aristocrat: again, he
is on the edge of very dangerous ground. Nicholas Watson has eloquently
argued that the *Canterbury Tales*, 'playing, as they so disruptively do, with
the most important contemporary arguments over teaching and religious
authority', are 'a product' of 'a world which is crucially pre-Arundelian'.[47]
It could be inferred from this that the post-Arundelian world was very
different, and certainly not conducive to the emergence of a Middle English
commentary-tradition.

   There is, I believe, much to recommend that argument, though it
requires substantial qualification. For a start, the contrast between the
pre- and post-Arundelian worlds should not be urged too strongly, for

there is substantial evidence of consistency and continuity in terms of establishment fear of Lollardy. King Richard II returned home early from Ireland (in 1394), allegedly responding to a plea by the archbishop of York and the bishop of London, to stamp out sympathy for Lollardy in high places. An example was made of Richard Sturry (chamber knight and friend of Chaucer), who was ordered to renounce his heterodox views, being threatened with 'a most horrible death' if he failed to comply.[48] Nigel Saul regards the king's treatment of Sturry as deadly serious, arguing that 'by 1389' King Richard 'was the vigorous and articulate defender of orthodoxy that he was to remain until his death'.[49] Archbishop Arundel, one may imagine, would have found Richard's robust reaction quite in keeping with the 'spirit of 1407', if so it may be called. We may recall that, when he was appointed archbishop (in 1397), Arundel 'appeared very much' King Richard's 'man', as Michael Bennett has put it;[50] early in the same year Arundel had written to the king, praising him for 'his efforts on behalf of the church' and offering 'wholehearted support'.[51] And Richard enthusiastically adopted the role of protector of religious orthodox as a vital part of his self-image; witness the 'hammer of heretics' phrase in the epitaph which he probably commissioned himself, and his desire (as expressed to the mayor of London in 1392) of having 'no heresies or errors to infect the people' within 'the bounds of his power'.[52]

Also in the 1390s, Chaucer showed himself acutely aware of the dangers of a zealous priest being accused of Lollardy. When his 'povre Persoun of a toun', a man 'riche . . . of hooly thoght and werk' (I(A) 478–9), takes Harry Bailly to task for his virulent swearing,[53] Harry retorts, 'I smelle a Lollere in the wynd', and warns the Canterbury pilgrims that this 'Lollere' is going to 'prechen us somwhat' (*Man of Law's Epilogue*; II(BI) 1173–7). Two priests of the early fifteenth century found nothing fictitious or funny in such a situation. First, we may consider the testimony of Alexander Carpenter, about whom hardly anything is known, though he may have been educated at Oxford. However, his *Destructorium viciorum* (apparently completed in 1429) was exceptionally well known, having enjoyed (as G. R. Owst once put it) 'an almost unrivalled succession of printed editions down to the year 1521'.[54] Herein Carpenter complains that, 'if anyone preaches or says anything against' the daughters of Avarice, 'immediately their lovers are enraged and call him heretic and Lollard'.[55] Later he claims that 'those who hear cursed transgressors of God's commandments daily blaspheming God with lies and horrible oaths' are 'ashamed to silence them and refrain from such transgressions themselves, lest they be called Lollards and heretics, or of the Lollard sect'.[56]

A more comprehensive protest had been made a little earlier, and in the
vernacular, by John Audelay, priest to 'þe lord Strange' (presumably Lord
Strange of Knokin, in Shropshire).[57] In the second of the poems (composed shortly before 1426) which survive uniquely in Oxford, Bodleian
Library, MS Douce 302, Audelay claims that it is impossible for those who
keep 'Cristis comawndmentis ny3t and day' to speak the truth against
the enemies of God, lest such 'trew Cristyn men' be labelled 'lollard'
(ll. 253–4) – no matter how impeccable one's doctrine may be. 'Here is
non error ne lollarde, / Bot postil and gospel, þe sauter treuly' (Poem 18, ll.
257–8).[58] In the second poem in the sequence, he complains of how layfolk
are similarly inhibited from protesting against clerical 'couetyse', for they
fear that ignorant people will mendaciously be told that their criticism is
an indication of Lollardy, and so they will end up 'preaching on the pillory'
and being burned (Poem 2, 669–75).[59] Poor devout priests can likewise be
branded as Lollards and hypocrites, and have their ardent devotions and
unceasing work for Holy Church valued as nothing.

> 3if þer be a pore prest and spirituale in spiryt,
> and be deuoute, with deuocion his seruyse syng and say,
> Þay likon hym to a lollere and to an epocryte;
> 3if he be bese in his bedus þe Prince of heuen to pay,
> And holde hym in hole cherche dule vche day
> Oute of þe curse of cumpane, and kepe his concyans clene,
> He ys a nyþyng, a no3t, a negard, þai say.
>
> (Poem 2, 131–7)[60]

Rien ne change. The accusation of Lollardy has lingered long in the wind.
Other continuities are equally evident. Richard II did not pursue Charles
V's strategy of political legitimation through patronage of 'commentated
translations' of high-prestige texts. Neither did his Lancastrian successors.
Vernacular hermeneutics became, and remained, a problem area. Writing in
the 1390s, Chaucer shows himself acutely aware of the orthodox insistence
that difficult 'scole-matere' and the deployment of authorities had to be
left to the Latinate experts, confined to 'prechyng and to scoles of clergye'
(*Friars's Prologue*, III(D), 1272, 1275–6). Writing in 1415, Thomas Hoccleve
vehemently affirmed that Biblical interpretation was the prerogative of
properly qualified and officially authorized clerics; layfolk should keep to
their own professions and read their own books.

> Bewar Oldcastel / & for Crystes sake
> Clymbe no more / in holy writ so hie!
> Rede the storie of Lancelot de lake,

Or Vegece of the aart of Chiualrie,
The seege of Troie / or Thebes / thee applie
To thyng þat may to thordre of knyght longe!
(Thomas Hoccleve, 'To Sir John Oldcastle', 193–8)[61]

All of this seems to indicate the ongoing, cumulative development of a cultural climate wherein church and state co-operated in the suppression of many manifestations of vernacular scholarship.

An obvious concomitant is that any activity which put scholarly tools – commentaries, concordances, reference-books – in the hands of the laity would have been viewed with deep suspicion. 'Symple soules' had to rest content with texts like Nicholas Love's *Mirrour of the Blessed Lyf of Jesu Christ* (*c.* 1409), a compilation of safe 'devoute ymaginacions' which bore the authorization of Archbishop Arundel himself.

That, at least, is a scholarly viewpoint which has achieved wide currency during the past decade or so. However, moves to appropriate Nicholas Love as a prominent member of Arundel's thought-police should be resisted, or at least moderated. For a start, and at the risk of stating the obvious, the Latin original of the *Mirrour*, the *Meditationes vitae Christi* which may be the work of Johannes de Caulibus, achieved a wide popularity throughout Western Europe in both its original form and in its several European translations, appealing to layfolk and clerics in countries which knew little if anything of Lollardy.[62] Generally speaking, the secret of its success seems to have been its spirited promotion of an affective, family-oriented piety; these are the core values of the text, and they remain powerfully present in Nicholas Love's version, whatever its effectiveness as anti-Lollard propaganda.[63] Besides, if we are seeking texts which (whether consciously or not) seek to keep layfolk away from the sites of official power, a plethora of possibilities present themselves – including works by a particularly brilliant 'vernacular theologian', Walter Hilton (d. 1396). Hilton may have been involved in the trials of Nottinghamshire Lollards, and a blatantly anti-Lollard treatise (in Latin), the *De adoracione ymaginum*, has been attributed to him.[64] *The Scale of Perfection*, Hilton's *magnum opus*, shows itself highly attentive to the needs and capabilities of those same 'symple soules' who were to become Love's target-audience. It is explained that they may experience the second part of contemplation, which lies principally in affection and is characterized by a fervour of love and spiritual sweetness in the remembrance of Christ's passion (*Scale*, I. 5). Hilton is certainly not patronizing about such people (see especially *Scale*, II. 30) and one of the treatise's governing assumptions is that most of us will never be able to climb to the higher rungs of the ladder of perfection. Of course, given divine omnipotence God can bestow the highest gift of contemplation on whoever He wishes – 'to lerid or to lewid, men or women occupied in prelacie, and to solitarie also'.[65] But, although a person living the active life may have this gift by a special grace, Hilton considers that no one can have the full use of it unless 'he be solitarie and in liyf contemplatif' (I. 9). There is nothing in the second book of the *Scale* to contradict this social and professional location of the spiritual élite, though there it is the differences between the various degrees of perfection which are at the centre of attention, with nothing being said about the status of people who, in normal circumstances, can expect to enjoy those various degrees.

Furthermore, in a text usually dated to the same period as Book I of the *Scale*, Hilton's *Epistle on the Mixed Life*, layfolk are offered as much 'contemplation' as is compatible with their busy 'active' lives. Their 'mixed' life is valorized by (*inter alia*) being set in parallel to that lived by 'men of holi chirche, as to prelates and oþire curates which have cure and souereynte ouer oþere men for to [kepe] and rule hem'.[66] But this comparison does not, of course, give 'temporal men' any 'lordschipe' over either the teachings or teachers of 'holi chirche'. Exceptional acts of divine grace apart, for layfolk 'mixed' life means enthusiastic participation in that same affective devotion which subsequently was promoted by Love's *Mirrour*. In that regard, the Augustinian canon and the Carthusian prior do not seem to be very far apart. Neither preached a doctrine of social or spiritual egalitarianism.[67]

A similar conclusion may be reached concerning a lesser-known text, the late fourteenth-century *Pore Caitif*, which presents itself as offering all that is sufficient for each Christian man and woman, and addresses its reader as a 'child willing to ben a clerk'. Nicholas Watson has praised the 'egalitarian language' of this 'opening', which, he suggests, points 'towards a readership liberated by the education' provided by the *Pore Caitif*, which functions as 'a tool for the autodidactic user'. 'This theme of liberation' is deemed to lie behind 'the text's use of the image of Christ's body as a charter':

This scripture is our lord Jhesu Crist, chartre and bulle of our heritage of heuene. Lokke nat this chartre in thy cofre, but sette it or wryte it in thyn hert, and alle the creatures in hevene, nor in erthe, ne in helle mow not robbe it neither brenne it fro the but yf thou wilt thiself, assentynge to synne. And yf thou kepe wel this chartre in thy cofre of thin hert, with good lyvyng and devoute love lastingly to thyn ende, and trustly and treuly as he is verray God, thorughe vertu of this chartre thou shalt have thyn heritage of blysse during withoute ende.[68]

Thus, in Watson's view, the *Pore Caitif* attempts to 'empower the vernacular reader', directing him beyond Christ's human flesh to his divinity, in contrast with the controlling corporeality of Love's *Mirrour*. Whereas Love wishes to tie his reader to his text's carefully approved imagery 'for a lifetime of reflection', the *Pore Caitif* sees its 'authority over the reader as *temporary*': 'Once the truths found' therein 'are written in the heart, the reader is no longer a child learning the ABC, but a clerk, finding his or her own way to heaven'.[69]

But the 'clerical education' offered by this treatise may be read as a skilful piece of spiritual spin-doctoring on a par with Hilton's creation of a mixed life for 'temporal men', as a means of recommending a programme of devotional self-help which leaves the institutional structures firmly in place and beyond criticism. The *Pore Caitif*'s clericism is allegorical, not literal. No argument can be drawn from the allegorical sense of Scripture, as legions of late medieval theologians were wont to say,[70] and it was hardly an effective means of educational empowerment. Writing the scripture which is Jesus Christ on one's heart will not create the level of actual literacy and book-learning necessary to achieve power and position whether secular or ecclesiastical. The *Pore Caitif* does not seek to subvert its readers' general dependence on the Church and its ministers, or to offer any 'autodidactic' substitutes for their orthodox rites; only ordained priests possess the privileges of expounding holy Scripture both in public and in private, and of administering all the sacraments, the most sacred of which is the sacrament of the altar: metaphorical discourse concerning 'a eucharistic act of eating'[71] is a very poor thing in comparison with the awesome priestly power of confecting the body and blood of Christ. And not even real-life clerks could (exceptional divine grace apart) find their own way to heaven, being obliged to avail themselves of those same ecclesiastical services which charted the life-cycle of every Christian from baptism to extreme unction.

So, then, it could be said that there is little difference between the *Pore Caitif*'s values and those of the *Mirrour of the Blessed Lyf of Jesu Christ*; if we are looking for purveyors of spiritual opium to the masses in late medieval England, Nicholas Love need not be singled out.[72] But I myself am wary of such totalizing judgements, believing that the spiritual ambitions and needs which these texts served are worthy of our respect even if they are not open to our understanding. Thousands upon thousands of individual late medieval experiences of religion are far too irreducibly plural (not to say unknowably private) to be reduced to simplistic or patronizing formulae. And neither need Arundel's authorization of his *Mirrour* be taken as the key to the cultural significance of the entire text, its worth to ordinary decent Christians seen as forever compromised by the *Constitutions*.

But is it possible that the impact of Arundel's *Constitutions* has been exaggerated in modern scholarship?[73] In the past few years a more sceptical view of their significance has emerged, well exemplified by comments in Kathryn Kerby-Fulton's latest monograph.[74] Here the 'draconian' interpretation of the *Constitutions* offered by Watson, Kantik Ghosh, and others is questioned, and the point emphasized that 'censorship in a manuscript culture is especially difficult to enforce'; hence the authorities may have been 'unrealistic' in their supposed ambitions.[75] The number of surviving manuscripts of the 'Lollard Bible' is a fascinating case in point. As already mentioned, approximately 253 copies of the whole or parts of this translation have come down to us.[76] Clearly, it achieved an extraordinarily high level of dissemination. And at least some of its owners seem to have been untroubled by (or at least, suffered no known legal consequences because of) its problematic origins.[77] Indeed, did they know or care about its problematic origins? The blatantly Lollard 'General Prologue' survives in a surprisingly small number of copies; only five are complete, while another three are substantially complete.[78] It could be argued that, divested of this dangerous document, the Biblical text itself was able to enjoy a relatively untroubled existence – particularly if it was owned by the great and the good, powerful people whose social status made accusation and ostracization difficult if not impossible. Some support for this hypothesis may be gleaned from the trials of Coventry Lollards during the period 1486–1522. Various books of the Bible are mentioned in the records: 'copies of the Old and New Testaments, . . . along with a Psalter, the Book of Tobit, the Gospels, the Acts, the Epistles of Paul and James, and the Apocalypse'.[79] Often it is specified that such texts are written in English; presumably we are dealing with portions of the Lollard Bible. Their possession had grave consequences for lower-status Lollards. However, members of the civic élite were, generally speaking, left alone. This leads Shannon McSheffrey and Norman Tanner to entertain the hypothesis that 'there may have been any number of high-status Lollards throughout England whose adherence to the sect remains obscure because their influential station left them immune from prosecution'.[80] At the very least, it seems quite clear that Geoffrey Blyth, bishop of Coventry and Lichfield, 'thought that it was dangerous for the lower orders to have direct access to the Bible'.[81]

Granted all of this, I feel that sufficient evidence remains to postulate the existence of a climate of fear in certain contexts and social sectors at certain times (both pre- and post-Arundel). The *Constitutions* may be seen as both a symptom and an important stage of the historical process, rather than an initiating and determining cause without which history would have been very different. And such a climate was not entirely absent from late medieval France, despite the much more positive attitude to vernacular hermeneutics which, as the present chapter is arguing, was a major feature of that country's textual culture. Let us return to the commentated translation of Augustine's *De civitate Dei* which, in 1375, Raoul de Presles contributed to Charles V's translation programme. Raoul explains his omission of theological questions from the second part of this work on the grounds that public disputation on such matters should be left to the schools, and certainly not conducted in his vernacular treatise: 'Il ne loist a aucun a desputer publiquement de la foy crestienne, se ce n'est escoles pour avoir la verite des matieres.'[82] (The parallel with the anxiety of Chaucer's Friar, who warned the Wife of Bath to leave 'scole-matere' and manipulation of *auctoritees* to 'prechyng and to scoles of clergye', is quite obvious.)[83] If a French scholar could express such concerns even in the context of the exceptional patronage of vernacular 'publication'[84] emanating from the court of Charles V, how much more pressing must they have been for vernacular writers in late medieval England, due to the very different message coming from the royal court (whether of Richard II, Henry IV, or Henry V). Raoul also set about making a French translation of the Bible, claiming at one point that no one could accuse him of arrogance in so doing, since the king's command put paid to any such imputation: 'vostre commandement m'en excusera en tout et par tout'.[85] The Wycliffite Bible enjoyed no such justification, not having been initiated by a royal command. And, although aristocratic status could well have put some of the owners of the Lollard Bible above suspicion, this certainly did not excuse the translation 'en tout et par tout'.

Besides, there are several substantial testimonies from fearful Englishmen, which make it quite clear that we should not move from over- to under-rating the significance of Arundel's *Constitutions*. The concerns of Alexander Carpenter and John Audelay (as discussed above) have the smack of authenticity. Then there is the curious case of the cleric who wrote the Middle English treatise on the Ten Commandments known as *Dives and Pauper* (dated between 1405 and 1410) and the set of sermons now preserved in MS Longleat 4. In the preface to the Longleat sermons, our anonymous author (who may have been a Franciscan) complains that despite Christ's order that his disciples and other preachers and teachers of God's law should teach the gospel to every man and woman in every language, in 'þese dayis' certain prelates are inhibiting preaching and teaching in English.[86] His 'leue frend' is fortunate because he (or she?) cannot be prevented from knowing the gospel in English, that being the addressee's 'kendely language' – presumably on account of that person's powerful social position? But he himself writes the gospel 'to ʒou in wol gret drede and persecucion', apparently living and working within a climate of fear to which the *Constitutions* contributed.[87]

There is, on the face of it, nothing in the Longleat sermons which would have aroused Arundel's ire. However, the earlier *Dives and Pauper* was a very different kettle of fish. Robert Bert, a chaplain of Bury St Edmunds, had his copy confiscated as a suspect book, Bishop William Alnwick declaring that it contained many errors and even more heresies. And yet – Abbot Whethamstede ordered a copy for the St Albans library.[88] Both of these reactions reflect parts of the truth about the book, which may be seen as a worthy successor to John Trevisa's dialogues; however, whereas Trevisa's *miles* or *dominus* had the best arguments and the last word, here it is the clerical Pauper whose judgement prevails. But this is not to say that Dives, who sometimes recalls Trevisa's 'fiction of magnate logical skill',[89] is a man of straw. He vehemently puts his point of view in the initial sharp exchange concerning riches and poverty, and is particularly outspoken on the topic of images in churches: 'I wolde þey weryn brent euerychon.'[90] Elsewhere, however, his views are impeccably orthodox, as when he accepts without any argument whatever that the wickedness of a sinful priest does not devalue the sacraments which he administers.[91] Dives is no latter-day Lollard knight. For his part, Pauper takes a quite orthodox line on (for instance) holy poverty, though in the eyes of suspicious readers that could perhaps have resembled a defence of Lollard 'poor priests'; however, subsequently he leaves us in no doubt of his support for the establishment view concerning the payment of tithes.[92]

In some measure *Dives and Pauper* carries over into English crucial aspects of the scholastic *sic et non* technique: dangerous opinions are heard and countered, divergent views are debated. Laymen are being encouraged, and to some extent enabled, to think and argue like real (rather than allegorical) clerics. And this is done in a clear and cogent vernacular style which finds no difficulty in rendering difficult concepts in idiomatic English. One may compare the lucidity frequently achieved by Reginald Pecock, who once remarked that certain 'ful hiʒe and worþi maters in her digynte touching booþ god his benefetis and his lawis' are easier to understand than such less dignified subjects as points of English law or business procedure. This follows a remark that he had encountered gentlemen of the laity who could 'conceive, vndirstonde, reporte and comune' the highest matters which he had written about.[93] In similar vein, in his preface to the Longleat sermons the *Dives and Pauper* author defends the poor preacher who dines with 'men of value': it is not the 'delicat metis' that he comes for but rather their 'speche of vertue and wisdam', this being found there more frequently than among the 'comounys'. On these occasions prelates and preachers should speak 'princepali wisdam of God's law', and 'answerin to doutis and questyonys þat men askin hem of Goddis lawe'.[94] The spiritual welfare of such intelligent and inquiring layfolk 'of value' deeply troubled the ecclesiastical authorities. Faced with the spread of Wycliffite heresy, the last thing they wanted was for the tools of the academic trade to pass into the hands of such people through their 'kendely language'.[95] Here, then, is the type of discourse which was most troubling to the establishment and, from the point of view of this present chapter, is most significant, rather than the rhetoric of those spiritual self-help books which were carefully prepared for 'autodidactic users'.

The implications for vernacular hermeneutics were immense. In an atmosphere of 'gret drede and persecucion' wherein just about any Middle English text, however innocuous its use of theological and philosophical doctrine, could be cited as evidence of heterodoxy (particularly in the cases of the socially weak and vulnerable), with the secular and ecclesiastical authorities colluding to maintain a clear division between the roles of *dominus* and *clericus*, *dives* and *pauper*, any attempt to develop an English commentary-tradition was doomed to failure. The fate of Reginald Pecock was hardly encouraging: even a prominent anti-Lollard polemicist could suffer the same fate as his opponents. In 1458 or 1459 Thomas Bourgchier, archbishop of Canterbury, instructed rectors and preachers in the province of Canterbury to hand over any of the bishop's books *in vulgari Anglico compositos* which they might possess.[96] Little wonder, then, that there is no fifteenth-century commentary on Chaucer's *Parliament of Fowls* of the type produced by Evrart de Conty, even though the mythography in that English poem merited exegesis every bit as much as that presented by the *Eschez amoureux*. In the prologue(s) to his *Legend of Good Women* Chaucer had provocatively raised the issue of the poetic ethics[97] of writing about a faithless woman, and had the God of Love complain that the *Roman de la Rose* is a heresy against his law – in other words, it supposedly functions as a *remedium amoris* rather than as an *ars amatoria*. Here is the key argument which Jean de Meun's defenders were to deploy in the *querelle de la Rose*. But, Thomas Hoccleve's translation of Christine de Pizan's *Epistre au dieu d'amours* apart,[98] that controversy found no English *campus duelli*,[99] and there is no evidence whatever of a *querelle de Criseyde*. When that extraordinary instance of Italian self-commentary and self-promotion, Dante's *Convivio*, impacted on Middle English literature it was as the source for quite traditional doctrine on true nobility, as featured in *The Wife of Bath's Tale*, rather than as the model for autoexegesis by Chaucer or any of his English contemporaries or successors.

Chaucer's French contemporaries spoke a very different language. As part and parcel of the 'state hermeneutics' sponsored by Charles V, French was regarded as 'the new Latin' whose hour had come. In Roman times, Nicole Oresme confidently explains, 'Greek was in relation to Latin what Latin is for us in relation to French. And at that time the students in Rome and elsewhere were introduced to Greek, and the sciences were usually presented in Greek; while the common mother language (*langage commun et maternel*) in that country was Latin.'[100] The mother language of his own country being French, Oresme can conclude 'that the project of our good King Charles, who has good and outstanding books translated into French, is to be commended'. Oresme is, in effect, proclaiming a *translatio studii*, the transition of scholarship from Rome to France, from Latin to French. Citing Cicero's *Academica*, he asserts that 'matters which are weighty and of great authority (*grant auctorité*) are delightful and agreeable to people when written in the language of their country'. Aristotle's *Politics*, a work previously translated from Greek into Latin, has now been rendered into French, at the king's command.[101] Christine de Pizan, enthusing about Charles V's translation programme, declares that 'it was a noble and perfect action' to have had such works 'translated from Latin into French to attract the hearts of the French people to high morals by good example'.[102] She proceeds to develop the *translatio studii* theme, making the point that France has taken possession of a heritage which in days of yore had passed from Greece to Rome.

But in late medieval England, the English language could hardly function in the same way within orthodox promotion of a transfer of learning and power as expressed in works written in the vernacular. John Trevisa and Geoffrey Chaucer had celebrated the transference of learning from Greek into Latin and from Latin into English,[103] but such discourse came to be associated with Wycliffite heresy:

Ierom, þat was a Latyn man of birþe, translatide þe Bible boþe out of Ebru and out of Greek into Latyn, and expoundide ful myche þerto. And Austyn and manie mo Latyns expounden þe Bible for manie partis in Latyn, to Latyn men among which þei dwelliden. And Latyn was a comoun langage to here puple aboute Rome and biʒondis and on þis half, as Englische is comoun langage to oure puple . . . Lord

God, siþen at þe bigynnyng of feiþ so manie men translatiden into Latyn and to grete profyt of Latyn men, lat oo symple creature of God translate into English for profyt of English men! [104]

Thus, the *translatio studii* ideal was tainted by the Lollards. It is not surprising, therefore, that there is no official affirmation of the *translatio auctoritatis* from Latin into English of the type which, most memorably, Dante had been able to make for his own 'illustrious vernacular'. And here is one possible solution to the mystery of the missing Middle English glosses.

CHAPTER 2

Looking for a sign: the quest for Nominalism in Ricardian poetry

Those who do not believe in Jesus Christ, declares Walter Hilton, are not eligible for the benefits made possible by His passion. Throughout time, no one was ever saved, nor will be saved, except through belief in Christ and His coming. He proceeds to attack certain men who 'gretli and grevousli erren' by saying that 'Jewis and Sarcenys and paynemes', who lack such faith, may nevertheless be saved. This erroneous view is described in terms which make it perfectly clear that Hilton is thinking of the *facere quod in se est* doctrine which has been associated with fourteenth-century Nominalism. 'Bi kepynge of hire owen lawe', convinced that their own 'trouth is good and siker and sufficient to here savacion', infidels may 'in that trouthe' perform many good and righteous deeds, and perhaps if they knew that the faith of Christ was better than theirs they would leave their own faith and follow it, to ensure their salvation. But this is not sufficient, Hilton retorts, because Christ is the mediator between God and man, and no one can be reconciled with God or come to heavenly bliss except through Him.[1]

This passage from the *Scale of Perfection* obviously bears comparison with Geoffrey Chaucer's praise of the pagan 'Tartre Cambyuskan', 'noble kyng' of Tzarev, for keeping the 'lay' (law) of the religion into which he was born to such a superlative extent that he exemplified all the virtues which are appropriate to the ideal ruler and knight, being 'So excellent a lord in alle thyng.' Chaucer keeps silent, however, on his prospects for salvation.

> Hym lakked noght that longeth to a kyng.
> As of the secte of which that he was born
> He kepte his lay, to which that he was sworn;
> And therto he was hardy, wys, and riche,
> And pitous and just, alwey yliche;
> Sooth of his word, benigne, and honurable;
> Of his corage as any centre stable;
> Yong, fressh, and strong, in armes desirous

As any bacheler of al his hous.
A fair persone he was and fortunat,
And kept alwey so wel roial estat
That ther was nowher swich another man.
(*Squire's Tale*, v(F) 16–27)[2]

Hilton's terminology is remarkably similar to that employed by William Langland in his treatment of the salvation of that paradigmatic virtuous pagan, the Roman Emperor Trajan, who 'took nevere Cristendom':

Ac truthe that trespased nevere ne traversed ayeins his lawe,
But lyveth as his lawe techeth and leveth ther be no bettre,
(And if ther were, he wolde amende) and in swich wille deieth-
Ne would nevere trewe God but threw truthe were allowed.
(B XII. 285–8)[3]

This chapter will concentrate on the ideas in these two passages, contextualizing them within the intellectual culture of their day and with reference to the relevant scholarly literature of ours. The term 'Nominalism' is a notoriously difficult one, of course; it has been stretched in many ways, as when (for example) it is taken as overlapping substantially with 'scepticism', a move which can be both confusing and sensationalizing. As W. J. Courtenay has recently reminded us, William of Ockham would almost certainly not have thought of himself as a Nominalist; for him the term would probably have denoted a supporter of the language-theory of Peter Abelard and/or his followers.[4] Elsewhere I have argued that some of Chaucer's ideas about language have many affinities with views expressed in twelfth-century treatises on terminist logic, including the work of Abelard;[5] this body of doctrine was later significantly developed by English rather than French scholars.[6] However, most if not all of the ideas in question are to be found in Jean de Meun's section of the *Roman de la Rose*, and it is this source which Chaucer seems to have been following.

So, the prospects of identifying Chaucer as some sort of Nominalist by this route are remote and unrewarding. Therefore I shall use the term 'Nominalist' here *improprie* and *secundum communem usum loquendi*, as found in much recent criticism. My concern will be with the 'Nominalist Questions' as termed and identified in Russell Peck's very helpful article,[7] questions which involved the dialectic of the divine power, the economy of grace and justification, the relationship between free will and destiny, and the nature of the covenant between God and man. The vexed question of salvation outside the Christian Church served, and will serve here, as a major focus for these controversial issues.

By way of focusing on the *facere quod in se est* principle, it should be said at the outset that this was neither an exclusively Nominalist nor indeed an exclusively fourteenth-century idea. Courtenay believes that it follows a general Franciscan tradition.[8] Indeed, versions of the doctrine appear in thinkers as far apart from William of Ockham, and from each other, as Alexander of Hales OFM, Albert the Great OP, and the secular masters Richard RitzRalph and Jean Gerson. The doctrine was controversial, certainly, as Hilton's attack makes abundantly clear. But that does not make it specifically Nominalist. It is more accurate to say that the idea was channelled, explored, and developed by certain so-called Nominalists, a good example of which may be found in the thought of the Oxford Dominican Robert Holcot (d. 1349).

It is generally assumed that Chaucer knew Holcot's popular commentary on the Book of Wisdom, a work which enjoyed a readership that went far beyond the clerical. The main proof that Chaucer consulted this work directly was offered in Robert Pratt's 1977 article on the Nun's Priest's knowledge of dream-theory, knowledge which, Pratt argued, derived from Chaucer's consultation of Holcot.[9] Having followed up Pratt's references and compared in detail Holcot's statements with Chaucer's text, I am rather less convinced than Pratt was. But let that pass for now; in principle I see no reason why Chaucer should or could not have read Holcot's Wisdom commentary. Now, here Holcot is generally more circumspect than he is in his *Sentences* commentary and his quodlibets, works written for a more specialist and select audience. Yet the Wisdom commentary does express clearly his belief that if a man 'does what is in him' God will not ignore him, but rather ensure that he is sufficiently informed concerning those things which are necessary for his salvation.[10] But if Chaucer did read the relevant passages, he has left no record of it. What he does share with Holcot – though he certainly did not have to go to Holcot for it – is 'classicism', if that term may be used in preference to the totalizing and potentially misleading term 'humanism'.[11]

This brings us to consider the general issue of the relationship between 'classicism' and Nominalism. As is well known, Holcot's Wisdom commentary offers an abundance of classical lore, as it draws extensively on exegesis of secular texts and mythographic treatises, and of course demonstrates his own extensive knowledge of many ancient authors. On the face of it, an interest in those supposedly 'Nominalist Questions' which bear on heathen virtue and prospects for salvation is utterly consonant with an interest in the texts and cultural traditions of pagan antiquity. It seems reasonable to suppose that such debates encouraged and stimulated the scholarly study of the relics of the past. But one did not have to be a Nominalist to be a classicist. There is not a trace of a Nominalist Question in, to take two highly influential works by 'classicizing friars', Nicholas Trevet's commentary on the *Consolatio philosophiae* of Boethius and John Ridevall's *Fulgentius metaforalis*. Or in the massive *Reductorium morale* by that classicizing monk, Pierre Bersuire OSB, one part of which, the *Ovidius moralizatus*, Chaucer seems to have known.[12]

To reinforce this argument, let me invite you to hear the testimony of one fourteenth-century witness who, for the moment, shall remain anonymous. There is, he claims, no substantial article of the Christian faith which God did not reveal many times before the actual advent of Christianity. A lengthy defence of the veracity of many pagan foretellings and confirmations of revealed truth follows, including reference to the sibylline prophecies, the discovery during the reign of Constantine of a tomb in which there lay a man wearing a golden medallion which bore the inscription 'Christ will be born of the Virgin Mary, and I believe in Him', the insight of the three wise men from the East who understood the significance of the star of Bethlehem, and Dionysius the Areopagite's admirable reaction to the solar eclipse which occurred at Christ's crucifixion, in the middle of the lunar month when such an event could not happen naturally. Are we dealing, then, with a Nominalist? Far from it: I have been paraphrasing a passage from the *De causa Dei* of Thomas Bradwardine,[13] a vociferous critic of the 'pestiferous Pelagians', as he termed those who dared to subvert the Augustinian explanation of the relationship between human merit and divine reward.[14]

The classicism of 'Bisshop Bradwardyn' – as Chaucer termed him in *The Nun's Priest's Tale* (VII. 3242) – has not received the attention it deserves. Moreover, his much-vaunted Augustinianism is not exclusively a matter of theological doctrine (involving the construction of a strict necessitarianism), though that is certainly true: it functions on the level of literary genre and strategy as well. For the model underlying Bradwardine's *De causa Dei* is not the *Sentences* commentary or *summa* or quodlibetal collection, but rather Augustine's *De civitate Dei*. The initials of the fuller title of Bradwardine's text, *De causa Dei contra Pelagium*, replicate those of Augustine's *De civitate Dei contra Paganos*. And the fourteenth-century text follows the style of the earlier work by introducing extensive quotations from classical writers into technical theological discussion, juxtaposing flights of rhetoric with rigorous logical inquiry, and strategically placing pagan virtue and knowledge in supportive and subordinate relation to definitive Christian doctrine, with the superiority of revealed truth regularly being proclaimed at the expense of heathen folly and falsehood. To some extent, then, *De causa Dei* should be seen as part and parcel of that same cultural movement which, in fourteenth-century England, produced no less than three commentaries on *De civitate Dei*, written by Nicholas Trevet, Thomas Waleys, and John Baconthorpe respectively.[15] It may be added that Bradwardine and Holcot had access to the same library, the exceptional collection amassed by the noted bibliophile Richard de Bury, which was well stocked with both sacred and secular texts.

But let us return to the passage from Chaucer's *Squire's Tale* which commends King Cambyuskan for doing the best he could. The Biblical text which is most apposite here is, of course, Romans 2:14–15: 'For when the Gentiles, who have not the law, do by nature those things that are of the law; these, having not the law, are a law to themselves. Who shew the work of the law written in their hearts, their conscience bearing witness to them.' Elaborating on this at the beginning of his *Compendiloquium de vitis illustrium philosophorum*, John of Wales OFM praises the lives of pagans who were virtuous despite the fact that they did not have the present Law: Christians promise but do not practise what they receive as precepts, while the Gentiles kept those things to which they were not bound by legal obligation.[16] This had been all said before, of course, by Gregory the Great, in his *Moralia in Job*, to which John of Wales is indebted.

Is there anything new here under the sun? Not thus far, I think. What is crucial is the argument context in which such material may be placed, the agenda which it is supposed to further. It is when one moves from praise of pagan virtue to consideration of the fate of the souls of virtuous pagans that the situation becomes critical. Chaucer, however, refuses to be drawn. At the end of the *Knight's Tale* the narrator professes ignorance regarding the destination of Arcite's spirit when it 'chaunged hous'. 'I nam no divinistre' (i.e. theologian) he protests; I find nothing about souls 'in this registre', i.e. the register of table of contents of the authoritative book he is allegedly following, this being an elliptical way of saying that his source is silent on the matter. 'Arcite is coold', may Mars guide his soul: but Chaucer does not speculate as to where Mars will guide his soul. Similarly, at the end of *Troilus and Criseyde*, we are told that the soul of Troilus goes to wherever it was that 'Mercurye sorted [i.e. allotted] hym to dwelle' (v. 1826–7). These passages contrast with the narrative which is in fact a primary source for them both, Boccaccio's account (near the end of the *Teseida*) of the ascent of Arcita's soul.[17] For the Italian text had hinted that Arcita's soul may dwell in Elysium; he is not worthy of heaven itself, but it is not appropriate that he should dwell among 'blackened souls'.[18]

However, Chaucer's attitude seems to be, 'To clerkes lete I al disputison' (here I borrow a phrase from Dorigen; *Franklin's Tale*, v(F) 890). It is worth recalling that a similar attitude is found in one of the major repositories of classicism in the European vernaculars, the 'romances of antiquity', those 'historical novels' about pagan antiquity which constitute the basic genre to which the *Knight's Tale* and *Troilus and Criseyde* belong.[19] There pagans are often commended, but the issue of their salvation is left very much alone – as when, for example, the *Roman d'Eneas* quotes Dido's epitaph as saying that no better pagan would ever have lived, had not 'solitary love seized her', without speculating about her afterlife.

> . . . Iluec gist
> Dido qui por amor s'ocist;
> onques ne fu meillor paiene,
> s'ele n'eüst amor soltaine . . .
> (2139–42)[20]

Turning now to Chaucer's interest in predestination and future contingents, which receives its fullest expression in *Troilus and Criseyde*, I would suggest that here also there is a lack of evidence which would demonstrate the specific relevance of Nominalist theology. Chaucer's knowledge of the text and gloss of the *Consolatio philosophiae* is quite sufficient to account for all the substantive statements about freedom and destiny which feature in his constructions of virtuous heathen. Here I am referring to the 'Vulgate' text of Boethius along with Jean de Meun's French translation and the extensive commentary by 'classicizing friar' Nicholas Trevet, these being the sources of Chaucer's *Boece*.[21] Moreover, Trevet seems to have been the direct source of at least one, and possibly more, passages of the *Troilus*.[22]

Chaucer's most crucial deviation from the *Consolatio* is particularly interesting. In Book IV of this poem, the most philosophical of all Chaucer's pagans, Troilus, falls prey to despair, as he contemplates the impending departure of his Criseyde to the Greek camp. Following a tortuous Boethian elaboration of the question, if a man sits, is this because God has preordained that action or is he acting out of free will (in which case, God's foreknowledge is dependent on human choice), Troilus proceeds to a conclusion which is certainly not in Boethius: 'al that comth, comth by necessitee: Thus to ben lorn, it is my destinee' (IV. 958–9).

These words could well have had a particular resonance for one of the addressees of the poem, 'philosophical Strode' (V. 1857), generally identified as the Ralph Strode who became a Fellow of Merton College, Oxford, before 1360. For Strode had debated this very subject with John Wyclif, who for his part affirmed the proposition that *omnia que evenient de necessitate evenient*: all that comes, comes by necessity.[23] The mantra is Bradwardine's; it permeates *De causa Dei*.[24] But it had become associated with Wyclif, to judge by the way his opponents used it against him.[25] Strode would probably have been intrigued, perhaps even amused, by the fact that Chaucer had put this strict necessitarianism into the mouth of a virtuous pagan (who, however virtuous, is still a pagan, and talking in a highly emotional state, his passions quite subverting his reason). Perhaps Troilus reminded Strode of someone he once knew.

Whatever the truth of this particular matter may be, the general picture seems quite clear. As far as Chaucer is concerned, there seems to be no necessity to allege the influence of radical, specifically Nominalist, ideas. And such influence should not be posited without necessity. Chaucer's eulogy for Cambyuskan stands alone, tantalizing and unsupported. It just might owe something to a reading of *The Travels of Sir John Mandeville* (originally written in French during the 1350s), a fantasy-filled travelogue which 'contains a startling degree of tolerance of the religious views of Saracens, Chinese, Indians, and others'.[26] For example, one of the Middle English versions declares that 'men schulde noght have many men in dispyt for theire dyverse lawis, for we wote not whom God loveth ne whom he hatith'.[27] There is no evidence that Chaucer knew this popular work. Its very existence, however, adds force to the point that in his day admiration for non-Christian virtue was by no means the prerogative of 'pestiferous Pelagians'. But whatever its source, influences, or inspiration, even the *Squire's Tale* passage does not include any speculation on the afterlife of a pagan whose life on earth was exemplary.

Moving on now to Langland, the main passages in question are B XI. 140ff (C XII. 73ff) and XII. 210ff (C XIII. 149ff and XIV. 148ff), together with the recuperation of many of the main issues at B XV. 385ff (C XVII. 117ff).[28] Trajan bursts into Langland's text by interrupting (most appropriately) a discussion of baptism which the Dreamer and Scripture are having. 'Baw for bokes!' As is witnessed by a pope, St Gregory the Great, the true knight Trajan 'was ded and dampned to dwellen in pyne / For an uncristene creature' (142–3). However, 'Gregorie ... wilned' salvation to his soul, on account of the

> ... soothnesse that he seigh in my werkes.
> And after that he wepte and wilned me were graunted grace,
> Withouten any bede biddyng his boone was underfongen,
> And I was saved, as ye may see, withouten syngynge of masses,

> By love and by lernyng of my lyvynge in truthe,
> Broughte me fro bitter peyne ther no biddyng myghte.
> 'Lo! ye lordes, what leautee did by an Emperour of Rome
> That was an uncristene creature, as clerkes fyndeth in bokes.
> Nought thorugh preiere of a pope but for his pure truthe
> Was that Sarsen saved, as Seint Gregorie bereth witnesse.
>
> (B XI. 147–56)

Langland proceeds to indicate his source for this story. In the *Legenda sanctorum*, he explains, may be found a fuller account (160), this being a reference to the *Legenda aurea* which the Dominican Jacobus de Voragine wrote around 1260, a work so popular that it survives in over a thousand manuscripts. The Trajan episode forms part of Jacobus's Life of St Gregory, which explains why Langland is adamant that a pope has witnessed to Trajan's salvation. This 'paynym of Rome' was pulled out of pain on account of 'leel love and lyvyng in truthe': blessed be the truth which broke hell's gates in this way, and saved the 'Sarsyn'[29] from Satan's power – something which 'no clergie' could (161–75). Trajan's subsequent monologue includes the citation of Christ's words at Luke 7:50 to the prostitute (generally identified as Mary Magdalene, following John 11:2) to the effect that *fides sua* should save her and cure her of sin (216–17). This is taken as proving that faith ('bileve') is a 'leel' (trusty, loyal) help, standing 'above logyk or lawe' (218).

> Of logyk ne of lawe in *Legenda Sanctorum*
> Is litel alowaunce maad, but if bileve hem helpe . . .
>
> (B XI. 219–20)

Similarly, in B XII, Ymaginatif argues that Trajan did not dwell 'depe' in hell, and so our Lord was able to get him out of there 'lightly', easily. A similar resolution may be offered to the problem of the penitent thief who was saved at the crucifixion – 'he is in the loweste of hevene' (212). There are, in other words, degrees of punishment and reward, and that fact should be taken into account when considering such difficult matters. Whether Socrates or Solomon are saved or not, no man can tell. But, particularly in view of the fact that God gave such teachers intelligence, whereby those who have come after have been instructed, we may 'hope' that 'God for his grace' may give 'hir soules reste' (270–3). But Christian clerics, protests the Dreamer, all believe that 'neither Sarsens ne Jewes' nor any creature who lacks 'Cristendom' may be saved (276–7) – a proposition which Ymaginatif disputes. He was not alone: as we shall see, many Christian clerics would have disagreed with the Dreamer's blanket statement; Langland is setting up an extreme statement in order that it may be challenged. So, 'Contra!', exclaims Ymaginatif. The 'just man shall scarcely be saved' on the day of Judgement (1 Peter 4:18), which must mean that he *shall* be saved.

> Troianus was a trewe knyght and took nevere Cristendom,
> And he is saaf, seith the book, and his soule in hevene.
>
> (281–2)

'The book' is generally assumed to be the *Legenda aurea*; the statement that Trajan 'took nevere Cristendom' emphasizes the fact that he was unbaptized. Ymaginatif then explains that there are three kinds of baptism, before going on to make the apparent allusion to the *facere quod in se est* principle (285–90) which was quoted at the beginning of this chapter.

According to Janet Coleman, 'What is most significant' in Langland's *exemplum* of Trajan (as it appears in both the B- and C-texts of *Piers Plowman*) 'is that God can and does respond to him who does his best *ex puris naturalibus* [i.e. in purely natural conditions, lacking the intervention of divine grace] and this response, this acceptance, is what ultimately matters in the fact of salvation.'[30] And Robert Adams avers that Ymaginatif 'revels in the naive Pelagianism of the story', using it to broach 'the possibility that God saves all whose lives conform to the natural law of Truth, regardless of sacramental support or explicit faith'.[31] I would like to approach such claims through, in the first instance, a consideration of what may advisedly be called the mainstream theological tradition relating to the different kinds of baptism, as alluded to at B XII. 283–4:

> Ac ther is fullynge of font and fullynge in blood shedyng,
> And thorugh fir is fullyng, and that is ferme bileve . . .[32]

This doctrine is expounded well in that most successful of all medieval theological textbooks, the *Libri sententiarum* of Peter Lombard, who will serve as a guide along this wicked way.[33]

The Lombard firmly distinguishes between the sacrament and the thing itself (the *res* or referent as opposed to the 'sacrament' or symbol). Some people have the sacrament but not the *res*, while others have the *res* but not the sacrament. In the case of the latter, he continues, it may be argued that martyrdom (*passio*) performs the function of baptism (*vis baptismi*). Furthermore, the Lombard quotes Augustine and Ambrose as being of the opinion that certain people can be justified and saved without baptism by water (*baptismus fluminis*). On the other hand, he continues, at John 3:5 Christ said, 'unless a man be born again of water and the Holy Ghost, he cannot enter into the kingdom of God'. If this is true in general, then the statements cited above cannot be correct. The Master demolishes this contrary opinion with the argument that Christ's condemnation applies to those who could be baptized but are contemptuous of the sacrament. Or the words may be understood as meaning that unless a man experiences the regeneration which comes through water and the Holy Ghost, he cannot be saved, the point being that *baptismus fluminis* is not the *only* possible means of achieving that regeneration. Support for this view is sought in the *Glossa ordinaria* on Hebrews 6:1–2, where it is said that baptism should be understood in several senses, 'because there is baptism by water, by blood, and by repentance'.

These statements were mulled over by generation after generation of *Sentences* commentators and compilers of *summae*. Only baptism by water is a sacrament, St Thomas Aquinas explains in his *Summa theologiae*, but a person can receive the effect of baptism, through either baptism by blood (*baptismus sanguinis*) or baptism by fire (*baptismus flaminis*).[34] *Baptismus flaminis*, which is baptism by the Holy Spirit, 'takes place when the heart is moved by the Holy Spirit to believe in and love God and to repent of one's sins. For this reason it is called baptism of repentance (*baptismus penitentiae*).' In his earlier *Sentences* commentary Aquinas gave an account of how *baptismus sanguinis* confirms Christ's passion not by sacramental representation but 'in reality' (*realiter*); therefore it is not the sacrament but the *res* itself. *Baptismus penitentiae* is here discussed with reference to someone who wants to be baptized but is prevented from receiving the sacrament; in that case someone can be saved 'by faith alone and contrition'.[35] A similar view is expressed in Bonaventure's commentary on the same passage of the *Sentences*. The fact that someone can be saved by means other than *baptismus fluminis* does not render it a non-essential sacrament, for it was laid down by divine precept, and insofar as precepts are necessary for salvation therefore baptism by water is necessary. But since God is not obligated to act by the precepts He himself has instituted, if someone has the will to receive baptism but not the opportunity then *baptismus flaminis* will suffice. However, a person who is able to receive *baptismus fluminis* but does not do so is not saved.

Returning to what Peter Lombard himself says, it is important to note that he proceeds to expound the *fides sufficit* ('faith is sufficient') doctrine which, as we shall see, was vitally important for Langland. If baptism suffices for the salvation of very young children who are unable to believe, argues the Lombard, how much more must faith suffice for adults who desire baptism but are unable to receive it? Augustine asks the question, 'which is greater, faith or water?' and answers, 'faith'. This is supported by Christ's words, 'he that believeth in me, although he be dead, shall live' (John 11:25). But what about those who were unable to believe in Christ specifically, because they could not possibly know of Him, due to their historical circumstances?[36] Could a special dispensation be allowed to them, just as it was to those who were unable to be baptized, though they wanted to be? Peter Lombard is silent on that issue; he is not talking about virtuous heathen, though of course his words easily lend themselves to being invoked in that context. Several of the *Sentences* commentators did precisely that. St Bonaventure, for instance, considered the case of the 'good pagan' Cornelius the Centurion (as described in Acts 10), who first received the Holy Spirit and subsequently was baptized with water.[37] This does not mean that *baptismus flaminis* cannot effect salvation, Bonaventure declares, but rather that if there is nothing to prevent one from being baptized by water then one should certainly receive the sacrament. Cornelius was in the right place at the right time. The clear implication is that if he had not been, then he would have been saved by *baptismus flaminis*. Earlier Bonaventure had quoted John 11:26, 'every one that liveth and believeth in me shall not die for ever'. The *iusti* believed and were of the faith before they were baptized; therefore, had they died in such faith they would not have been eternally damned. *Gratia gratum faciens* is a disposition sufficient for salvation, when one returns to God with one's whole heart and withdraws from error. This can occur through divine grace without baptism by water, and therefore it is possible for a person to be saved by *baptismus flaminis* alone.

In bringing the doctrine of the various types of baptism to bear on the issue of the salvation of the heathen, Langland was following the tradition of the *Sentences* commentaries in general; he did not need Nominalism in particular to help him find that thread. Trajan was a tougher test-case than Cornelius, but Langland did not need to read Neopelagian theology to be aware of the depth and extent of the controversy surrounding this figure. For that was made abundantly clear by the *Legenda aurea* itself, in a passage which represents one of that text's few forays into the area of speculative theology.

On this subject some have said that Trajan was restored to life, and in this life obtained grace and merited pardon: thus he attained glory and was not finally committed to hell nor definitively sentenced to eternal punishment. There are others who have said that Trajan's soul was not simply freed from being sentenced to eternal punishment, but that his sentence was suspended for a time, namely, until the day of the Last Judgment. Others have held that Trajan's punishment was assessed to him *sub conditione* as to place and mode of torment, the condition being that sooner or later Gregory would pray that through the grace of Christ there would be some change of place or mode. Still others, among them John the Deacon who compiled this legend, say that Gregory did not pray, but wept, and often the Lord in his mercy grants what a man, however desirous he might be, would not presume to ask for, and that Trajan's soul was not delivered from hell and given a place in heaven, but was simply freed from the tortures of hell . . . Then there are those who explain that eternal punishment is twofold, consisting first in the pain of sense and second in the pain of loss, i.e. being deprived of the vision of God. Thus Trajan's punishment would have been remitted as to the first pain but retained as to the second.[38]

Moreover, Langland's constant reference to the *Legenda* is remarkable in a text which is notorious for the way in which it covers the tracks of its sources. Why should he be so concerned to refer us to Jacobus? Because this was a safe source to cite, given its author's high reputation and unimpeachable orthodoxy, or simply because it was the main determinant of his own discussion? Or even both?

The situation is further complicated by the fact that, when a card-carrying Nominalist (still using that term according to the common *usus loquendi* of recent criticism) treats of the three types of baptism, the results may seem far from controversial. In a quodlibet wherein he insists that observance of the Mosaic Law merited eternal life, Robert Holcot affirms the importance of grace.[39] An unnamed colleague (*socius*) had suggested that a person can be saved without baptism or grace. If one is thinking of baptism by water, Holcot argues, it may be pointed out that no Catholic believes such baptism to be necessary for salvation in the sense that without it a man cannot be saved. Building on Peter Lombard, Holcot notes that two other kinds of baptism (by the shedding of blood and by fire) are equally efficacious. However, as far as grace is concerned, there is no doubt that a man who lacks it is damned. Apparently it is the *socius* who is the radical rather than Holcot. Who, then, is the Nominalist; will the pestiferous Pelagians stand up and be counted? Apparently not. At least, not here.

But Bradwardine certainly had a point. The clerics he was opposing were far from being mere rhetorical men of straw. At least some Neopelagian ideas (or what were perceived as such) were definitely current, and figures like Walter Hilton worried about them. It is also indubitable that aspects of Nominalist thought put great pressure on the conventional ideology of baptism. Some of them must therefore be considered at this point.

In exemplifying the subversive teaching of the alleged ringleader of the gang of 'Nominalists', William of Ockham, it is *de rigueur* to cite instances of his invocation of the absolute power of God.[40] And it is perfectly true that, according to Ockham, through the exercise of his *potentia absoluta* God can condemn the best of saints and save the worst of sinners. However, the extent to which such a claim is genuinely subversive is very debatable. It is evidently true that some of Ockham's contemporaries were troubled by it. The masters who condemned fifty-one articles from his *Sentences* commentary at Avignon in 1326 refused to accept the excuse that God's absolute power functioned most infrequently; Ockham's argument, they declared, proceeded equally well without that condition as with it. This I take to mean that the impact of what Ockham was saying was not lessened by his appeal to *potentia absoluta*; it did not justify the extreme, perhaps even shocking, claims he made concerning what God could do.[41] In sharp contrast, a far more positive approach has been taken by one of the most influential of Ockham's modern advocates, Philotheus Boehner, who believed that the *potentia absoluta* should be seen in terms of ultimate possibility.[42] On this interpretation, what is at issue are things which God is able to do but might never do. For most of the time one can be confident of the predictable and secure governance which we perceive as the result of the *potentia ordinata*. Furthermore, W. J. Courtenay has robustly dismissed the spectre of 'arbitrary divine intervention' functioning to 'undermine certainty both in the physical order of nature and in the order of salvation', claiming that here we are dealing with 'a mistake of modern historical interpretation'.[43] To put it another way, the realm of the *potentia absoluta* is best understood not as one of action but rather as one of capacity, comprising all the possibilities open to God, out of which He chose or chooses to do certain things, or to establish certain laws or procedures. Whatever God has done, does, or will do, falls within His ordained will, and most of this is understood as the present orders of nature and salvation. In certain cases, however, God can act in ways which are unusual or unexpected, to say the least. For instance, He could make an essence without existence, produce an accident without its subject, make the body of Christ be present in the absence of the host, or remit guilt and punishment without created grace.[44] Indeed, God can do anything which does not involve a contradiction. But one should not, so to speak, hold one's breath in eager expectation of such an occurrence. We can have confidence in the *status quo*, trust the operation of God's established laws or procedures. According to this argument, then, the somewhat sensational claims which some have made for the *potentia absoluta* are highly misleading.

The Ockhamist theory of merit *de congruo* presented much more of a challenge to the traditional economy of grace and salvation: significantly, Bradwardine spent a lot of time attacking that particular doctrine.[45] Congruent merit involved 'half merit', 'an act performed in a state of sin, in accordance with nature or divine law' which was 'accepted by God as satisfying the requirement for the infusion of first grace'.[46] (By contrast, actions informed by grace, with established supernatural 'habits' behind them, merited *de condigno*, i.e. were fully meritorious.) Men could perform individual good deeds without a fixed supernatural *habitus* of charity behind those actions and God could accept them as meritorious *de congruo*. In this regard Ockham defended himself against the charge of Pelagianism by saying that God is not *obliged* to accept men who have rendered themselves acceptable to him (here the appeal to *potentia absoluta* came in very useful).[47] The crucial point, however, was that God had freely bound himself to reward such good deeds; under the *potentia ordinata* a righteous man living *in puris naturalibus* was inevitably rewarded with an infusion of grace: 'de potentia Dei ordinata non potest non infundere'.[48] Robert Holcot worked this vein of thought further. In his Wisdom commentary we find the argument that actions done out of natural goodness are meritorious *de congruo*; they meet the standard required to ensure a generous divine response. If a man 'does what is in him' God will reciprocate by doing what is in Him.[49] According to God's ordained power, if a good pagan walks by the best light he has, he will merit, and receive, his eternal reward. Here, then, is the ideological context in which Holcot's insistence on grace (as noted above) may be placed. It is not so traditional after all.

All this, I believe, is far removed from the attitudes which Langland expresses at B XV. 385ff (C XVII. 117ff), which may now be discussed, after which we will consider the relationship of that passage to *Piers Plowman*'s version of the Trajan story. At B XV. 385–9 Langland's treatment of the notion that faith alone can ensure salvation makes it utterly clear that here he is thinking, at least in the first instance, of how this functions within, rather than outside, the Christian Church – in short, at this point his perspective is very similar to that of the 'Master of the Sentences' as described above. Sometimes clerics do not perform their proper functions, and fail to teach the 'folk of holy kirke' adequately. In this case, *sola fides suffit* to save such uneducated people. However, then the speaker, Anima, proceeds to add the remark that *sola fides suffit* can function for non-Christians also: 'And so may Sarasens be saved, scribes and Jewes' (388). Are we, then, back in the world of B XII. 285–8 (as quoted at the very beginning of this chapter), which voices the hope that genuine 'truthe' will be rewarded by God, no matter what 'lawe' is being followed? Apparently not – for Anima quickly explains exactly what is meant by this last remark. Muslims have a belief which approximates to Christianity, inasmuch as they also believe in one creator-God. Indeed, Langland declares, Mohammed was a Christian himself, who, having been frustrated in his ambition of becoming pope(!), set about misleading the people of Syria to whom he preached. Therefore the clear implication is that any hope of salvation which Muslims may have is based on the extent to which their beliefs are fundamentally or residually Christian; that salvific *sola fides i*s solely the faith of Christianity.[50]

A little later, in the context of a discussion of the conversion of England by St Augustine, Anima remarks that the heathen are like 'heath' or uncultivated land. This evokes a vision of a 'wilde wildernesse' in which 'wilde beestes' spring up, 'Rude and unresonable', running around without keepers (457–9). So much, then, for the restraining and civilizing force of *lex naturalis*. Likewise, Anima declares, a newly born child is thought of as a heathen as far as heaven is concerned, until it is baptized in Christ's name and confirmed by the bishop. Here the importance of baptism is affirmed. And all of these comments, I believe, serve as a contrast with what was said about Muslims, who have, so to speak, received some cultivation, and therefore are in a different situation from pagans and newly born children. It is logical for Anima to go on to say that since 'Sarsens', with 'pharisees', 'scribes and Jewes', are 'folk of oon feith' in that they honour 'the fader God', it is relatively easy for them to add the other tenets of the Christian creed to this the first one, 'Credo in Deum patrem omnipotentem' (B xv. 605ff). Once again, the necessity of believing in specifically Christian doctrine is being hammered home. True, 'faith alone' may suffice for the salvation of 'Sarsens', 'scribes and Jewes' (here Langland does not pursue that thought), but Christianity alone brings security, and the main advantage which such people have is clearly defined in terms of the extent to which they have been prepared to receive the full Christian message, because of what they know already.

Langland makes his views even more clear in the c-text's version of this excursus, which I see as an amplification and elaboration of his views rather than some later shift in his thinking in sympathy with a 'Lollard enthusiasm for conversion', as Coleman has argued.[51] The point about *sola fides* being sufficient for the salvation of Christians is extended with the remark that, if priests do their job properly, we shall 'do the bettre'. Moreover, Muslims may be saved also – but now the condition is made fully and uncompromisingly explicit. Within their lifespan they have to come to believe in Holy Church:

> Saresyns mowe be saued so yf thei so by-leyuede,
> In the lengthynge of here lyf to leyue on holychurche.
>
> (C XVIII. 123–4; Skeat text)[52]

Thus, the necessity of conversion receives more emphasis. Jews, gentiles, and Muslims live in accordance with law, though their laws are diverse, and they all love and believe in one and the same God Almighty. But our Lord 'loueth no loue' unless 'lawe be the cause' (136). The meaning of 'lawe' is rather unclear here, and Liberum Arbitrium (for he has taken over the role of Anima) proceeds to talk of law in rather a broad sense. Lechers and thieves are identified as people who love against the law, whereas those who love 'as lawe techeth' behave in a way which is in accord with charity. Seeking clarification, the Dreamer asks if Muslims know what charity is (150), to be told that they may love in a way which approximates to it, thanks to the law of nature. It is perfectly natural for a creature to honour its Creator. But many men do not love Him in the correct way; neither do they live in accordance with trusty belief, for they believe in a 'mene', i.e. a false mediator:

> Ac many manere men þer ben, as Sarresynes and Iewes,
> Louyeth nat þat lorde aryht as by þe Legende *Sanctorum*
> And lyuen oute of lele byleue for they leue on a mene.
>
> (C XVII. 156–8)

Muslims live after the teaching of Mohammed 'and by lawe of kynde', this being a good example of how, when nature takes its course 'and no contrarie fyndeth' (i.e. finds no belief system to restrain and cultivate it), both law and loyalty suffer: 'Thenne is lawe ylefte and leute vnknowe' (162). Clearly, Langland is here a lot less confident about the efficacy of what may be achieved *ex puris naturalibus* than Ockham and Holcot seem to have been on several occasions. Followers of 'Macumeth' live in a state in which they are partly educated and partly uneducated ('as wel lered as lewed', 182), continues Liberum Arbitrium, and since our Saviour allowed such people to be deceived by a false prophet, it is up to 'holy men' to put matters right by converting them. Once again, the point is being made that clergymen should be doing their job properly.

> Holy men, as y hope, thorw helpe of the holy goste
> Sholden conuerte hem to Crist and cristendoem to take.
>
> (C XVII. 185–6)

In the C-text's reformulation, then, Langland's excursus is concerned to affirm the superiority of Christianity over other belief-systems rather than to explore the possibilities for salvation outside the Church – as were adumbrated earlier by both the B-text and the C-text. There is no trace of an appeal to the *potentia absoluta*. Indeed, so conservative is Langland's maintenance of the standards of what some called the *potentia ordinata* that there seems to be no reason to bring the 'power distinction' to bear on the above-mentioned passages at all.

If it may be granted that in B XV. 385ff, and more conclusively in the corresponding C-text passage, Langland's thought is at least avoiding or at most opposing certain theological doctrines which have been identified as Nominalist, the crucial question then arises, what is the structural and argumentative relationship between this material and the earlier passages in which we are offered 'naive Pelagianism'?[53] Janet Coleman stresses the dialectical aspect of *Piers Plowman*,[54] an idea which I would wish to elaborate. When reading a scholastic *quaestio* one must not make the assumption that the initial definition of the proposition, and the arguments offered whether pro or contra, express the personal views of the disputant. Rather those are to be sought in the ultimate *determinatio*.[55] Clear evidence of this strategy is often to be found in *Piers Plowman*, though (unfortunately for Langland's modern exegetes) what is speculative research and what is determination lacks the clear structuring and labelling which is characteristic of the formal academic *quaestio*. On this approach, then, B XI. 140ff (C XII. 73ff) and XII. 210ff (C XIV. 148ff) propose a radical solution to the problem of salvation outside Holy Church, while the passages we have just discussed offer, however obliquely and imprecisely, Langland's last – and much more conservative – word on the matter.

I have much sympathy with this methodology, but feel obliged to enter one major caveat, namely that the difference between the supposedly 'radical' thesis and the supposedly 'conservative' resolution may not be as great as some have supposed. The role of St Gregory as mediator (at B XI. 140ff) has, in my view, been undervalued by those readers who wish to highlight those elements which may be seen in terms of the allegedly Pelagian view that Trajan has merited his salvation and that God is obliged to accept him (*de potentia ordinata* at least. Obviously, in theory and *de potentia absoluta* he could reject him). But I believe that the passage can be read quite differently. Here Langland is fundamentally concerned with making a contrast between love and learning, and therefore Gregory's own clerical credentials are conveniently forgotten. Indeed, the saint is credited with having been fully aware of the fact that love, loyalty, and merit weigh a lot more (as it were) than the power of the entire Christian clergy:

> . . . al the clergie under Crist ne myghte me cracche fro helle
> But oonliche love and leautee and my laweful domes.
> Gregorie wiste this wel . . .
>
> (B XI. 144–6)

And because Gregory knew this well, he desired salvation for Trajan's soul:

> . . . and wilned to my soule
> Savacion for soothnesse that he seigh in my werkes.
> And after that he wepte and wilned me were graunted grace . . .
>
> (B XI. 146–8)

Clearly, there is a lot of 'willing' going on here, and note also the expression of the fact that St Gregory saw, and wept. The saint, in other words, was the initiator. It was he who made the judgement that Trajan's achievements were worthy of some reward: here is no exclusive reliance on congruent merit, no illustration of the principle that *facientibus quod in se est Deus non denegat gratiam*. For no matter to what extent Trajan had done what was in him, if Gregory had not intervened God would not have given the pagan His grace. There was nothing normative about this case, as is implied in Holcot's formulation of the general principle. Neither is there any evidence here of a 'baptism by fire' – once again, that would make Gregory's patronage of Trajan quite superfluous. For Trajan would have been saved already, and certainly not in need of a rescue from hell.

Indeed, the 'love' which helped Trajan to salvation must surely be, at least in part, the saint's love rather than Trajan's. That would seem to be what is meant in the following lines, where this notion is coupled with the idea that it was Gregory who discovered (or 'learned') that this virtuous heathen had lived in truth:

> Withouten any bede biddyng his boone was underfongen,
> And I was saved, as ye may see, withouten syngynge of masses,
> By love and by lernyng of my lyvynge in truthe,
> Broughte me fro bitter peyne ther no biddyng myghte.
>
> (B XI. 149–52)

If Holcot's views are right, then this discovery was utterly redundant, for God would have responded to Trajan's truth within the usual order of things; an extraordinary operation of *potentia absoluta* was quite unnecessary. But what about the apparent emphasis on the lack of efficacy (in this case) of prayer ('bede biddyng') or the singing of masses? After all, as the text goes on to specify, it is not just anyone's prayer that is in question here, but the prayer of a pope:

> Lo! ye lordes, what leautee did by an Emperour of Rome
> That was an uncristene creature, as clerkes fyndeth in bokes.
> Nought thorugh preiere of a pope but for his pure truthe
> Was that Sarsen saved, as Seint Gregorie bereth witnesse.
>
> (B XI. 153–6)

These lines can easily be taken to mean that Trajan was saved not on account of Pope Gregory but because of his 'pure truth', with Gregory playing the role of mere witness and confirmer of an event in which he was fundamentally uninvolved. But that, I believe, is to make a part-cause of Trajan's salvation into the whole. The other part-cause was not, as the text makes abundantly clear, any prayer made formally by Gregory. Rather it was the pope's other actions. He saw ('seigh'), wept ('wepte'), and desired ('wilned'), and 'his boone was underfongen',[56] 'withouten any bede biddyny' and 'nought thorugh preiere'. For prayer simply did not come into it – Gregory's 'boone' or request was conveyed by other means, and duly granted ('underfongen') by God. The distinction I am drawing attention to here is utterly precedented in Langland's source, the *Legenda aurea*: 'Still others, among them John the Deacon who compiled this legend, say that Gregory did not pray, but wept, and often the Lord in his mercy grants what a man, however desirous he might be, would not presume to ask for.' Jacobus also reports the opposite point of view, that Gregory was indeed 'pouring forth prayers for Trajan', and so it would seem that Langland has made a definite decision here, in face of the various options.

The originality of this recontextualizing of Trajan should be recognized. The emperor often appears in scholastic discussions of the efficacy of suffrages for the dead;[57] perhaps that (in part at least) is why, in his desire to break new ground, Langland is so emphatic that 'bede biddyng' and 'syngynge of masses' do not provide a ready answer to the problem. Trajan does not feature in the major scholastic discussions of the different types of baptism; rather it is the centurion Cornelius who tends to appear when *baptismus flaminis* is at issue. But why did Langland strike out on his own, and privilege tears over prayers?[58] Because this is utterly appropriate here, within the context of this particular discussion in its entirety. In B XI. 140ff feelings (particularly love) are being privileged over learning and clerical ritual, the *affectus* over intellectual *aspectus*, and actions are supposed to speak louder than written words. Law without love is not worth a bean (cf. XI. 170). Hence the later remark that Trajan's salvation was something which 'no clergie ne kouthe, ne konnyng of lawes' (B XI. 165). That last phrase could be taken as implying that even the most assiduous following of the *lex naturalis*, or indeed some heathen code of behaviour which elaborated upon it, does not guarantee a spiritual reward, a thought which is utterly consonant with the views found in B XV, as summarized above. By the same token, *fides* stands 'above logyk or lawe', the *Legenda aurea* being cited as a proof-text (B XI. 219–20; quoted above, p. 45); I take that to mean that according to all logic or law Trajan should have remained in hell. Hardly consonant with fourteenth-century Neopelagianism, but utterly consonant with one of the interpretative possibilities offered by Langland's main source for the Trajan legend, the *Legenda aurea*.

Also in keeping with the *Legenda aurea* is Ymaginatif's statement that 'Troianus the trewe knyght tilde noght depe in helle', so 'Oure Lord' was able to get him out easily ('lightly'; B XII. 210–11). Jacobus, echoing Aquinas's *Sentences* commentary, had suggested that Trajan 'was not finally committed to hell or definitively sentenced to eternal punishment'. A similar suggestion is included in William of Auvergne's *Summa aurea*.[59] And in one of his disputed questions on truth, Aquinas declares that 'although Trajan was in the place of the damned, he was not damned absolutely'.[60] (The matter is complicated by the fact that in Middle English 'helle' can refer to either hell or purgatory; the Medieval Latin term *infernus* can be ambiguous in the same way.) In other words, at that point in Passus XII Langland is concerned to make relatively 'light' of the divine rescue of Trajan. Had he been concerned to emphasize the absolute power of God surely he would have placed Trajan in the deepest pit of hell – thereby allowing the Almighty a real chance to show what He could do.

But, all due allowance having been made for these arguments, may we not still suspect that lurking behind – however far behind – Langland's construction of Trajan is the notion of congruent merit, that being a feature of Neopelagian thought which I have described as being more genuinely subversive than the power distinction? The case is weak. Even if one were to isolate the statement that 'for his pure truthe / Was that Sarsen saved' (B XI. 155–6) from its qualifying context (as described above), there is insufficient evidence to enable its identification with a specifically Ockhamist or Holcotian version of the theory of divine acceptability. One could equally well invoke Bonaventure's statement that as far as the *iusti* are concerned *gratia gratum faciens* is a disposition sufficient for salvation (p. 48 above). To be sure, questions could be asked about what a person required to be counted among the *iusti*: did membership entail certain *explicit* beliefs in doctrines essential to Christianity or was *implicit* belief sufficient on the part of the righteous who lived under the guidance of such knowledge and religious precepts as were available to them? That was where God's helping hand, so to speak, intervened. 'It pertains to divine providence to furnish everyone with what is necessary for salvation', declares Aquinas, providing there is no obstruction on the human's part. Thus, if someone who had been brought up 'in the forest or among wild beasts' followed 'the direction of natural reason in seeking good and avoiding evil, we must certainly hold that God would either reveal to him through internal inspiration what had to be believed, or would send some preacher of the faith to him as he sent Peter to Cornelius'.[61] Ockham and Holcot pushed this sort of doctrine further by their insistence that in the usual run of things God *had* to reward such righteous followers of natural reason; hence their controversial line on merit *de congruo*. So, where does Langland's Trajan stand here? In obvious contrast with Cornelius, he lacked a St Peter figure. On the other hand, if my view of St Gregory's definite role in Trajan's salvation be accepted, could Gregory be regarded as a Peter who arrived very late, 'many years after that emperor's death'?[62] But better late than never, of course, and still (so the argument would run) to be taken as an instance of how God is willing to provide the crucial supplement necessary to effect the salvation of a just man.

Then there is the issue of whether Trajan can be regarded as having received some sort of divine illumination, a veritable *baptismus flaminis*. The text is silent on that matter. However, it could be argued that the statement that Trajan lived as his law taught and believed there to be no better (B XII. 286) indicates that he did not receive such assistance. As does the problematic and much-emended line B XII. 289, which Kane and Donaldson give as 'wheiþer it worþ of truþe or noȝt, þe worþ of bileue is gret' and Schmidt as 'wheither it worth or noght worth, the bileve is gret of truth'.[63] Whatever Langland actually wrote there, he seems to have meant that, even though the truth which a pagan held was partial and incomplete by Christian standards, the fact that he had such a faith was meritorious. Now, if Trajan's world-view lacked a lot, surely he could not have experienced a divine revelation? And would that not place Langland's text well within the Neopelagian band of the ideological spectrum? The less God has to work on, so to speak, the greater the opportunity for an action *de potentia absoluta*.[64] But Langland's emphasis on the great worth of belief and the divine respect for truth seems to point rather to the dispensation of the *potentia ordinata*.[65] Yet if we apply its terms of reference to Langland's text the result is inconclusive – for the very good reason that traditionalists and radicals alike (if we may use those categories) were often imprecise about what pagans had to believe in order to be saved. Certainly they did not have to believe the whole truth and nothing but the truth, but exactly *how much* truth was needed was generally left vague. (Aquinas suggested that 'it was enough for them to have implicit faith in the Redeemer, either as part of their belief in the faith of the law and the prophets, or as part of their belief in divine providence itself'.)[66] Which meant that the extent to which they had to be divinely helped was left vague also. The following statement by Alexander of Hales – no 'Nominalist' he – which links the principle of *facere in quod se est* to the belief in God's helping hand is quite typical: 'Si facit quod in se est, Dominus illuminabit eum per occultam inspirationem aut per angelum, aut per hominem.'[67] That sounds remarkably like what Holcot has to say on the same subject in his Wisdom commentary[68] – yet further proof that in the areas here under investigation, exclusively Nominalist doctrines are very elusive.

Finally, while it is quite correct to say that Langland uses Trajan to raise the issue of the salvation of the heathen in general, it should be recognized that he is a lot more tentative about what has happened to Socrates and Solomon than he is about the fate of Trajan's soul. Gregory, both pope and saint, witnesses to the salvation of Trajan, but as far as the rest are concerned Langland contents himself with hopeful imaginations – no more than that. It is, after all, Ymaginatif who in B XII (C XIV) argues that the just man may scarcely but definitely be saved; it is he, rather than a personification representing the highest theological authority, who adduces 1 Peter 4:18.[69] William of Ockham and Robert Holcot were a lot more confident, as we have seen. The distance between them and Langland is quite considerable.

In order to gauge this distance more fully, and to locate Langland more precisely on the intellectual map of his day, a comparison may be made between the relevant passages of *Piers Plowman* and John Wyclif's treatment of Trajan, viewed in relation to Wyclif's unusual version of the *baptismus flaminis* doctrine. In his *De ecclesia* Trajan is considered within a typical scholastic context, namely in a discussion of the value of prayers for the dead.[70] Wyclif supposes that Trajan had dwelled in purgatory rather than in hell, and that God had predestined him to glory and predestined Gregory to save him through intercession.[71] Both these resolutions have the status and power of eternal decrees, for we must believe that neither Gregory whilst alive nor a saint in heaven could change the divine judgement or alter or redirect the divine through prayers. It is evident, Wyclif declares, that Trajan died in a state of grace whereby he was predestined to glory. Moreover, Wyclif cannot believe that Trajan died in a state which would not satisfy the present requirements of justice; presumably here he means justice as understood in the contemporary Christian situation, rather than some sort of shadowy, pre-Christian justice. For in his opinion many people outside Judaism, such as Job, Nebuchadnezzar, and others like them, were Catholics, and the same goes for certain people that we judge to be outside our Christian faith: they were, and are, actually within the true Church, its rightful members. Trajan and just people like him, declares Wyclif, are part of the *vera ecclesia* and have received *baptismus flaminis*, baptism by the Holy Spirit.

The version of those views found mainly in Wyclif's *Trialogus* was vociferously attacked in the vast *Doctrinale antiquitatum fidei catholicae ecclesiae* of Thomas Netter (*c.* 1377–1430), Carmelite theologian and confessor of King Henry V.[72] Wyclif, complained Netter, concealed his doctrine under ambiguous words, but there was no doubt in Netter's mind that the heretic had denied the necessity of baptism. As quoted (and somewhat simplified) by Netter, Wyclif had argued that it would detract from the divine freedom and divine power if God could not intervene to save an infant or adult within the Christian faith unless some old woman or some other person who had come in off the street should baptize them; moreover, he applied the same principle to infidels. Wyclif therefore theoretically dispensed with baptism by water, believing that all that was necessary was *baptismus flaminis* and the influx of 'material water' from the Saviour's side, an allusion to the idiom of John 19:34.[73] Romans 6:3 claims that 'all we who are baptized in Christ Jesus are baptized in his death'; Wyclif took this to mean that Christ's merit and passion were sufficient for the baptism of the *congregatio predestinatorum*. Netter replied with a vehement reinstatement of the importance of *baptismus fluminis*. Wyclif had devalued both *baptismus fluminis* and *baptismus sanguinis*, he complains, in regarding them as mere 'antecedent signs' of *baptismus flaminis*, and arguing that unless this imperceptible (*insensibilis*) baptism is bestowed, the baptized person is cleansed from guilt, whereas if it is lacking the other two are insufficient. This, Netter exclaims, breaks all the pronouncements of the fathers and the Scriptures to the effect that man will perish unless he is regenerated through water. As an imperceptible form of baptism, *baptismus flaminis* would be unknown to us, and indeed be a lesser thing among Christians than that Jewish circumcision which was the figure of our own baptism.

Very similar phrasing occurs in one of Wyclif's *Responsiones* to the arguments of Ralph Strode.[74] This 'friend of truth', as Wyclif terms him, had asked a question which highlighted the problems incumbent on Wyclif's theory of predestination: if a *prescitus* (a person foreknown to be damned) were to die immediately after having enjoyed the spiritual benefits of baptism, would this not interfere with his destiny? No one, replies Wyclif, should presume to deny the regular practice of baptism by water. Yet without it a man can be predestined to glory, providing he has experienced *baptismus flaminis*. *Baptismus fluminis* should be regarded as necessary only if the water in question is understood as the water that flows from the side of Christ.[75]

A powerful critique of such views is mounted in Netter's *Doctrinale*, with reference to the crucial test-case of the virtuous pagan, Cornelius the Centurion appearing yet again.[76] When St Peter preached to Cornelius and certain other (unnamed) people, 'the Holy Ghost fell on all them that heard the word' (Acts 10:44). But this, Netter emphasizes, was not sufficient, for subsequently Peter commanded that they should be baptized (Acts 10:47–8). The visible sacrament is crucial: 'quamvis bonus fuerit plena fide, dico tamen, sine visibili sacramento, vel re ipsa, salvus esse no poterat'. Cornelius had to enter into the Church, participate in its sacraments – and baptism is the fundamental entry requirement. Membership of the Church does not come about simply by grace of predestination or by *baptismus flaminis*. When the Saviour himself said, 'unless a man be born again of water and the Holy Ghost, he cannot enter into the kingdom of God' (John 3:5), he was speaking of 'material' water as used in *baptismus fluminis*, and not of the water which flowed from the side of the Saviour on the cross. As the case of Cornelius illustrates, faith is *conceived* through the influx of the Holy Spirit, but it is *born* in the reception of the visible sacrament.

Wyclif's views on baptism were quite consistent with his eucharistic theory, as Netter shrewdly observed. As an 'empty sign' (*signa vacua*) Wyclif believed the host contained no supernatural grace, but merely functioned to 'signify' or 'figure', and similarly he called the seven sacraments seven 'signs'.[77] And Wyclif's elevation of *baptismus flaminis* over *baptismus fluminis* was one among many manoeuvres whereby the authority of the orthodox priesthood was seriously undermined. Indeed, he suggested to Strode that just as the only water utterly necessary for baptism is that which flows from the side of the crucified Christ, so the 'true sons of God' who have received the spiritual oil of predestination are best equipped to perform the priestly office, even though they may not have been anointed with material oil at a bishop's service of consecration, and lack the *character* which formal ordination imposes, along with the traditional tonsure.[78] Lollard theology elaborated upon such ideas. According to Netter, William White held the view that infant baptism was unnecessary,[79] and William Swinderby was accused of the belief that baptism was of no effect if the priest or the godparents were in mortal sin.[80] Infant baptism is not required where the mother is Christian because the Holy Ghost is transmitted to the child in the womb, according to Thomas Bikenmore, a clerk who was investigated by Bishop Aiscough of Salisbury in 1443.[81] And the Welsh Lollard Walter Brut famously posed the question, if women have the ability to baptize (allowed them in an emergency situation, when a child is near death), and if baptism is the chief sacrament, why should women not administer the other sacraments as well, and take upon themselves all the priestly duties and functions?

Even more significant for us is the curious case of Sir Lewis Clifford, one of the group of 'Lollard Knights' with which Chaucer had some association. It may be recalled that it was Clifford who brought Deschamps's poem in praise of Chaucer from France. Clifford is himself mentioned in it, and elsewhere Deschamps gives him the epithet 'amorous', which I presume means that he could speak well of love, being well-versed in the fashions of *fin amor*.[82] When he renounced his Lollard views in 1402, Clifford conveyed to Archbishop Thomas Arundel a list of Lollard conclusions, wherein the seven sacraments are devalued as 'dead signs' (the sacrament of the altar being described as 'a morsel of dead bread').[83] Most bizarre of all is the statement that baptism is not to be performed by churchmen on a boy, because 'that boy is a second Trinity, not contaminated by sin, and it would be the worse for him if he were to pass into their hands'.[84] K. B. McFarlane regarded this entire account as slightly 'fishy', feeling that 'the views Clifford is made to ascribe to the Lollards are wilder than usual'.[85] Perhaps, under duress, Clifford exaggerated such Lollard views as he knew of, in an attempt to distance himself far from them and impress upon Arundel the strength of his repudiation? However, it should be noted that all the Clifford conclusions may be paralleled (in some shape or form) in other records of Lollard belief, and indeed can be traced back, however circuitously, to the thought of the arch-heresiarch himself. At least part of Clifford's rejection of baptism may be explained with reference, yet again, to Wycliffite doctrine of predestination. Maybe what we are dealing with here is a reflex of the belief that the child of a man and woman who are members of the *vera ecclesia* has been purified by the Holy Spirit and therefore is not in need of material baptism. Indeed – to apply Wycliffite theory of predestination – the churchmen in question could well be in a state of mortal sin (perhaps even 'foreseen' to eternal damnation), and hence less pure than he; therefore it would quite inappropriate for them to minister to the boy. So, there seems to be some logic in Clifford's list of heretical horrors after all.[86]

Langland once complained about how 'heighe' (i.e. noble) men presume to talk 'as thei clerkes were' about Christ and his powers, finding fault with the Father who formed us all, and with 'crabbede wordes' contradicting clerics by raising casuistical theological questions. Men who 'muse muche' about their words, Langland concludes sadly, are brought into 'mysbileve' (B X. 103–15). It would seem that, as far as laymen were concerned, a little learning could be a dangerous thing. But Langland's professional contempt for layfolk who dabble in theology should be recognized for what it is. (As should McFarlane's impatience with views which he saw – too hastily, in my view – as a dumbing-down of Wyclif's sophisticated thought.) In Langland's day, certain laymen achieved impressive levels of proficiency in theology. An excellent example is provided by James Palmer, a London bureaucrat, who compiled the vast *Omne bonum* (within the period *a.* 1327 through 1375) and was the scribe of a manuscript containing William of Nottingham's Gospel Harmony.[87] Other obvious examples include Walter Brut and Geoffrey Chaucer.

If a little learning was a dangerous thing, a lot of learning could prove very dangerous in Ricardian England, given the climate of fear and repression which, as I argued in Chapter 1 above, was then current (in certain times, places, contexts), and by no means unique to the age of Henry IV and Archbishop Arundel. Chaucer's reticence about appearing as a 'divinistre', his profession that most 'disputison' should be left to 'clerkes', was quite sensible, a means of playing safe. Moreover, in light of the wide range of opinions canvassed above (whether Neopelagian or Wycliffite, heterodox or orthodox, sublime or specious), all the major Ricardian poets, no matter how eccentric their formulations could sometimes be, appear as relatively, indeed remarkably, orthodox. True, David Aers has vociferously attacked the *Gawain*-poet as 'Pelagius redivivus', finding his works permeated by the secular values of the 'honourmen' who were his masters, to whom Aers attributes a 'virtually Christless Christianity, good enough for this world'.[88] There was, in my view, a general growth of 'secularity' and a laicizing of many aspects of intellectual conversation in late medieval European 'high culture'.[89] And the *Gawain*-poet is indeed immersed in upper-class values, and professes what Nicholas Watson has nicely called an 'aristocratized theology'.[90] But that need not panic us into announcing a major outbreak of Pelagianism, or (and here I move beyond Aers's specific concerns) convince us that the ideas associated with the *Pelagiani moderni* can be sought and found 'In every bussh or under every tree', like the fairies 'In th'olde dayes of the Kyng Arthour' (to borrow a phrase from the Wife of Bath; *Canterbury Tales*, III(D) 857, 879).

We are, I hope, on safer ground in noting how traditional views on baptism are given new life in *St Erkenwald* and *Pearl*. In the latter poem the Pearl-maiden is safe and sound in heaven, having received *baptismus fluminis.*

> Bot innoghe of grace hatz innocent:
> As sone as þay arn borne, by lyne
> In þe water of babtem þay dyssente.
> Þen arne þay boroȝt into þe vyne.[91]
>
> *(Pearl,* 625–8)

In the former the body of a pagan judge is miraculously preserved in order that its virtuous owner may receive the sacrament of baptism.[92] However, in this case any suggestion of narrow legalism is brilliantly avoided by the device of having St Erkenwald weep over the corpse – in this case a saint's tears actually become the material water needed for *baptismus fluminis* – and anticipate the words he will say in performing the rite.[93] The virtuous heathen joyfully recognizes that his long-awaited baptism has now been effected.

> ffor þe wordes þat þou werpe & þe water þat þou sheddes   – *utter, shed*
> þe bryȝt bourne of þin eghen – my bapteme is worthyn![94]   – *stream, brought about*

All the conditions for the sacrament having been met, his soul ascends to partake in the heavenly banquet whilst his body blackens and corrupts.[95]

And Langland, I believe, avoided both Neopelagianism and Wycliffite predestinarianism in constructing a Trajan who is given full credit for his 'truthe' yet needs some help from a saint; here due recognition is given to both God and man (or more precisely, to both the men involved, with Gregory's role being carefully negotiated and respected). Trajan 'took nevere Cristendom'. There is no suggestion in Langland (as there is in Wyclif) that although Trajan may have seemed to be outside the Church he was actually within it, as a member of the *vera ecclesia.* Rather he 'trespased nevere ne traversed ayeins *his* lawe', the pagan code of behaviour which was the best law he had. But Langland never went so far as to assert unequivocally that this pagan in particular (and certainly not pagans in general) won salvation simply and exclusively by keeping such law. St Gregory, that great willer and weeper, had his part to play.[96]

Lewis Clifford told Arundel of a Lollard view which undermined the efficacy of penance, 'because, as they say', faith is what matters; thus Christ assured Mary Magdalene that her faith had made her safe (cf. Luke 7:50).[97]

That is to say, faith alone suffices for the salvation of a righteous person, the traditional instruction and guidance of the church hierarchy being dispensable. In marked contrast, Langland was a great believer in the efficacy of the sacrament of penance (see especially B XX. 280–7, 305–9). And the *fides sufficit* principle functions very differently in *Piers Plowman*. Though the idea initially appears in the guise of a major challenge (see p. 45 above, noting particularly Langland's invocation of the Magdalene), later it is contained within a quite unthreatening conception of educational deficiency. Faith does suffice in the case of those Christians who have not been properly instructed by their clergymen, or in the case of heathens who possess some but not complete knowledge of Christian truth. In short, special cases are being provided for here; Langland is not undermining either the Church's hierarchical apparatus or the traditional process of salvation, in contrast with on the one hand the Nominalist notion of congruent merit and on the other the Wycliffite notion of the predestined *electus* who deals directly with his God. Concomitantly, Langland's Trajan is not presented as a beneficiary of God's *potentia absoluta* or as one who merited *de congruo* (with his paganism being emphasized). Neither is the emperor seen as one of the *electi*, with the emphasis falling on his membership of the *vera ecclesia* (his paganism being minimized).[98] Therefore, as far as baptism is concerned Langland cannot be accused of being in deep sympathy with either Neopelagianism or Lollardy,[99] *pace* those who have detected the substantial influence of one or other of those ideologies in *Piers Plowman*. The fact that both – generally inconsistent and incompatible[100] – influences have been alleged may be taken as a clear and visible sign that neither is easily discernible in the poem.

So, then, is Nominalism simply 'all in the mind' (like Ockham's universals), as far as the major Ricardian poets here discussed are concerned? I am certainly not saying that. In respect of Chaucer, my point is that there is insufficient evidence to go on. When we begin to enter those areas in which we could discover Chaucer's advocacy (or lack thereof) of some distinctively Nominalist view, the poet stops in his tracks, gesturing vaguely towards those problem regions without exploring them himself. He is content, he declares ostentatiously, to leave such matters to the experts. Whether in actuality he was or was not, we will never know, because in his texts he is just not telling. In other words, the signs run out at the crucial stage, leaving us without direction.

As far as Langland is concerned, the problem regions are certainly under investigation, but the outcome is far from clear. The signs are there but they are all too ambiguous; much depends on the viewpoint of the *viator*.

Are false trails being laid, trails which are meant to be recognized as false? Or are dangerous speculations being carefully ringfenced, contained within a dialectic which proceeds to affirm conclusions that offer consensus and conformity? Or is there indeed something Pelagian or at least Semipelagian about aspects of Langland's thought? My own opinions may be summed up as follows. It is difficult if not impossible to disentangle a sufficient number of views which would place Langland (however briefly) in the Neopelagian camp, especially in view of the complicated cross-currents of theological thought which characterize Ricardian England. Passages which look Nominalist on inspection turn out to be capable of less radical readings, and/or to have been placed within a dialectical framework which does not allow them the last word. Moreover, in Langland there are no Middle English terms which point to the real erogenous zones of Nominalism, i.e. the distinctions between the absolute and ordained powers of God and (more crucially in my view) between condign and congruent merit. In sum, there is no extensive 'Neopelagian Sect Vocabulary' to be identified in *Piers Plowman*. True, the *facere quod in se est* principle does appear at B XII. 285–8, as it does in Chaucer's *Squire's Tale* and Hilton's *Scale of Perfection*. But, as we noted at the very beginning of this chapter, it was not exclusive to the thought of Ockham *cum suis*. The Nominalist Questions accentuated and elaborated upon issues which had been the currency of speculative theology for generations, but their minutiae did not trouble very deeply the hearts and minds of a wider audience: that dubious privilege belonged rather to Wycliffite thought.

I myself doubt if Langland was profoundly involved with Neopelagian doctrine. To me it is highly significant that when he does adumbrate ideas which were associated with it, his citations are limited to issues which had, so to speak, hit the headlines of his day. Ideologically speaking, all that Langland needed to generate the ideas underlying his treatment of Trajan in particular and good pagans in general was knowledge of the *Legenda aurea* and familiarity with the vernacular 'virtuous heathen scene' (as Grady calls it),[101] plus some technical theological information about the *facere quod in se est* doctrine: on this he brought to bear his quirky and obsessive talent. (In the following chapter, I will be arguing that Langland sought to make spiritual sense out of the vernacular theology of pardoning *a pena et a culpa* along with the demotic praxis of pilgrimage commutations.)[102] To focus on that more technical aspect for a moment: the scandal of the 1368 condemnation of Uthred of Boldon's opinions[103] would have helped broadcast certain controversial ideas concerning the fate of the unbaptized (assuming this episode was as well known as some scholars have claimed).[104]

Vernacular reactions against such ideas (however correctly or incorrectly understood) were often ferocious, and this also seems to testify to their fame. I have particularly in mind Walter Hilton's attack (as quoted at the very beginning of this chapter) on those who suppose that non-Christians are able to attain salvation 'Bi kepynge of hire owen lawe'. John Trevisa was even more brusque. Anyone who holds that St Gregory delivered Trajan from hell on account of the pagan's 'greet riʒtwisenesse', he exclaimed, is worse than mad and 'out of riʒt bileve'.[105]

It would seem, then, that a few – just a few – radical theological ideas relating to unconventional baptism and salvation outside the Christian Church had travelled beyond the confines of the schools, and the specialist Latin genres which scholasticism produced, to impact on vernacular literature. The extent of that impact is highly debatable, not least because vernacular literature had already developed sophisticated ways of depicting virtuous heathen.[106] But its shock-waves had certainly reached Geoffrey Chaucer, whose deep interest in the *roman antique* genre made him particularly receptive. However, Chaucer – like Langland, who inscribed arguably Nominalist notions in *Piers Plowman* without affirming them – was anxious to remain within the parameters of 'riʒt bileve'.

In sum, when we consider the possibility of Neopelagian influence on Ricardian poetics, the best attitude is one of scepticism.

CHAPTER 3

Piers's protean pardon: Langland on the letter and spirit of indulgences

In May 1377 Catherine of Siena enthusiastically urged a visitor to Rome – quite the best place on earth for indulgences – to 'Bathe, bathe in the blood of Christ crucified! Go on lapping up the blood of Christ crucified through these pardons (*perdoni*). For when people go to the pardons they are doing nothing less than harvesting the blood, since the pardon is granted us because of the blood of the spotless Lamb.'[1] Christ was the main contributor to a vast *thesaurus mysticus*, filled superabundantly with His own merits and those of His Saints, which made such pardoning possible. Clement VI's bull *Unigenitus* (1343), wherein the idea was promulgated as dogma, had declared that 'Christ shed of His blood not merely a drop, though this would have sufficed . . . to redeem the whole human race, but a copious torrent', thereby 'laying up an infinite treasure for mankind'. This treasure was 'entrusted to Blessed Peter, the key-bearer, and his successors, that they might, for just and reasonable causes, distribute it to the faithful in full or in partial remission of the temporal punishment due to sin'.[2] Powerful words, which express well the emotive force of the originary theology of indulgences (or 'pardons' as they were called in Middle English), the depth of its belief in the largesse of divine love. At its very centre was an affirmation of religious communality: the spiritually rich helped the spiritually poor, the strong the weak, though a transfer of merit from their surplus-supply in the heavenly treasury.[3]

Within the process of pardoning, however, the relationship between the material and spiritual economies was a deeply problematic one, difficult to explain even in the most distinguished schools of theology, and impossible to communicate with sufficient clarity to the public at large – assuming, of course, that those who 'published' or preached the terms of reference of pardons actually wanted their clients to know the whole truth, for it was frequently in their financial interest to exaggerate what was on offer. The depth of semi-comprehension, and downright confusion, was extraordinary. Such a situation was ripe for exploitation – and exploited it was, by learned and lay, by high and low, by popes and pardoners. It afforded a major business opportunity for the real-life models of the *quaestores*[4] presented by Langland, Chaucer, and the Tudor dramatist John Heywood (*c.* 1497–*c.* 1580). In Heywood's play of *The Foure PP* the pardoner-figure is intimately associated with falsehood:

> Ryght selde is it sene or never
> That treuth and pardoners dwell together.
>
> (109–11)[5]

In the crux-laden 'tearing of the pardon' episode in *Piers Plowman*, however, a pardon – albeit an allegorical one – is associated with truth: for in Passus VI (B-text) Piers prepares the folk of the field for a journey to Saint Treuthe, and at the beginning of Passus VII Treuthe responds with the award of a very special pardon. The following chapter will seek to explain the nature of that relationship, by throwing light on the discourses relating to indulgences which Langland is manipulating both literally and allegorically.

My textual commentary – for this is the *modus procedendi* followed in the present chapter – will begin with the final part of the Pardon Passus, for the simple reason that it is the easiest to understand, at least from the perspective of the present inquiry. Whatever Langland said or may have meant earlier in Passus VII, at this point it seems quite clear that he has in mind ordinary, everyday indulgences, the kind on offer at many a medieval shrine and on many a feast-day. And his Dreamer has two major points to make about them.

First, we have to believe in their efficacy. The fact that the pope has 'power' to 'graunte' pardon to 'the peple' is 'is a leef of our bileve', taught us by 'lettred men' (VII. 174–6). As one might expect, this statement is very much within the mainstream of medieval justification and rationalization of the system of indulgences. The Universal Ruler of the Church is not supposed to be fallible, declares Albert the Great, particularly with regard to those things which the whole Church receives and approves. Since the pope has ordered that indulgences be preached, they must be valid.[6] Likewise, Thomas Aquinas is confident that 'the universal Church cannot err'. Therefore, if it approves and grants indulgences, we may be confident that they must 'have some value'.[7]

To be more specific, the 'power' whereby 'the peple' are enabled to pass 'into joye' without 'penaunce' (whether exacted in this life or in purgatory) derives from the power of the keys, as Langland carefully acknowledges: *Quodcumque ligaveris super terram erit ligatum et in celis.* At Matthew 16:19, Christ had said to St Peter, 'I will give you the keys of the kingdom of heaven, and whatever you bind on earth will be bound in heaven, and whatever you loose on earth will be loosed in heaven.' According to a standard late medieval exegesis of this passage, two keys were bequeathed to St Peter, as the first pope, and to his successors in perpetuity. One was the key of *ordo* (as exercised in priestly ministry) and the other, the key of jurisdiction. The former authorized a priest to officiate in (for instance) the 'tribunal of penance' (*forum penitentiale*): hearing confession, judging if a sinner was truly contrite, granting absolution, and setting the terms of the satisfaction which had to be rendered. Thereby men were freed from their *culpa*, or moral guilt.[8] The latter, the key of jurisdiction, constituted the authority for the issue of indulgences, this being an extra-sacramental means of liberating the sinner from part or all of his 'temporal' punishment or *pena*. Hence ordination did not confer on priests the authority to issue indulgences; that was the prerogative of those officials who had the legal right to do so in the 'judicial tribunal' (*forum iudiciale*), namely the pope and bishops acting under his delegated authority.[9] In sum, the power of the keys covered, *inter alia*, two crucial operations of the Church – the power to grant indulgences (as described near the end of Passus VII) and the power to absolve from sin in the tribunal of penance (that being, I believe, what Langland mainly has in mind in Passus XIX. 183–91).[10]

The Dreamer's second major point is that, in the final judgement, trust in indulgences 'is noght so siker [sure] for the soule . . . as is Dowel'. 'A pokeful [bagful] of pardon', 'indulgences doublefold' and membership of all the fraternities of friars,[11] may be rated as worth a mere piecrust if Dowel does not help you, if you are lacking in respect of good works. Mere possession of indulgences will certainly not be sufficient for the sinner at judgement day – a point which takes on added poignancy if it be realized that indulgences and fraternity letters were sometimes used as grave-goods, buried with their owners as passports to the next world.[12] Once again, the Dreamer's pronouncement is utterly orthodox, with generations of theological discussions behind it. Langland's Middle English poetry is carrying on the business of Latin theology, staying well within its terms of reference and reiterating its verities. The importance of good works was made abundantly clear by the commonplace scholastic doctrine that indulgences were useless without them. Before any release from *pena* was possible the sinner had to be cleansed of moral guilt or *culpa*, which involved contrition, confession, and absolution, with a properly ordained priest officiating. As that most popular of all Middle English poems, *The Pricke of Conscience* (c. 1350), succinctly puts it,

> ... pardon of papes and bisschopes,
> Þat es granted here als men hopes,
> May availe þair saules in purgatory,
> Þat has purchaced it here worthyly,
> If þai of þair syn had contricion
> And war shrifen byfor þat pardon,
> Þan may pardon after þair dede
> In purgatory þam stand in stede.
>
> (IV, 3804–11)[13]

The question of whether the individual was in a state of grace was crucial.

> Bot na man may here pardon wyn,
> Bot he be out of dedly syn ...
>
> (IV, 3880–1)[14]

Had he not passed successfully through the tribunal of penance, his indulgences were indeed worth nothing more than a piecrust.[15]

The importance of the recipient's spiritual condition was emphasized by, *inter alia*, William Lyndwood (*c.* 1375–1446), bishop of St Davids and right-hand man of Archbishop Chichele in his proceedings against the Lollards. In his *Provinciale seu constitutiones angliae* Lyndwood poses the question, if people are impenitent, how can giving them indulgences be defended, particularly in view of St Paul's assertion that before Christ's tribunal each one will receive what he has won, according to his works, whether good or evil (2 Cor. 5:10)?[16] While sinners retain their guilt (*culpa*) it's impossible to remit their punishment (*pena*). Now, the power of binding and loosing was handed down to ministers for edification and not for destruction: but does not an indulgence, which is a gratuitous remission of sin, tend to destruction, because by this process sin remains unpunished?[17] Indeed, it could be said that the facility of pardon encourages men to sin: it's very easy to obtain an indulgence, so why worry?

In response to these arguments Lyndwood stresses the importance of contrition on the part of the penitent, which relates to justice, and the satisfaction which is rendered through the Church's communication of the merits of the saints, which relates to mercy. Hence both justice and mercy are given their due in the process. Mere possession of pardons – even plenary pardons – does not make one immune from divine punishment. The recipient has to be in the correct spiritual state, and devoutly carry out the designated spiritual activities. Furthermore, people should beware of neglecting good works in the future simply because they have obtained indulgences.[18] They may think themselves immune, but they can still be 'bound' or convicted on the charges of negligence and contempt. Proper satisfaction has to be made, Lyndwood emphasizes; penitence which has been enjoined must be performed. Langland would certainly not have quibbled with that.

So much for the poet's comments on 'normal' pardons, as found at the end of Passus VII. Explaining the opening lines of this same passus is a far tougher assignment.

> Treuthe herde telle herof, and to Piers sente
> To taken his teme and tilien the erthe,
> And purchaced[19] hym a pardoun *a pena et a culpa*
> For hym and for his heires for everemoore after;
> And bad hym holde hym at home and erien hise leyes . . .
>
> (*Piers Plowman*, B VII. 1–5)

My aim is to distinguish and describe the literal/historical discourses relating to regular indulgences which are being transformed and transcended in Langland's construction of his allegorical pardon. I most certainly do *not* wish to reduce Langland's allegorical pardon to a literal one, confuse the spirit with the letter, or muddle the tenor of what Langland says with the vehicles he uses to say it. The principle on which I am proceeding is that an understanding of the significance of those very vehicles, and an appreciation of their valence in literal/historical contexts, are major steps towards comprehension of the allegorical tenor which Langland has them bear.

'A PARDOUN *A PENA ET A CULPA*'

This is the most controversial of all the discourses here deployed by Langland. As already explained, indulgences appertained to *pena* but not to *culpa*; the latter could be forgiven only through the sacrament of penance, as administered by a priest who possessed the 'key' of ministry.[20] However, the phrase *a pena et a culpa* seems to have come into common use with reference to indulgences, particularly plenary ones. (The fact that Langland is allegorizing a plenary indulgence in particular is indicated by his reference to 'pleyn pardon' in l. 102.) I suspect that this was in some measure due to a blurring of the two senses of the term *absolutio*, which could mean either priestly absolution – following confession, as part and parcel of the sacramental process whereby *culpa* was remitted – or release from obligation or debt in a strictly legal sense. That is to say, pardons could be said to 'absolve' insofar as they released their possessors from the debt of sin and hence its punishment (*pena*).[21]

Whatever the causes, the evidence for the magnitude of the confusion is compelling. Francis of Meyronnes OFM (*c.* 1285 – after 1328) remarks that it is commonly taught ('communiter docetur') that indulgences *a pena et a culpa* may be granted. In fact, this cannot be, he explains, because *culpa* is a matter repugnant to indulgences, and can be remitted only through contrition and confession.[22] Similar treatments of the topic are afforded by Bonifatius de Amanatis and William of Montlaudun.[23] According to the former, the belief that indulgences can deliver absolution *a pena et a culpa* is a 'vulgar' misunderstanding rather than a legal fact (*est non a iure, sed a vulgo*), and the latter spoke of how such remission of sin as was granted by jubilee year indulgences offered absolution merely from *pena*, though 'vulgarly' they were supposed to afford release from both guilt and punishment (*vulgo a pena et a culpa dicitur*).

A similarly 'vulgar' misunderstanding seems to have developed in relation to the plenary indulgence issued by Urban VI in connection with the (quite disastrous) 'crusade' mounted in 1383 by Henry Despenser, bishop of Norwich, against Clement the Antipope. This indulgence 'ab omnibus peccatis tuis' was offered to participants, with the necessity of confession and contrition ('ore confessionis et corde contritis') being emphasized in the *forma absolutionis* that formed part of the papal documentation. Here I quote from Thomas Walsingham's *Historia anglicana*.[24] The likes of Francis of Meyronnes, Bonifatius de Amanatis, and William of Montlaudun could have found nothing to complain about there. However, in Henry Knighton's chronicle this same indulgence is described as granting absolution from both punishment and guilt ('a poena et culpa absolvebat').[25] The latter opinion seems to have been a widely held one; it reappears in a Wycliffite sermon which complains about the claim of Urban's followers 'to han power of Crist to assoile alle men that helpen in her cause, for to gete this worldli worshipe to assoile men *of peyne and synne* bothe in this world and in the tothir'.[26] The Lollard writer is assuming that absolution from both punishment and guilt is a doctrine held and promoted in all seriousness by the establishment, and as such is an appropriate object of his wrath.

For Langland, it may therefore be suggested, the phrase *a pena et a culpa* carried no major negative charge. No doubt he had heard it commonly used of indulgences by learned and lewd alike. The fundamental meaning of the allegorical pardon issued by Treuthe is that 'all Christians who follow the model' of the exemplary Piers will share in his pardon; i.e. those who act well may reasonably hope for salvation.[27] It is highly unlikely, then, that Langland would have used a phrase he deemed suspicious or suspect as the vehicle for such an auspicious tenor. As James Simpson says, Treuthe must be using the formula 'without deceit'. To admit this reading is not, however, to relegate Langland to the vulgar lumpenproletariat (as constructed by a buck-passing establishment) who failed to comprehend the true nature of indulgences, or to disparage his poem for its vernacularity.

On the contrary, it could be argued that a vernacular theology had developed concerning pardons *a pena et a culpa*, which transcended the boundaries of class, educational status, and language. The occasional denigration of the *vulgus* by those who thought they knew better should not obscure the extent of the communality of belief and practice which existed, right across medieval Europe, in respect of saints' cults. Rich and poor, clerical and lay, highborn and commoner alike, sought relief from the trials and tribulations of this life (and hoped for a secure passage to paradise in the next) through the veneration of relics, and were equally eager to obtain the benefits of indulgences. The theology relating to indulgences in general and plenary indulgences in particular was complex and potentially confusing, and troubled even the most subtle theologians of Western Europe. From the viewpoint of those subtle theologians, Langland would have seemed confused, misinformed, or at best technically incorrect. But he was in very good company.

'FOR HYM AND FOR HIS HEIRES FOR EVEREMOORE AFTER . . .'

What, then, of the line which declares that the pardon has been granted to Piers and his successors for evermore? Here, Simpson suggests, is 'an offer which no literal pardon could ever make'. That is not strictly accurate, given the existence of the *indulgentia perennis* in Langland's day, the idea being that a person could gain a pardon as often as he or she visited a given church, there being no set time-limit. (This sort of indulgence came to be known as the *toties-quoties* type.)[28] Discussing the issue of temporal restriction on the availability of indulgences, Aquinas cites as an example of a continual pardon the 'perpetual indulgence' appertaining to 'the church of the Blessed Peter' in Rome.[29] In contrast, other indulgences were granted for a set period of time – a particularly interesting case concerned those issued within the duration of a jubilee year. Then again, certain indulgences were perpetual in the sense that they were on offer from year to year, albeit limited to a special day or days in the church calendar; once instituted they were there to stay, lacking any sort of 'use by' date and not subject to built-in obsolescence.[30] It would seem, then, that Langland's readers would have had little difficulty with the notion that at least some indulgences would (so to speak) long outlive them and be available to their children and children's children.[31] If such pardons – as issued by actual popes and their delegated representatives – can last so long and offer so much, how much more compelling must be the allegorical pardon on offer from the figural 'pope', Treuthe, who is to be identified with God Himself?

Furthermore, Piers's pardon is a communal or 'group' pardon, for which real-life models may be sought. When a pope, bishop, or some other authorized person granted the request for an indulgence to support some charitable cause (refurbishment of church or hospital buildings, repair of roads and bridges, and the like), of course everyone who was issued individually with an indulgence formed a group which shared its spiritual benefits. However, in the late fourteenth century there was a significant change of practice,[32] whereby certain indulgences – instead of being issued on the basis of papal (or episcopal) grants directly associated with the church or hospital in question – fell within the purview of authorized confraternities which offered collective indulgences to their members, along with the right to choose their own confessors.[33] Individual indulgences did not have to be given to each and every member. Rather, fraternity letters would be issued, stating the various privileges which membership brought, including participation in the collective indulgence.[34] Langland might well have regarded the folk from the fair field (or at least some of them) as members of an allegorized fraternity, all of whom share in the special pardon Piers has obtained from Saint Treuthe. And when the sons and daughters of members of this group reach the age of discretion, they too can 'join the club' and avail themselves of the privileges of membership.

Piers is granted, and holds, the crucial text on behalf of his community. Copies have not been distributed among his fellow-workers, it would seem, and neither have they been issued with individual pardons. The priest asks to examine this (apparently unique) document and proceeds to translate it into English. The Pardon's contents, and particularly its brevity, come as something of a surprise. For we have been led to expect a far more substantial and comprehensive certificate, an allegorical version of a papal 'bulle' (cf. ll. 38, 65) which includes statements to the effect that not every-one will receive the same amount of remission or *relaxatio* from 'yeres' in purgatory (cf. 18–19, 39, 60, 102), which has a marginal apparatus that expresses certain qualifications (18–20), and which is accompanied by a 'lettre' sent under Treuthe's 'secret seel' (23) instructing Piers how to imple-ment the pardon in respect of one troublesome group of supplicants, the merchants. Actual bulls often explained that different groups got different rewards from one and the same indulgence; for instance, why should someone who lives relatively near to Rome receive the same spiritual benefits as a person who has to make an arduous journey to get there?[35] Langland seems to have allegorized along the following lines a real-life scenario relating to indulgences. Essentially he has in mind a 'pleyn pardon' (102) or plenary indulgence, a type of document which, within vernacular religious culture, was often termed a pardon *a pena et a culpa*, as explained above. In the material world, such a pardon gave its recipients – or at least its properly qualified recipients – *full* release from the pains of purgatory. Some of those who share Piers's pardon do indeed receive full remission, along with Piers himself. For example,

> Alle libbynge laborers that lyven with hit hondes,
> That treweliche taken and treweliche wynnen,
> And lyven in love and in lawe, for hir lowe herte
> Haveth the same absolucion that sent was to Piers.
>
> (VII. 60–3)

In similar vein, 'olde men', 'wommen with childe', and those who are blind, bedridden or crippled (all these falling within the category of people who are physically unable to work), 'Han as pleyn pardon as the Plowman hymselve', because they have experienced 'hir penaunce and hir purgatorie' already, here on this earth (98–104). Fake beggars are not included in the bull's provisions, however ('ne beth noght in the bulle', 64), and while 'men of lawe' have managed to make it, they receive the 'leest pardon' of all (39). Merchants, on the other hand, come off rather better. A marginal gloss grants them 'manye yeres' of remission, 'Ac noon *a pena et a culpa* the Pope nolde hem graunte' (18–19). That is to say, Pope Truth does not grant them the plenary remission which the indulgence allows for at best, full *relaxatio* from *pena* (here misunderstood – typically – as pardon *a pena et a culpa*). But they get a good deal nevertheless, one unparalleled in their business dealings: 'manye yeres' release from appalling purgatorial pain is a considerable discount from spiritual debt, particularly when they seem to be doing relatively little in return. No wonder, then, that they should be 'murie', weep for joy, and praise 'Piers the Plowman, that purchased this bulle' (37–8). That is, after all, the whole point of an indulgence – the recipient is released from all or part of what he owes.

> Pardon properly noght elles es
> Bot of payne, þat es dette, forgyfnes.
> (*Pricke of Conscience*, IV. 3816–17)[36]

One may imagine their shock when, on hearing the Pardon translated into English, they discover that they have been freed from nothing at all, for each must pay his 'dette' in full. But more on that later.

'AND BAD HYM HOLDE HYM AT HOME . . .'

In Passus VI, we see Piers and his fellow-pilgrims planning to set off to seek Saint Treuthe. But at the beginning of Passus VII they are told to stay right where they are – and apparently they will not lose out in any way by so doing. Instead of undertaking a journey to worship at some shrine, where indulgences could have been obtained (that being the goal of, for example, Chaucer's fictional Canterbury pilgrims), they will receive a pardon for keeping the home-fires burning, so to speak. Matters will get even more complicated later in the Passus, when Piers *does* presume to leave his post – is he acting here against the express command of Treuthe, i.e. against the will of God?

In order to trace the movements of these shifting semantic sands, we may turn yet again to the specific historical circumstances and ideological concerns which shaped the discourses that Langland made the basis of his allegory. In the thirteenth century, a host of legalistic questions had arisen – and not just in the rarefied atmosphere of the *Sentences* commentaries and *summae* – concerning people who genuinely wanted to travel to places of 'holy war' and/or pilgrimage but were unable to do so, through no fault of their own. For instance, if a crusader dies before he can take the journey across the sea, has he gained full forgiveness of sins? That all depends on the form of the papal letter, Aquinas explains. If 'an indulgence is conceded to those taking the cross in aid of the Holy Land, a crusader has an indulgence at once, even if he dies before he takes the journey'. But if the letter specifies that an indulgence will be 'given those who cross the sea, he who dies before he crosses lacks the cause of the indulgence' and hence does not benefit from it.[37] Bonaventure wondered if a person who takes the cross, makes the vow, and has the perfect intention of going overseas, obtains remission of all sins by dint of that alone, what is crucial being the intention rather than the act. His answer is that, according to the experts (*periti*) and despite what certain 'vulgar preachers' say, such a person does *not* have a total indulgence. Indulgences are not given just because one wishes to do something; actual performance is also necessary. Only the penitent who combines both will enjoy the full indulgence, though Bonaventure concedes that one with the desire alone may gain great merit through his devotion.[38]

However, despite what the *periti* said, on numerous occasions the desire was taken for the deed. The Fourth Lateran Council had granted plenary indulgences to those who sent 'suitable men' to Palestine at 'their own expense' rather than going themselves.[39] Furthermore, despite Pope Clement VI's initial efforts to ensure that people actually went on pilgrimage to Rome to earn the benefits of the indulgences he had issued for the 1350 jubilee, he found it expedient to dispense with this in the case of Queen Elizabeth of Hungary.[40] The same privilege was bestowed upon King Edward III of England, his wife, his mother, Edward prince of Wales, and Henry earl of Lancaster – not to mention the entire population of Mallorca![41] These are but a few aspects of an economy of pilgrimage 'waivers' or substitutions which, in Langland's day, was well established. Here is no mere fantasy of 'vulgar preachers' but a vernacular practice which high-ranking churchmen were willing to condone, at least in certain circumstances, though the professional theologians had little to say about it.

Of course, people had to have good reason and just cause to be granted special dispensations from participation in the actual expedition (whether it entailed a military venture or a visit to some shrine or other holy place); their staying at home had to be deemed of equivalent, or indeed greater, value to church and society, and hence to their individual souls. Or so the argument went. But the system was open to abuse, and abused it certainly was. The extravagant commutations of vows associated with the antipope, Clement VII, were mocked by Lollard writers, as in the caustic remark that a man might stay at home and get himself forty thousand years' pardon by noon: 'It were ydil to traveile for ony pardoun, siþ a man my3te at home gete him fourty þousand 3eer bi noone.'[42] This refers to a provision allegedly made by Clement VII, at the request of the king of France, whereby in exchange for the saying of a specific prayer any contrite person was granted the relaxation of

two þousand 3eer of indulgencis fro þe peyne of purgatorie. And so men neden not to go to Rome to get hem plein indulgence, siþ a man mai gete here indulgence for many þousand 3eer after domesday, siþ he may geten in half a day an hundrid þousend 3eer and more. Bot who wolde traveil þan so folily to þe Courte of Rome in perel, for to gete hem indulgences?[43]

Clement, alas, was not alone, in this misplaced spiritual generosity. In desperate need of money, Boniface IX recklessly offered indulgences *ad instar*, meaning that many minor (indeed some quite insignificant) shrines were allowed to dispense the indulgences of major ones; hence, as Jonathan Sumption says, 'most Christians were able to win the [papal] Jubilee Indulgence of 1390 at churches within a few miles of their homes'.[44]

The most trenchant criticism known to me of the avoidance of arduous pilgrimage appears not in any Lollard tract but in John Heywood's play of *The Foure PP*. Here a Palmer and a Pardoner argue over whether one really has to travel afar to receive major spiritual benefits. Heywood devotes some forty-two lines to a listing of the many shrines the Palmer actually has visited in England, Wales, Ireland and even farther afield, including Amiens, Armenia, Compostella, Jerusalem, Palermo, Paris, Rhodes, Rome, and Venice (ll. 9–50). According to the Pardoner, this is sheer stupidity – 'here at home' (l. 96) is an easy remedy, 'with smale cost and without any paine' (l. 145), in the many indulgences he has on offer.[45]

> Nowe marke in this what wyt ye have
> To seke so farre and helpe so nye –
> Even here at home is remedy.
> For at your dore my selfe doth dwell,
> Who coulde have saved your soule as well
> As all your wyde wandrynge shall do
> Though ye wente thryes to Jericho.
> Nowe syns ye myght have spedde at home,
> What have ye wone by ronnyng at Rome?
>
> (94–102)

In response, the Palmer angrily condemns pardoners in general for enlarging 'with . . . lyes' (ll. 112–13) the power of their indulgences, and declares that, even if his opponent's pardons were ever 'so great' (l. 111), he himself is more confident about having received pardon by dint of the great 'labour' expended on his travels. God knows full well how people spend their time, and will reward them accordingly (ll. 115–18, 123–6).

Returning to *Piers Plowman*: I believe that, at this point in his construction of the allegory of the pardon, Langland had in mind a pilgrimage-commutation of a kind which was common in his day, a regular feature of the demotic praxis of pardoning. It involved a person who did not actually go on a pilgrimage receiving, by special dispensation, the benefits which would have accrued had he or she actually done so.[46] The plowman's work is, after all, essential for the good of the community and the health of the half-acre's economy; he has just cause to be granted the reward which the expedition would have brought. Similar arguments may be made about the other figures who share in Piers's 'pleyn pardon', though Langland (as already noted) baulks at the inclusion of beggars, lawyers, and merchants in the allegorical 'bulle' which publishes his very special indulgence. The poet seems to have no reservations about the literal/historical state of affairs (in marked contrast to Heywood's vitriolic outpourings), and so the discourse of pilgrimage-commutation may, quite inoffensively and unprovocatively, serve as the vehicle for his allegorical realization of Piers the Plowman staying at home, an action which can hardly brook any criticism since Saint Treuthe Himself has commanded it. Or, to make the same fundamental point in a more cautious manner, if Langland had any qualms about the actual practice of pilgrimage-commutation he does not share them with us here (or, indeed, at any other point in any of the versions of his poem). As was the case with his apparent acceptance of the (academically suspect) phrasing *a pena et culpa* in vernacular description of a certain kind of indulgence, Langland seems willing to accept the *status quo*. Maybe he simply saw no problem in either instance. Or he was willing to put his misgivings on hold, given the objective of his higher argument – the construction of the allegorical dispensation which an abstract and impeccable authority-figure bestows upon Piers.

This dispensation seems to be true in its own, elevated terms, no matter what kinds of dubious dealings its mundane counterparts might have involved. We can say that with confidence, I believe, though clear understanding of the nature of that truth remains difficult if not impossible to attain, given the poem's refusal to remain at rest long enough for a definitive resolution to emerge. In Passus VI the pilgrimage to Saint Treuthe was assumed to involve a journey from one geographical location (the half-acre) to another (Treuthe's shrine), with the half-acre being set to rights as a prelude to pilgrimage, a somewhat tiresome task which has to be performed before Piers and his fellow-pilgrims can set off on their exciting, albeit highly demanding, spiritual adventure. At the beginning of Passus VII, however, a major semantic shift occurs, as the text moves from pilgrimage understood as a movement through time and space, through Treuthe's command not to set out on such a journey after all (which is where the allegorical pilgrimage-commutation comes in), to a master-narrative based on the notion that life itself is a pilgrimage, and the half-acre its locus. Piers becomes the collective *status*-symbol for all plowmen, just as the woman who is lightly sketched in VI. 7–14 represents all women, and the idealized knight described in VI. 20–56 serves as a symbol for the entire knightly class. Understood in these terms, Piers the Plowman definitely must stay at home – the social consequences of all the world's plowmen downing tools and going off to seek spiritual advancement would be dire; by the same token, the knight and the woman must continue to perform their traditional roles within the half-acre, now understood as a microcosm of society at large.

After the tearing of the pardon, the lead-meaning of the text's key concepts changes yet again. Piers ceases to represent plowmen in general, having mutated into a more individualized figure who trades insults with a petulant though knowledgeable priest, and – having vowed not to work so hard within the domain of *activa vita* – looks forward to a life of 'preires and of penaunce' (l. 120). The idea of the pardon mutates along with the idea of the plowman, since in the final lines of Passus VII it is the literal sense, the standard theology, of indulgences which is in focus, as explained at the beginning of this chapter. But, what had Piers's pardon become just before this moment of high drama and seismic semantic shift; exactly *what* was torn up? Langland's intentions here remain elusive, enigmatic – and the fact that in the C-text the actual tearing of the pardon is excised may be taken as evidence that Langland himself was uneasy about a passage which made for good drama but bad (or at least unclear) theology. However, I will risk the following remarks.

Detractor though he may be[47] – and his aggressive, supercilious treatment of the uneducated but enlightened plowman brings no credit to his profession – the priest who is given the task of reading and translating Piers's pardon knows a regular indulgence when he sees one. And what he sees here is nothing like a regular indulgence. Hence his statement, 'I kan no pardon fynde' (l. 111) is, in this sense, quite accurate. It may be deemed accurate in another sense as well: there is no *relaxatio* or *absolutio*, no transfer of merit from the vast heavenly treasury to the humble sinner's personal account, on offer here, as I shall now proceed to argue.

Piers's protean pardon seems to have started out as an encoding of the principle that, in the normal course of events, those who practise the good *activa vita*, working hard and praying hard, may have some confidence in their ultimate salvation. That is the principle which permeates lines 1 through 104 of Passus VII. And Piers's 'document' may seem to encapsulate it, when what it says is finally revealed (though, as already said, this was certainly not the sort of text we were led to expect; during this Passus it seems to have changed in size and content). Those who practise the good *activa vita*, by 'doing well', will have access to eternal life (*qui bona egerunt ibunt in vitam eternam*). The converse is that those who do evil will go into everlasting fire (*qui vero mala, in ignem eternum*).[48] As deployed here, this statement – true in itself, but not expressive of the whole truth – is shocking in its utter simplicity and uncompromising rigour. Piers's Pardon is no pardon at all; it simply says that each and every one of us stands alone, and will get what he deserves, no more and no less.

But real-life indulgences could do much better than that; their economy of reward and punishment was a lot more accommodating. Purgatory existed as a place of temporary and 'temporal' punishment, by which I mean finite punishment which took place in time, in contrast with the everlasting torments of hell (or indeed with the everlasting pleasures of heaven). And indulgences functioned – assuming all the necessary conditions were met – to enable a sinner 'thorugh purgatorie to passen ful lightly, / With patriarkes and prophetes in paradis to be felawes' (to enlist one of Langland's own phrases, at B VII. 11–12). Prudent acquisition of pardons could remit part or indeed all of the *pena* which lay in store – thanks to the generosity of the divine love, which was the very foundation of the theology of indulgences. The consequences of this doctrine were considerable. (And little wonder that the acquisition of indulgences was so popular a religious practice.) On the one hand, sinners are judged according to their merits; justice must have its day in court. As St Paul says, before Christ's tribunal each one will receive what he has won, according to his works, whether good or evil (2 Cor. 5:10).[49] In similar vein, the psalmist claims that God repays all according to their works (Ps. 61:13). On the other hand, the resources of divine mercy are superabundant. Sinners need not face their judgement alone and in utter isolation. Others can lend a helping hand, to judge from the recommendation of Galatians 5:2 that we should 'bear one another's burdens'; *alter alterius onera portate.*[50]

St Bonaventure is an eloquent witness (among many others) who saw in indulgences an endorsement of this principle. Interpreting the 'burdens' mentioned in the Galatians passage as spiritual burdens, he suggests that, if a heavy penance is imposed on someone, it is quite possible for someone else to 'bear it for him in part or in whole'.[51] A comparison is offered with what happens in nature. In the case of the animal body, one member may expose itself to mitigate the hurt which threatens another member, as when the arm seeks to shield the head. Assuming 'there is a connection and likeness between the mystical body and the natural body, it seems that one member can and should bear the burdens of the other'. A comparison with human conduct is also offered. A creditor does not care who pays what he is owed, whether the debtor himself or someone else; he is happy to accept payment from either source. Likewise God, being at once 'more indulgent and yet more eager to receive payment than a man of this world', is content to have one person make satisfaction for another. Finally, Bonaventure notes

that Christ 'was punished and by His punishment he made satisfaction' –
not, of course, for His own sin, but for another's, indeed for the sins
committed by all of us. Since 'we are all one in Christ and are His members,
we ought also to be imitators of Him'. Following Christ's example, then,
one individual can and should make satisfaction for another. For all these
reasons, Bonaventure concludes, it is quite reasonable for a penalty to be
commuted to another person, insofar as it pays the debt of punishment.[52]
Here is a humane rationale for the dispensation of merit from the *thesaurus
mysticus*, that vast repository of spiritual wealth which may be distributed
in relation to the needs and capabilities of all its beneficiaries, whether
they be rich or poor in material terms. This doctrine implicates a solidarity
which is at once natural, human, and divine, an inclusiveness deriving from
shared membership of the Saviour's mystical body, which is the Christian
Church. 'Truthes tresores' are available 'trewe folk to helpe', to borrow a
phrase from the very heart of the Pardon-Passus (54). And, as Langland
says in a different but related context,

> . . . alle are we Cristes creatures, and of his cofres riche,
> And bretheren as of oo blood, as well beggeres as erles.
>
> (B XII. 198–9)[53]

Such doctrine is some distance away from the notion that those who sin
will inevitably be punished, suffering every last consequence of their evil
actions (*qui vero mala, in ignem eternum*). Actual medieval pardons offered
far more hope than does the allegorical pardon which Piers physically
destroys. Little wonder, then, that he should tear it up, particularly when
its inadequacy is made abundantly clear by a priest who insists on rubbing
salt in the wounds. But little, if anything, is lost by this act of righteous
indignation ('pure tene'). The poem has a long way to go; the Dreamer –
who now resumes his role as the text's mediating consciousness – has much
to learn; many questions must be asked and many answers heard. In Passus
XVIII will come the supreme reconciliation of justice and mercy, truth
and righteousness, as Langland vividly depicts Christ's crucifixion and the
Atonement. Piers's protean pardon is left far behind.

A recapitulation of the present argument is in order now – to check
just how far it has taken us, and to allow a major challenge. The term
indulgentia derived from the Latin verb *indulgeo*, meaning to be forbearing,
patient, kind, or tender. This does not seem to fit the two lines of Latin
which ultimately constitute Piers's Pardon. At this point, as on several
earlier occasions in Passus VII, Langland – or at least his Dreamer – makes
comments which evince a deep suspicion of anyone getting away with

anything, the idea being that we all have to work hard for what we get, both materially and spiritually. Insofar as the allegorical pardon comprises such attitudes, we may point to a remarkable paradox: some of its values stand in direct, indeed stark, opposition to those of literal/historical pardons. Regular indulgences actually pardon, offer a little or a lot of help from one's (spiritual) friends, those magnanimous donors to the heavenly treasury of merit. But Piers's allegorical pardon (at least on the face of it) warns us that each of us will be judged according to our individual works, in accordance with what we have merited personally.

Sed contra . . . With Langland, there is always a 'contra'. It may be protested that the pardon which Piers has obtained from Treuthe need not, indeed should not, be taken at such a face value. At its ultra-allegorical level (so to speak) it may be seen as the Atonement, man's reconciliation with God through a sacrifice which rendered superabundant satisfaction for sin, here understood as a pardon which Christ 'purchased' for us by dying on the cross.[54] Before this turning-point in history, each and every human was condemned to hell; now, thanks to our Lord's act of supreme self-sacrifice, only the obdurately evil suffer such a terrible fate, and the good are able to enter heaven. When the priest can find no pardon here he is revealing his spiritual obtuseness; thus he represents 'ignorant learning' in contradistinction to the plowman's 'learned ignorance'. For here we are dealing with Christ's pardon – the best pardon of all, as even Chaucer's criminal Pardoner has to admit.

> . . . Jhesu Crist, that is oure soules leche,
> So graunte yow his pardoun to receyve,
> For that is best; I wol yow nat deceyve.
> (*Canterbury Tales*, vi(c) 916–18)[55]

While fully appreciating the appeal of such an interpretation, I must admit to some uneasiness about it. First of all, in Passus VII there is no clear textual signal from Langland that he expects us to read the Pardon of VII. 105–14 in this way. This contrasts with the far more explicit technique of another species of 'documentary allegory' which images aspects of the Atonement, the 'Charters of Christ' which are written on the Lord's cruci-fied body (as parchment), sealed with steel and iron (= the spear and nails), witnessed by the two thieves crucified alongside Him, and so forth.[56] Sec-ondly, it seems premature to read the Pardon in such a manner, since Lang-land will return to the idea later, in Passus XIX, where Piers/St Peter and his successors ('heires', if you will) receive 'power' and 'pardon' from Christ, i.e. the power of the keys ('to bynde and unbynde bothe here and ellis') which authorizes priests to offer 'mercy and foryifnesse' through the *forum peniten-tiale* and to confect[57] the Eucharist (183–91, 390–4). (True, the Atonement as such is not at issue here in Passus XIX, but some of its direct consequences certainly are: Christ purchases pardon for mankind and passes it on to the heads of His Church for management and distribution.[58]) My point is, then, that any attempt to reduce the Pardon of VII. 105–14 to the Atone-ment requires of its readers a major hermeneutic operation of a type which is quite unnecessary, for the poet himself will provide us with the relevant doctrine later. Maybe we should wait for *Piers Plowman* to run its course.

However, I propose to set aside those qualms for what are, I hope, good reasons. First, information from the theology of literal/historical pardons can certainly help us to a more nuanced version of Piers's Pardon under-stood as a figure or foreshadowing of the Atonement. It would be perverse to refuse that interpretive purchase. Furthermore, reading the text *qui bona egerunt*... with reference to the Atonement helps us to gain what is, in my view, the most comprehensive and coherent possible understanding of Langland's treatment of the letter and spirit of indulgences. For the Atone-ment was understood as the very *fons et origo* of the ecclesiastical practice of dispensing pardon. Hence the following discussion.

It is misleading to speak of *qui bona egerunt*... as an 'absolute' pardon, if by that is understood a complete and utter *relaxatio*, free from any qualifications or conditions. A 'plenary' indulgence entailed full release from *pena* – but not in an absolute sense, as the earlier part of this chapter has explained. For the pardon's owner had to pass through the *forum penitentiale* in order to ensure the immediate efficacy of his indulgence, and subsequent sinful behaviour could damage or destroy its future efficacy, as William Lyndwood's disquisition makes quite clear. Piers's Pardon = the Atonement has similar conditions; it certainly does not offer the sinner *carte blanche*. Thomas Aquinas's help may be enlisted in explaining this point. Discussing whether or not the spiritual keys are necessary to the Church, Aquinas notes that in a manner of speaking the door of heaven is already open to Christians, particularly since Christ Himself is the door (cf. John 10:7). However, while the door of heaven 'considered in itself' is indeed open, it is said to be closed to someone in the sense of there being an obstacle which prevents entry. That obstacle is sin, both original and actual. 'Hence we need the sacraments and the keys of the Church.'[59] The sacrament of baptism removes original sin; the sacrament of penance serves to effect absolution from the guilt of sin (*culpa*) as committed by errant mortals after baptism. In the 'tribunal of penance', the penitent has to do his part, in being sincerely sorry for his sins and making amends. To adopt a phrase which had a particular resonance for Langland, he has to render what he owes (*redde quod debes*; cf. Matthew 18:28).

This conditionality is made abundantly clear in *Piers Plowman* B xix, where Christ appoints Piers/St Peter as his registrar or debt-collector, the agent who receives what is owed by sinners (260–3). Men may be absolved from 'alle manere synnes', *providing* ('in covenaunt') that 'thei come and kneweliche to paye / To Piers pardon the Plowman – *Redde quod debes*' (186–8). Thus they avail themselves of the necessary sacrament of penance. Similarly, they may avail themselves of another necessary sacrament, the Eucharist, if they have paid their dues 'To Piers pardon the Plowman, *Redde quod debes*' (390–4). Comparable caveats are entered in the 'Charters of Christ'. In the Vernon *Testamentum Christi* Christ grants mankind life with Him in the 'rewme of heuen-blis' on 'condicion' that His love is reciprocated and that man renders Him a four-fold grace, viz. shrift, repentance, the resolution to sin no more, and fear of God (109–26). If, as Traugott Lawler has eloquently argued, 'to do ill but repent is to do well' (that idea being implicit in the statement, *qui bona egerunt ibunt in vitam eternam*),[60] then in the conditional clauses here under investigation may be found an affirmation of the importance of penance for doing well – and the Pardon (or at least this half of it) does not seem so harsh after all.

Lawler also suggests that, through the argument between the priest and Piers, Langland is dramatizing 'the difference between what Chaucer's Pardoner calls "Christ's Pardon" and paper pardons'.[61] This is symptomatic of a long-established tendency in Langland studies to keep literal/historical indulgences and Piers's special Pardon well apart, indeed to drive a wedge between them. According to R. W. Frank, the scene advocates doing well and attacks papal indulgences; 'In tearing the parchment, Piers is symbolically tearing paper pardons from Rome.'[62] For Susan H. McLeod it proves that 'The only *true* pardon [her italics] is to be gained by doing well, and that man cannot expect to buy indulgences for his sins.'[63] Indeed, she believes that the scene gets so close to heresy that Langland has to 'temper' it 'with orthodoxy'; hence he introduces a 'disclaimer' to the effect that 'pardons do save souls, as the Church teaches'.[64] I would question such binary thinking, for – as I hope the evidence offered in the earlier part of this chapter has made clear – literal/historical indulgences were more readily and directly allegorizable in Langland's terms than has generally been recognized. Indulgences *a pena et a culpa* (that phrase lacking any subversive force), 'perennial indulgences' which the recipient could be confident of his 'heires' obtaining in their turn, pilgrimage commutations which enabled those who stayed at home to gain the benefits of the attached indulgences: it took no quantum leap to transform these ideas into the special pardon which, at the beginning of Passus VII, Treuthe grants to Piers. However – and here is where the real problem arises – the pardon there envisaged is difficult to square with the document which, later in the same Passus, the priest translates; hence my claim that real-life indulgences were far more tender and tolerant than the (apparently) rigorous statement to which Piers's Pardon is reduced.

However, the incompatibility disappears if the two crucial lines (*qui bona egerunt . . . qui vero mala . . .*) are read and glossed with reference to the Atonement. For the Atonement was at the very centre of the theological rationale for indulgences – and therefore on this argument also, binary thinking must be rejected. It was Christ's sacrifice which had made possible all the individual dispensations of pardon made by successive heads of His Church through the power of the keys, as is indicated vividly by the two quotations with which the present chapter began. The 'copious torrent' of Christ's blood laid up 'an infinite treasure for mankind' (in Clement VI's words), which successive key-bearers had the prerogative of dispensing to the faithful. Each and every indulgence had been rendered possible by 'the blood of the spotless Lamb', which was there to be bathed in, lapped up, harvested (in Catherine of Siena's words). Such religious idealism seems perfectly consonant with Langland's own. True, the poet declared that possession of indulgences was no substitute for godly living, but there is no hint of heresy to be detected here, since the greatest schoolmen of the later Middle Ages, including Sts Thomas Aquinas and Bonaventure, thought so too. And one did not have to be a heretic to be concerned about the widespread abuse of indulgences, the gross misrepresentation of what was really on offer.

In conclusion, another comparison of Langland's attitude to indulgences may be ventured, this time with that of a figure whose cultural formation could hardly have been more different, Desiderius Erasmus Roterodamus (d. 1536). In Erasmus's colloquy on rash vows (*De votis temere susceptis*, first printed in 1522)[65] the character 'Arnold' tells 'Cornelius' of how, on pilgrimage to Rome and Compostella, two of his companions died, and another was left behind at Florence, terminally ill. Although this man was 'a complete good-for-nothing', he 'had a purse bulging with the most generous indulgences'. Therefore he is now safe in heaven, 'Arnold' and 'Cornelius' mockingly conclude. In the edition of this text which was published in August 1523, Erasmus has 'Arnold' spell out his intention as follows: 'I certainly don't disparage indulgences, but I laugh at the foolishness of my fellow drinker. Though in other respects the most foolish trifler, he pinned his whole hope of salvation, so to speak, on a piece of parchment instead of on a moral life.' This passage was probably added in face of the reaction of Nicholaas Baechem, prior of the Carmelites in Louvain, who found heresy in *De votis temere susceptis* on the grounds that it mocked religious vows. Erasmus's defence was that it mocked only rash, drunken vows. In any case, he was hardly at risk, having enlisted powerful allies against his detractor: two popes in succession, Adrian VI and Clement VII, afforded him their protection. (It should be recalled that Erasmus always refused to come out in support of Luther, retaining his belief that the Church could be reformed from within.) However, in his *De utilitate colloquiorum* Erasmus felt obliged to make his position even clearer.

> Nor do I condemn papal indulgences or briefs (*pontificias indulgentias aut diplomata*) there [i.e. in *De votis temere susceptis*], but I do reprove the utterly frivolous man who, without even a thought of amending his life, puts his whole hope in human pardons (*in condonationibus humanis*). If, in this connection, a person but reflected on how much men's devotion is impaired, partly by the fault of those who hawk papal indulgences (*prostituunt pontificias indulgentias*), partly by the error of those who receive pardons otherwise than as they should, he will admit it is worth while for youth to be warned about this matter.[66]

This brings us back to the Langland passage with which my commentary started, the end of Passus VII (B-text, 174–95). While as 'a leef of our bileve' we must accept that pardons possess the powers being claimed for them,[67] nevertheless at the day of judgement they should not be relied upon exclusively. All the indulgences in the world will be of little use if your good works are insufficient. Pinning your hopes on a piece of parchment rather than on moral behaviour is utterly frivolous; filling your purse brim-full with generous indulgences is no substitute for amending your life. Here the 'radical conservative'[68] Middle English poet and the pioneering Latin humanist seem to be at one. In neither case need we imagine the tones of religious dissent; rather both authors see in the theory and practice of indulgences, as abused by certain (all too many) individuals, a major and utterly appropriate target for their satire. Quite obviously, such satire may be achieved in both Latin and in the vernacular. Language-difference is not the issue; success is largely dependent on the talent of the individual writer.

Orthodox rationalizations of, and anxieties concerning, late medieval systems of pardoning should be given their due, appreciated in all their complexity and sophistication. That is no easy task, given the long history of antagonism towards indulgences, as fed by Protestant propaganda from the time of Luther onwards – a tradition which, indeed, appropriated both Erasmus and Langland as morning stars of the Reformation,[69] and continues to exercise a major, though usually unacknowledged, influence on literary criticism of Middle English writers. The waters have been further muddied by the recent tendency to privilege proto-protestant polemic (the heritage of Wyclif and the Lollards) as the premier repository of social wisdom and religious insight in Langland's day. But the attempt should be made, for the rewards of such recuperation are obvious. One obvious benefit is the potential for greater understanding of the letter and spirit of Langland's theology of indulgences. We may gauge with greater confidence the extent to which our clerkly maker was aware of the strengths and weaknesses both of literal/historical indulgences and of the elaborate allegorical pardon which he constructed so carefully and then destroyed – at least materially – so quickly.

CHAPTER 4

Making bodies: confection and conception in Walter Brut's vernacular theology

Byhold opon Wat Brut · whou bisiliche þei pursueden
For he seyde hem þe soþe · & ȝet, syre, ferþere,
Hy may no more marren [hym] · but men telleþ
Þat he is an heretike · and yuele byleueþ,
And prechiþ it in pulpit · to blenden þe puple;
Þei wolden awyrien þat wiȝt · for his well dedes;
And so þei chewen charitie · as chewen schaf houndes.

(657–63)[1]

Thus *Pierce the Ploughmans Crede* lauds Walter Brut, who has told the friars many home truths about how they have moved far away from Christ's 'lore and his lawe'. He seems to have been quite a celebrity among the religious dissenters of his day, since he is the only contemporary figure named in this Lollard poem apart from John Wyclif himself. But there is no mention therein of Brut's most radical ideas, including the belief that 'women have power and authority to preach and make the body of Christ, and they have the power of the keys of the church, of binding and loosing'.[2]

Here I am quoting from the register of John Trefnant, bishop of Hereford, who tried Brut for heresy in 1391–3.[3] It preserves a fascinating series of self-justifications written in Latin by this 'sinner, layman, husbandman (*agricola*) and Christian', as Brut styles himself, adding that he was a Welshman – a fact of which he seems to have been proud, since he explains that both his parents were Welsh.[4] His opponents called him a 'son of Belial',[5] declaring that under a show of holiness this *laycus literatus* had seduced the people, 'nobles as much as plebeans', by teaching them privately and in secret.[6] To refute Brut's opinions Trefnant recruited an impressively large number of university men: fifteen masters of theology (including Nicholas Hereford, himself once a heretic), three baccalaureates in theology, and two canon lawyers.[7] In addition to the extensive account and refutation of Brut's views in the bishop's register, a set of four *quaestiones* has survived, presumably the work of members of that team.

The relationship between the *quaestiones* and the five 'diverse paper documents' (*diversas papiri cedulas*)[8] submitted by Brut and notarized in Trefnant's register is highly problematic. In contrast with the two blow-by-blow, if rather rambling and repetitive, refutations included in the register (the first by the Cambridge masters William Colville and John Necton, the second without any name attached to it)[9] they are highly selective, and ignore many matters which are treated at length in Brut's documents. Arguments in favour of what may be called the laicization of priestly prerogatives are presented with surprising fullness – but of course their refutation is equally thorough. Could this be seen as the product of a relatively tolerant period of reasoned opposition to Wycliffite views, as also evidenced by the 1401 Oxford debate on Bible translation, a far cry from the repressive era characterized by the infamous *Constitutions* of Archbishop Arundel (drafted 1407, formally issued 1409)? Against that suggestion stands the fact that the *quaestiones* were, quite clearly, prompted by the Brut trial, and hence had a significance – or at least a potential significance – which extended far beyond academic point-scoring within the privileged and protected milieu of the schools.[10] They had a public function, akin to the identification and refutation of the heretical views of Wyclif, Repington, and Hereford in 1382. (And it should be remembered that 1401, the year of the Oxford debate on Bible translation, also saw the enactment of the statute *De heretico comburendo* and the execution of William Sawtry.) Trefnant's team of theologians may have extended and amplified certain crucial principles of Brut's Lollard theology in a cool-headed and unpolemical manner, and may well have come up with propositions that the Welshman himself had not developed. (It is, however, impossible to tell if they had information about Brut's opinions in addition to what has been preserved in the register.) But this can hardly be mistaken for intellectual disinterestedness or tacit collusion. They found themselves faced with highly dangerous views, which could spread like wildfire: Brut was preaching to all and sundry, and had done so for many years. His doctrines had to be understood in all their ramifications, the better to critique and condemn them. Of course, not all the views thus analysed were to become staples of later Lollard thought, but Trefnant's team could hardly have known that.

Only one of these questions, which asks 'Whether women are permitted to instruct men assembled in public', has thus far enjoyed full scholarly scrutiny.[11] It has been shown to draw extensively on material from the *Summa theologiae* of St Thomas Aquinas and the *Summa quaestionum ordinariarum* of Henry of Ghent, works which had been written over a century previously.[12] The present chapter will draw on aspects of two of the others, 'Whether women are suitable ministers to confect the sacrament of the Eucharist'[13] and 'Whether women confect or can confect as true priests the sacrament of the Eucharist.'[14] I use the technical term 'confect' to preserve the form and meaning of the Latin verb *conficere*, which describes the 'making' of the body of Christ in the sacrament of the altar. My interest is in the stark challenge to orthodoxy presented by certain implications of Brut's 'vernacular theology' (I shall return to that obviously problematic term later), as seen by Trefnant's panel of experts. If women can make bodies in conception, why cannot they make bodies in confection? In the womb of the Virgin Mary the Christ-child was conceived; is it not strange, then, that Mary should be denied the power to make yet again the body of her son, this time in the holy mystery of the mass?

In the *quaestio* on the suitability of women as ministers of the Eucharist, the arguments in favour start with citation of 1 Peter 2:9, 'You are a chosen people (*genus electum*), a royal priesthood, a holy nation.'[15] Every 'elect' or chosen woman is holy; therefore, every such woman is a priest, and so she can confect the Eucharist. Secondly, there is the analogy with baptism. A lay man or woman can baptize *in necessitate* – in an emergency situation, as when a child is on the brink of death. But, as Peter Lombard makes clear in his *Libri sententiarum* (IV, dist. vi), the power to baptize belongs to priests by dint of their priestly office. Therefore, on the same argument women can confect the Eucharist in the case of necessity. Third, is a quite extraordinary interpretation of Exodus 12:3, 'let every man take a lamb by their families and houses'. A figurative expression should correspond to the truth: that is to say, its details should conform to significant specifics of the dogma which it is believed to express. Now, in Exodus we read of how a lamb is sacrificed within one's own house. This is a figure of the true and immaculate Lamb of God, and so it too should be sacrificed *in domo propria*. Since lay men and women rule their own house, it is appropriate that they should perform this sacrifice.

The fourth argument in favour of female confectors raises the spectre of Donatism, the heresy which holds that the effectiveness of the sacraments depends on the moral character, the state of grace, of the minister.[16] A good lay man or woman is of greater worth than a bad priest; therefore, they are more suitable to carry out a worthy task. Confection of the body of the Lord is the most worthy task possible; therefore the good lay man or woman is more suitable for it. Fifth, the Holy Spirit operates more through those in whom it is (i.e. good lay people in whom the Holy Spirit

is present) than in whom it is not (i.e. for example the wicked priest);
therefore it would rather work through the former than the latter. The
sixth argument rests on the principle that whatever can be done in the
more important case can also be done in the less important case. Being
able to communicate worthily – i.e. to receive the body of Christ in the
appropriate spiritual condition – is more worthy than to consecrate it. And,
just as a good woman can communicate worthily, so should she be able
to consecrate. Seventh: imagine the occasion on which a bishop ordains a
woman, uttering with an intercessory prayer the words of the sacrament
of the Eucharist, 'do this in memory of me; take, eat'. Here she (allegedly!)
receives the *character* (i.e. the indelible mark or imprint) of priesthood.[17]
Why then cannot she herself confect, saying with the intercessory prayer,
'this is my body'? The eighth and final argument is that, if an evil ordained
priest cannot confect this can only be due to a defect of goodness. As
Anselm says, 'Christ by Himself gives the power of confecting, and not to
all, but solely to the apostles and their successors in life, knowledge and
power.' It follows that those who are deficient in life cannot confect. Power,
as ordained by God, extends throughout the Church and by the Church to
its individual members. But the evil are not true members of the Church,
and therefore that power does not extend to them. In nature a severed
member lacks the agency of the body, being nothing other than a rotten
limb. The evil are rotten members cut off from the Church. Given that
the consecration of the body of Christ is the most sublime act possible,
there is no way in which the evil may have the power of consecrating. Our
anonymous *quaestio* proceeds to pose sharply the question, if a woman has
goodness of life and can be ordained, why cannot she consecrate? After
all, in canon law we discover that in the ancient Church female presbyters
and priests existed.[18] Thus it appears that, once upon a time, women were
ordained. Add that to the obvious and uncontentious fact that women can
achieve goodness of life, and sufficient requirements for the capability to
consecrate have apparently been met.

Then, out of the blue, a quite different type of idea makes an
appearance.[19] A woman can make (the Latin verb used being *efficere*) the
body of Christ in the sense of bearing him as a child; therefore she can
confect (*conficere*) the body of Christ in the sacrament of the Eucharist. No
elaboration of this startling argument is offered here; instead the *quaestio*
shifts into refutation of the above propositions, drawing on canon law. A
properly ordained priest and no one else can consecrate the body of Christ.
And women who were called presbyters among the Greeks do not seem

to have been ordained. Similarly, Christ did not confer upon his mother the power of binding and loosing, and hence he did not confer the power of confection upon her either, that being an equal consequence of priestly power. If he did not confer those powers upon Mary, there is no way in which they could be conferred on any lesser woman. All these arguments had been deployed in the classic scholastic debates on female ordination, wherein such theologians as Thomas Aquinas, Bonaventure, Henry of Ghent, and Duns Scotus had systematically denied priestly office to women. Those same theologians had also amplified the doctrine, ably summarized by Peter Lombard in his *Libri sententiarum*, that personal merit or demerit was irrelevant as far as the consecration of the sacraments were concerned, since the requisite power came from God and was bestowed upon the priest (male, of course) at his ordination.[20] The *officium* of the priesthood is here being celebrated and rigorously defended – this term having the sense of a hierarchical office or *magisterium* which marks off the priest from many other men and from all women, authorizing him to perform an exclusive repertoire of sacerdotal tasks, including preaching and the consecration of all the sacraments, with the rigidly restricted prerogative of making the body of Christ being the most awesome power of all.

However, my primary interest here is not in the refutation of Brut's (alleged) ideas but rather in the formulation of one issue which arose in the course of the debate: the proposed connection between two ways in which Christ's body was made, through conception and through confection. And this connection is subjected to further scrutiny later in the *quaestio* under discussion.[21] Women and virgins preached the word of God with constancy and converted many to the faith. To preach the word of God is greater than, or at least equal to, ministering the body of Christ (a common Lollard belief).[22] Therefore, women can administer the body of Christ. This proposition is supported with rather lugubrious reasoning along the lines of 'if you can act in the major case then you can act in the minor', which produces an extraordinary chain of argument that links the spirituality of the Father and Son to the materiality of woman:[23]

1. It is more holy to preach the word of God and to keep it than to hear it and keep it, because of the principle that it is more perfect to give than to receive.
2. But whoever hears the word of God and keeps it is more blessed than, or equally blessed to, the womb which bore Christ and the breasts which he sucked.[24]

Therefore,

3. Whoever preaches and keeps the word of God is more holy than, or equally holy to, the womb which bore Christ and the breasts which gave him suck.
4. But to generate the word of God and bear it and feed it with milk from one's own breasts is as holy as, or equally holy to, the confection and ministration of the body of Christ.

So in conclusion,

5. To preach the word of God and keep it is equally blessed to, or more holy than, the confection and ministration of the body of Christ.

Here, then, is a convoluted way of reinforcing the point that if women can preach they can certainly perform the lesser task of confection.[25]

Connections between conception and confection are also explored in the related *quaestio*, 'whether women confect or can confect as true priests the sacrament of the Eucharist'.[26] Several of the major arguments in favour of this proposition turn on the definition of *concipere* as *facere*, i.e. that 'to confect' means 'to make'.[27] Since the Blessed Virgin 'made' the body of Christ in co-operation with the Holy Spirit, it would seem to follow (so the argument runs) that she 'confected' the body of Christ. In other words, a woman confected the body of Christ because a woman generated the body of Christ, nourished and gave it suck. Furthermore, confection involves the conversion of bread into flesh and wine into blood. Now, a woman can do this by virtue of her nutrient power. (Here Brut's opponent is referencing scholastic opinion concerning the way in which food is processed by the human body. It was commonly believed that 'The body is the agent of digestion, for it converts food into itself. The body turns food, which is potential flesh, into actual flesh.')[28] It would seem to follow, then, that a woman by virtue of her nutrient power can confect.

The meaning of this statement is clarified in the proposition which immediately follows. If a woman can make a certain (human) body which can be joined to Christ in true unity, then she can make and confect (*facere et conficere*) the body of Christ. A woman, by virtue of her nutrient power, can convert food into female seed (seed being a byproduct of blood, which is generated from food),[29] and by virtue of her generative power then she can activate (*excitare*) that seed through the agency of a man (i.e. by having sex with a man, and mingling her seed with his) or by the agency of the Holy Spirit (as when Mary was impregnated with the Christ-child). The Holy Spirit, the creator of souls, can infuse a soul into the body which has thus been generated and disposed, and the second person of the Godhead (the Son) can unite with that animated body. All that being done, we have the body of Christ. In this sense, then, it can be said that a woman confects the body of Christ. Therefore women should not be barred from consecrating the sacrament of the altar. The implication, though it is not spelled out here, is that a woman who confects the Eucharist is, as it were, replicating the process by which the body of the Christ-child was generated to enter into union with the divine.

In addressing this and interconnected issues raised (however minimally) by Brut, his opponent distinguishes between four kinds of possibility or potency, relating to logic, politics, physics, and law (*judicium*) respectively.[30] Logical possibility means that anything can be done which does not involve a contradiction, whereas political possibility covers everything which a friend may do to help another by reason of friendship or love. If something contains within itself the principle or possibility of acting in a certain way, no matter how strange or startling it may seem, then that may indeed be done: and this is what is meant by 'physical' possibility. Finally, judicial possibility concerns the power to do everything and anything that is legally possible. So, then, when it is asked if women can confect, one must inquire into the meaning of that crucial word 'can' (*posse*). In terms of logical possibility, it must be conceded that a woman can indeed confect, since this does not involve a contradiction. But such reasoning must not be preached to layfolk, declares Brut's opponent, clearly worried about 'frightening the horses'. For if they were told such things, then on the same principle it could publicly be taught that a daughter could contract marriage with her own father or with her own son. Indeed, continues our theologian, really getting into his stride, a nun consecrated with the sacred veil could contract a marriage with a professed religious or even with the pope himself! And that woman could make the sun and stars, and any woman could conceive and give birth to God and redeem the world. But the tongue of the preacher who would say such a thing should be cut out! Clearly, it is socially disruptive to speak openly of such logical extreme possibilities.

Here, as elsewhere, Trefnant's team is deploying the notion of the two powers of God, 'ordained' and 'absolute', a distinction which is well known to us from recent scholarship on fourteenth-century Nominalist theology and philosophy, particularly the thought of William of Ockham – though the idea is of both earlier and wider currency, and one certainly did not have to be a 'Nominalist' of the Ockhamist stamp to use it.[31] It may look radical in the context under discussion. Indeed the 'power distinction' often has an air of intellectual dash and dare about it. But in this context it functions to close down rather than open up possibilities for female confection. Theoretically being granted powers in the never-never land of absolute possibility (the imagining of extreme test-cases which do not involve a contradiction thereby being licensed) does little or nothing to further the cause of women priests. Womankind in general hardly benefits from the extraordinary events which may be occasioned in the case of a select few. What was deemed impossible by the 'ordained' power of God (then as now in orthodox Catholic theology) was the routine entry of women to the priesthood, the imprinting of the sacerdotal *character* on the female body at ordination.[32]

Brut's opponents, then, do admit the logical possibility of female confection. But they seek to reduce it to absurdity by emphasizing the horrors that certain applications and operations of this same principle would produce. Of course, the absolute power of God, by definition, can work above and beyond nature and Natural Law. But here the suggestion is that it can work *against* nature (as commonly understood), and thereby its power within a defence of women priests is cleverly undermined. It is not just that a woman would need an exceptional act of divine intervention to enable her to confect the Eucharist; the further suggestion is that this could look like, and could well be, an unnatural act, on a par with her having incestuous sexual relationships.

More of the same follows. Politically, thanks to the power of her lover God a woman can create angels, or a single woman at one and the same time can conceive and give birth to a thousand sons by a thousand men.[33] None of these test-cases involves a contradiction, according to the speculation of Brut's opponent. We are back in the world of logical possibility: all such marvellous things can be done by God. Therefore they can be done by God in response to the invocation of a woman. It follows that a woman who is holy, and whose prayer is therefore beloved by God, can confect the Eucharist in terms of political possibility.

What, then, of the possibility in relation to physics? The proposition may be formulated as follows. A woman has within her (*in se*) the principle and the power of confecting the bread into flesh and the wine into blood sacramentally, which principle or power is called 'the priestly *character*', without which God does not give the sacramental words the power of confecting the Eucharist. This is a quite extraordinary claim, to be sure, and it will not survive for long within the intellectual economy of the present *quaestio*. Finally, 'legal possibility' is said to relate to the law of the Church as now instituted, which rules out the possibility of women confecting.

That prohibition is perfectly clear, it seems, so Brut's opponent concentrates on the other possibilities.[34] He argues that, for the Virgin Mary, the processes of conception and generation were very different from what

happens normally in such cases, and so they cannot be related to the sexual activities of men and women in general; no general case can therefore
be made for the confection of the Eucharist by women. Furthermore, it
is impossible for a particular woman to conceive the body of Christ or
to confect the Eucharist unless she is given special power to enable that
conception and confection. 'The power was given to the blessed Virgin to
conceive and generate the body of Christ but I do not read of the power of
confecting the body of Christ being given to the blessed Virgin or to other
women.' True, a woman conceives that body, but she is not consecrated as
a priest, nor does she confect by turning the bread into the body of Christ
and the wine into blood. Although Mary was able to conceive she was not
able to confect; divine conferral of the one type of power, it would seem,
does not imply the conferral of the other. Here Brut's opponent is playing
him at his own game – Lollards believe only what is written in the Bible,[35]
and since the Bible has nothing to say about female confection, they should
not believe in such a thing.

Furthermore, Brut's opponent continues, the confection of the Eucharist
is an unusual, special occurrence, not to be confused with due natural
process (as occurs in conception).[36] It is by virtue of the sacramental words
that the conversion of bread into flesh and wine into blood occurs, and
therefore no woman can do this, the point being that women lack the
power to utter those words sacramentally. Speaking in terms of logical and
political possibilities, a woman other than Mary can confect and make the
body of Christ, he admits, but speaking in terms of physical and judicial
possibilities, this is not so. True, another woman could generate a body
which Christ could assume in the unity of His person, and this would then
be the body of Christ. But this would not be the body of the Christ who
was born of the Virgin Mary and suffered on the cross for the redemption
of mankind, that being the very body and blood into which bread and wine
are converted during the sacrament of the altar. It is that body and that
body alone which is confected by the power of the sacramental words. But
those words, if spoken by a woman, would lack that power, since women
cannot be ordained to the priestly office.

One can only wonder how much of this extraordinary *tour de force* was
the work of Walter Brut's skilled scholastic opponent, since the account of
the Lollard's own views as found in Trefnant's register gives us so little to go
on. Maybe Brut's opponent had little to go on too? Certainly the material
in the Harley *quaestiones* is unparalleled in the records of Lollard theology.
Analogues to at least some of the arguments *sic et non* may, however,
be found in attempts to honour and authorize the Virgin Mary without

subverting the traditional economy of priestly power, to which members of Trefnant's team could have had access. The most challenging disquisitions known to me are included in the *Mariale super Missus est* which Albert the Great wrote around 1245, and so now we may turn to that text.

Here a major effort is made to show that the Virgin Mary was not demeaned or undervalued in any way when her son chose not to bestow upon her the sacrament of holy orders. Albert's authorizing strategy involves a dialectic of comparability, substitution, equivalence (*aequipollentia*). A bishop 'consecrates churches by dedicating corporeal holy places', while the Blessed Virgin 'consecrates spiritual temples by inspiring chastity', of which she herself is the prime exemplar. Furthermore, 'the most blessed Virgin shares continuously with the pope' the care of all the churches and the plenitude of spiritual power: the former because while 'the pope is the father of fathers' she is 'the mother of all Christians, indeed of all good people', and the latter because while 'the Lord Pope holds the plenitude of power in this life' the 'most blessed Virgin holds all power in heaven, purgatory and hell'.[37] And so on and so forth. Most interesting of all is Albert's attempt to find prestigious roles for Mary which are comparable with the priestly prerogatives of confection and absolution.

Habet cum sacerdotibus Dominici corpus per seipsam formationem, tractationem, communicationem, hoc est, quod corpus Domini mediante ejus verbo et ejus carnibus et sanguinibus formatum fuit, et ipsum familiarissime, et diutissime tractavit, et in cibum et potum nobis communicavit, et per hoc omnes ad jugum suum suave et onus suum leve charitate ligavit, et ab omnibus culpis et pœnis non solum solutos ostendit, sed etiam absolvit, juxta illud: *Qui manducat meam carnem*, etc.

[She shares with priests the formation of the Lord's body through herself, its handling and communication. That is to say, the body of the Lord has been formed through the mediation of her word, and her flesh and blood, and she handled his body most intimately and for the longest time, and communicated it to us in food and drink. Through this she bound us all to his sweet yoke and his light burden with charity; and not only did she show that sins and punishments were removed from all, but she even absolved them, according to this: 'He that eateth my flesh and drinketh my blood hath everlasting life' (John 6:55).][38]

The radicalism of this (quite striking) statement is more apparent than real. Confection may be compared with confection as types of body-formation, and with the priest's handling of the host with the Virgin's handling of the flesh-and-blood Christ-child, as she took care of him in the traditional maternal manner. Presumably in the case of the Virgin Mary the mediating 'word' was what she said on the occasion of the Annunciation, in humble acceptance of the divine will ('Behold the handmaid of the Lord'; Luke 1:38). Albert is likening this to the language of priestly consecration. The notion that she 'communicated' her son's body 'to us in food in drink' is harder to sustain; Albert seems to have in mind the Virgin's role in the process whereby God became man, the crucial part she played first in the formation of the child's body and subsequently in its 'handling' or care, so a healthy male body was 'communicated' to the world, ready to take on its divine mission. Eventually this led, in a manner of speaking, to his followers partaking of the body of Christ in the Eucharist. His startling comparison may therefore be reduced to the (somewhat banal) point that, had Mary not given birth to Christ, priests could not confect Christ's body when they celebrate the sacrament of the altar. Albert's casuistry also allows a kind of analogous power of *absolutio* to be claimed for the Mother of God, based on the way in which those who receive the Eucharist may gain eternal life (certain conditions having been met, of course).

None of Albert's ingenious analogies amounts to the suggestion that the Virgin Mary engaged in activity which was priestly in the strict sense of the term, the sense which appertained when medieval theologians rationalized their denial of public office to women. On the contrary, we are in the dehistoricized realm of *aequipollentia*, Albert having guided us there in order that he may honour the blessed Virgin, allow her to possess *by other means* 'whatsoever there is of dignity or grace in the sacraments of the Church', including the sacrament of holy orders.[39] This may be compared with those late medieval paintings in which Mary is depicted wearing priestly vestments – images which, as Bynum has explained, 'have nothing to do with claiming sacerdotal functions for ordinary women'.[40] Or indeed for Mary herself. Mary is presented as a priest 'because it is she who offers to ordinary mortals the saving flesh of God, just as the celebrant does in the mass'.[41] That 'just as' bespeaks irreducible distance, irresolvable difference. Behind the reverential casuistry of conjunction lies the stark, non-negotiable doctrine of disjunction. Mary was not ordained, could not have been ordained. And that fact has rendered the future priesthood of (lesser) women impossible.[42]

In an earlier *quaestio* Albert had remarked that forming the Christ-child from one's own flesh (*de carne propria*) is a greater thing than ministerially transforming bread into that same body.[43] Since the Virgin Mary achieved the former, why could she not also achieve the latter? His subsequent discussion separates out these two actions, however, the Virgin's conception being elevated over and above the confection which Christ's ministers perform – and in the process, the basis on which a claim for female ministerial power might be made is demolished. Within the debate on Walter Brut's views, the comparison between Mary's role in the conception and nurturing of the body of Christ and the priest's role in confecting that very body in the Eucharist moved beyond the normalizing parameters of *aequipollentia* to take on a new significance, present a fresh challenge. But the conclusions were the same. The roles played by Christ's Mother and Christ's ministers are judged as irreducibly different and distinctive, and all the clever comparisons in the world cannot change that fact.

John Wyclif himself had little to say on the subject of women priests. It is true that Thomas Netter once accused him of having shamelessly laboured 'on behalf of woman, . . . to the end that she might be suitable as a priest of the Church, or a bishop, or a pope'.[44] But the text against which Netter is fulminating here, part of Wyclif's *De potestate pape* (1379), does not live up to such hype. Wyclif's disquisition is inchoate and hard to follow (mainly because he tries to score several different points at once), marred by loose ends and substantial gaps, and interspersed with discussions of other topics (such as the symbolism of priestly vestments) which seem equally, if not more, important to him.[45] What Wyclif does provide here (and elsewhere) is a comprehensive assertion that authority derives from personal righteousness rather than in official position and hierarchical appointment. This follows from his theory of dominion,[46] and here the basis of many of Brut's controversial ideas may be found.

Which brings us to the question of the nature and significance of Brut's contribution to Lollard theology. K. B. McFarlane, whose succinct account of Bishop Trefnant's trial of Brut has done so much to bring him to contemporary scholarly attention, was dismissive of both the style and substance of what Brut had to say: the Lollard is denigrated as a Welsh windbag. According to McFarlane, Brut's first 'essay' (in Trefnant's register) proceeds to conclusions which 'were supported by strings of not very intelligible quotations from scripture'[47] – an unfair charge, I believe, since read within the interpretative parameters of Lollard thought their sense, and consistency, is quite apparent. Brut's Latin is functional yet highly effective, and capable of some eloquence – as McFarlane recognized, though unfortunately he fell into heavy-handed jocularity concerning his Welshness: 'Brute claimed that both his parents were Britons, as he called Welshmen. His oratorical style and his fondness for the language of *Revelation* bear him out. He was evidently a fellow-countryman of Owen Glendower.' McFarlane proceeds to complain of Brut's 'verbosity', declaring that he was clearly Wyclif's pupil in respect of his reliance on divine grace and rejection of transubstantiation, but 'his cloudy grandiloquence was his own. Not even John Foxe, who thought almost any utterance by a heretic worthy of a place in his *Book of Martyrs*, could be bothered to quote all of Brute's.' In fact, the only utterances by Brut which Foxe omitted are those which concern women priests.[48] His tolerance of the Welshman's 'cloudy grandiloquence' was therefore far greater than McFarlane allows. It was issues of gender rather than matters of style which prompted Brut's Protestant hagiographer to part company from him.

Nowadays we are in a better position to appreciate Brut's intellectual achievement, thanks in large measure to recent study of the *quaestiones* which were written against him, though much remains to be done. He is emerging – I myself believe he should emerge – as one of the most interesting and impressive of the early Lollards,[49] a thinker who added much to the doctrine he acquired from his associate William Swinderby,[50] and had strong intellectual affiliations with John Purvey, who included a justification of women preachers and priests in his (no longer extant) treatise, *De Compendiis scripturarum, paternarum doctrinarum et canonem*.[51] Much of Brut's theology was shared, but his Latin was his own; he devised a discourse which conveyed powerfully the challenge of his dissident theology. If Trefnant was really concerned by Brut's obscurity (as McFarlane thought),[52] that may be attributed to a failure to grasp the internal consistency of a value-system quite different from the one he had imbibed, a theology which stood normative dogmas on their heads and made crucial orthodox concepts work in a way which moved them some considerable distance away from orthodoxy.[53] But the anti-Brut *quaestiones* which Trefnant commissioned reveal no problem in comprehending Brut's ideas, which are easily placed within the scholastic *sic et non* structure, and the bishop's team seems to have experienced no technical difficulty in elaborating those ideas, the better to refute them. With all due respect to McFarlane, the number of experts recruited by Trefnant would have been 'absurdly large' only if Brut's ideas had been unworthy of their attention, and they themselves do not seem to have thought so; there is not a scrap of evidence that they found their task a waste of time.

Brut's 'Latin was his own'. But, if he was writing in Latin, how can one speak of his 'vernacular theology'? Given that intellectually and stylistically Brut achieved many of the things recently claimed (too exclusively, I believe) for theology specifically written *in vulgari*, this term might well be justified. Alternatively, one could offer the argument that in the house of Medieval Latin there were many mansions, and locate Brut *in domo propria*. Totalizing comments or assumptions about Latin theology – when placed in opposition to 'vernacular theology' – may mask the capaciousness and flexibility of Medieval Latin, the many forms it could take, in respect of technical requirements, genre, audience, and indeed of speaker (for the structures of Wyclif's native Middle English have been detected behind his Latin expression). Indeed, Medieval Latin could be seen as the great medieval European vernacular. 'Popularitas, communitas vel publicatio, manifestatio': surely all of those terms, which feature in Firmin le Ver's definition of *vulgaritas*,[54] may appropriately be applied to a language held in common by a large international community, which enjoyed major success in making public or manifest many bodies of information. And part of the secret of Latin's success was its receptivity to a wide range of appropriations and idiolects.[55]

At the very least, the Latin of the schools of philosophy and theology may be recognized as markedly different from those of the neoclassical epic, satire, or drama, and different again from the language of the will or of the charter, of the *historia* or of the chronicle. Canon lawyers had idioms all of their own, as did the grammarians, rhetoricians, logicians, astrologers/astronomers, medical doctors, and speculative theologians, while the experts on such secular 'arts' as warfare and hunting purveyed a jargon which is bewildering to the novice. There were many Medieval Latins. Even within a given subject-area the amount of variation can be remarkable – familiarity with the logical schema of the theological *quaestio* is of little help in approaching, for example, the prosametric elegance of Thomas Bradwardine's *De causa Dei* (written in proud and ostentatious imitation of Augustine's *De civitate Dei*, as noted in my previous chapter) or the Dionysian superlatives of Hugh of Balma and Denys the Carthusian, and of no help whatever in seeking to comprehend the vigorous grammar-abuse (or rhetorical innovation, if you prefer) of Richard Rolle's *Melos amoris*. And many medieval authors produced versions of Latin which are as distinctive as fingerprints – among women religious writers, Hildegard of Bingen, Elisabeth of Schönau,[56] and Claire of Assisi stand out, and I myself admit to admiration of the style of Gertrude of Helfta, which combines pellucid expression of personal experience with careful deployment of images which retain vestiges of the power which they palpably held for her.[57]

Of course, in the later Middle Ages holy women frequently expressed themselves in their vernaculars rather than in Latin (though some of them had a degree of competence in Latin); one may recall Bridget's Swedish, Catherine of Siena's Italian, Hadewijch's Dutch, Marguerite Porete's French, Mechtild of Magdeburg's German, etc. This is hardly surprising, given the exclusion of so many women from even the most elementary forms of education, and utterly regrettable. But Latin as a language cannot be blamed for that. *Latinitas* may be understood as a culture which held deeply entrenched patriarchal views of women, for which support was drawn from secular science and sacred Scripture – and the discourses of this culture could be expressed in the various European vernaculars as much as in Latin. Conversely, Latin offered a vehicle for radical teaching as least as much as did the vernaculars – indeed, it may be acknowledged that Latin offered *more* possibilities for the powerful expression of radical thought, since dangerous doctrines expressed therein knew no European frontiers, and the tares of heresy could thus be scattered more easily and take root the more readily in foreign fields. An excellent example is afforded by the Latin Lollard commentary on the Apocalypse known as the *Opus arduum*. Clearly composed in England *c.* 1389–90, no English manuscript survives, and the text's survival is due to the fact that it had travelled to Bohemia.[58] Latin heresy could have more impact than vernacular, really make the masters of theology sit up. Walter Brut's Latin certainly got the full attention of the bishop of Hereford and his associates. The examination and refutation of this heretic generated the single largest body of documentation concerning any Lollard trial which has survived. And the sheer number of experts called in by Trefnant is further testimony to the seriousness with which Brut was taken. Unorthodox views on the Eucharist in particular were likely to provoke a strong reaction, as Wyclif had learned to his cost.[59]

In the Oxford debate on Bible translation of 1401, the possibility that English was linguistically incapable of conveying the Word of God, since it lacked the requisite expressional capabilities and competencies, was mooted.[60] In the international scholarly debate on medieval 'vernacular theology' of 2008, surely we should seek to avoid the promotion of this kind of linguistic essentialism and determinism concerning Latin.[61] 'Vernacular theology' is a brilliant soundbite which has encouraged intertextual study of vernacular religious texts and underlined the point that theology in the vernacular need not and should not inevitably be taken as the poor relation (the poor female relation, indeed) of its rich and famous Latin cousin.[62] The term's use has been timely and utterly necessary: nowadays it is difficult if not impossible (*deo gracias*) to assume that theology written in Middle English is a dumbed-down or semi-understood version of what had been conveyed much better in Latin.[63] But, of course, we should not make the service greater than the God. English clerics moved easily from Latin into one or other of the vernaculars of fourteenth-century England. Walter Hilton could just as readily have written his *De tolerandis imaginibus* in

English[64] or his *Treatise on the Mixed Life* in Latin (though it made practical sense to issue the latter in English, to ensure the widest possible readership among the layfolk who were its target audience). While *The Cloud of Unknowing* makes powerful use of the resources of Middle English, it is a highly elitist text with a learned – and recondite – Latin theological tradition behind it. Addressed only to the person who is determined 'to be a parfite folower of Criste'[65] and imbued with the Dionysian *via negativa*, it deploys concepts of love and *affectus*[66] which have nothing in common with the populist 'affective piety' advocated and illustrated by (for example) Nicholas Love's *Mirrour of the Blessed Lyf of Jesu Christ*[67] and *The Book of Margery Kempe*.[68] Indeed, the *Cloud* author orders his 'goostly freende in God' to put away all recollection of earthly things, no matter how good they may be; even thoughts of 'þe kyndenes or þe worþines of God' or of 'oure Lady' or of 'þe seintes or aungelles in heuen' are ruled out.[69] The obvious implication is that the true contemplative must avoid thinking of any action performed here on earth by Christ in His humanity, including His passion.[70] Such emotive empathy was, of course, the life-blood of those meditational exercises recommended in legions of treatises, whether written in Latin or *in vulgari*, which appeared throughout late medieval and Counter-Reformation Europe. Little wonder, then, that some of the *Cloud* author's readers found his work 'harde' and 'hei3'.[71] One might well be sceptical of the existence of a coherent 'vernacular intellectual community' which found the products of fourteenth-century English theology equally accessible.[72] In any case, at least some literate layfolk were, like their clerical fellow-countrymen, profoundly multi-lingual; one need only cite Geoffrey Chaucer's mastery of English, French, Italian, and Latin, and the ease with which John Gower could move from French to Latin to English, writing (in that sequence) a poem in each language.

Is the term 'lay theology' preferable? It does have some purchase, particularly because it avoids the fallacy of linguistic exclusivity. But clear demarcation lines cannot be drawn between innovative layfolk and conventional clerics. Not all literate laymen were like Walter Brut, as may be illustrated with reference to the monumental *Omne bonum* of James Palmer (produced *a.* 1327–75), clerk of the Exchequer.[73] The *distinctio* on *Femine* reiterates well-worn clichés.[74] Women should cover their heads in church and certainly should not speak therein, on account of the sex's inferior subject-position following the Fall. Neither can women be judges, or teach. True, we read of how the prophetess Deborah judged the people of Israel, but that was in Old Testament times, and in this era of 'perfection of grace, judgement by women has been abolished'. St Bernard is quoted as saying that to be familiar with a woman and not have sex with her is about as likely as waking the dead; little wonder that women cannot be ordained as deacons. Business as usual, then.

The phrases 'non-institutional theology' and 'anti-institutional theology' are probably better, since they avoid any rigid demarcation on linguistic grounds whilst enabling a high degree of precision in positioning a problematic text in relation to the institution (however specifically or generally defined) beyond or against which it functioned and/or which might brand it as a deviant or indeed heretical production. A case could also be made for 'unofficial theology', since that too denotes theology which has an existence beyond the normative and may well be in confrontation with it. However, 'unofficial' has a rather bland meaning nowadays, and in order to make the term work properly we need to recuperate the force of the medieval notion of *officium*,[75] as designating a hierarchically conferred and rigidly policed status. Walter Brut, then, produced 'unofficial theology' inasmuch as he himself was not an ordained priest and cultivated a world-view which was at variance with the 'official' ideology of the Church. The term also works well in respect of holy women, for the only way in which their teaching and prophesies could become 'official' and achieve publication was through the approval of male office-holders, the *officium sacerdotis* having been denied them. Men who possessed that high *officium* could nevertheless place themselves beyond the pale through 'unofficial' or dissenting doctrine which might be judged heretical; thus they destroyed the very basis of their power and position. Their subversive discourses could be expressed either in Latin or in the vernacular, not being exclusive to or bound by either language. 'Witte stondis not in langage but in groundynge of treuthe.'[76]

Whatever degree of usefulness the terms offered above may or may not possess, the fact remains that making 'the vernacular' (understood as exclusive of Latin) the basis of our crucial distinction is deeply problematic, as the situation of England's arch-heretic, John Wyclif, makes abundantly clear. Until relatively recently, there would have been no difficulty whatever in designating him as a vernacular theologian, and the most important one of all as far as Middle English is concerned. Rudolf Buddensieg, writing in 1884, could claim that Wyclif 'stepped in at Chaucer's side as the father of later English prose'.[77] But nowadays the scholarly consensus is that we may not possess any English text written by Wyclif himself; most if not all of the English treatises and sermons once printed under his name are deemed to be Lollard translations from his Latin originals.[78] Quite a paradox – the prime mover of the single most substantial, and certainly the most radical, corpus of Middle English vernacular theology has not left a single word in the vernacular which may be verified as his own.

However, Mary Dove, whose recent monograph on the Lollard Bible is set fair to replace Margaret Deanesly's monumental study of 1920,[79] has made a valiant attempt to restore Wyclif to the position of prime mover of the Middle English Bible project (so to speak). Reacting against Anne Hudson's sharp but utterly fair remark that Wyclif's attitude towards translation was 'amazingly nonchalant',[80] Dove reads that same attitude as one of 'over-confidence'. 'Probably' this was 'a virtue during the early stages' of the translation project, she continues, given that it was so 'enormous' an enterprise; hence over-confidence may have been necessary to get it off the ground.[81]

The person who decided to make the entire Bible in the vernacular, so that 'simple men of wit', the growing body of people literate in English but not in Latin, would have full access to God's law without the need for a Latin-literate intermediary, was someone with rare boldness and tenacity. I believe this person was Wyclif. [82]

Dove characterizes Wyclif as being 'well-placed to organize the gathering of the necessary resources'; while he 'was in Oxford the translation was surely made there'. Furthermore, 'Wyclif was probably a contributor' to the early version; 'It would be odd if he did not want to take a turn at translation, having set the project up.'[83]

The great problem with all of this is that hardly anything can be found in Wyclif's vast corpus in support of a vernacular Bible. He seems to have been quite uninterested in theorizing the 'Latin *versus* vernacular' issue. There is nothing of the kind in his masterpiece of hermeneutic theory, *De veritate sacrae scripturae* (1378). On the contrary, this treatise expresses a dismissive attitude to the Bible as a physical book and the skills needed for its material production (the matter of which language it is written in simply not featuring). A highly revealing distinction between the various grades of meaning of the term 'Holy Scripture' identifies 'the Book of Life' as the highest sense, while in the lowest sense the Bible consists of codices, words, and other signs which are necessary aids to the memory of man.[84] Such *signa* are of importance only insofar as they signify the Word. Contemporary sophists worried too much about mere signs, Wyclif often argued. And the consequences for his hermeneutics were considerable. Holy Scripture is more than a delineation of words on parchment; a syllable in Scripture is not a fragment of speech or writing, but a (quite inadequate and distant) reflection of eternity.[85] Whereas Nicholas of Lyre OFM (*c.* 1270–1349), arguably the best equipped and most influential Biblical exegete of the late Middle Ages, had worried about the correct placing of punctuation marks in manuscripts of the Bible,[86] Wyclif believed that concern for such things invites comparison with those palm-readers who consider the lines on a hand and geomancers who scatter earth on the ground and prognosticate in accordance with the pattern of dots thereby formed.[87] 'Individual manuscripts are of no greater value than the beasts from which they are made'; if all of them were burned, the faith would not perish.[88] 'Scripture is not merely some sort of sign'; if that 'were the case, then all Holy Scripture could be damaged by a leather-worker, authorized by a scribe, torn apart by a dog, and corrected by a buffoon'.[89] Moreover, the writing in an actual Bible is as ephemeral as the trace of a tortoise-shell on a stone.[90] Given such remarks, I have much sympathy with Kantik Ghosh's view of this entire excursus: 'Scripture is identical with Christ and the will of God', whereas 'the book itself is quite irrelevant'.[91]

One may easily imagine the anonymous author or authors of the General Prologue to the Lollard Bible having some difficulties with this. There the virtues of 'good lyuynge and meeknesse' are affirmed, 'simple men' being advised to avoid disputes with 'proude clerkis of scole and veyn religions'.[92] However, meekness and humility have their limits. Would those 'simple men' have been edified by hearing a subtle clerk of school put their scribal and editorial work on a par with the menial labour of a leather-worker or the destructive act of some irrational beast? I wonder. Not a tactful form of expression, particularly from a team-leader. But tact was never one of Wyclif's strong points. It is quite true that, in a late work, the *Trialogus*, Wyclif unequivocally states that 'manuscripts of the New Testament or the Old Testament' should 'be read and studied in the common tongue', a sentiment which is attributed to the Holy Spirit.[93] But this is very little, very late. It hardly compensates for the denigration of material Bibles which characterizes *De veritate*. And on the face of it, that denigration is hard to square with the notion of Wyclif as instigator, organizer, and participant in a project that involved much manuscript collection, study, and production.

Mary Dove, attempting to bolster Wyclif's position as 'the person who decided to make the entire Bible in the vernacular', takes a different line: 'although the Bible as book is Scripture in the fifth and lowest mode, it cannot be called insignificant'. She reads the five modes of Scripture rather in terms of 'an awareness of the incommensurability of material and spiritual value'.[94] Wyclif 'protests too much', Dove continues. 'If the potentially defective biblical text is where enquiry into the truth of Scripture begins, it surely follows that each and every Bible is a pearl without price.'[95] My own feeling is that Wyclif was troubled by the idea that our 'enquiry into the truth of Scripture' has to begin from a 'potentially defective biblical text', and so he was eager to find means of transcending, perhaps even dispensing with, that fallible material object. There is no evidence (to judge by *De veritate*) that he regarded it as a pearl of great price. Rather it was grit that he denied had anything to do with the formation of the oyster. Indeed, for Wyclif the oyster of Biblical Truth seems to exist in some strange ethereal sea where the presence of grit is quite unknown.[96]

However, this does not mean that Wyclif was actively opposed to the notion of a vernacular Bible, or minded getting his hands dirty, so to speak, in the great 'trauaile' of gathering 'to gedere manie elde biblis, and othere doctoris, and commune glosis', in order to 'make oo Latyn bible sumdel trewe', from which the English Bible was in turn made.[97] I myself do not think it is necessary to attempt to square Wyclif's mature exegetical theory (as in *De veritate*) with his alleged involvement in this enterprise. For a start, it should be noted that discussion of the 'Book of Life' was common in scholastic exegesis. Nicholas of Lyre worried about the imperfections of material Bibles in his second prologue to the *Postilla litteralis*, as already noted, but in his first prologue he offered an elaborate – allegorical and abstract – exposition of Ecclesiasticus 24:32, 'all these things are the Book of Life'.[98] Here the Bible is set above all other books, the products of merely human agency. Lyre's major precedent in matters hermeneutic, Thomas Aquinas, had devoted an entire *quaestio de veritate* to the *liber vitae*.[99] Is the Book of Life something created? Aquinas's answer *inter alia* defends the metaphorical use of the term 'book' in 'divine matters' (*in divinis*), explores the appropriateness of Christ Himself being called the Book of Life, and explains that in a material book *figurae* serve to make known 'what was written in that book and what is read there', but the divine *ideae* 'whereby God recognizes things are nothing other than the Divine Being', and that 'uncreated nature cannot be called a book'. It is true that, whereas Aquinas reduces apparently dissonant ideas to actual consensus, Wyclif prefers to leave the dissonance unresolved in his own discussion *de veritate*. However, the point remains that Wyclif was not breaking any new ground in addressing the topic of the Book of Life, but following (though not being constricted by) well-developed procedures for dealing with it.

Furthermore, one does not need to produce an abstract theoretical justification in order to get involved with a major practical project; it is not a necessary price of admission, the *sine qua non* for participation. It is perfectly possible to imagine Wyclif, as Biblical exegete, developing a hermeneutic based on Scripture understood in a supra-textual sense, whilst encouraging, and perhaps also working on, the production of vernacular

Scriptural texts. The appeal of the stereotype of the absent-minded professor, lost in abstract theories and somewhat incapable of coping with
the demands of everyday life, should be resisted. Wyclif was very much a
political animal, for most of his life deeply mired in university, church, and
state controversies.

Besides, the abstract theory can be read differently. If Wyclif regarded the
Bible as 'an emanation of the Supreme Being transposed into writing' (as J.
A. Robson puts it),[100] then it hardly mattered what form the writing took –
English was just as valuable as Latin. (To put the matter in a positive light.
The negative or 'glass half empty' version would be that both languages were
equally inadequate transpositions of the Supreme Being.) If, considered in
the fifth and lowest sense, Holy Scripture consists of mere codices, words,
and other mundane signs, and collectively such *signa* are of importance
only insofar as they signify the Divine Word (cf. p. 107 above), it may
easily be inferred that whether the linguistic *signa* are in Latin or in English
is a matter of little or no consequence. As Anne Hudson has noted, for
Wyclif language 'was a *habitus*'; 'whatever the language, whether Hebrew,
Greek, Latin, or English, the same gospel message should, and could be
delivered'.[101] Hardly a ringing endorsement of English as a fit language for
delivery of the gospel message. But not a rejection of it either. We are dealing
with an indifference to language-transference or *translatio* at the level of
high theory – whether this be termed nonchalance, over-confidence, or
whatever. Hostility it certainly is not.

The Welshness of Walter Brut affords further food for thought in respect
of language-transference and interchangeability in fourteenth-century England. Brut was proud of his Welsh identity, secure in the belief that his
countrymen had been early converts to Christianity, in the time of King
Lucius (apparently he had read Geoffrey of Monmouth).[102] No doubt Brut
could speak Welsh. Yet he wrote his replies to Bishop Trefnant in Latin,
and recanted in English:

I, Walter Brut, submitte me principaly to the evangely of Jhesu Criste and to the
determinacion of holy chyrche, to the general consayles of holy chyrche and to
the sentence and determinacion of the four doctors of Holy Wryt, that ys Austin,
Ambrose, Jerom, and Gregory, and I meklyche submit me to your correccion as a
soget ought to his byschope.[103]

Those are the only words of English attributed to Brut in Trefnant's
register.[104] Yet his extraordinary Latin *cedulae*, together with the *quaestiones*
which amplify and refute his teaching, deserve inclusion in any anthology
of texts constitutive of *theologica anglicana*, in the company of the essential

writings of his master John Wyclif,[105] who seems to have felt the need to justify vernacular Scripture only very belatedly, as he neared the end of his life. The English language did not have a monopoly on the development and dissemination of 'The English Heresy'. And, as an anonymous Lollard once remarked, 'there is moche heresie in bookis of Latyn, more than in Englische bookis'.[106]

CHAPTER 5

Spiritualizing marriage: Margery Kempe's allegories of female authority[*]

One of the devil's more ingenious interventions, as he laboured to impede the spiritual progress of Catherine of Siena, was the argument that she could well get married, since many married women were saintly.

Live the life that other women do. Take a husband. Be a mother of children. Bow to the law of human nature to increase and multiply. None of this can hinder the fulfillment of your desire of pleasing God. Have not saintly women been wives and mothers? Think of Sarah and Rebecca; think of Leah, too, and Rachel. Why should you make yourself an exception, taking on a kind of life in which you will never be able to persevere?[1]

But Catherine was not fooled. She recognized this dangerous temptation for what it was, a means of compromising her status, effectiveness, and general credibility as a holy woman. Margery Kempe was not so lucky, having married long before her spiritual vocation became clear. Her claim that the Bible gave her leave to speak of God was met with doubt, downright hostility, and frequent accusations of heresy. This chapter will discuss the vernacular hermeneutics which Margery practised in respect of Luke 11:27–8 and Genesis 1:28, *auctoritates* which she recognized as being crucial for that claim. At its centre is a desire to transcend material, conventional marriage whilst remaining respectful of marriage as a sacrament and a normal life-choice for ordinary women. In this sense, then, Margery's reading of these two Biblical passages in terms of *sensus spiritualis* may be seen as an attempt to spiritualize her own complex situation as a wife with a divine mission, through the construction of allegories of female authority which remain well within the parameters of orthodoxy as defined in her day.

The interpretive context for the first of these scriptural passages is provided by Margery's examination at York by Archbishop Henry Bowet. Accused of being a Lollard, and having had St Paul's prohibition of female preaching (1 Cor. 14:34–5) hurled at her, Margery is anxious to assert that she does not engage in public address: 'I preche not, ser; I come in no pulpytt. I use but comownycacyon and good wordys, and that wil I do whil I leve.'[2] The distinction to which she appeals was a well-established one, with a *locus classicus* in the *Summa theologiae* of St Thomas Aquinas.[3] 'Scientific' or wise speech can be used in two ways, Aquinas had explained: privately, with one person speaking to a few others, familiarly conversing (*familiariter colloquendo*) with them, and publicly, in church. Women may speak in the first manner but not in the second. Teaching and persuasion in church must be done by superiors, he continues, and not by inferiors. Moreover, if women presumed to speak before an audience which included men their words would lead those men into lecherous thoughts, as Ecclesiasticus 9:11 indicates when it warns that female 'conversation burneth (*exardescit*) as fire'.

Similar arguments are found in Henry of Ghent's treatment of the question, 'Whether a woman can be a teacher (*doctor*, *doctrix*) of theology.'[4] Women cannot teach *ex officio*, he declares, given St Paul's prohibition and the natural weaknesses of the female sex, but *ex beneficio* it is perfectly permissible for a woman to teach, providing she has sound doctrine and that this is done privately and *in silentio*[5] rather than publicly and in church. It is true that Mary Magdalene and Martha received the gift of different tongues along with the Apostles, and were sent out to teach and preach publicly just as the menfolk were. But this was due to the exceptional circumstances of the early days of the Church, when there were many harvests (of converts) to be made and a small number of labourers (cf. Luke 10:2). The aid of women was necessary then, but this affords no precedent for female preaching in the present-day Church.

The arguments of Thomas Aquinas and Henry of Ghent are drawn on in one of the *quaestiones* which were prepared, it would seem, by theologians commissioned by John Trefnant, bishop of Hereford from 1389 until 1404, to refute arguments raised by the Welsh Lollard Walter Brut (as discussed in Chapter 4). A comparable dismissal of female preaching is included in the *Doctrinale* of Thomas Netter, one of Lollardy's most astute opponents.[6] With reference to a (now lost) treatise which Netter, on his own account, took from John Purvey in prison,[7] Purvey is attacked for having extended the office of preaching (*officium praedicatoris*) very widely, allowing it to many different kinds of layfolk, including women. St Jerome's strictures on those unqualified persons who think that they can understand holy writ are quoted with warm approval. Garrulous old women, doting old men and wordy sophists rend the Scriptures in pieces and teach them before they have learned them. Some philosophize concerning the sacred Scriptures among weak women. Others learn from women what they are to teach men.[8] It is one thing, Netter continues, to teach *ex officio et auctoritate* and quite another to teach *ex necessitate et amicabiliter*. The women teachers mentioned in holy Scripture are placed in the latter category. Netter explains *ex necessitate* teaching through the analogy that even though the safety of a ship is entrusted to its captain, when a storm strikes it is a case of all hands on deck, with every sailor doing whatever he can to help.[9] Thus, Judith instructed certain priests at a time of extreme peril (Judith 8:9–31). This was done not *ex officio* but as one rendering assistance. Here is the rationale for Mary Magdalene's preaching in the time of the early Church.[10] After Christ's Ascension the Virgin Mary did teach the Apostles, but this was done *amicabiliter*, in the manner in which a friend teaches a friend – as a friend of the faith Mary shared those secrets concerning the Incarnation which only she knew. But this is very different from a woman assuming the *magisterium* of teacher, that being contrary to the sexual hierarchy.[11]

That gives us some idea what Margery was up against. Little wonder, then, that she carefully should claim to be engaged in 'holy communication' rather than preaching in the formal, dangerous, sense of that term.[12] She could also have claimed to be teaching *amicabiliter* (and perhaps *ex necessitate*?) rather than *ex officio*, and privately (in fact a quite elastic category) rather than publicly.[13] It is, however, Luke 11:27–8 to which Margery turns, in response to Bowet's demand that she should not 'techyn ne chalengyn [call to account] the pepil' in his diocese:

the Gospel makyth mencyon þat, whan the woman had herd owr Lord prechyd, sche cam beforn hym wyth a lowde voys[14] and seyd: 'Blyssed be the wombe that þe bar & þe tetys that yaf þe sowkyn.' Than owr Lord seyd ayen to hir: 'Forsothe, so ar thei blissed that heryn the word of God and kepyn it.' And therfor, sir, me thynkyth that the Gospel yevyth me leve to spekyn of God.[15]

Karma Lochrie has suggested that Margery's '"reading" of Luke and her assertion of her own teachings could be labelled Lollard. They are, in fact, Lollard arguments.'[16] Lochrie's only evidence for this consists of an alleged parallel with the following statement by Walter Brut, as found in one of his trial records. Christ, recounts Brut,

respondit mulieri dicenti: 'Beatus venter qui te portavit et ubera que suxisti dicendo quin ymmo beati qui audiunt verbum Dei et custodiunt illud', si beati qui audiunt et custodiunt, magis beati qui predicant et custodiunt verbum Dei, quoniam beacius est magis dare quam accipere.

[responded to the woman who said, 'Blessed be the womb that bore you and the breasts which gave you suck', saying, 'Rather, blessed are they who hear the word of God and keep it'. If they are blessed who hear and keep it, they are even more blessed who preach and keep the word of God, because it is more blessed to give than to receive.][17]

At this stage in his testimony Brut is considering whether preaching is superior or inferior or equal to confection (cf. the Latin verb *conficio*, used to describe the priestly 'making' of the body of Christ in the sacrament of the Eucharist).[18] The deft manoeuvre whereby greater praise is won for preaching, rather than merely hearing, the word of God does not help us understand why Luke 11:27–8 should feature in such a context.

However, this apparent non-sequitur can be explained thanks to a passage in the second of the anti-Brut *quaestiones* as preserved in London, British Library, MS Harley 31, namely *Utrum mulieres sunt ministri ydonei ad conficiendum eukaristie sacramentum*. Returning to this passage (previously cited on pp. 94–5 above), it may be recalled that the excursus starts with the claim that preaching and keeping the word of God is more holy than hearing it and keeping it, since it is more perfect to give than to receive. Second, it is asserted that whoever hears the word of God and keeps it is more blessed than, or equally blessed to, the womb which bore Christ and the breasts which he sucked – a statement which keeps quite close to Luke 11:27–8. Brut's opponent then yokes these two assertions together: whoever preaches and keeps the word of God is more holy than, or equally holy to, the womb which bore Christ and the breasts which gave him suck. In other words, the hierarchy seems to be (in ascending order): giving birth to and nurturing Christ, keeping and hearing the word of God, and keeping and preaching the word of God.[19]

The next stage in Brut's argument-process (as elaborated by his opponent) involves dramatic semantic shifts. From material motherhood we move to preaching understood as a kind of allegorical body-making and nurturing, with this being deemed superior to yet another kind of spiritual body-making, the confection of Christ in the sacrament of the altar. To generate the word of God and bear it and feed it with milk from one's own breasts is as holy as, or equally holy to, the confection and ministration of the body of Christ. What exactly is meant here by generation and nurturing of the word of God? The idea of material motherhood is certainly present (which would put Mary's conception and maternal care of Christ's body in direct comparison with priestly confection of Christ's body). But there is also, I believe, a definite allusion to 1 Cor. 4:15, 'In Christ Jesus, by the gospel, I have begotten you', which was commonly read as designating preaching.[20] This helps explain the transition to the next and final stage of the argument: to preach the word of God and keep it is equally blessed to, or more holy than, the confection and ministration of the body of Christ. In other words, preaching is equal or even superior to the making of Christ's body through priestly confection, just as preaching was previously deemed superior to conception, the making of Christ's body in His mother's womb.

This entire excursus is governed by the principle, 'if you can act in the major case then you can act in the minor'. If women can preach (this being the major case) they can certainly perform the task of confection (the minor case).[21] Quite provocatively, confection is judged to be inferior to preaching – a sentiment very much in line with the Lollard belief that 'rigt preching of goddis word is þe mooste worþy dede þat prestis don here among men'.[22]

Here, then, are actual 'Lollard arguments'. And such arguments are quite absent from Margery's statement. That is hardly surprising, given that she is on her best behaviour during her appearance before the archbishop of York – at least exegetically, for as a holy woman Margery assumes the right to chastise churchmen[23] who are a disgrace to their high calling (hardly a tactful move, given the circumstances).[24] The last thing she would want to do would be to risk an exegesis that might be construed as Lollard. In any case, Margery does not make or imply either of the dangerous connections which were spelled out by Brut's opponent – between conception and confection, and between confection and preaching. In her text there is no trace of the crucial link in Brut's argument-sequence, viz. the comparison between preaching and ministration of the body of Christ.

A simple – and perfectly orthodox – explanation is available. The point of Margery's citation of Luke could well be that, while childbearing (undertaken within marriage) is a highly commendable activity, so also is keeping the word of God, and the fact that she, as a mother, has done the former does not mean that she cannot do the latter. (Furthermore, the fact that Christ is addressing a woman here[25] may be taken as proof that He did not suppose that men alone should keep the Word of God.) True, Margery makes a leap of logic from hearing the Word of God to speaking it – for her, presumably, this is part and parcel of 'keeping' it. The *Glossa ordinaria* on Luke 11:27–8 is quite helpful here, for it asserts that the Virgin Mary is to be praised not just because she carried the Word of God in her womb; more important is the fact that she maintained the divine precepts *in opere*, in her actions.[26] In his *Postilla litteralis* on the same passage Nicholas of Lyre explains that Christ was not seeking to drive a wedge between the different activities of which He spoke; the point seems to be that motherhood and spiritual work are not in essential opposition. 'Non dicitur aduersatiue sed concomitatiue.' Not only was the one who bore Him in her womb blessed, but so also are those who hear the Word of God, believing it in their hearts and implementing it in their deeds. Lyre then refers to Augustine's *De sancta virginitate*, where the saint asserts that Mary bore Christ 'more blessedly in her heart than in the flesh'.[27] Lyre's *Postilla moralis* also cites Augustine's treatise, affirming that the Blessed Virgin conceived Christ more fruitfully *spiritualiter quem corporaliter*, by her faith and devotion.[28] As a mother of fourteen children, Margery could hardly be faulted on her reproductive record. But she wished to go beyond what were regarded as normative female biological functions, by expressing the divine precepts *in opere*, conceiving and 'keeping' Christ *spiritualiter*. For Margery that included speaking of God. And she ardently believed that there was nothing adversarial (to apply Lyre's term) in this spiritual progression.

On her own testimony, Margery's speaking of God consisted of 'comownycacyon and good wordys'. She certainly did not seek Biblical authorization to engage in formal preaching, to come into some pulpit – a point which may be substantiated further by contrasting Margery's exegesis of Luke 11:27–8 with that found in the Lollard treatise *De officio pastorali*.[29] (This intersects, and has some interesting parallels, with the Harley question's elaboration of Brut's exegesis of that same text, as quoted above – a fact which serves to emphasize further the distance between Lollard hermeneutics and anything in *The Book of Margery Kempe*.) We judge the worth of actions by the fruit that comes from them, asserts the anonymous Wycliffite. And 'more fruyt comeþ of good preching þan of ony oþer werk' – for 'bi þis werk a prest getiþ goddis children & makiþ hem to come to heuene'. As St Paul says, 'in crist iesu y haue gendrid ʒou' (1 Cor. 4:15). And therefore, the author continues, 'crist preisiþ more preching of þe gospel þat gendriþ þis chirche þan gendering of his oune body' (i.e. the material engendering of his body), though 'þey boþe ben gode werkis'. Priestly begetting, which saves many, is better than the nursing undertaken by a mother, which saves but one individual. Obviously, the Lollard has Luke 11:27 in mind here. He proceeds to cite it. Christ's response to the woman who blessed his mother's procreative and nurturing achievements is expanded thus: 'ʒe but blissid ben þey þat heren goddis word & kepen it. & bi the same skile or myche more þei ben blissid þat prechen goddis word. lord, how worþy werk it is to gendre god in mannus soule bi seed þat is goddis word'. Margery would no doubt have agreed heartily with that last sentiment, but in asserting her own right 'to spekyn of God' she keeps well clear of the masculinist imagery of semination which characterizes the

Lollard's exegesis, not least because of the prominence given therein to St Paul's affirmation of spiritual fatherhood. Margery's concern is rather to project a self-image (at once a self-promoting and a self-preserving image) of a woman who has decorously heard and is appropriately keeping the Word of God. She is, so to speak, careful to distance herself from that seminating process which is the prerogative of the male clergy, namely formal preaching.[30] Thus she constructs her vernacular allegory of distinctly female authority.

Margery's exegesis of Luke 11:27–8 is grounded on its literal sense, which she well understands. And on this she builds an allegorical reading which values her spiritual labours, authorizes transcendence of the childbearing and childrearing functions which would keep her within the normal run of women. However, Margery's exegesis of the second Biblical passage under consideration in this chapter, Genesis 1:28, seeks to part company from the literal sense as quickly as possible. Earlier in her eventful visit to York, a 'gret clerke' had asked how the words 'Crescite et multiplicami' should be understood. While noting and accepting the literal interpretation, Margery quickly moves into the allegorical understanding or *sensus spiritualis*, emphasizing that the corporal begetting of children is not the only fruit:[31]

Ser, thes wordys ben not undirstondyn only of begetyng of chyldren bodily, but also be purchasyng of vertu, whech is frute gostly, as be heryng of the wordys of God, be good exampyl yevyng, be mekenes and paciens, charite and chastite, and swech other, for pacyens is more worthy than myraclys werkyng.

A wonderfully diplomatic answer – not least because of the (reassuring, deferential) feminine passivity implied by the 'ghostly' fruits of listening, setting a good example, being meek and patient, and, of course, preserving one's chastity.

But the assertion that patience – to be understood in terms of forbearance, endurance, and the resigned acceptance of God's will[32] – is more worthy than the working of miracles is *prima facie* somewhat surprising, since it seems to question a crucial manifestation of medieval sainthood (and Margery herself was not averse to having her name associated with miraculous events). I suggest, however, that the ultimate source of this *sentence* is a quite unthreatening text: the tale of Libertinus, a sixth-century prior of the Abbey of Fondi in southern Italy, as told in the *Dialogues* attributed to St Gregory the Great.[33] Although perfectly capable of working miracles, Libertinus was renowned for his patience: so much so that Gregory (or

Pseudo-Gregory?) affirms his belief that the virtue of this monk's 'patience far excelled all his signs and miracles'. *Ego enim uirtutuem patientiae signis et miraculis maiorem credo.*[34] To prove this, Gregory recounts how Libertinus took a severe beating from his abbot without complaint, and even covered up the incident by claiming that his swollen and bruised face was the result of an accident. Whereupon the abbot repented of his deed, being won over by his victim's 'humility and meekness' (*humilitatem ac mansuetudinem*). The point of the story is that Libertinus stands as a notable example, his virtues being offered for imitation (*imitari*) by others within the cloister[35] – and, of course, by anyone reading this narrative. Maybe the 'gret clerke' recognized the source of Margery's allusion (the *Dialogues* being a medieval 'bestseller'); maybe Margery's scribe has made her reply a lot more opaque than it was on the actual occasion. What is abundantly clear is that all of the instances of 'frute gostly' she identifies are activities which a holy woman can practise appropriately, without causing offence or arousing suspicion. Margery's list may appear as somewhat anodyne (particularly once the apparent denigration of 'myraclys werkyng' is explained), but in this context an emphasis on her 'humility and meekness' is politic. And it should be recognized that the task of 'good exampyl yevyng' is no small one (as anyone who recalled the tale of the passive-aggressive Libertinus could well attest). Here, then, Margery is subtly but surely offering an allegory of female authority.

But why was she asked about Genesis 1:28 in the first place? Alcuin Blamires has suggested that here we may have the faint impress of a Lollard 'test question' that never got fully developed.[36] Some support for this view may be found in Roger Dymmok's response to the eleventh of the Wycliffite *Twelve Conclusions* which were displayed, in English, during the session of parliament from 27 January to 15 February 1395. The Lollards had said that vows of continence 'mad in oure chirche of wommen' is the cause of bringing 'most horrible synne' to mankind – the killing of illegitimate children, abortions, lesbianism, bestiality – since women, being 'fekil and vnperfyth in kynde', cannot bear the burden imposed by those vows.[37] In reply, Dymmok asserts that Lollards used the text 'Crescite et multiplicami' to attack female vows of chastity, which (he claims they say) obstruct women's natural inclinations and bodily functions.[38] He immediately trivializes the argument by stating that unscrupulous people use it to deceive simple souls and uneducated women, leading them into sin. Perhaps Margery's interlocutor hoped that she would come out with some rash remark which could easily be turned into a recommendation of sexual promiscuity. In the following paragraphs I will explore, and offer further evidence in support of, this possibility – though I do not think that the answer is necessarily to be found there, for reasons which will soon emerge.

Further traces of the undeveloped 'test question' postulated by Blamires may be found among the records of heresy trials conducted in the diocese of Norwich between 1428 and 1431. Given that Margery was an East Anglian woman these trials throw some light on the kinds of dissident belief she may have encountered. Furthermore, William Sawtry, the first Lollard to be burned (in 1401) following the enactment of the statute *de heretico comburendo*, had been a priest in Margery's home town, King's Lynn, where he publicly abjured his heresies before moving to a London parish. (Subsequently Archbishop Arundel tried him as a relapsed heretic.) In the Norwich records we find several testimonies to the Lollard advocacy of clerical celibacy, some of which include the assertion that marriage is a more meritorious state than chastity. For example, John Skylly recanted the belief that 'it is leful prestes to take wyves and nunnes to take husbondes and dwelle togeder as wyff and husbond, holding that lyff more commendable than to lyve chaste'.[39] Even closer to the Dymmok passage is the belief attributed to Edmund Archer: 'Y have holde, beleved and affermed that chastite of monkes, chanons, freres, noones, prestes and of ony other persones is not commendable ne meritorie, but it is more commendable and more plesyng unto God al suche persones to be wedded and bringe forth frute of hare bodyes.'[40] The reference to women bringing forth fruit from their bodies could easily have been substantiated with reference to Genesis 1:28, but this scriptural text is not actually cited. Perhaps this was due to the concise, sometimes quite curt, way in which the trial proceedings were recorded.

If one considers the corpus of Lollard thought as a whole, however, defences of clerical marriage are few and far between. Indeed, Lollardy never developed a full theology of marriage. Such matters seem to have been quite low down the order of priorities for Wycliffite thinkers. Wyclif himself spent little time on the subject. In his most substantial treatment, in the *Trialogus*, the tone seems impatient, dismissive. The character 'Phronesis' (Wisdom), Wyclif's usual spokesperson, grumpily remarks that he does not take much pleasure in discussing the matter of how mutual consent should be expressed in the making of a marriage, because this 'is humanly instituted, often without [good] foundation'; a little earlier, he had declared that he takes no pleasure in multiplying reasons for divorce, since many of them are 'humanly ordained without [good] foundation'.[41]

This pleasure-deficit seems to have been shared by most of Wyclif's fol-lowers. Such statements as actually were made[42] pale into insignificance in face of the substantial dissident theology concerning the Eucharist, for example, or concerning the sacrament of penance. It is highly revealing that, when Thomas Netter sought to attack Wycliffite views on clerical marriage (simply because he had come to that topic in the course of his comprehensive attack on Wyclif's heresies), he found very slim pickings in the writings of Wyclif himself, and had to consolidate his attack with fulminations against the views of William White (of which, alas, he clearly lacks detailed knowledge).[43] White had practised what he preached by tak-ing a wife, even though he was an ordained priest, and his name features prominently in the Norwich heresy trials from which I have been quoting – indeed, White himself was tried at Norwich on 13 September 1428.[44] We can discern clearly the impact of this charismatic Lollard's teaching against clerical celibacy in the trial records of members of his East Anglian audi-ence. Other parts of the country were less obviously affected, though the zealous White did cover a lot of ground, having moved to Norwich from Kent.[45] One may wonder at what even a 'gret' clerk in the north of England could have known about an issue which does not appear 'with any frequency elsewhere [i.e. apart from the Norwich records] in texts or from suspects' (to quote Anne Hudson).[46] It was not at the forefront of the orthodox attack on Lollardy. Presumably that is because it was not deemed to constitute a major threat – at least, not everywhere.

We are dealing, then, with a small band of historical information – and it is salutary to note that, even within that small band, considerable differences of opinion may be discerned. This point may be illustrated with reference to the only Wycliffite tract on the subject of marriage to have survived. (More accurately, this is a work which contains some passages that bear the unmistakable impress of Lollardy, the remainder appearing to be quite orthodox.) So, let us turn, then, to *Of Weddid Men and Wifis and of Here Children Also.*

Its author complains that many men who are 'yong and strong of com-plexion' become priests to have a lustful and easy life. They 'faren wel of mete and drynk', and will not work either in penance or in study-ing God's law; neither will they labour with their hands. Whereupon 'thei fallen into lecherie in dyverse degrees, and in synne agenst kynde'. This, then, is what happens when they 'forsaken wifis bi Goddis lawe', i.e. legal marriage as approved by God, here seen as the best method for containing male – and female – desire.[47] As in the Wycliffite *Twelve Con-clusions*, male clergymen and female religious – seen as constituting social groups particularly vulnerable to lust – are being offered a means of sexual restraint and normalization which had long been used to justify marriage for layfolk.[48]

Total rejection of marriage was, after all, itself a heresy, as held for instance by the Cathars. 'The felt need of orthodox thinkers to defend it against the attacks of heretics' has been identified (by Marcia Colish) as a major reason why marriage was the sacrament that 'received the fullest discussion on the part of canonists and theologians alike' in the first part of the twelfth century.[49] Writing over 200 years later, the author of *Of Weddid Men and Wifis* expresses that same 'felt need':

the Holy Gost warneth Cristen men, hou in the laste daies summe heretikis schullen departte fro feith of Goddis lawe, gevenge entente to spiritis of error, and to techynge of develis, spekynge lesyngis in ypocrisie, forbedynge men and wymmen to be weddid, and techynge men to abstene hem fro metis, the whiche God hath maad to be eten of trewe men, with thankyngis and heriyng of God . . . he that forbedith or lettith verrey matrimonye is enemye of God and seyntis in hevene and alle mankynde.[50]

This connection of food-prohibitions with the rejection of matrimony may be taken as proof positive that the Middle English author had Catharism in mind (or at least a view which had become known due to the corpus of orthodox literature directed against Catharism). For Cathar *perfecti* refused to eat any of the products of coition (e.g. meat, milk, eggs, and cheese), though they permitted the consumption of fish, on the mistaken assumption that these creatures grew from water itself. And of course, all sexual contact was firmly forbidden.[51] This stands in intriguing contrast to the Lollard connection between clerics' indulgence in good 'mete and drynk' and their sexual lusts, as postulated in *Of Weddid Men and Wifis*. The third of the *Twelve Conclusions* puts it even more graphically, by declaring that the 'delicious metis and drinkis' which idle-living clerics enjoy must have 'nedful purgaciun or werse'. If no women are available, men whose desires have been inflamed by their luxurious diet will inevitably seek to vent their lusts with other men.[52] In both these Wycliffite texts, clerical marriage is offered as a solution – the contrast with Catharism could hardly be more blatant.

Of Weddid Men and Wifis also attacks the way in which many sons and daughters of gentlemen are obliged to enter religious orders against their will.[53] But it stops far short of recommending a blanket abolition of religious orders. Here it seems to differ from the propositions quoted above from the Norwich heresy trials, though (once again) one should urge caution given the curtailed nature of those accounts. Indeed, it goes on to extol virginity as the superior state: 'though matrimonye be good and gretly comendid of God, yit clene virgynité is moche betre'.[54] Thus the treatise moves back within the boundaries of orthodoxy.

There is no reason to suppose that Margery ever left those boundaries. As far as marriage is concerned, she seems to steer well clear of both the Scylla of (occasional) Lollard elevation of marriage over chastity[55] and the Charybdis of Cathar misogamy. Of course, Catharism had been well and truly crushed on the continent long before Margery's lifetime, and it had never made any significant inroads into England.[56] But its dangers were well known in England. We have seen that the author of *Of Weddid Men and Wifis* regarded at least some of its subversive opinions as viable targets for his invective. Consider also the strange case of the 'Pythagorean moment' which occurs in the second of the Harley *quaestiones* against Brut.[57] This arises in the course of one of the many arguments elaborated there in favour of women priests. It runs as follows. Sex is of the body whereas the priestly *character* (as impressed at ordination) directly affects the soul. If the priestly *character* is stamped on a man's soul, and that man dies and his soul passes into the body of a woman, surely that woman would then be a priest, or at least her soul would bear the priestly imprint? Where does *that* idea come from? There is nothing in Trefnant's notarized record of Brut's own words to parallel this crucial passage, and (to the best of my knowledge) there is no precedent whatever in the writings of other Lollards. However, there is an abundance of relevant information in writings against Catharism – in Alan of Lille's *De fide catholica* and Bernard Gui's *Manuel de l'Inquisiteur*, for instance, or (at more length) in Moneta of Cremona's comprehensive treatise against Cathars (although it should be noted that its circulation in England is problematic).[58] Theologians of the distinction of Brut's adversaries no doubt had access to such information. And they could easily have deployed it in their elaboration of Brut's testimony – all heresies had the same source, after all; therefore they were all interconnected, and those connections could justifiably be brought out. Indeed, why not use a Cathar heresy to help catch a Lollard heretic? In sum, the fact that there were no Cathars in England certainly does not mean that there were no Cathar views in England. And a 'gret clerke' might have wondered, however briefly, if any of them had reached Margery Kempe.

But such a thought could only have been brief, something to be set aside following an examination of Margery's life. Margery had been fruitful and multiplied quite successfully, and her *Book* contains no statement denigrating the marriage state in general. No one could seriously accuse her of Catharist subversion of marriage. Switching over to the opposing heretical view (i.e. the Lollard line), there is no evidence whatever that Margery felt marriage was a fit state for clergymen and religious women.[59] Far from challenging the vows of chastity undertaken and maintained by priests and nuns, she sought to emulate them as best she could, though her marital status constituted a major legal impediment. Hence her anxiety to secure the approval of Philip Repington, bishop of Lincoln,[60] for the 'spiritual marriage' which her husband John eventually allowed her to request from the ecclesiastical authorities.[61] The *Book of Margery Kempe* is pervaded with conventional respect for marriage, along with the conviction that chastity is by far the higher form of Christian living. 'The state of maydenhode be mor parfyte and mor holy than the state of wedewhode, and the state of wedewhode mor parfyte than the state of wedlake.'[62]

It remains to consider the possible relevance of the 'artificial' heresy (as Malcolm Lambert has termed it)[63] of the Free Spirit for an understanding of Margery's exegesis of Genesis 1:28. The alleged adherents of this movement (if indeed it can be called that) were not an organized group at all, it now seems, but rather a motley crew of individual mystics, dissident spirits, and credulous layfolk, 'some of whom wrote or said some dangerous or extravagant things'.[64] Yet they were all put 'into the jar of the "Free Spirit"' in the belief that 'there was a wide-spread, rightly organized sect of that name'.[65] Here, then, is yet another case of paranoid fantasy on the part of fearful churchmen. The slanderous testimony against their victims included (all too predictably) charges of promiscuity, aberrant sexual practices, and deviant attitudes to marriage. Which brings us back to Margery Kempe's *translatio auctoritatis*, particularly because Anne Hudson has suggested that the question she was asked about the text 'Crescite et multiplicami' was 'designed to detect in her any leanings towards the belief of the Free Spirit'.[66] An 'artificial' heresy it may have been, but if great clerks (with knowledge of what supposedly was happening on the continent) believed in its existence, that would have been more than enough to put Margery at risk, had she said the wrong thing.

Two clear instances of continental incursion are to hand. *The Chastising of God's Children* (*a.* 1408) includes a thoroughgoing attack on heretics who 'wenen þat þei haue fredom of spirit', which means that if they are 'stired to any kust or likyng' they must 'fulfille þe wil of þe kynde'; such people are described as more dangerous than the Lollards.[67] Walter Hilton's *Eight Chapters of Perfection* similarly warns its readers to 'be-war of hem that seyn herself han geten the spirit of freedom and that their have to moche grace of love that thei mai liven as hem list. Thei thenken hem so free and so siker, that thei schal not synne.'[68] The *Chastising* author is following an account of the Free Spirit movement by the Flemish mystical writer Jan Ruysbroeck,[69] while the Hilton text is an English translation of a (now lost) treatise by an Aragonese Franciscan friar, Lluis de Font, who taught at Cambridge during the 1380s and early 1390s.[70] So, then, 'the ideas of the Free Spirit were available in England',[71] and Hudson's suggestion concerning Margery Kempe must be taken very seriously.[72]

Hudson's main evidence consists of a putative parallel between the great clerk's question and supposedly Free Spirit propositions condemned at the trial of William Ramsbury (a lay Lollard, probably from Wiltshire) before John Waltham, bishop of Salisbury, in 1389. Proposition 9 states that it is better for clergymen to take wives rather than live in chastity, and the same can be said of nuns. This seems familiar enough, of a piece with the material quoted above from the trials of Norwich Lollards. But then come certain heresies which, Hudson suggests,[73] 'did not derive from Wyclif'.[74] Proposition 10 states that a man can legitimately divorce a barren woman and marry another; proposition 13, that it is not sinful to have sex with a nun; and, proposition 14, that it is legal for priests and others to know carnally any number of women and indeed nuns, virgins, and wives, *propter multiplicationem generis humani* (presumably an allusion to Genesis 1:28).[75]

However, it may be argued that these opinions *did* derive from Wyclif. Attacking a few (incomplete and inadequate) comments on marriage included in the *Trialogus*, Thomas Netter accused his opponent of having defined marriage too narrowly as necessarily involving the propagation of children.[76] This, according to Netter, ruled out the marriage of old people and others who, for good reason, could not have children, and implied that the sexless marriage of Mary and Joseph was not a true marriage.[77] Furthermore, he argued, Wyclif was opening the door to easy divorce and remarriage in the case of childless couples. Such 'modern errors' are secretly breaking out in Kent, Netter continues; certain people there say that if after three years a couple have not had children, for instance because either part-ner has some deformity or is too old or past the age of childbearing, then the marriage must be dissolved.[78] (Here we may detect the influence of that *presbyter uxoratus*,[79] William White – who, as already noted, had preached in Kent before moving to Norwich.) So, then, it is evident that, within at least some strands of Lollardy, the belief that marriage must entail the propagation of children developed alongside the (quite consonant) belief that marriage is superior to chastity – we do not have to look to the (real or imagined) heresy of the Free Spirit to find them.

And from those core beliefs the others follow. If religious vows of chastity are not to be observed then of course men (including priests) can marry, and have sex with, nuns. The same principle supports priests and other men having sex with any number of women (including nuns). A man may have sex with more than one woman inasmuch as, if his wife is barren, he may divorce her and marry another. Procreation is essential for marriage; if there is no procreation there is no marriage. This behaviour may ultimately be justified on the grounds that mankind must be multiplied. Now, in the extant documents no single Lollard (and certainly not Wyclif) says all of that in such a joined-up way; here I am piecing together what fragments actually have survived in order to find a pattern, to discover their inner logic.

In conclusion, there is no reason to suppose that 'a non-Wyclif element has entered' into Ramsbury's heresies,[80] because the ideas in question can indeed claim their origin from the arch-heresiarch himself, however convoluted the process of transmission and amplification may have been, and however imperfectly they may have been recorded. (A tendency to sensationalize may be attributed to the heresy-hunters.) And, by the same token, Lollardy affords a sufficient basis for speculation about what may have been worrying the 'gret clerke' who asked Margery to comment on 'Crescite et multiplicami'.[81] Besides, in the *Book of Margery Kempe* there are no terms or phrases which are unique to the description of the Free Spirit heresy – in contrast with Hilton's *Eight Chapters of Perfection* and *The Chastising of God's Children*, where a distinctive 'sect vocabulary'[82] is indeed present. Heresies should not be multiplied beyond necessity.

That seems a good note on which to end this review of heresies which have been cited in attempts to explain why Margery was questioned on Genesis 1:28. None of them, in my view, offers a clear parallel or convincing explanation – not even the prime suspect, Lollardy. Of course, we have access to the entire *Book of Margery Kempe* and therefore are in a better position to know Margery's beliefs and aspirations than her clerkly interlocutor could possibly have been, but there is no reason to suppose he suspected Margery of promoting promiscuity[83] and/or harbouring negative views about marriage in general (from whatever source they may have come). So, let us try another tack. The 'gret clerke' might have had something quite different in mind. One of the major undercurrents behind so many of the attacks on Margery is the prejudice that she should behave like other women. As she is escorted towards Beverley certain 'men of the country' say to her, 'Damsel, forsake this lyfe that thu hast, and go and spynne and carde [i.e. card wool] as other women don.'[84] A little later in the narrative Margery is accused of having counselled Lady Greystoke, daughter of Jean of Beaufort and wife to John of Greystoke, 'to forsakyn hir husbonde'.[85] Therefore the above-mentioned clerk might, in effect, be asking Margery, why are you not staying at home with your husband, like a dutiful wife and a normal woman, bringing forth children to the glory of God, as well as performing those other tasks which are appropriate to womankind?[86]

And maybe he suspects that Margery is leading other women, like Lady Greystoke, astray, encouraging them to leave their husbands at home and go roaming the countryside – not necessarily as Lollard proselytizers, for holy women like Margery could be disruptive without being heretical.[87] One may recall the accusation of her enemy the mayor of Leicester that Margery had 'comyn hedyr to han away owr wyvys fro us and ledyn hem with the'.[88] Perhaps such a concern for social control and order prompted the clerk's question. That explanation certainly makes sense of the answer which Margery gives. Instead of referring to the bodily children she had begotten (in abundance) Margery seeks an allegorical interpretation of Genesis 1:28 as a means of justifying the 'ghostly fruit' she has brought forth, which are far more important to her – this being done in a way which is perfectly respectful of the literal sense of the Genesis passage (which she freely accepts) and without in any way denying the value assigned by the Church to material motherhood.

What makes this reading even more convincing is that it is of a piece with the way in which Margery appropriated Luke 11:27–8 ('Blyssed be the wombe that the bar & þe tetys that yaf þe sowkyn') to affirm that, while childbearing is a highly commendable activity, so too is hearing and keeping the word of God – activities which she believes God now wants her to perform. If my interpretation of Margery's interpretation of 'Crescite et multiplicami' is correct, then it may be said that, far from saying or doing anything to support the charge that she advocated sexual promiscuity (as allegedly justified by either Lollardy or Free Spirit doctrine),[89] Margery held and expressed attitudes quite in line with traditional doctrine concerning the bridling of desire. Furthermore, while Margery regarded herself as a special case, called by Christ as His Bride (and therefore required to withdraw from sexual relations with her husband John), there is nothing in her *Book* to suggest that she contested the orthodox belief that marriage is a fit state for the normal run of women, or actually advised Lady Greystoke or any other wife to leave her husband. Margery cites Christ as saying that there are 'many wifys . . . in this worlde that wolde lovyn me and servyn me ryth wel and dewly, yyf thei might be as freely fro her husbondys as thu art fro thyn'. But the main point of this passage is its emphasis on Margery's special situation. Thanks to Christ's gift of a 'man that wolde suffryn the levyn chast, he being on lyve and in good hele of body', she has been set apart from those other wives.[90] Christ promises that the 'gret peyne' which they suffer will have 'ryght gret reward in hevyn', the clear implication being that while alive on earth they must accept their lot. Neither He, nor Margery as his agent, is in the business of encouraging wives to leave husbands who were less compliant than John Kempe.

In any case, she seems to have convinced the 'gret clerke' of her good intent (at least, according to Margery's own account – which proceeds to enlist him in the ranks of men who were made by 'owr Lord, of hys mercy' to 'lovyn hir and supportyn hir'). Apparently Margery's exegesis of Genesis 1:28 passed muster, since the clerk professes himself 'wel plesyd' with her answer.[91] Little wonder that Margery refers to him so warmly as a '*gret* clerke'. And, in reality, perhaps he was less worried about Margery's understanding of 'Crescite et multiplicami' than I (and others before me) have been.

Married women found it harder to be taken seriously as visionaries and emissaries of the divine will – hence Catherine of Siena's robust dismissal of the devil's attempt at marriage guidance (as cited at the beginning of this chapter). An equally telling comment occurs in the *quaestio* about female preaching and teaching, 'Utrum mulier praedicando et docendo mereatur aureolam', which was composed around 1263–6 by the Franciscan Eustace of Arras.[92] It canvasses the opinion that, when St Paul prohibited women from preaching or teaching, he was speaking of married women, because married women belong within the 'common state of women' (*in statu communi mulierum*) rather than being grouped with those women who were specially elected and privileged (*specialiter electae et privilegiatae*) by God. That opinion may well redound 'to the praise and glory of all women saints', as Eustace puts it, but this is at the expense of ordinary women and those activities (marriage, childbirth) which were deemed to be normatively 'womanly', constitutive of what Eustace calls the 'office of woman' (*officium mulieris*). Here the *officium mulieris* stands in stark, uncompromising opposition to the *officium praedicatoris*.

One can only wonder what Eustace would have made of St Bridget, married woman and mother – a major role-model for Margery Kempe.[93] Throughout her *Book* we see Margery struggling to lift herself beyond the 'common state of women', to be recognized as specially elected and privileged by God. Hence her appropriation of Luke 11:27–8 and Genesis 1:28 – a *translatio auctoritatis* which, I believe, does not transgress the limits of fifteenth-century orthodox Catholicism.[94] 'I am non heretyke, ne ye schal non preve me', Margery tells the archbishop of York, a man well known for his loathing of Lollardy.[95] He failed to find her guilty. In Margery's vernacular allegories of female authority there is nothing to suggest that we should reverse his judgement. Besides, it is unclear which (if any) heresy some of Margery's interlocutors were trying to 'preve'.

CHAPTER 6

Chaucer and the relics of vernacular religion

Having asked Harry Bailly to 'com forth' and be the first to 'kisse' his spurious 'relikes everychon', the Pardoner suffers what is probably the most robust put-down in the entire *Canterbury Tales*.

> 'Nay, nay!' quod he [i.e. Bailly], 'thanne have I cristes curs!
> Lat be', quod he, 'it shal nat be, so theech!
> Thou woldest make me kisse thyn olde breech,
> And swere it were a relyk of a seint,
> Though it were with thy fundament depeint!
> But, by the croys which that Seint Eleyne fond,
> I wolde I hadde thy coillons in myn hond
> In stide of relikes or of seintuarie.
> Lat kutte hem of, I wol thee helpe hem carie;
> They shal be shryned in an hogges toord!'
>
> (VI (C), 946–50)

This passage has been the subject of substantial exegesis recently, particularly by those who wish to claim that the Pardoner's alleged homosexuality does indeed matter. Monica McAlpine, whose 1980 article on that subject[1] set the course of much subsequent criticism, saw it as the result of the Pardoner's assault on 'Harry's heterosexual sensibilities'.[2] Following up on this initial outing of the Host as a homophobe, Steven Kruger argued that at this point he 'could not stand farther from Christian spirituality'. That is to say, Harry 'is drawn strongly away from the spiritual' as he 'fully involves himself in the debased physical world presented by the Pardoner as his own'.[3] In the Host's 'revulsion' at the thought of kissing the Pardoner's soiled pants may be found 'a moment of homosexual panic'; thus, according to Kruger, the Pardoner 'perhaps gains a certain kind of victory' insofar as he presents an ongoing challenge to societal norms and the 'procedures of signification and interpretation' that support them. This chapter will argue for a quite different relationship between 'Christian spirituality' and the 'debased physical world' in which the real-life equivalents of Chaucer's characters lived.

Harry's genital discourse has frequently been compared to the passage in the *Roman de la Rose* where Dame Raison explains the conventional, *ad placitum*, nature of language to Amant, by remarking that the term '*coilles*' could denote *reliques* while the term '*reliques*' could denote *coilles*, if we all agreed to talk like that (ll. 7076–85).[4] And, at the end of the *Rose*, a comparable substitution takes place – albeit through allegory rather than the application of *ad placitum* theory – when Amant adores the Rose's genitalia as if they were relics, devoutly kissing an image close to the *saintuaire* in which they are kept (ll. 21553–73). However, Chaucer's concern is not with linguistic substitution but rather with the substitution of a *relyk* of debatable power for the real thing: i.e. the problematic item is afforded the space which is appropriate only for the genuine one, treated with the respect (ironically, of course) which an authentic relic of great value deserves. He has Harry move from a strident rejection of the Pardoner's relic-collection – why, if you had your way, you'd make me kiss anything, even your worthless breeches! – to a fantasy in which the Pardoner's *coillons* are treated *as* a (very special) relic, enshrined in a reliquary which he, Harry, will help him carry. My purpose is to explore the cultural sources and significance of the humour in play here, by investigating the ways in which, in Chaucer's day, relics were supposed to cure various diseases of what we now call the urogenital tract, which includes the kidneys and the testicles. Those diseases could include impotence, infertility – and the more mundane (perhaps) but equally pressing pains caused by kidney stones.

My inquiry has a much wider significance, however, inasmuch as I see it as a test-case of the difficulty of sourcing ideas and practices which are, so to speak, under the radar of high-culture texts (whether produced by schoolmen, clerkly makers, or courtly poets). It is impossible to disagree with Gurevich's general proposition that 'an aristocratic, élitist view of medieval culture, based only on the thoughts of "high-brows" – theologians, philosophers, poets and historians' has become 'firmly established and has dominated scholarship'. The problem is, what can be done about this situation, since we are inevitably dependent on the sources 'produced by a clerical élite'?[5] In response I seek to offer an illustrative excavation from sources both high-brow and low-brow, serious and silly, official and subversive, of vestiges, relics, relicts, remains of what I am calling 'vernacular religion' (a term preferable, in my view, to 'popular religion' or 'folk religion', terms used in the past to categorize information of the kind I am seeking here). By vernacular I do not mean 'as opposed to Latin', because such traces as we do have of demotic religious practices are recorded both in Latin and in one or other of the medieval European vernaculars. If, to follow the *OED*'s definition of 'vernacular', it may be regarded as 'the informal, colloquial or distinctive speech of a people or a group', then the group in question here comprised ordinary, decent late medieval Christians who had little, if any, access to the learned theological disputations of the schools. Even more *au point* is the entry under the headword *vulgo* in Firmin Le Ver's dictionary (as quoted at the very beginning of this book), where the relevant terms are explained with reference to notions of being 'public', common', 'manifest', 'popular' – the property of a community. And also 'disordered' – which I am going to interpret in the sense of being disordered in relation to high-culture paradigms,[6] though the practices of vernacular religion usually have (so to speak) their own logic. Whether we can always understand it is a moot point.

The kissing of even genuine relics could be a stomach-turning experience, to judge from the reactions of Erasmus's character 'Gratian Pullus' (based on John Colet) in his thinly fictionalized account of a visit to Canterbury made during the period between late 1512 and the summer of 1514. A large quantity of bones was brought before his party, 'skulls, jaws, teeth, hands, fingers, whole arms; all of which we adored and kissed'. However, when he was presented with an arm 'with the bloodstained flesh' still attached, Gratian looked 'rather disgusted' and shrank from kissing it.[7] He may soon have recovered his composure, however, for a few lines later he is not specifically excluded from the group which renders all due reverence to certain relics of St Thomas à Becket that have been brought out especially for them: 'We were shown a *pallium*,[8] silk to be sure, but coarse, without gold or jewels, and there as a face-cloth (*sudarium*),[9] soiled by sweat from his neck and preserving obvious spots of blood. These memorials of the plain living of olden times we gladly kissed.'[10] However, Gratian's aversion resurfaces when he is presented with one of the rags with which, 'they say, the holy man wiped the sweat from his face or neck, the dirt from his nose, or whatever other kinds of filth human bodies have'. 'Gratian was hardly grateful for it. He touched the piece with his fingers, not without a sign of disgust, and put it back scornfully.'[11]

Some expression of gratitude would have been quite in order, however, given that Gratian and his companions were being given exceptional treatment. Not everyone got to kiss that *pallium* and *sudarium*, or was honoured with such a wonderful present as Becket's *depeinted* rags. But even Erasmus and his distinguished company did not gain access to most of the really special relics of Becket, as is made clear later in the *Peregrinatio religionis ergo.* 'Ogygius' – Erasmus's persona in this colloquy – describes how the chest 'in which the holy man's body is said to lie' was indeed opened for them, but they did not see the actual bones. 'That's not permitted', Ogygius continues, 'nor would it be possible without the use of ladders.' (It seems that the first chest, a wooden structure, concealed a 'golden chest' which could not be seen unless it was 'drawn up by ropes'.)[12] True, in the crypt they were shown 'the martyr's skull, pierced through'; the 'top of the cranium is bared for kissing, the rest is covered in silver'.[13] But Erasmus's party was not allowed to kiss those very special 'contact relics',[14] the 'hair shirt, girdle and trousers (*cincilia, cingula subligariaque*) by which the bishop used to subdue his flesh hang in the gloom there – horrible even to look at and a reproach to our softness and delicacy (*mollitiem ac delicias*)'.[15] So, then, Gratian *cum suis* can look but not touch. And certainly cannot kiss.

Visitors of lesser social status would have received far more perfunctory treatment. In the fifteenth-century *Canterbury Tales* continuation known as *The Canterbury Interlude and Tale of Beryn*, we read an account of how the pilgrims

> ... preyd to Seynt Thomas, in such wise as they couth.
> And sith the holy relikes ech man with his mowth
> Kissed, as a goodly monke the names told and taught.
> (ll. 165–7)[16]

However, it is highly likely that, in the case of at least some relics, the poem imagines 'the pilgrims kissing the ornamented (opaque) containers . . . rather than the precious contents themselves'.[17] Here I quote Robyn Malo's important discussion of the way in which many major relics were occluded, hidden from sight (even from the likes of Erasmus and Colet) in richly ornamented reliquaries which affirmed the sanctity of their contents – and (to add a practical point) which helped their custodians maintain firm control over them. In sum, medieval conventions of relic veneration were many and various; it would be inappropriate as well as impossible to impose any uniformity on shifting, developing practices – which, in any case, took on different shapes and forms in different times and places, that being the very nature of vernacular culture.

Traditions and techniques of occlusion must therefore be given their due, particularly since they have been neglected in contemporary scholarship. That said, there is abundant evidence that relics both major and minor were put on display for the adoration of the *vulgus*, at least on special occasions, and the number of crystal or glass reliquaries which survive from the later Middle Ages were, quite evidently, designed to display their spiritually rich (though physically grisly) contents to best advantage.[18] And there were plenty of relics (and/or the reliquaries which contained them) available for kissing. Including the top of Thomas à Becket's cranium. Then there was the drinking. The practice of drinking water or wine in which relics or related objects had been dipped, washed, or dissolved, was a common medieval method of healing. Jonathan Sumption notes that at Norwich Cathedral, pilgrims 'drank water mixed with scrapings of cement from the tomb of St William', while 'at Reading abbey the hand of St James was dipped in water, phials of which were sent off to cure the sick'.[19] Some found this hard to stomach – like the monk of Mont-St-Michel who 'refused a draught of the wine which had washed the skull of St Aubert, "preferring to die than drink wine swilled in the head of a corpse"'.[20] Following Becket's martyrdom the Canterbury monks collected some of Becket's blood and diluted it in a large cistern of water; with such a precious medicine in their possession, they were keen to ensure there 'was plenty available and that it would not be too repulsive to drink'.[21] A small *ampulla* of 'Becket's blood' became one of the *signa* of a Canterbury pilgrim. However, their production had ceased by the end of the thirteenth century, and so they could not have been bought by the real-life equivalents of Chaucer's pilgrims.[22]

This change cannot be attributed to what Sumption calls a 'growing sensitivity' in respect of physical contact with relics; the records offer few precedents for the 'disgust' and 'contempt' felt by 'Gratian Pullus'. *Pace* Sumption's argument, 'macabre beverages' did *not* pass 'out of fashion after the twelfth century'.[23] Water in which a finger of 'Saint' Douceline of Digne (c. 1215–74) was dipped supposedly cured many ailments, including the swollen abdomen of a two-year-old child, a stomach ailment that kept a servant woman from eating, and a fellow-beguine's breathlessness and hiccups. 'Many other people were healed in the same way: when they drank some of the water in which the holy mother's finger had been dipped, they were immediately cured of the infirmities from which they suffered.'[24] The fact that the Pardoner's clients are in the habit of drinking similar concoctions also indicates a then-current trend, and indeed vestiges of the practice have survived until the present day. Besides, the Canterbury monks described in Erasmus's account seem unaffected by the sensitivity Sumption has postulated.

So, then, oral contact with relics was common – and not for the squeamish, though profession of distaste was rare, at least according to the written record. (Which is hardly surprising, given any supplicant's wish not to offend the saint he or she was petitioning.) That insight does not, of course, confer any odour of sanctity on the Pardoner's pants. But – strictly in material terms – it may serve to diminish the distance between the authentic and the fake relic. And also support the view that, far from Chaucer seeking to present the Host as standing far away from Christian spirituality,[25] his humour in the above passage depends on the verisimilar connections between authentic 'relikes' and the cod-relic (the Pardoner's *coillons*) which, in Harry's fantasy, comes to occupy the very place (*stide*) that rightly belongs to the genuine article. Knowledge of the powers some 'real' relics were believed to possess may help us understand the manner in which the Host fictionalizes his opponent's testicles as the prize exhibit in his collection.

It is possible to detect a specific joke in the Host's statement that the Pardoner is the kind of man who would make him kiss his shit-stained breeches, swearing that they were the 'relyk of a seint'. This may be an ironic allusion to the famous relic of Becket's hair-breeches, which is mentioned, together with his girdle and shirt, in a passage from Erasmus's *Peregrinatio* which has already been quoted above (p. 133). When the Canterbury monks removed the clothes from their 'holy blissful martyr', they were amazed to discover that his breeches and hair-shirt were covered with lice and vermin.[26] Thus Becket had mortified his flesh.[27]

Here I follow Daniel Knapp, who proposed the Becket allusion in an article published in 1972.[28] The matter was taken further in Richard Firth Green's subsequent article on 'The Pardoner's Pants (and Why They Matter)',[29] where it is suggested that the Host's reference to his adversary's soiled breeches also recalls a well-known folktale (of the 'Adulteress Outwits Husband' type) wherein a friar or some other lecherous clergyman cuckolds a husband who then discovers his discarded trousers; the wife's honour is saved when this garment is taken to be the relic of a saint.[30] In one version of the narrative (which goes back at least to the mid-thirteenth century, appearing in the *fabliau* known as *Les Braies au cordelier*), the pants are seen as a cure for infertility, and, more specifically, in the renderings of the Knight of La Tour Landry (*c.* 1371), Franco Sacchetti (mid-1380s), and Poggio Bracciolini (mid-fifteenth century), they are presented as a holy relic. Closest of all to the ending of Chaucer's *Pardoner's Tale* is the French farce *Frère Guillebert*, printed in the mid-sixteenth century but perhaps of earlier composition.[31] Green draws particular attention to the fact that here 'the word *reliquère/reliquaire*, rather than *relique*', is used 'to refer to the holy pants', comparing the wish of Chaucer's Host to have the Pardoner's *coillons* in his hand, 'In stide of relikes or of *seintuarie*'. 'In both instances the comic effect is the same: the pants are not precious in themselves but for what they contain.'[32] I want to build on this remark by arguing that, as part of his ridicule of the Pardoner, Harry Bailly treats the contents of the Pardoner's pants as if they were indeed a precious relic, capable of curing disorders of what we now call the urogenital tract (understood to include the kidneys and the testicles), not least the afflictions of impotence and infertility. This was an age which regarded the kidneys or loins 'as the seat of sexual potency',[33] a belief well illustrated by the Vulgate Latin Bible's reference to the 'fruit' of one's loins (Acts 2:30, *de fructu lumbi eius*). So, then – once more into the breech.

The first part of this argument must comprise brief demonstrations of the fact that many late medieval men and women actually visited specific shrines, and kissed relevant relics, in their search for relief from the above-mentioned disorders. Eamon Duffy's sensitive account of the shrine of St Walstan of Bawburgh (near Norwich) affords an excellent point of departure.[34] Allegedly a king's son, Walstan chose to live in poverty, working in the fields as a humble labourer. 'All catell & corne encrease in his hond'; miraculous fecundity attends all his works. When he is rewarded by his employers with a cow, this animal produces two fine bullock calves. Near to death, Walstan asks a gift of God. Any person who invokes him should be cured 'of sicknes or ache of bones', and the same should also apply to sick beasts, so they may be more useful in 'Mans labour'. God readily grants this petition, and appropriate miracles follow: a priest's rupture is healed when the wound is washed with water from a vessel on Walstan's tomb, a knight's 'bone ache' is cured by water from Walstan's well, and so forth. However, it was his fecundating prowess that was the key to Walstan's popularity; 'the appeal of a holy man who can bring healing and fertility to man and beast, and who can bless the harvest and the harvesters', was very considerable.[35] This is borne out by the belief that 'both Men and Beastes which had lost their Prevy partes, had newe members again restored to them, by this Walstane'.[36] Here, then, is some good news for the Pardoner (assuming for the moment that he suffers from some genital lack, deformity or malfunction),[37] though perhaps he should be heading for Bawburgh rather than Canterbury.[38] Our source for this information is, however, the reformer John Bale, who likens Walstan, as the 'god of their feldes in Northfolke and Gyde of their Harvestes', to the pagan god Priapus. We should be wary of trusting the testimony of Protestants in whose interest it was to exaggerate the superstitions and stupidities of popery. They are hardly a reliable guide to the vernacular practices of Catholic believers – a point to which we shall return.

One did not have to be a Protestant, however, to find absurdity in the practices associated with certain saints' cults (though it certainly helped). In the *Dialogue concerning Heresies* which Sir/Saint Thomas More published in 1529, the More-persona converses with a confidential Messenger sent by a right worshipful friend who seeks advice on certain matters of faith, including the problems caused by false relics, going on pilgrimage for the wrong reasons, and asking inappropriate petitions of the saints. Clearly, the (possibly fictional) Messenger is aware of Chaucer's Pardoner, for he expresses concerns about people mistakenly venerating 'pygges bones',[39] an allusion to the General Prologue, I(A) 700. The Chaucerian reference is confirmed a few lines later: 'For what reuerent honoure is there dayly done vnder the name and oppynyon of a sayntes relyke / to some olde rotten bone yt was happely some tyme as Chaucer sayth a bone of some holy Iewes shepe.'[40] Here the allusion is to the *Pardoner's Prologue*, VI(C) 350–65, where the Pardoner is advertising the miracle-working properties of the shoulder-bone of 'an hooly Jews sheep', in terms reminiscent of the fecundating prowess that was associated with St Walstan, as described above. Just as the water from Walstan's tomb-vessel and well can cure many disorders in beast and man, so too can the water in which the Pardoner's 'boon' is washed, and if the animal's owner himself drinks from the same source, once a week, early in the morning before he has eaten, then his animals and his possessions shall increase and multiply.[41]

> 'Goode men', I seye, 'taak of my wordes keep;
> If that this boon be wasshe in any welle,
> If cow, or calf, or sheep, or oxe swelle
> That any worm hath ete, or worme ystonge,
> Taak water of that welle and wassh his tonge,
> And it is hool anon; and forthermoore,
> Of pokkes and of scabbe, and every soore
> Shal every sheep be hool that of this welle
> Drynketh a draughte. Taak kep eek what I telle:
> If that the good-man that he beestes oweth
> Wol every wyke, er that the cok hym croweth,
> Fastynge, drynken of this welle a draughte,
> As thilke hooly Jew oure eldres taughte,
> His beestes and his stoor shal multiplie.'

In the next chapter this very allusion is repeated, as More's interlocutor sharply asks, 'May the takyng vp of a mannys bones / & settyng his carcas in a gay shryne / and than kyssyng his bare scalpe / make a man a saynt?' Yet there are some saints who lack shrines, for no one knows where they are buried. Or indeed, whether they had any body at all (i.e. perhaps they didn't exist). Then again, sometimes one body lies in two places far apart, and in both places the monks claim possession of the authentic body, and cite miracles to prove it. Either the miracles at one place are false or performed by the devil, or one saint actually had two bodies – which would be the greatest miracle of all! And therefore, the Messenger continues, it is likely that somewhere a bone is 'worshypped for a relyke of some holy saynt / that was peraduenture a bone as Chaucer saythe of some holy Iewes shepe'.[42]

Protesting that the Messenger risks taking 'the reuerence from all relyques bycause that som be doubtfull', the More-persona proceeds to address all of these concerns.[43] Perhaps different parts of one and the same body reside in different places, perhaps two holy men shared the same name, perhaps some true relics are now 'vnknowen and mysnamed' – as in the case of certain items discovered at Barking Abbey some thirty years previously, when an 'olde ymage' was moved to a new tabernacle, and found to have a secret compartment. When he gets to the matter of those 'pygges bones' being venerated as if they were 'holy relyques' he couples it with the problem of damned wretches mistakenly being venerated as saints, and gives the same answer to both questions.[44] If such a thing indeed has happened, it did not in any way harm 'the soules of them that mysse talke it', any more than if we venerate a host in the mass which perchance 'the neglygence or malyce of some lewde preste hathe lefte vnconsecrate'. Besides, he finds it impossible to believe that God would allow such a thing to 'laste and endure in his chyrche'.

The Messenger then returns to the attack, emphasizing how some people while on pilgrimage behave scandalously, 'roylynge about in ydlenes / with the riot / reuelynge / and rybawdry / glutony / wantonnes / waste / and lechery'.[45] Surely God and the holy saints would rather they would stay at home than come seek them with such appalling 'seruyce'! A point the More-persona readily accepts. The Messenger proceeds to claim that we afford the saints little worship by setting each of them to his particular task and assigning 'hym a crafte suche as pleaseth vs'. For example, we turn St Loy (= Eloi) into a horse-doctor,[46] engage St Hippolytus to assist at a blacksmith's forge,[47] make St Apollonia into a dentist,[48] and have 'Saynt Sythe' (= Zita) help women find their lost keys.[49] St Roch 'was set to se to the great sykenes' (i.e. the plague) 'bycause he had a sore',[50] and 'with hym they ioyne saynt Sebastyan / bycause he was martyred with arowes'. Furthermore, some saints 'serue for the eye onely. And some for a sore brest. Saynt Germayne onely for chyldren.' Ridiculous offerings are deemed necessary to enlist a saint's help – a white loaf and a pot of good ale in the case of St Germain and oats in the case of St Wylgeforte (Wilgefortis),[51] otherwise known as 'Saynt Vncumber' because women believe that for an offering of oats she will 'uncumber' them of their husbands. Why oats? Perhaps, suggests the Messenger, because Wilgefortis would provide a horse for the wicked husband to ride to the devil on!

An even more bizarre anecdote follows, clearly meant to be amusing – one of those 'mery tales'[52] which, again and again, we see the discussants laughing at. What I am about to tell you, begins the Messenger, 'I dare as boldely make you sure of / as yf I hadde sene it my selfe' (a remark that leads us to expect a tall tale). In Picardy there is a shrine to St Valery, who is especially sought out 'for the stone' (i.e. kidney stones),[53] and not just by people from the regions round about but also from England as well. A young English gentleman who, having taken his new wife overseas to see Flanders and France, visited the chapel, and found it far stranger than he had expected.

For lyke as in other pylgrymages ye se hanged vp legges of waxe or armes or suche other partes / so was in that chapell all theyr offrynges yt honge aboute the walles / none other thynge but mennes gere & womens gere made in waxe.[54]

Here More is referring to the votive offerings which were a common feature of medieval shrines, effigies of complete bodies (pierced with arrows or knives, for instance) or of body parts, such as a foot, leg, arm, eye, teeth, heart or breast, together with the crutches or bandages left by those who had been cured, and perhaps a model anchor or ship (indicating that its donor had survived a shipwreck, or some other nautical disaster).[55] Images of animals (particularly cows and horses) were also made, indicating the anxieties of men and women who depended on such creatures for their livelihood.[56] Usually these *ex votos* were made of wax, but sometimes wood was used – or even silver or gold, depending on the wealth of the grateful pilgrim.[57] Such images were, as Eamon Duffy puts it, 'the most eloquent of all possible testimonies to the reality of healing, assurances of the triumph of life in a world which must often have seemed dominated by suffering and death'.[58] The particular form of suffering in which St Valery specializes concerns the urogenital tract; the wax images of genitalia hanging on the chapel walls are testimonies to the success of his healing. No doubt they were reassuring to the young English gentleman in this yarn who, we are told, was particularly fearful of the 'stone'.

A graphic account is given of how this condition is treated in the chapel. On the altar there are two round rings of silver, one much larger than the other:

Thrughe whiche euery man dyd put his preuy membres at the aulters ende. Not euery man thrughe bothe / but some thrughe the one and some thrughe the other. For they were not bothe of a bygnes / but the one larger than the other.

In their wisdom the monks have catered for two sizes of male genitalia. But there is more to be done. At the altar stands a monk, blessing threads made of Venetian gold, and teaching the pilgrims how to use them 'agaynst the stone'. They are to 'knytte' the thread 'aboute theyr gere' and say various prayers. On learning this, the gentleman's servant ('a maryed man and yet a mery felawe') lowers the tone by asking how 'he sholde knytte it aboute his wyues gere'. Unless the monk has some special skill, this will prove a difficult matter 'bycause her gere was somwhat shorte'. Whereupon everyone laughs – save the monk, who leaves angrily, taking his rings and threads with him.

There is a second part to this story, which the Messenger recounts with relish.[59] As this gentleman was kneeling in the chapel with his wife, 'a goode sadde woman' came to him, asking him if he knew about a certain other practice used in that pilgrimage, which was the surest measure possible 'agaynste ye stone'. She offers to measure his 'gere' and make a wax candle the same length, which would be placed to burn in the chapel, with certain prayers being said the while. But the gentleman's wife, who has raised no objection to the other goings-on in the chapel, baulks at this one: 'lyke a good faythfull crysten woman' she 'loued no such superstycyons'. Some 'wychecrafte' is involved, she warns her husband, and if he took part in the ritual 'it wold wast vp' his 'gere'. The obvious irony here is that this good Christian woman may be worried less about superstitious veneration than about the dimunition of her husband's 'gere', which clearly would be to her disadvantage.

How seriously are we to take More's account? More himself offers no judgement; indeed he refuses to comment, given that this shrine is in France, and so it is up to the University of Paris to pronounce on the situation. 'But nowe as for our mery matters of saynt wallery bycause the place is in Fraunce we shall leue the matter to the vnyuersyte of Parys to defende.'[60] I read this as jocular – the 'mery matters of saynt wallery' are beneath the notice of the distinguished scholars at the University of Paris. But does the statement that these matters are 'mery' imply that More is rejecting the tale of St Valery out of hand? We cannot assume that, given that he proceeds to pay serious attention to another apparently 'mery' yarn, the tale of 'St Uncumber' (Wilgefortis), who had a shrine at St Paul's in London. 'We wyll come home here to Poules to put one ensample of both /

that is to say the superstycyous maner and vnlefull petycyons / yf women there offer otys vnto saynt wylgefort in trust yt she shall vncomber them of theyr housbondys'.[61] The extent to which More tries to make some sense of this vernacular practice (while admitting that the Messenger is right to be concerned about it)[62] is remarkable. Priests can hardly be blamed for what 'folysh women' do, and they don't get much if any profit out of the practice – a point with which the Messenger readily agrees, remarking that all the oats offered in whole year wouldn't feed three geese and a gander for a week.[63] Furthermore, priests can't hear what 'peuyshe women' pray for. Indeed, when they pray to be 'uncumbered' this isn't necessarily harmful or sinful: for example, if they prayed that their husbands should change their 'comberous condycyons', or that they themselves should change their 'comberous tounges / which is happely the cause of all theyr combraunce'. And finally if they can be uncumbered only by death, then it may be by their own death, their husbands being safe enough. The Messenger baulks at that: the women aren't such fools, they really do pray 'bytter prayers' and won't throw away their oats for nothing. Whereupon More offers his definitive general argument. If praying to saints, going on pilgrimage, and venerating relics and images may be done well (which of course More believes is the case), then the fact that some engage in these practices in a wicked manner is immaterial. We shouldn't put away the good use just because of the bad. If we did, there would be some marvellous changes in the world. In some countries, they go hunting (as a common custom) on the morning of Good Friday. Will you break that evil custom or throw away Good Friday? We wouldn't wish to abolish Lent because some get drunk then, on 'wygges and craknels' (little buns and biscuits dipped in wine).[64] Christmas is commonly abused, yet is not to be cast away; rather we should admonish men to mend their manners and behave in a more Christian fashion. Just because some people ask evil petitions of saints, or fail to understand the true manner in which images should be venerated, doesn't mean that all Christians think and act in that way. 'A few dotynge dames make not the people.'[65]

The (often earthy) humour in More's *Dialogue concerning Heresies* is more than merely entertaining: it functions as a highly effective means of defending the faith. Dubious practices are reduced to absurdity and laughed out of court, to the end that all Christians should not suffer calumny because of the ridiculous antics of the few. This is not to say that More is patronizing about ordinary Christians – indeed, the opposite is true. The sympathy and fellow-feeling he brings to the practices of vernacular religion are quite remarkable, as may be illustrated by the following exchange.

More's persona asserts that to pray to St Apollonia if we have toothache is not witchcraft, considering that she had her teeth pulled out for Christ's sake. And, since St Loy was a farrier, it is not a great fault 'to pray to hym for the helpe of our horse'.[66] The Messenger sceptically retorts that, in this case, we should get St Crispin and Crispiane to sit down and mend our shoes, since they were shoemakers,[67] and pray to St Dorothy for some flowers, since she always carries a basket full.[68] More patiently explains that the cases are different. What is crucial is whether certain things are essential to us, and whether we ourselves can perform the action in question or find someone else who can, rather than seeking divine assistance. God commanded that we should chiefly seek for heaven, reassuring us that, if we do so, the other things that we need shall be given unto us (Matthew 6:32–3). Our heavenly father feeds 'the birds of the air', and we are of much more value than they (6:26); His will is that we should not live in anxiety and trouble our mind with fear. God desired also that we should ask of Him what we cannot achieve by our own labour. He did not reckon a horse to be of so little value that he deemed it a breach of the Sabbath to pull it out of a pit. And therefore, the More-persona continues, devotion to St Loy goes too far if a smith will not, on his feast day, for necessity set a shoe on a poor man's horse. If the horse is sick and even a good 'leche' is unable to cure it, St Loy's assistance may rightly be sought, given that the animal's loss would be a great financial blow to its owner. As for your teeth, if they ached badly you would not think it a simple and unworthy thing to ask help from 'saynt Appolyn and of god to'! The obvious implication is that you should not be condescending about others seeking remedies which desperation might force you yourself to try. It just might be added – though More does not – that a person suffering because of 'the stone' could well be driven to visit a shrine that offered the same service as that wondrous chapel of St Valery.

As an account of actual practice at shrines which offered relief to those suffering from urogenital disorders, More's story is suspect, to say the least, but as an indication of the kind of humour which could arise from 'popular' (I use this term in the sense following the Latin *popularis*)[69] beliefs about the healing powers of certain shrines it inspires trust. Hence it may advisedly be applied in an investigation of Chaucer's comic discourse concerning the Pardoner – and the fact that More references this very character on three occasions (as reported above) seems to indicate that he found Chaucer's humour congenial. The next sources are of a different order, even though like More's tale of St Valery they fall into the category of 'strange but perhaps partly true and/or possibly exaggerated' – I refer to the accounts given of priapic shrines by continental Protestants, in whose interest it clearly was to highlight and heighten any Catholic practices which they deemed scandalous.

Agrippa d'Aubigné's *Confession de Sancy* (1597–1617) is interesting for the way in which it manages to combine staunch Calvinism with a willingness to use fiction in the service of the Protestant faith, at least inasmuch as its author speaks in the person of Sancy, a nobleman who has converted to Catholicism in the hope of personal gain.[70] D'Aubigné's own feelings show through in his account of the shrine of 'Saint Foutin' at Varailles in Provence, which is adorned with wax effigies of male and female sexual organs ('des parties honteuses de l'un et l'autre sexe formees en cire').[71] Suspended from the ceiling of his chapel, when the wind blew them against each other this somewhat interrupted the devotions being performed in honour of the saint. During his visit there, the narrator continues, he was surprised to discover how many men there were named 'Foutin', and the daughter of his hostess had as her godmother one 'Mademoiselle Foutine'. Thus d'Aubigné underlines the evident derivation of 'Foutin' from the French verb *foutre*, 'to fuck'. Furthermore, at a nunnery at Fontaine in Perigreux, barren women, in addition to offering wax models of the genitalia of both sexes, place candles on the virile member of an image known as 'Saint Chose' (i.e. 'Saint Thing'),[72] which they watch burning down. This last story recalls both parts of Thomas More's account of the amazing chapel at St Valery.[73] D'Aubigné also recounts how, when the Huguenots took the town of Embrun in the lower Alps (which, historically, occurred in 1585), they found among the relics in the main church an ancient wooden phallus, its head turned red due to the amount of wine which had been poured over it. Thus women made 'holy vinegar' – which they put to some (unspecified) strange use, d'Aubigné coyly remarks. An even bigger wooden phallus was discovered and burned by the troops who destroyed the temple of St Eutropius at Orange (an incident which had taken place earlier, in 1562). D'Aubigné rounds off his account of phallic saints by claiming that there are other St Foutins at Auxerre and Vendre (in the Bourbonnais), while the diocese of Viviers has a 'St Foutin de Cives'.

Comparable accounts may be found in Henri Estienne's *Apologie pour Hérodite* of 1566 and the *Tableau des differens de la religion* which the Belgian Calvinist Philippe de Marnix, Seigneur de Sainte-Aldegonde, composed in 1599. Estienne sets about defending Heroditus by a novel method: there is no reason to question the truthfulness of the ancient Greek historian, he claims, in view of the amazing events which may be found in recent history (and which the Huguenot writer records with satiric relish). One of his tales is reminiscent of D'Aubigné's account of the church at Embrun. In the Berri area, St Guerlichou is venerated by women who scrape powder from the large penis on his statue; from this they make a potion which helps women who cannot conceive.[74] St René of Anjou is added to the pantheon of phallic saints; he too has 'fine priapic weapons' around which women conduct themselves in a manner Estienne is too ashamed to describe. Following Malcolm Jones, it seems reasonable to suggest that 'St René's fecundating power is due to the folk-etymological connection of his name with the kidneys, loins or "reins" (French *reins*; cf. the Lat. *renes*, which is a synonym of *lumbi*, as in "fruit of one's loins").'[75] Philippe de Marnix produces a saint who works by gaze alone: women who lift the apron on the image of St Arnaut to gaze upon its genitalia will thereafter be fertile.[76] Yet another way in which women can ensure fecundity, according to Marnix, is of particular interest to us – they can kiss the breeches either of St Francis or of St Ioost in Flanders.[77]

It would seem, then, that a corpus of anecdotes concerning the fecundating powers of certain saints, statues, and relics was in circulation by the end of the Middle Ages, a source of merry tales among the faithful which later became grist to the mill of Protestants who used it for propaganda purposes. It is a matter of historical record that Huguenot soldiers sacked churches at Orange in 1562 and at Embrun in 1585, but their discovery of large wooden phalli may well be a tall tale. To speak of 'burlesque' saints in this context is somewhat misleading, however, if by the term is understood caricature of a kind so extreme that the imitation is far distanced from the genuine article. For, in the cases under review, it is the direct connections to (rather than any disjunctions from) the genuine article that are most crucial. John Bale's account of St Walstan's ability to restore the testicles of man or beast (as quoted above) may smack of Protestant malice, but a few centuries earlier miracles of this kind were believed to have happened and to have met the highest standards of proof. One of the miracles attributed to Thomas à Becket by William of Canterbury concerns one Ailward from Western in Bedfordshire, who was punished for housebreaking by castration and blinding. Thanks to the intervention of the (recently martyred) Becket along with the Virgin Mary, Ailward grew small testicles and eyes to replace his missing body parts.[78] In Benedict of Peterborough's more optimistic version of the same incident, Ailward's testicles are restored to their former size, as are his eyes.[79] (The real-life equivalents of Chaucer's pilgrims would have seen this miracle, depicted in stained glass, in the Trinity Chapel at Canterbury; the relevant three roundels have survived, and may still be viewed in the Cathedral today.)[80]

Ailward's amazing experiences have been dated to the period 1170–4. A remarkably (indeed suspiciously) similar incident is recorded at some length in the *Vita Sancti Willelmi* which, Christopher Norton has convincingly argued, was written *c.* 1225 as part of the formal canonization process involving William of York.[81] (Given the deep rivalries between York and Canterbury, one may suspect that the *Vita's* author was keen to ensure that his saint was not outshone by Becket.) Having been convicted on a trumped-up charge of arson, a man (named Ralph in another record) was blinded, and then his enemy (one 'Besing') 'with bestial ferocity . . . forcefully and completely cut off his virile parts and, horrible sight, publicly threw them to the people, together with the pupils of his eyes, so that children and adults were astounded by his rage'. At St William's tomb Ralph 'poured forth fragrant prayers', whereupon he 'received new privy parts and fresh little eyes'.[82] Yet another case was reported from Worcestershire in the 1230s, concerning one Thomas of Eldersfield, whose testicles and eyes grew back to their full size, thanks to the agency of St Wulftan and the Virgin Mary. The Worcester monk who recorded the event proudly noted the parallel with Becket's miracle.[83] Little wonder, then, that 'Thomas' was regarded as 'the best doctor for the worthy sick'.[84] So, in travelling to Canterbury the Pardoner was going to the right place after all – though he can hardly be deemed one of the 'worthy sick'.

But it must be admitted that the written records cannot give us much sense of what really went on at the level of vernacular religion. For we are seeking access to what Gurevich has called a '"low" layer of medieval culture which was barely if at all influenced by schools of classical or patristic tradition but which had preserved vital links with the mythopoetic and folkloric-magic consciousness'. 'Folkloric elements were suppressed by the church or distorted or partially adapted to the demands of official ideology', as the work of Jacques le Goff has admirably demonstrated. The dominant civilization was unable to eliminate resistant vernacularity and hence 'partially absorbed it', though in certain cases this meant that 'the themes of folklore radically changed their meaning in their new Christian form' – and there was much clerical incomprehension of 'popular' culture.[85] Hence research by present-day folklorists and social anthropologists can be of great value, allowing us occasional glimpses of a world we have lost (though it would be naive to think in terms of unbroken or unreconstructed tradition). To offer one example: nowadays, at Gondomar in Portugal, barren women gather dust from the floor of St Simon's chapel (previously, they scraped limestone from his holy hill).[86] This might be seen as a modern, and altogether more decorous, version of the practice of scraping powder from the large penis on the statue of St Guerlichou. If Philippe de Marnix is to be believed, of course. Even if he is not, the practice of taking scrapings from images, and indeed from relics, of saints is well documented for the later Middle Ages. Pierre Sanchis has noted the near-disappearance in modern Portugal of 'those aggressively indecent or scatolological actions' which 'used to feature prominently in the cult of saints especially connected with sexual matters or fertility', such as Sts Gonçalo, John, and Anthony.[87] However, certain vestiges remain, such as the selling at Amarente, on St Gonçalo's day, of phallic cakes popularly known as 'St Gonçalo's cocks' – these being, as Sanchis puts it, 'stylized versions of biscuits that used to be more realistic'.[88] Again at Amarente, women seeking husbands used to pull at the belt of St Gonçalo's robe – 'or embrace a mysterious statue near the chapel of São Braz at Matozinhos'.[89] Perhaps in the past more intimate engagement with statues was deemed permissible, at least by some. The practice of praying to certain saints for marital assistance is certainly well known throughout contemporary Europe, St Anthony of Padua probably being the best-known 'marrying saint'; he is also patron saint of barren women, and believed to find rich husbands for women who light candles on his holy day.[90] A fifteenth-century English analogue to such practice is found in John Paston's letter to his wife of 14 September 1465, in which he expresses the hope that his sister should visit two crosses (one at the north door of St Paul's Cathedral, the other at St Saviour in Bermondsey Abbey) to 'pray to them that sche may have a good hosbond'.[91]

Going back even earlier, another type of marital problem is illustrated in the *Lai de desiré* (c. 1200), which begins with a wise but barren wife recommending to her husband that they should travel (from Scotland) to Provence, where they will find the relics (literally, the body) of a celebrated saint who has received from God the gift of granting children – no one who prays there has been disappointed.

> 'Sire, je ai oï parler
> k'en Provence, dela la mer,
> ad un cors seint mut glorius;
> dames i vunt od lur espus;
> nul nel requert pur tel besoing,
> quel quë il seit ou pres ou loing,
> ke sa requeste ne li face;
> de Deu en ad ottrei e grace
> nomeement d'aver enfant'.
>
> (27–35)[92]

In Chaucer's day, the same service was performed by Our Lady of Walsingham. One of England's most popular shrines, it was regularly visited
by both kings and commoners (Richard II and his queen seem to have
gone there twice in 1383), and proved a big draw for women. This is hardly
surprising, given Mary's special expertise in matters relating to fertility,
childbirth, and children. Elizabeth of York (1465–1503), who was Edward
IV's daughter and Henry VII's wife, visited the shrine following the deaths
of two children, a son and a daughter.[93] Walsingham possessed, as its most
precious relic, some of Mary's milk, become hard like powdered chalk,
which was kept on the high altar in a crystal container to avoid 'being
defiled by the kisses of men' (the container itself could be kissed).[94] Pilgrims could buy ampullae filled with holy water mixed with a little of this
milk, 'presumably to aid in fertility, childbirth, or lactation'.[95] The Milk
Grotto at Bethlehem (records of which begin in the twelfth century) also
claimed possession of some of Mary's milk; this was a popular shrine until
the early twentieth century, though nowadays visitors are few. Those who
still come preserve the belief that eating the white powder from the grotto's
walls will increase their milk supply.[96]

The medieval (and indeed, pre-medieval) tradition of leaving replicas
of afflicted body parts at shrines has also survived. Wax votives are most
prevalent in modern Spain and Portugal; wooden models were once common in Switzerland, whereas metal ones (which have a long ancestry) are
still used in Italy and Spain. To take one specific example, the wax votives
at the Spanish shrine of Nuestra Señora de Cortes are almost life-sized, and
include images of female breasts (left by sufferers from breast cancer).[97]
Votives of (ungendered) breasts are frequently referred to in records of
now-defunct (or transformed) English shrines.[98] There is nothing erotic
about such imagery; rather it signifies a 'heart-rending stream of desperate
men and women'[99] who sought (and continue to seek) whatever relief was
(and may be) available.

The display of *ex votos* touches the very nerve and centre of the meaning of the
cult of the saints in the late Middle Ages. The miracle stories associated with the
shrines of the saints . . . opened a window of hope on a daunting world of sickness,
pain, and natural calamity . . . We catch glimpses of a whole gallery of devastating
diseases – bone cancer, gangrene, epilepsy, paralysis – of homes wrecked by insanity,
and entire families or villages decimated by plague or famine.[100]

Disorders of the urogenital tract, together with impotence and infertility,
can be added to this list of horrors. As Boccaccio once memorably remarked,
in time of plague even the most sedate of men will do absolutely anything,

even walk abroad with his breeches for headgear, if he thinks it may save his life.[101] Similarly, in respect of the contents of those same breeches, even the most sedate of men will do anything he thinks might relieve his distress. Damaged testicles were not deemed unworthy of divine intervention, to judge by the cases of Ailward of Western, Ralph of York, and Thomas of Eldersfield; evidently their repair fell under the category, as defined by Thomas More, of things which we ourselves cannot do. Fear of the 'stone' was very real, and therefore fell under the related category of things that God does not want to see troubling our minds.[102]

But can we really believe the lurid tales of Thomas More and the continental Reformers? Only when sixteenth-century 'high culture' is motivated by some purpose of its own, such as ridicule, satire, or propaganda, does it deign to pay attention to the evidence of vernacular religion – in which case we cannot be confident about the testimony of witnesses with an obvious axe to grind. On the other hand, better to have an exaggerated account than no record at all. It was only because More wanted to illustrate the problems caused by asking inappropriate petitions of, and making inappropriate offerings to, the saints that we know so much about the strange cult of 'St Uncumber'. It is therefore impossible to rule out the possibility that wax models of male and female genitalia once adorned the roofs or walls of certain shrines: how unfortunate that More ducked the issue. Sometimes an artifact turns up which provides some support for that possibility, such as the late medieval wooden phallus dug up on the Norwegian coast near Bergen.[103] Could it have been a votive offering? Could images made of wood or stone of the type described (however inaccurately) by the likes of d'Aubigné, Marnix, and Estienne have existed after all? And can any truth be discerned in or behind those amazing stories involving wax and virile members – measuring a man's 'gere' and preparing a candle the same length, making 'a waxen image to the liknes of hir husbands bewitched member', and so forth?

Perhaps. At the very least we may point to a tradition of long standing, whereby the ill were measured with a piece of thread, that often became the wick of a candle that was taken to a shrine. 'Measure me to St. Thomas!' exclaimed a girl who had been rescued from a well – meaning that she wanted a candle to be 'made to the measure of the length of her body' and offered to Becket at Canterbury.[104] When the unfortunate Ailward of Western was awaiting his punishment, a priest suggested that he should seek the assistance of Becket in particular, and 'measured the length and breadth of his body with a thread with which to make a candle to be offered to the martyr'.[105] It was essential, as Ronald C. Finucane explains, that 'the length of the wick was right – the candle had to "contain" the person's height and sometimes width, usually from one outstretched hand to the other'. But would this practice not have produced very large, and hence quite expensive, candles, affordable only by the wealthy? The problem was solved by folding the wick back upon itself several times, or rolling it into a coil, before applying the wax. Babies and small animals presented no problem. Neither did small body-parts, like hands, feet, and heads. Nor would the 'gere' of men and women, had people with problems in that region decided to make candles which accurately represented their size. What, then, of 'St Foutin', surely he was just an imaginary saint? Indeed, but imaginations have lives also. In the first quarter of the twentieth century, a fair in honour of 'St Foutin' was a regular event at Avranches, in Normandy. He was held to have a special interest in families without children. 'St Foutin vivait'![106]

An even greater interpretive challenge is posed by the late medieval metal badges which feature graphic images of phalli and vulvae. Could they have been pilgrim badges, or (at least) badges closely associated with pilgrims in some way or other? There has been considerable scholarly resistance to that notion. However, it is an inescapable fact that the so-called 'erotic' badges are found alongside 'their more strictly religious fellows'.[107] Cast in cheap materials like tin and pewter, they were produced in substantial quantities (so we can hardly speak of a marginal subculture). The River Seine and the drowned villages of the Schelde estuary have yielded many fine examples of both types of badge.[108] The British evidence is hard to get a handle on simply because, as Nicola McDonald has recently put it, 'the most complete catalogue of badges produced and/or circulating in medieval England and a magnum opus of its kind . . . completely obliterates all genital or sexual material from the visual record'. Indeed, its compiler, Brian Spencer, deems the continental finds 'pornographic', and takes comfort in the thought that medieval Londoners 'preferred to reveal their attitudes to sex through subtler, less offensive motifs' – even though the British finds include badges which take the forms of belled and winged phalluses.[109]

First, a few words on those artifacts which are universally accepted as pilgrim badges – such as the scallop-shell badge from Compostella, the representations of Becket from Canterbury, and the images of the Magi from Cologne. Palm-leaf badges came to be associated with the Holy Land, and by the twelfth century they could be bought from stalls in Jerusalem. Rome got into the market relatively late; in 1199 Pope Innocent III granted the canons of S. Pietro the monopoly of producing badges which 'bore the double image of St Peter with a key and St Paul with a sword and the inscription *Signa Apostolorum Petri et Pauli*'.[110] By the fourteenth century another badge was on sale there, depicting the veronica, i.e. St Veronica's cloth, bearing the marks of the suffering face of Christ. Chaucer's Pardoner sports such a badge sewn on his cap (1(A), 685), proof that he visited Rome before setting out on the present pilgrimage to Canterbury. Generally speaking, these badges were the signs of pilgrimages actually completed, in contrast with the scrip and staff which pilgrims acquired at the beginning of their journey.[111] In *The Canterbury Interlude* which prefaces the *Merchant's Tale of Beryn* we see the 'Chaucerian' pilgrims engaging in this traditional form of behaviour, acquiring 'signes' to show the folks back home that they have 'soughte' Thomas à Becket.

> . . . as manere and custom is, signes there they boughte,
> For men of contre shuld know whom they had soughte.
> Ech man set his sylver in such thing as they liked.
>
> (171–3)[112]

It is evident that these souvenirs include 'signes of Caunterbury broches' (175), for the Miller and the Pardoner seem to have shoplifted a large number of them, no doubt hoping to sell them for personal gain.[113]

So much is clear. The second type of artifact is much harder to interpret, and appears in many forms. A relatively simple one presents the male phallus, sometimes adorned with wings[114] and sometimes with bells.[115] Iconographically these resemble the decorative phalli and phallic animals which are well known from Greek and Roman antiquity, though the medieval examples are, in contrast with their classical predecessors, 'almost absurdly realistic', to borrow another phrase from A. M. Koldeweij.[116] However, there has been considerable reluctance to admit that such artifacts are late medieval products; they have frequently been mis-labelled as 'antique', 'Roman', or 'pagan'[117] – which makes them at once more comprehensible and acceptable. But medieval they certainly are – and therefore more of a puzzle. The phallic images with bells on may indeed have Roman antecedents[118] but in the later Middle Ages they perhaps recalled the bells carried on at least some pilgrimages (the 'winged willies' are, to be sure, harder to interpret). Therefore they seem to have some connection with pilgrimage, whether serious or parodic (on which, more later). Others manifest that connection even more blatantly, as in the case of a large phallus with pilgrim's staff and scrip and a crown in the form of a woman,[119] or a legged vulva wearing a pilgrim's hat and carrying a staff with a penis-shaped tip.[120] Other items have no obvious connection with pilgrimage, such as the fifteenth-century 'penis in a purse' badge excavated from the Thames at Custom House Quay, London.[121]

What is to be made of these prolific images of disembodied genitalia?[122] Could it be possible that at least some of them provide support for Gurevich's proposition that 'the transition from paganism to Christianity involved a reorganization of existing beliefs rather than a clean sweep'?[123] That conclusion may be drawn if the badges are judged to have had an apotropaic function; i.e. if 'they were intended to disarm that ever-present yet vague malevolence known as the Evil Eye' by the 'exposure of the genital icon, whether male or female'. Here I quote a suggestion by Malcolm Jones, who believes that consequently 'almost all such sexual badges were not intended as "erotic" in the sense of provoking sexual arousal'.[124]

However, he and others are prepared to canvass other explanations, such as the suggestion that the sexual badges may be 'frivolously "carnivalesque"', 'celebratory of that licensed misrule that obtained during periods of carnival and in which brazen sexual display was almost *de rigueur*'.[125] Another possible motive on offer is social satire, specifically concerning what Jones describes as medieval 'sex-tourism', the practice of going on pilgrimage for quite the wrong reasons[126] – as indicated by Chaucer's remark about that veteran pilgrim, the Wife of Bath, having done much 'wandrynge by the weye' (I(A) 464–7).[127] Thus he reads the vulva-as-pilgrim badge as possibly 'satirical of women's alleged mixed motives for undertaking pilgrimages', with the phallus-as-pilgrim badge as the male equivalent.[128]

Yet another possible motive was nascent Protestant criticism of Catholic excess. Jones seeks this in the case of an elaborate badge in the form of three phalli walking on human legs and carrying a crowned vulva on a litter on which rides a vulva crowned with a three-phallus diadem. Despite the early date of this artifact (*c.* 1400–50), he is 'tempted to suggest' it 'may be seen as a satirical proto-Protestant attack on a Catholic procession in honour of the Virgin Mary'.[129] Jones interprets in similar vein a little fifteenth-century lead badge excavated in Bruges, which is of special interest to us given the topic of the present chapter. The top section represents a phallus, with a woman on either side, whereas the bottom section represents a pair of breeches.[130] Those breeches, Jones proposes, may relate to a relic associated with St Rombout of Mechelen in Belgium. In 1624 Thomas Scott, preacher to the English garrison at Utrecht and hence knowledgeable about the Netherlands, published the second part of his anti-Catholic *Vox Populi*, which includes a discussion of the vernacular belief that 'a young married wife shall have a child in the same yeare if she can stride ouer at once Saint Rombauts breeches at Mechlin'.[131] So, then, perhaps what we have here is 'a Protestant badge satirizing credulous Catholic belief in the fecundating power of such absurd relics'.[132] A precocious Protestant indeed, given that the badge is dated *c.* 1400–50. The hypothesis that we are dealing here with Reformation polemic before its time seems unlikely. It would have taken an awful lot of nascent Protestants to produce the thousands of badges in circulation at the time, and I do not know of any heretics who went into the badge business – certainly not England's Lollards, who occasionally did make (rather bad) jokes about the shrines at Walsingham and Canterbury. John Wyclif would, I suspect, have felt that to be a very indirect way of making his point – and I cannot imagine him advising his followers to mint genital badges as a means of attacking ecclesiastical decadence! The 'carnival' theory would account for more (but enough?) badges, although there is a major difficulty with that hypothesis – the fact that so many 'erotic' badges are found along with 'their more strictly religious fellows'.

Perhaps it is a mistake to see the 'erotic' badges as designed to work in opposition to the obviously religious artifacts. Given the belief that Christian shrines could cure all kinds of disorders, including urogenital ones, and granted that some of them specialized in matters relating to loins and the fruit thereof, could it not be the case that at least some of those problematic badges were sold at the same shrines as were the more decorous ones, perhaps even at the same stalls by the same tradesmen? Like Jones I suspect that the badges in question were not at all '"erotic" in the sense of provoking sexual arousal', but I feel that his apotropaic hypothesis does not quite hit the mark. Rather they may have been indicative of the hopes and fears of that 'heart-rending stream of desperate men and women' described so eloquently by Eamon Duffy. Far from being self-indulgent 'sex-tourists' perhaps they were seeking relief from a vast array of urogenital diseases of a chronic kind, and/or racked with anxiety about the grave consequences of impotence or sterility. So, then, rather than being parodies of 'popular' devotion[133] our controversial badges may be, in some measure, an expression of it.

But is this not too serious an explanation for badges which frequently seem to be intentionally humourous? Not necessarily – for humour, then as now, was a good medicine[134] (and no doubt medieval shrines readily lent themselves to black humour). Besides, the genital images may not have been officially sanctioned (in contrast with those badges of Sts Peter and Paul for which the canons of S. Pietro held the monopoly)[135] but were rather the productions of local entrepreneurs who knew a good thing when they saw it. One may compare the 'alternative culture' souvenirs available at today's secular tourist attractions, which may parody local assets but yet are dependent on them. A closer analogy, perhaps, for both the humour and the un- (or semi-)official status of the genital badges may be found in the cakes known as 'St Gonçalo's cocks', which, on that saint's day, are sold at Amarante in Portugal (cf. p. 146 above). Pierre Sanchis writes that, because 'their sale is in theory forbidden', 'some of the women stall-holders go through a curious procedure when the procession passes by, covering the cakes discreetly with a white cloth so that the saint may not see them'.[136] I suspect that medieval vendors were less inhibited. And what was 'in theory forbidden' was a larger and more elastic category in their time. My own research into that other major adjunct of medieval pilgrimages, the indulgences which afforded pilgrims release for all or part of the punishment (*pena*) incurred through sin, has afforded ample evidence that theory and practice were frequently far apart. The argument that the pope (or his subordinates) may tolerate certain activities which they do not authorize or explicitly permit was put forward in all seriousness in a debate on whether plenary indulgences had actually been granted to certain churches which had claimed them – the clear implication being that, even if the claims were doubtful, no official action would be taken to curb local practice. In another case, it was argued that, in the case of some holy place for which an indulgence had been granted by several bishops, all comers should receive the same indulgence, even though some of them were not subjects of those same bishops (and therefore, a lawyer might argue, were not entitled to receive it).[137] Thereby the appearances were saved, accusations of deceit pre-empted, and scandal avoided. The principle of *laissez-faire* was a powerful one. It may also have operated in the case of problematic pilgrim badges.

If genital badges were indeed believed to avert ill fortune and/or bring good luck, if some apotropaic intention had survived (from God knows when or where), surely this would have enhanced rather than diminished their appeal. Deflection of demons, relief from disease, freedom from fear – all of these functions move in the same direction, work to the same end. All could have contributed to the appeal of a healing shrine and the badges associated with it. Furthermore, we must beware of applying modern notions of taste and decency to an earlier culture – a useful warning having been provided by the manner in which Renaissance artists' depictions of the full physical manhood of Christ (his genitalia being clearly delineated in infancy and again after death) were censored in subsequent centuries.[138] And Christ had supposedly left on earth the greatest genital relic of them all – the holy foreskin, as cut away at his circumcision. But, several school-men asked, how could this relic, or any drop of blood shed by Christ at the passion, possibly be present in some medieval shrine, since (as Thomas of Chobham put it) 'Christ was resurrected in glory and his whole body was glorified'?[139] Pope Innocent III reviewed various opinions concerning the relic, including the belief that it 'was borne by an angel to Jerusalem, to Charlemagne who carried it off to Aachen, and that later it was placed by Charles the Bald in the church St Sauveur at Charroux'. But he refused to be drawn on its authenticity: 'Rather than attempt rash answers to such questions, it is better that they be left entirely to God.'[140]

However, some theologians did attempt an answer, as when Thomas of Chobham noted that the body of Christ (in the Eucharist) 'can be at one and the same time in several places'. Likewise, 'that same body can exist in several forms'. It is quite possible, therefore, that 'Christ's foreskin, glorified as part of his integral body [i.e. his resurrected body, which is in heaven] may exist in another place unglorified [i.e. in some sanctuary on earth]'.[141] And Gervase of Tilbury (writing during the mid-1210s) reported a tradition that the Lateran possessed the holy foreskin, together with the Lord's umbilical cord, protected 'in a cross of purest gold, ornamented with gems and precious stones'. He adds that 'this cross is anointed with balsam, an anointing which is repeated every year when the lord pope, with his cardinals, goes in procession from that oratory into the church of St John Lateran on Holy Cross Day'.[142] It is hard not to recall the rather more suspect anointings carried out by the women of Embrun, as described by Agrippa d'Aubigné. Some true words were said in jest – or, to use a more precise formulation, Catholic legends and Protestant libels had much in common.

The precious prepuce also fed the visions of several *mulieres sanctae*, including Catherine of Siena and the Viennese beguine Agnes Blannbekin (d. 1315). In her mystical marriage with Christ, Catherine received the holy foreskin as her ring, and, on one occasion when she was receiving the Eucharist, Agnes felt 'a little piece of skin alike the skin in an egg' on her tongue, which she swallowed 'about a hundred times'.[143] (Once again, we note the crucial connection between the Eucharist and the holy foreskin as manifestations of the body of Christ.) Are these instances of bad taste? Not to Catherine and Agnes, for whom the foreskin represents 'flesh that bleeds' – and, by taking on this suffering physicality, they became Christ's flesh, an experience quite different from 'erotic fusing with a male figure'.[144] When He 'veiled' his divinity in what Catherine called 'the wretched dung heap of Adam', God provided a means of leading us 'to salvation through suffering' (as Bynum nicely puts it).[145] To invert Steven Kruger's comment (as quoted at the beginning of this chapter): full participation 'in the debased physical world', with all its suffering, may be a means of accessing the 'spiritual' rather than a strong drawing-away from it; here is a meeting point for the children of Adam and their incarnated creator. Christ's holy foreskin not only symbolizes but also participates in that world; little wonder, then, that *mulieres sanctae* wanted to possess it. In sharp contrast, the Pardoner's relics (including the one imagined by Harry Bailly) lead nowhere and lack any contact with the spiritual.

So, then: from St Rombout's breeches and Christ's foreskin we may move back to the Pardoner's pants and their controversial contents. For reasons soon to become clear, we will do so via the Host's words to the Physician:

> I pray to God so save thy gentil cors,
> And eek thyne urynals and thy jurdones,
> Thyn ypocras, and eek thy galiones,
> And every boyste ful of thy letuarie;
> God blesse hem, and oure lady Seinte Marie!
> So moot I theen, thou art a propre man,
> And lyk a prelat, by Seint Ronyan!
>
> (VI(C) 304–10)

In case we fail to notice the reference to 'Seint Ronyan', the Pardoner repeats Harry Bailly's oath (albeit with a different pronunciation of the name, and one syllable less)[146] as he responds to the request to 'telle us som myrthe or japes right anon': "It shal be doon", quod he, "by Seint Ronyon!"' (320).

Following a suggestion originally made by Frederick Tupper in 1915,[147] and developed by Malcolm Jones, it may be that Ronyan is another of those phallic saints, like 'St Foutin' and 'St René' as investigated above. Indeed, the parallel with St René is particularly apt, given the possible pun there on the French word *reins* which, as already noted, corresponds to the Latin *renes*, a synonym of *lumbi* (which means 'loins' or indeed 'testicles').[148] By the same token, 'Ronyan/Ronyon' may be a pun on the French word *roignons*, which has the same etymological derivation as *reins*.[149] Though today, in Modern French, *rognons* and *reins* are differentiated, in the Middle Ages and Renaissance the corresponding words were largely synonymous. In Chaucer's day, then, a set of words was available which constituted a discourse concerning one's kidneys or loins, understood as the seat of sexual potency and the means of procreation.[150] Kidneys were closely associated with testicles, conjoined materially, metaphorically, jocularly – a good example of the last being found in a *fabliau* which refers to 'deux coillons / Autresi grans con deus roignons'.[151] The kidneys could have problems all of their own, of course, as the English gentleman constructed in More's

Dialogue concerning Heresies knew all too well; one may compare the case of Albreda of Gisburn who, being unable to retain urine following excision of the stone, was healed by St William of York, in York Minster, in 1177.[152] To these examples may be added the sufferer described in Montaigne's *Essais*, III. xiii, where doctors' widely varying diagnoses are being ridiculed. A member of the medical faculty, who recently died of the stone (*pierre*), had starved himself to combat his condition; according to his colleagues, this was the worst thing he could have done, since his fast dried up his kidneys (*rognons*) rather than curing them. Returning to an earlier doctor: it may be noted that, although the Host is rather vague about the tools of the Physician's trade in the passage (quoted above) containing his reference to 'Seint Ronyan', two items, 'urynals' and 'jurdones' (the latter term probably meaning 'piss-pots'),[153] have clear associations with urine, concerning which it would be quite appropriate to invoke 'Saint Kidney'.

The *Riverside Chaucer*'s note to l. 310 (which heaps confusion upon confusion) flatly rejects Tupper's suggestion: 'The OED offers no support'; 'there are no citations for this form before Shakespeare nor for this sense before 1635'.[154] I presume the date 1655 is meant here, that being the year in which Sir John Mennis and Dr James Smith published their *Facetiae: Musarum deliciae*, which includes a cumbersome Chaucer pastiche in mock-memory of a certain William Nelson:

> He faire could gloze among the country wives.
> A lusty runnyon ware he in his hose,
> Loud could he speak, and crackle in the nose.[155]

The use of 'gloze' in the first line here cited shows the author pushing a word beyond its range of meaning in Chaucer, and there is no way of being sure that he got the (hypothetical) joke about 'Saint Kidney', with its allusion to the whole urogenital area, including the testicles. On the other hand, he seems to have detected some sexual humour surrounding the word, which may be significant. The Shakespeare reference is no help at all, since his two uses of the term *runnion/ronyon* seem to designate 'a mangy creature', following the French *rogne* ('scab').[156] Far more telling is the reference to 'Saint Runnion' in the scurrilous *Choise of Valentines* attributed to Thomas Nashe (1576–1601), a poem which reveals some knowledge of Chaucer.[157] On the hallows of blessed St Valentine, a 'poore pilgrim' named Tomalin goes to visit 'his lady's shrine', the lady being Mistress Francis, a prostitute, and her shrine, a brothel. Having given his all, Tomalin is horrified to hear Francis plan to replace cowardly men with a dildo – which, she says, has many advantages, for it will give her total satisfaction and won't make her pregnant. 'Poore Priapus' – his triumph will now fail, unless she banishes this 'Eunuke dilldo', who is 'senceless', 'counterfet', and 'beardles' (ll. 247–8, 263, 291).[158] Such is the context in which the 'Saint' is invoked.

> For, by Saint Runnion he'le refresh me well,
> And neuer make my tender bellie swell.
>
> (245–6)[159]

The way in which Mennis and Smith understood 'runnyon' gains considerable support from this usage.

A third citation lends even further support. A passage in Geoffrey Fenton's *Certain Tragical Discourses* (1567) refers to how 'Papistes in Fraunce performe their ydolatrous pilgrimage to theyr ydoll Sainct Tronyon uppon the mont Avyon besides Roan, or our supersticious catholikes of England of late dayes to the holye Roode of Chester, or ymage of our Ladye at Walsingham'.[160] 'Tronyon' is almost certainly a variant form of 'Ronyan/Ronyon'.[161] Here the narrator is describing how the hero of his story, Cornelio, is preparing himself for an assignation with his beloved Plaudina, the point being that he is doing so with 'no lesse devocion' than the above-mentioned Catholics perform their ridiculous rites. It seems evident that 'Ronyan/Ronyon/Tronyon' is a 'saint' with a particular appeal for lovers.

Given the link made between 'Seint Ronyan' (as first invoked by the Host) and the Physician's expertise in matters urinary, the fourth of our citations is particularly interesting. This comes from Sir Thomas Elyot's *Pasquil the Playne* (1533), a treatise against excessive stylistic ornamentation which is cast in the form of a dialogue between 'Pasquil' and 'Gnato'. At one point Gnato defends one of the targets of Pasquil's vituperation by reminding him of a principle which he himself had expressed, that some men 'wolde be in the bowels of diuinite or [before] they know what belongeth to good humanite'. It is the mention of 'bowels' which seems to determine the way Pasquil begins his response: 'It is well raysoned of you by swete saint Ronyon'.[162] As the Wife of Bath memorably said, the 'thynges smale' of men and women were made for both 'purgacioun / Of uryne' and 'engendrure' (III(D), 119–34), and Saint Ronyan/Ronyon, understood as referencing the kidneys and loins, has great expertise in both spheres.

Furthermore, 'Saynt Tronion' is alliteratively coupled with 'Saynt Toncomber' in John Heywood's *Playe Called the Foure PP* (first printed *c.* 1533).[163] 'Toncomber' may be identified with the St 'Uncumber' (Wylgeforte/Wilgefortis) about whom Thomas More had so much to say. A 'Saincte Tronnion' is also mentioned in *Respublica*, v.ix. 1694.[164] While it is true that neither of these last two references provides enough context to support the 'kidney theory', the fact that our problematic figure appears in association with other suspicious saints does strengthen the suggestion that Chaucer was making a urogenital joke here, rather than invoking a quite reputable saint – such as the Breton St Ronan[165] and the St Ninian whose cult had spread by Chaucer's time from Scotland and the North of England to Kent.[166] These proposed identifications are unconvincing, since there is nothing in the characteristics associated with the (hardly famous) saints in question that explains why Chaucer would have wanted Harry Bailly, and then the Pardoner, to mention either of them. So, then, a joke concerning 'Saint Kidney' remains a definite possibility.[167] It is pleasing to speculate that, when the Pardoner concludes his tale, Harry returns to develop a type of humour which he had instigated at its very beginnning, the transition from *roignons* to *coillons* being an easy one. But this time the Pardoner is too angry to engage in banter (or even to trade insults), and so Harry must cease to 'playe' with him.

However, this speculation is not a necessary prop for my claim that the Pardoner's *coillons* are ultimately presented a cod-relic: the argument works perfectly well without it. 'Kutte of' just like the disembodied phalli of those mysterious metal badges, the Pardoner's privates will (in Harry's lurid imagination) become public property, an object of reverence to men who wish to enhance their sexual potency and women who wish to conceive. Or to people who seek relief from genital disorders, including those kidney stones which so troubled Albreda of Gisburn and the sufferers described by More and Montaigne. If that latter explanation sounds too prosaic, one might recall More's remark that, if a person has severe toothache (and no other relief is to hand), of course he will pray to the relevant saint. Faced with acute pain or a major deficiency in the *roignons* and/or *coillons*, a man can hardly be choosy or condescending.

The Pardoner is, of course, no saint, and the point of the Host's joke (as analysed thus far) is that his enshrined *coillons* are 'in stide of relikes or of seintuarie', i.e. they are put in the position properly occupied by genuine relics and other kinds of saintly intervention which address infer-tility in man or beast, ranging from Thomas à Becket, William of York, and Wulfstan (as curers of *castrati*) through the species-crossing miracles of Walstan of Bawburgh to the hearsay images or relics associated with 'St Foutin' and his phallic fellows. This is, of course, to take the Pardoner at his word – to be specific, the words he uses when claiming to have a jolly wench in every town, even as he contemplates marriage. (At the very least, he is happy to encourage the Wife of Bath's heterosexist rant on the pleasures and pains of marriage.) Such a tread-fowl (to borrow a phrase the Host uses of the Nun's Priest – may his 'breche' and 'every stoon' be blessed!)[168] would surely produce a potent relic, which eager worshippers would flock to visit. On this reading, then, far from 'casting aspersions on the Pardoner's virility'[169] the Host is paying it a compliment – for the purpose of his jest, of course.

This interpretation evidently supports a reading of Chaucer's construction as based on the stereotype of the immoral preacher, the corrupt cleric who preaches for personal gain and commits all the sins he preaches against (with lechery high on the list). If, however, we believe that the Pardoner is all talk and no action, a failed womanizer like the Pardoner of *The Canterbury Interlude* and that other Chaucerian 'womanly man', Absolon in the *Miller's Tale*, then the Host's relic joke works rather differently. Harry Bailly is ironically praising something which has little or no actual value; as a relic, the Pardoner's *coillons* would fail to satisfy, in accord with their lack of potency when joined to their owner.[170] Any pilgrim who came seeking a remedy for his 'stoon' (as vented through the testicles or as the actual testicular area itself) would be sorely disappointed. On this reading, the Pardoner's *relyk* is the prize fake in a collection of fakes.

In similar vein, if Chaucer's character is judged to be some sort of eunuch in material (as opposed to metaphorical) terms, i.e. if he suffers from a testicular deformity or deficiency, then it is the Pardoner himself who should be visiting the relevant shrine and reverently kissing the appropriate relic, rather than setting up in business himself, with the Host helping to carry the reliquary containing his precious parts.[171] Furthermore: should the Pardoner visit the shrine of some St Foutin, and should he be fortunate enough to be cured, no doubt he would leave behind a votive offering in the form of a wax effigy of his restored members – a celebratory image of disembodiment which inversely marks the Pardoner's return to what his society regards as normative in physical terms.

What, then, of the 'queer' Pardoner whose sexual preference is for men rather than women, whose references to townswomen of lax morals, and to a possible wife, are either a cover-up or camp humour or a bit of both? (On this reading the Pardoner is, once again, seen as sexually active as opposed to sexually inadequate or even impotent; now the problem is that he is practising the wrong kind of sex, engaging in intercourse with the wrong kind of body.) If the traditional binary between heterosexuality and homosexuality is affirmed (and many medieval texts do precisely that), then we might substitute the terms 'sexual deviance' for the term 'testicular deformity or deficiency' in the argument above, the point being that the

Pardoner should be seeking a cure for behaviour which his society regards as unacceptable, and indeed as punishable by the actual removal of those offending members.[172] Following such a cure, the Pardoner could return to what his society regards as normative in behavioural terms.

However, the notion of 'sexual preference' understood in an exclusive sense is utterly anachronistic in relation to much late medieval thought about human sexuality, and many texts, rather than affirming the above-mentioned binary, seem to present a moral continuum. Lust is lust, no matter on which body it is discharged. Illicit sex with a woman is bad; sex with a man (always illicit) is very bad.[173] Hence one way to eradicate homosexuality among clergymen (and among nuns as well) is to allow them to marry – that being the key Lollard argument for the abolition of clerical celibacy.[174] By this means, desire would be controlled and contained within heterosexist parameters. That was, of course, a heretical view, but orthodox thinkers endorsed the underlying principles. To find an example of this we need look no further than the widely disseminated *Speculum vitae*, wherein William of Nassington (d. 1359) offers an elaborate hierarchy of fourteen branches of lechery, in ascending order of awfulness.

> Litchery of body als men may here.
> It shewes in fourtene braunches sere
> After ye state es mare and lesse
> Of yam yat dose swilk writchednes.
> Ya braunches springes and waxes vpward
> Fra wicke to wers yat ye saul feles hard.
> (9245–50)[175]

The fourteenth and worst branch is, quite predictably, sodomy:

> Ye fourtened braunche als falles in mynde
> Es a foul synne mast agayne kynde,
> Ye whilk es ful wlatsom to neuen
> Yat gretly greues Godde of heuen.
> For yat synne Godde had vengeaunce tane
> When he did rayne fyre and brunstane
> Opon Sodom and on Gomor . . .
> (9447–53)

Thus Nassington wraps up his discussion of 'litchery / Bathe of hert and of body', having measured desire in terms of degree rather than of kind.

A certain amount of desire was usually deemed necessary (albeit with many caveats and conditions) within marriage, so that the work of procreation could be promoted. A husband and wife had legal rights over each other's bodies, each being obliged to pay the marital debt (and a woman had the right to be given a child). If no children ensued, for whatever reason, prayer to the right saint and recourse to the right relic could well help the process. Hence the attractiveness of such a boon as the Pardoner would bestow upon the world, according to the Host's vivid imagination (as here interpreted). But that relic should come with an official health warning – kiss at your own risk. There is no telling what kind of mischief and mayhem it could induce. Desire, once unbridled, can get out of control, as it may well have done in the Pardoner's case, however he may choose to vent his lusts.

Whichever of these interpretations one prefers, it seems reasonable to assign Harry Bailly's put-down of the Pardoner to that group of texts which express disgust about kissing a *relyk* which is both spurious and repellent. As such it may usefully be compared with a passage in Heywood's *Playe Called the Foure PP* where an unscrupulous pardoner, who has clear affinities with Chaucer's character,[176] encourages his companions to kiss 'hardely with good devocion' the 'blessyd jaw bone' of All Hallows (497–8; perhaps this is Heywood's attempt to improve on the shoulder bone of a holy Jew's sheep).[177] The Potycary does so, and is quite disgusted:

> Fogh! By Saynt Savyour, I never kyst a wars!
> Ye were as good kisse All Hallows ars,
> For by All Halows, me thynketh
> That All Halows breth stynketh.
>
> (500–3)[178]

Whereupon the devout Palmer remarks that if any breath stinks, it is the Potycary's own; to which the Potycary grumpily replies that he can tell the difference between his own breath and that of All Hallows – kissing that relic is like kissing a gallows! (504–7). The Pardoner then offers another relic, the toe of the Trinity: roll this just once in your mouth, and it will cure the toothache. But the Potycary declines. So the Pardoner produces the buttock bone of Pentecost – to which the Potycary responds:

> By Chryste, and yet for all your boste,
> Thys relyke hath beshyten the roste.
>
> (522–3)[179]

That is to say, it has befouled the perch or 'nest' in which it is kept – just like a chicken or some other domestic fowl. Could that be Heywood's version of Chaucer's crack about enshrinement 'in an hogges toord'?[180] A few lines later we have another turd-joke, though no animal is specified. On being presented with a slipper allegedly worn by one of the Seven Sleepers, the Potycary remarks that its owner seems to have 'trode in a torde' (533). 'Shall I prayse relykes when they stynke?' he angrily asks his associates.

'Relykes' which 'stynke', whether they be true or false, provide the cultural context in which we should seek to place Harry Bailly's visceral comments on the Pardoner's *coillons*. The problem is that so much of the necessary evidence is generally beneath the notice of official written sources. The 'mery matters of saynt wallery' are a long way from the quodlibets and *summae* wherein the masters of the 'vnyuersyte of Parys' pursued theological inquiries which sometimes seem to have little relevance for the 'debased physical world' in which men and women lived, feared, and visited shrines. 'Debased' that world may have been, but it was their world. A world wherein they venerated relics and images, and listened to miracle stories, of a kind which related to their loins and the fruits thereof. 'A few dotynge dames make not the people', and priests cannot be blamed for what 'folysh women' do (to echo remarks by Thomas More). But it is through the recuperation of what such women (and their male counterparts) actually did and believed that we may gain, *inter alia*, a better understanding of the comic discourse surrounding Chaucer's Pardoner and his ridiculous relics – and measure the extent to which they were ridiculous, the points at which they became ridiculous. The English poet is, to be sure, writing fiction, and allowing the lurid imagination he has fathered on one of his characters, Harry Bailly, to run riot. But this is fiction with a large dose of verisimilitude, fantasy wherein the 'fals' and 'soth' are complexly 'compouned' (to draw on *The House of Fame*, 2108).

Top-down research, based on high-culture texts, will not get us very far into the breech. Rather we need to work from the bottom up – reading between the lines of the élite documents, becoming familiar with the research (and the research techniques) of social anthropologists and folklorists. By such means, we may attempt to access the rich mother lodes of vernacular religion, and allow them their true value.

Notes

PREFACE

1. Frank Birbalsingh, 'Interview with David Dabydeen (1991)', in Kevin Grant (ed.), *The Art of David Dabydeen* (Leeds, 1997), pp. 177–98 (p. 182). On another occasion Dabydeen remarked, 'I found writing the notes as complex and as fascinating as writing the poems.' Wolfgang Binder, 'Interview with David Dabydeen (1989)', in Grant (ed.), *Art of Dabydeen*, pp. 159–76 (p. 169). His crack about writing a 'spoof gloss' (in the style of Eliot) should not obscure the cheekily competitive nature of that project. The clear implication is that Creole poems can sustain the same kind of interpretive framework, and the same kind of high-cultural humour, which everyone associates with that modernist monolith, *The Waste Land*.
2. On whom see my article, '*Amor* and *Auctoritas* in the Self-Commentary of Dante and Francesco da Barberino', *Poetica* [Tokyo], 32 (1990), 25–42.
3. *Slave Song* (Mundelstrup, 1984), p. 13.

INTRODUCTION: VALUING THE VERNACULAR

1. Firmin Le Ver, *Dictionarius: dictionnaire latin-français de Firmin Le Ver*, ed. Brian Merrilees and William Edwards, CCCM, Lexica Latina Medii Ævi, I (Turnhout, 1994), pp. 539–40. Firmin is following in the footsteps of those great dictionary-makers Hugutio of Pisa, who compiled his *Magnae derivationes* between 1192 and 1201, and Giovanni de'Balbi of Genoa, whose *Catholicon* dates from 1286: cf. Hugutio, *Derivationes*, ed. Enzo Cecchini *et al.* (Florence, 2004), II. 1292–3 (U 46), and Giovanni de'Balbi, *Catholicon* (Mainz, 1460; repr. 1971), s.v. *uulgo*, unfol.
2. Following Hugutio of Pisa's definition; *Derivationes*, ed. Cecchini *et al.*, II. 968 (P 120).
3. The *MED* (s.v. 'popular', adj.) cites the following fifteenth-century instance: 'populer, i. knowen to þe comon pepul [L popularia]'. Cf. *OLD*, s.v. *popularis*, p. 1404; C. T. Lewis and C. Short (eds.), *A Latin Dictionary* (Oxford, impression of 1975), p. 1398; and the *OED*, s.v. 'popular' (adj.).

4. Felicity Riddy, 'Publication before Print: The Case of Julian of Norwich', in Julia Crick and Alexandra Walsham (eds.), *The Uses of Script and Print, 1300–1700* (Cambridge, 2003), pp. 29–49 (p. 40). Cf. the Classical Latin senses of the verb *vulgo*, 'to make available to the mass of the population, make common to all'; 'to make widely known, spread a report of, make public, broadcast'; 'to make general, common, or universal'; *OLD*, s.v. *vulgo*, pp. 2121-2; Lewis and Short (eds.), *A Latin Dictionary*, p. 2015. While the term *Biblia Vulgata* ('Vulgate Bible') came into widespread use as a means of designating St Jerome's fourth-century *magnum opus* of translation and compilation only following the Council of Trent in 1546, Jerome himself and Augustine thought of the Septuagint and its Latin translation as the *uulgata editio*, thereby indicating its 'general, common, or universal' status – the term being used positively and respectfully. Cf. the *Dictionnaire latin–français des auteurs chrétiens*, ed. Albert Blaise (Turnhout, 1954–67), s.v. *uulgatus*; consulted via the Brepols Database of Latin Dictionaries. In other contexts, *vulgaris* meant plebeian, lacking in urbanity and refinement, rustic (*plebeius, inurbanus, rusticus*). Hugutio explains that *vulgo* is derived from *volo* ('I wish/want') because the unruly *vulgo* or multitude do whatever they want; *Derivationes*, ed. Cecchini *et al.*, II. 1292–3 (U 46). Such are the associations which Dante and Charles V's translators were challenging.

5. For instance, 'the vulgar' was the way in which, for centuries, English speakers referred to their native language, as when John Lydgate, writing probably before 1439, spoke of Geoffrey Chaucer as having made 'a translacioun' in 'our vulgar' (he has *Troilus and Criseyde* in mind; cf. *MED*, s.v. *vulgār(e)*, n). Subsequently (in the seventeenth century) the term 'vernacular' came into use, from the Latin *vernaculus*, meaning 'domestic, native, indigenous', though also 'low-bred, proletarian' (*OLD*, p. 2038). Shaking off much of its negative implication, 'vernacular' displaced 'vulgar' as a means of designating a language, and hence distanced English from associations of 'vulgarity', coarseness, or even obscenity, senses which continue to be borne by the term 'vulgar'.

6. Transcribed by Caroline Boucher from Paris, Bibliothèque nationale de France, MS fr. 1792, fols. 1r–3v, in her doctoral thesis, 'La mise en scène de la vulgarisation: les traductions d'autorités en langue vulgaire aux XIIIe et XIVe siècles', École Pratique des Hautes Études, 5e section (Paris, 2005), pp. 513–14.

7. C. R. Sherman, *Imaging Aristotle: Verbal and Visual Representation in Fourteenth-Century France* (Berkeley and Los Angeles, 1995), p. 6. See further C. R. Sherman, 'Les thèmes humanistes dans le programme de traduction de Charles V: compilation des textes et illustrations', in Monique Ornato and Nicole Pons (eds.), *Pratiques de la culture écrite en France au XVe siècle: Actes du Colloque International du CNRS, Paris, 16–18 mai 1992*, Textes et études du Moyen Âge, 2 (Louvain-La-Neuve, 1995), pp. 527–37. A (partly inaccurate) list of the works commissioned by Charles V is provided in Christine de Pizan's adulatory *Livre des fais et bonnes meurs du sage roy Charles V*, ed. S. Solente (Paris, 1936), II. 42–5. Obviously, these translations contributed substantially to the development of 'royal propaganda' in this period, on which see Gilbert

Ouy, 'Humanism and Nationalism in France at the Turn of the Fifteenth Century', in B. P. McGuire (ed.), *The Birth of Identities: Denmark and Europe in the Middle Ages* (Copenhagen, 1996), pp. 107–25 (p. 110).

8. On Oresme's milieu and works see Sherman, *Imaging Aristotle*, pp. 6–33; also Nicole Oresme, *Le livre de politiques d'Aristote*, ed. A. D. Menut, Transactions of the American Philosophical Society, n.s. 60, pt 6 (Philadelphia, 1970), pp. 5–33.

9. Nicole Oresme, *Le livre de éthiques d'Aristote*, ed. A. D. Menut (New York, 1940), p. 99.

10. *Parliament of Fowls*, 75.

11. *Livre de éthiques d'Aristote*, ed. Menut, p. 100; cf. Oresme's *Livre de politiques d'Aristote*, ed. Menut, p. 27.

12. *Il convivio*, IV.10 and IV.14–15, ed. Cesare Vasoli and Domenico de Robertis, in *Dante Alighieri Opere minori*, 1.2 (Milan and Naples, 1979–88), pp. 637–44, 687–709; trans. Christopher Ryan, *Dante: The Banquet*, Stanford French and Italian Studies, 61 (Saratoga, CA, 1989), pp. 146–47, 157–64.

13. *Canzone terza*, 101, in *Il convivio*, ed. Vasoli and de Robertis, p. 515; trans. Ryan, p. 121.

14. It was spelled out at great length in the fifteenth-century Florentine *questione della lingua*, wherein a wide range of opinions concerning the relationship between Latin and vernacular was canvassed, including the belief that linguistic effectiveness was due not to a language's natural capacity but rather to its careful cultivation by illustrious writers and speakers. For example, Cristoforo Landino claimed that Dante had taken the Florentine idiom, 'a coarse, untried language', and 'transformed it into an efficient, elegant linguistic instrument, just short of being perfect'. Angelo Mazzocco, *Linguistic Theories in Dante and the Humanists: Studies of Language and Intellectual History in Late Medieval and Early Renaissance Italy* (Leiden, 1993), p. 95.

15. *De vulgari eloquentia*, 1.1, ed. and trans. Steven Botterill (Cambridge, 1996), pp. 2–3.

16. However, at one point in *Il convivio*, Latin is valued at the vernacular's expense: it is said to excel in terms of nobility (Latin is stable and incorruptible), of *vertù* (Latin makes manifest many things conceived in the mind which the vernacular cannot), and of beauty (in Latin, words correspond more regularly in respect of grammar and therefore are more harmonious). *Convivio*, 1.6–7, ed. Vasoli and de Robertis, pp. 37–49; trans. Ryan, pp. 23–7. Cf. the discussion in Alastair Minnis and A. B. Scott with David Wallace (eds.), *Medieval Literary Theory and Criticism, c. 1100–c. 1375: The Commentary Tradition*, rev. edn (Oxford, 1991; repr. 2001), pp. 380–1. So, then: writing in Latin, Dante affirms the superiority of the vernacular; writing in the vernacular, he affirms the superiority of Latin. The details of Dante's sophisticated polemics on the status and capacities of different forms of language are beyond the scope of my discussion here. Suffice it to say that they manifest the fact that, in the later Middle Ages, the relationship between Latin and vernacular was a highly complicated one, certainly not to be reduced to simplistically oppositional

discourse (though it must be acknowledged that oppositional discourse is often to be found, as when the *translatio studii* topos is deployed to award victory to some newly empowered language). See further Sarah Stever Gravelle, 'The Latin-Vernacular Question and Humanist Theory of Language and Culture', *Journal of the History of Ideas*, 49.3 (1988), 367–86; and Zygmunt G. Barański, 'Dante Alighieri: Experimentation and (Self-) Exegesis', in *CHLCMA*, pp. 561–82. Fifteenth-century Italian humanists became concerned with the question, was the Italian vernacular a derivative of Latin or an ancient language that had co-existed with Latin? For a comprehensive discussion see Mazzocco, *Linguistic Theories in Dante and the Humanists.*

17. Cf. Michael Bennett, *Richard II and the Revolution of 1399* (Thrupp, Stroud, 1999), pp. 42–3. However, I believe that Bennett exaggerates Richard's 'bookish interests' (p. 43); for a discussion of the problem (and a summary of the scholarly debate) see Alastair Minnis, *Oxford Guides to Chaucer: The Shorter Poems* (Oxford, 1995), pp. 11–14, 19–35.

18. *Livre de éthiques d'Aristote*, ed. Menut, p. 99.

19. Lawrence Beaston, 'The *Pearl* Poet and the Pelagians', *Religion and Literature*, 36 (2004), 15–38 (pp. 24, 23). Other scholars who have argued impressively for the (at least partial) presence or pressure of Pelagianism in the works of the *Gawain*-poet include David Wallace, '*Cleanness* and the Terms of Terror', in R. J. Blanch, M. Miller, and J. Wasserman (eds.), *Text and Matter: New Critical Perspectives of the 'Pearl'-Poet* (Troy, NY, 1991), pp. 93–104; Lawrence M. Clopper, 'The God of the *Gawain*-Poet', *Modern Philology*, 94.1 (1996), 1–18, and Jim Rhodes, *Poetry Does Theology: Chaucer, Grosseteste, and the 'Pearl'-Poet* (Notre Dame, IN, 2001). In these studies, the 'power distinction' informs nuanced literary criticism which is untrammelled by the burden of proving a reductive thesis. Davis Aers's wonderfully trenchant characterization of the *Gawain*-poet as 'Pelagius redivivus' is discussed in Chapter 2.

20. On this point see especially W. J. Courtenay, 'The Dialectic of Divine Omnipotence in the Age of Chaucer: A Reconsideration', in Hugo Keiper, Christoph Bode, and Richard J. Utz (eds.), *Nominalism and Literary Discourse: New Perspectives* (Amsterdam and Atlanta, GA, 1997), pp. 111–21 (pp. 114, 116–17). It is also salutary to note that Rega Wood has been able to build a convincing case for 'Ockham's Repudiation of Pelagianism'; see her article of that title in P. V. Spade (ed.), *The Cambridge Companion to Ockham* (Cambridge, 1999), pp. 350–73 (esp. pp. 356, 357–61, 365–6). Some of Ockham's adversaries did not see it that way, of course.

21. Cf. Beaston, 'The *Pearl* Poet and the Pelagians', pp. 16, 18, etc.

22. As is well argued by Rhodes, *Poetry Does Theology*, see esp. pp. 120–2, 138–9.

23. *Pace* Philip F. O'Mara, 'Robert Holcot's "Ecumenism" and the Green Knight', *ChR*, 26.4 (1992), 329–42 (p. 329). This is the first part of a two-part article, the second being 'Holcot and the *Pearl*-Poet', *ChR*, 27.1 (1992), 97–106.

24. O'Mara, 'Holcot and the *Pearl*-Poet', 104.

25. Here I echo the title of Sheila Delany's study, *Chaucer's 'House of Fame': The Poetics of Skeptical Fideism* (Chicago, 1972).

26. Frank Grady, *Representing Righteous Heathens in Late Medieval England* (New York, 2005), pp. 6, 7. Nicholas Watson has gone much further, in a thought-provoking article, 'Visions of Inclusion: Universal Salvation and Vernacular Theology in Pre-Reformation England', *Journal of Medieval and Early Modern Studies*, 27.2 (1997), 145–87. Here he proposes that 'universal salvation' (including the salvation of virtuous heathen) is 'a theme that somehow *belongs* to the vernacular in late medieval England' (169). In response, David Benson has argued that 'two distinct ideas about salvation' are being 'conflated' here. 'The first, an appeal to mercy, *hopes* [my emphasis] that all humans will somehow be saved regardless of their sins' (an issue famously raised by Julian of Norwich), 'whereas the second, an appeal to justice, posits the possibility that non-Christians may obtain salvation as a reward for faithful adherence to their own laws.' *Public 'Piers Plowman': Modern Scholarship and Late Medieval English Culture* (Pennsylvania, 2004), p. 148. There is a world of difference between pious, non-subversive hoping for the best for all mankind and the troubling (and perhaps *prima facie* Pelagian) belief that humans – no matter what religion they live and die in – can merit their own salvation. If there are indeed 'signs that eternal damnation was neither so fixed in lay belief nor so commonly preached as we might assume' (Watson, 'Visions of Inclusion', 149), that is probably due less to hopes concerning universal salvation as to the commanding position which the doctrine of purgatory maintained in devotional praxis. Here was a place of temporal punishment and purgation which could make sinners fit for heaven, and give men and women hope in their (and their ancestors') ultimate salvation. But, short of a special divine revelation, no one could be sure of the time at which the cleansing process was complete, or indeed if, in the case of certain heinous sinners, it could ever suffice. In *Piers Plowman*, B XVIII, Christ speaks of how those who 'diden ille' will be 'clensed clerliche and [clene] wasshen of hir synnes / in my prisone Purgatorie' (391–3). Thus, He continues, 'my mercy shal be shewed to manye of my bretheren' (394) – not to *all* of my brethren, we may note. In any case, hope of ultimate salvation (for Christians) should not be confused with hope of universal salvation (for everyone irrespective of religion).

27. See especially his agenda-setting study, 'Censorship and Cultural Change in Late Medieval England: Vernacular Theology, the Oxford Translation Debate and Arundel's *Constitutions* of 1409', *Speculum*, 70 (1996), 822–64. See also, in addition to the article discussed in my previous note, 'The Middle English Mystics', in David Wallace (ed.), *The Cambridge History of Medieval English Literature* (Cambridge, 1999), pp. 539–65; and 'Conceptions of the Word: The Mother Tongue and the Incarnation of God', *New Medieval Literatures*, I (1997), 85–124. Independent use of the term 'vernacular theology' has been made by Bernard McGinn; see especially his article 'Meister Eckhart and the Beguines in the Context of Vernacular Theology', in McGinn (ed.), *Meister Eckhart and the Beguine Mystics: Hadewijch of Brabant, Mechthild of Magdeburg, and Marguerite Porete* (New York, 1994), pp. 4–14. A review of its origins and recent scholarly adventures is included in Vincent Gillespie's

essay, 'Vernacular Theology', in Paul Strohm (ed.), *Middle English*, Oxford Twenty-First Century Approaches to Literature (Oxford, 2007), pp. 401–20. Cf. the collection of short essays in *English Language Notes*, 44 (2006), 77–126.

28. On which we now have a comprehensive book, Robert W. Shaffern, *The Penitents' Treasury: Indulgences in Latin Christendom, 1175–1375* (Scranton, PA, and London, 2007).

29. *Tractatus de ecclesia*, ed. J. Loserth (London, 1886), pp. 549–87.

30. *Le jubilé de Saint Thomas Becket du XIIIe au XVe siècle (1220–1470): études et documents*, ed. Raymonde Foreville (Paris, 1958), pp. 115–60 (the above quotation may be found on p. 119); cf. Minnis, *Fallible Authors*, pp. 91–3, 263, 385n, 386n.

31. Cf. n. 29 above.

32. To quote from Barbara Newman's remarks as found on the jacket blurb and the relevant University of Notre Dame Press web page, www3.undpress.nd.edu/exec/dispatch.php?s = title,P01082 (accessed 15 Aug. 2007). Cf. Ian Forrest's (rather more modest) claim that 'England was not completely immune from the major heretical movements of continental Europe'; *The Detection of Heresy in Late Medieval England* (Oxford, 2005), p. 23.

33. For this idiom see Felicity Riddy, '"Women Talking about the Things of God": A Late Medieval Sub-Culture', in Carol M. Meale (ed.), *Women and Literature in Britain, 1150–1500* (Cambridge, 1993), pp. 104–27.

34. To borrow a phrase from Ruth Shklar, 'Chobham's Daughter: *The Book of Margery Kempe* and the Power of Heterodox Thinking', *Modern Language Quarterly*, 56.3 (1995), 277–304 (p. 293). However, in my view, Shklar's contention that Margery 'establishes her own path of dissent, neither strictly orthodox nor heterodox' (p. 304), confuses rather than clarifies the situation.

35. But see the recent reappraisal of Margery's language competency by Melissa Furrow, 'Unscholarly Latinity and Margery Kempe', in M. J. Toswell and E. M. Tyler (eds.), *Studies in English Language and Literature. 'Doubt Wisely'. Papers in Honour of E. G. Stanley* (London and New York, 1996), pp. 240–51. This suggests (quite plausibly, in my view) that Margery understood more Latin than hitherto supposed.

36. The others are: *Utrum liceat mulieribus docere viros publice congregatos* (London, British Library, Harley 31, fols. 194v–196r), and *Utrum quilibet laicus iustus sit sacerdos noue legis* (fols. 216r–218r). Two of this set of four, *Utrum quilibet laicus iustus sit sacerdos noue legis* and *Utrum mulieres conficiunt vel conficere possunt*, also appear in London, British Library, MS Royal 7 B III, fols. 1r–4v.

37. Including writings by Thomas Aquinas and Peter of Tarantasia; cf. Alastair Minnis, '*Respondet Walterus Bryth*... Walter Brut in Debate on Women Priests', in Helen Barr and Ann M. Hutchinson (eds.), *Text and Controversy from Wyclif to Bale: Essays in Honour of Anne Hudson*, Medieval Church Studies 4 (Turnhout, 2005), pp. 229–49 (pp. 238, 245–6, 247), and the shorter account in *Fallible Authors*, ch. 3.

38. Cf. the Latin term *popularis*; defined in n. 3 above.

39. 'If Brut did not attend university, he studied with someone who did', as Fiona Somerset has said; '*Eciam mulier*: Women in Lollardy and the Problem of Sources', in Linda Olson and Kathryn Kerby-Fulton (eds.), *Voices in Dialogue: Reading Women in the Middle Ages* (Notre Dame, IN, 2005), pp. 245–60 (p. 248).
40. This is not, of course, to deny or undervalue the 'association of the vernacular with clerical suspicion', which Anne Hudson has well documented in her paper 'Lollardy: The English Heresy?', in Hudson, *Lollards and their Books*, pp. 141–63.
41. This comes from the point in Thomas Hoccleve's *Dialogue* (22–4) at which his 'Friend' asks if he has made his mental breakdown *public* knowledge. *'Complaint' and 'Dialogue'*, ed. J. A. Burrow, EETS OS 313 (Oxford, 1999), p. 35; and cf. Riddy, '"Publication" before Print', p. 41, to whom I am indebted here.
42. For instance, Dante remarks that 'few...achieve complete fluency' in the use of Latin, 'since knowledge of its rules and theory can only be developed through dedication to a lengthy course of study'; in contrast, the vernacular is learned by infants by hearing it spoken around them. *De vulgari eloquentia*, I.I, ed. and trans. Botterill, pp. 2–3.
43. Both perspectives are well illustrated in John Trevisa's *Dialogue* on translation. 'Clericus' places the matter within the wider European perspective, pointing out that Latin 'is used and understonde a this half Grece in alle the naciouns and londes of Europa. And comynliche Englisshe is not so wide understonde, iused, and iknowe, and the Englisshe translacioun is not so wide understonde but Englisshe men al oon'. In response, 'Dominus' argues from the narrower English perspective. If Latin chronicles (he has Ralph Higden's *Polychronicon* specifically in mind, the *Dialogue* being one of the prefaces to Trevisa's translation of that work) were 'translated out of Latyn into Englisshe, than by so meny the moo men shuld understonde hem as al thoe that understonde Englisshe and no Latyn'. Cf. Jocelyn Wogan-Browne, Nicholas Watson, Andrew Taylor, and Ruth Evans (eds.), *The Idea of the Vernacular: An Anthology of Middle English Literary Theory, 1280–1520* (University Park, PA, 1999), p. 132.
44. Anne Hudson, 'Wyclif and the English Language', in Anthony Kenny (ed.), *Wyclif in his Times* (Oxford, 1986), pp. 85–103 (p. 90).
45. Jean le Danois, *Summa grammatica*, ed. Alfred Otto, Corpus philosophorum Danicorum Medii Ævi (Copenhagen, 1955), p. 54.
46. Alfonso Manierù, 'The Philosophy of Language', in Giulio Lepschy (ed.), *History of Linguistics*, II: *Classical and Medieval Linguistics* (London and New York, 1994), pp. 272–315 (pp. 280–1). See also K. M. Fredborg, 'Universal Grammar according to Some Twelfth-Century Grammarians', in K. Koerner, H.-J. Niederehe, and R. H. Robins (eds.), *Studies in Medieval Linguistic Thought Dedicated to G. L. Bursill-Hall* (Amsterdam, 1980), pp. 69–84, and Alastair Minnis, *Magister amoris: The 'Roman de la Rose' and Vernacular Hermeneutics* (Oxford, 2001), pp. 121–2.

47. Cf. my discussion in *Medieval Theory of Authorship: Scholastic Literary Attitudes in the Later Middle Ages*, 2nd edn (Aldershot, 1988), pp. 118, 145, 149, 151, 154, 158, 162, 171, 268n, 269n.

48. *Vita nuova*, xix.22, ed. Domenico de Robertis (Milan and Naples, 1980), p. 132; trans. Barbara Reynolds (Harmondsworth, 1969), pp. 58–9.

49. To borrow a phrase from the introduction by János M. Bak and Paul A. Hollingsworth to their translation of Aron Gurevich, *Medieval Popular Culture: Problems of Belief and Perception* (Cambridge, 1988; repr. 1997), p. ix.

50. Jacques le Goff, *The Birth of Purgatory*, trans. Arthur Goldhammer (London, 1984); cf. Gurevich, *Medieval Popular Culture*, pp. ix, 149.

51. Gurevich, *Medieval Popular Culture*, p. 148.

52. This view was expressed by the monks of Fleury in the late eleventh century, who ardently prayed for the recovery of a mason who, while working on their new church, had fallen from scaffolding. They worried that, if he died, the *vulgus* would believe that 'St Benedict did not care about his own monastery' – with grave consequences for the building fund. Jonathan Sumption, *Pilgrimage: An Image of Medieval Religion* (Totowa, NJ, 1976), pp. 69–70.

53. Gurevich, 'Foreword' to his *Medieval Popular Culture*, p. xvi. Here Gurevich cites Jacques le Goff, who has asserted that 'clerical culture did undoubtedly accept folklore to some degree', this being 'a practical and tactical necessity for evangelical purposes': *Time, Work and Culture in the Middle Ages*, trans. Arthur Goldhammer (Chicago, 1986), pp. 156–7. Le Goff proceeds to emphasize the extent to which 'folkloric culture was *refused* by ecclesiastical culture', through processes of 'destruction', 'obliteration', and 'adulteration'. Such opposition resulted not only from 'conscious and deliberate hostility but equally out of incomprehension' (pp. 15–58). An opposing view is offered in Eamon Duffy's dramatically revisionist *The Stripping of the Altars: Traditional Religion in England, 1400–1580* (New Haven, 1994), which argues that 'no substantial gulf existed between the religion of the clergy and the educated élite on the one hand and that of the people at large on the other' (p. 2). Unfortunately, Duffy's totalizing construction of a 'traditional religion' shared by all results in the occlusion of many issues and activities which, in my opinion, could and often did divide élite religion (including scholastic theology) from 'popular' religion.

54. André Vauchez, *Sainthood in the Later Middle Ages*, trans. Jane Birrell (Cambridge, 1997), p. 413. See further J.-C. Schmidt, '"Religion populaire" et culture folklorique', *Annales ESC*, 31 (1976), 141–53.

55. There are two editions: by F. Stegmüller, *Annali della biblioteca governatica et libreria civica di Cremona*, Monumenta Cremonensia 2 (Cremona, 1955), pp. 1–17, and D. Trapp, 'The Portiuncula Discussion of Cremona (ca. 1380)', *Recherches de théologie ancienne et médiévale*, 22 (1955), 79–94. For discussion see Minnis, *Fallible Authors*, pp. 94–5, 387n. The authenticity of a plenary indulgence supposedly granted to Canterbury by Pope Honorius III in 1220 was also a matter of considerable controversy, as noted above.

56. In such a context 'scandal' denotes something which occasions a general feeling of outrage or indignation, causes a public affront. St Thomas Aquinas defines the term in terms of a 'stumbling' whereby something done or said may occasion someone's spiritual downfall: *Summa theologiae*, 2a 2ae , qu. 43, art. 1 (xxxv. 110–11). Fear of scandal was a major concern. Thomas of Chobham went so far as to argue that a priest can, quite commendably, hide his wickedness out of reverence for God and benefit to his neighbour, thereby avoiding the scandal which 'publication' of his wicked works would cause. *Summa de arte praedicandi*, ed. F. Morenzoni, CCCM 82 (Turnhout, 1988), p. 58. For other uses of the term see Katherine Gill, '*Scandalia*: Controversies concerning *clausura* and Women's Religious Communities in Late Medieval Italy', in S. L. Waugh and Peter D. Diehl (eds.), *Christendom and its Discontents: Exclusion, Persecution, and Rebellion* (Cambridge, 1996), pp. 177–203.

57. Robert W. Shaffern, 'A New Canonistic Text on Indulgences: *De quantitate indulgenciarum* of John of Dambach O.P. (1288–1372)', *Bulletin of Medieval Canon Law*, n.s. 21 (1991), 25–45 (p. 41); and also Shaffern, *The Penitents' Treasury*, pp. 181–4.

58. As when the Tower Hill site on which the Lollard Richard Wyche was burned in June 1440 was promoted as a pilgrimage destination; cf. Duffy, *The Stripping of the Altars*, p. 197.

59. Vincent, *The Holy Blood*, pp. 87–101. One of the most intriguing features about Grosseteste's tract is the apparent influence of Romance tradition (perhaps some version of the Grail legend) on its account of Joseph of Arimathaea; cf. pp. 89–91.

60. Vincent, *The Holy Blood*, pp. 123–34.

61. Vincent, *The Holy Blood*, pp. 136–51, 153–4, 171–6.

62. Chaucer, *Pardoner's Tale*, vi(c) 652; Vincent, *The Holy Blood*, pp. 186–201.

63. Perhaps with some regret on Henry VIII's part. Bishop Latimer complained that it took a 'great while' to get the 'great abomination of the blood of Hailes' out of the king's mind. Cf. Vincent, *The Holy Blood*, p. 198. On the shrine's destruction see *Letters to Cromwell on the Suppression of the Monasteries*, ed. G. H. Cook (London, 1965), pp. 206–7, 228–9.

64. Thomas More, *A Dialogue concerning Heresies*, II.II, ed. T. M. C. Lawler, G. Marc'Hadour, and R. C. Marius, in *The Yale Edition of the Complete Works of St. Thomas More*, executive ed. R. S. Sylvester (New Haven and London, 1963–97), vi, pt 1, p. 234.

65. Sumption, *Pilgrimage*, p. 44.

66. Sumption, *Pilgrimage*, pp. 71, 69.

67. Gurevich, *Medieval Popular Culture*, p. 45.

68. Gurevich, *Medieval Popular Culture*, p. xviii.

69. Peter Burke, 'Editorial preface' to Gurevich, *Medieval Popular Culture*, p. ix.

70. Here I borrow phrases from the definition of 'vernacular' in the *Concise Oxford Dictionary of Linguistics*, consulted via Oxford Reference Online.

71. This term goes back to the nineteenth century, according to the *OED*; however, its frequency in current critical conversation is largely due to Rita Copeland's highly influential *Rhetoric, Hermeneutics and Translation in the Middle Ages: Academic Traditions and Vernacular Texts* (Cambridge, 1991).

1 ABSENT GLOSSES: THE TROUBLE WITH MIDDLE ENGLISH HERMENEUTICS

1. Cf. Julian Weiss, *The Poet's Art: Literary Theory in Castile, c. 1400–60*, Medium Ævum Monographs, n.s. 14 (Oxford, 1990), p. 122; see further Weiss's account in *CHLCMA*, pp. 523–4. Unfortunately, this work has not survived in its entirety.

2. See especially the thesis by Stephen Partridge, which includes reference to previous scholarship on the subject: 'Glosses in the Manuscripts of Chaucer's *Canterbury Tales*: An Edition and Commentary' (Harvard University, 1992). Chaucer himself does not seem to have been interested in producing systematic commentary on any of his works, in contrast with Gower.

3. Recent discussion includes two articles by R. F. Yeager, '"Oure englisshe" and Everyone's Latin: The *Fasciculus morum* and Gower's *Confessio amantis*', *South Atlantic Review*, 46 (1981), 41–53, and 'English, Latin, and the Text as "Other": The Page as Sign in the Work of John Gower', *Text*, 3 (1987), 251–67; also Derek Pearsall, 'Gower's Latin in the *Confessio amantis*', in Alastair Minnis (ed.), *Latin and Vernacular: Studies in Late-Medieval Texts and Manuscripts* (Cambridge, 1989), pp. 13–25, and Siân Echard, 'Glossing Gower: In English, in Latin, and *in absentia*: The Case of Bodleian Ashmole 35', in R. F. Yeager (ed.), *John Gower: Recent Readings* (Asheville, NC, 1998), pp. 237–56. Cf. my own discussion of the topic in *Medieval Theory of Authorship*, pp. 188–90, 275.

4. Wogan-Browne *et al.* (eds.), *The Idea of the Vernacular*, p. 241.

5. *The Court of Sapience*, ed. E. Ruth Harvey (Toronto, 1984). The apparatus is included in the earlier edition by Robert Spindler, *The Court of Sapience: Spät-mittelenglisches allegorisch-didaktisches Visionsgedicht*, Beiträge zur englischen Philologie, 6 (Leipzig, 1927). See further the study of Curt F. Bühler, *The Sources of 'The Court of Sapience'*, Beiträge zur englischen Philologie, 23 (Leipzig, 1932), which incidentally demonstrates the accuracy of the Latin commentary's source-identifications.

6. On the techniques and terminology of the Latin commentaries on authoritative texts, as studied in the medieval schools, see Minnis, Scott, and Wallace (eds.), *Medieval Literary Theory and Criticism*.

7. *Virgil's Aeneid Translated into Scottish Verse*, ed. David F. C. Coldwell, Scottish Text Society (Edinburgh and London, 1957–64), IV. 191.

8. With the following review cf. the chapter 'Latin Commentary Tradition and Vernacular Literature' in *CHLCMA*, pp. 363–421, written jointly by Ralph Hanna III, Tony Hunt, R. G. Keightley, Alastair Minnis, and Nigel Palmer.

9. Cf. Minnis, Scott, and Wallace, *Medieval Literary Theory*, pp. 439–519; Robert Hollander, 'Dante and his Commentators', in Rachel Jacoff (ed.), *The Cambridge Companion to Dante* (Cambridge, 1993), pp. 226–36.

10. Cf. Minnis, '*Amor* and *Auctoritas* in the Self-Commentary of Dante and da Barberino'.

11. Rosalind Brown-Grant, *Christine de Pizan and the Moral Defence of Women* (Cambridge, 1999), pp. 7–51; Minnis, *Magister amoris*, pp. 26–8, 209–56. The documents have been edited by Eric Hicks, *Le débat sur le Roman de la Rose* (Paris, 1977).

12. Cf. Minnis, *Magister amoris*, pp. 234–47. On medieval Ovid commentary see especially Ralph J. Hexter, *Ovid and Medieval Schooling. Studies in Medieval School Commentaries on Ovid's 'Ars Amatoria', 'Epistulae ex Ponto', and 'Epistulae Heroidum'* (Munich, 1986).

13. Edited by Françoise Guichard-Tesson and Bruno Roy as *Le livre des eschez amoureux moralisés*, Bibliothèque du moyen français, 2 (Montreal, 1993). Evrart's authorship was established by F. Guichard-Tesson, 'Evrart de Conty, auteur de la *Glose des Echecs amoureux*', *Le moyen français*, 8–9 (1981), 111–48. For discussion of this commentary, and further bibliography, see Minnis, *Magister amoris*, pp. 257–319. For the argument that Evrart wrote the original poem – the *Echecs amoureux* itself – as well as the commentary on it, see Caroline Boucher, 'Des problèmes pour exercer l'entendement des lecteurs: Évrart de Conty, Nicole Oresme et la recherche de la nouveauté', in Pieter De Leemans and Michèle Goyens (eds.), *Aristotle's 'Problemata' in Different Times and Tongues* (Leuven, 2006), pp. 175–97 (pp. 195–6). If Boucher is right (and I myself find her argument very convincing), then we are dealing here with a magnificent French example of 'self-commentary' or 'autoexegesis'.

14. On this work, of which we have an autograph manuscript of some 500 folios, see especially F. Guichard-Tesson, 'Le métier de traducteur et de commentateur au XIVe siècle d'après Evrart de Conty', *Le moyen français*, 24–5 (1990), 131–67. It is not to be confused with the occasional Latin glosses which survive in the Venice manuscript of the *Eschez amoureux*. One of the two extant manuscripts of John Lydgate's Middle English translation (*c.* 1410) of the first part of the *Eschez amoureux*, namely Oxford, Bodleian Library, MS Fairfax 16, contains a redaction of those same Latin glosses, and it is evident that Lydgate drew on them in making his translation (cf. Minnis, *Magister amoris*, pp. 289–91). They are included in E. Sieper's edition of John Lydgate, *Reason and Sensuality*, EETS ES 84 (London, 1901).

15. For an excellent general account of the king's life and works see Françoise Autrand, *Charles V: le sage* (Paris, 1994).

16. *Livre de politiques*, ed. Menut, p. 20.

17. Cf. Peter Dembowski, 'Scientific Translation and Translators' Glossing in Four Medieval French Translators', in Jeanette Beer (ed.), *Translation Theory and Practice in the Middle Ages* (Kalamazoo, 1997), pp. 113–34 (p. 126).

18. *Livre de politiques*, ed. Menut, pp. 26–7.

19. Dembowski, 'Scientific Translation and Translators' Glossing', pp. 125–6.

20. C. C. Willard, 'Raoul de Presles's Translation of Saint Augustine's *De civitate Dei*', in Jeanette Beer (ed.), *Medieval Translators and their Craft* (Kalamazoo, 1989), pp. 329–46 (p. 331). Willard notes (p. 336) Raoul's interest in the problem of authentic book division in Augustine's text, which had been discussed by Trevet and Waleys; cf. Minnis, *Medieval Theory of Authorship*, p. 154. On this translation see further Jeanette Beer, 'Patronage and the Translator: Raoul de Presles's *La Cité de Dieu* and Calvin's *Institutio religionis Christianae*', in Jeanette Beer and K. Lloyd-Jones (eds.), *Translation and the Transmission of Culture between 1300 and 1600* (Kalamazoo, 1995), pp. 91–141.

21. Cf. Guichard-Tesson, 'Le métier de traducteur'. On Abano's commentary see especially Joan Cadden, '"Nothing Natural Is Shameful": Vestiges of a Debate about Sex and Science in a Group of Late-Medieval Manuscripts', *Speculum*, 76 (2001), 66–89.

22. Cf. Minnis, *Magister amoris*, pp. 296–8. Here I draw on information provided by the late Ronald G. Keightley, who published studies on Spanish translations of *De consolatione philosophiae* and the Eusebius commentary of Alfonso de Madrigal. Cf. especially his article, 'Alfonso de Madrigal and the *Cronici canones* of Eusebius', *Journal of Medieval and Renaissance Studies*, 7 (1977), 225–48, and also the material he contributed to ch. 14 of *CHLCMA*. I am deeply grateful to Ron for a long and invaluable correspondence concerning the matters here discussed.

23. Cf. Hollander, 'Dante and his Commentators', p. 229.

24. On which see William J. Kennedy, *Authorizing Petrarch* (Ithaca and London, 1994), esp. pp. 25–81. Despite its title, this admirable study has little to say about either medieval or Renaissance notions of textual authority.

25. See Daniel Javitch, *Proclaiming a Classic: The Canonization of 'Orlando Furioso'* (Princeton, NJ, 1991), esp. pp. 9, 15, 21–48, and Paul F. Grendler, *Schooling in Renaissance Italy* (Baltimore, 1989), p. 298.

26. Cf. David Wallace's account in Minnis, Scott, and Wallace, *Medieval Literary Theory*, pp. 456–8.

27. On the family's literary patronage see especially Ralph Hanna III, 'Sir Thomas Berkeley and his Patronage', *Speculum*, 64 (1989), 878–916. See further his article, 'The Difficulty of Ricardian Prose Translation: The Case of the Lollards', *Modern Language Quarterly*, 51 (1990), 319–40. Mention should also be made of John of Gaunt's patronage of two Anglo-Latin writers, Richard Maidstone and Walter of Peterborough. The latter produced for Gaunt a Christian allegorization of Ovid's *Metamorphoses*, which has been lost. See George Rigg, *A History of Anglo-Latin Literature, 1066–1422* (Cambridge, 1992), pp. 276–8, 285–6.

28. On this work see especially Ian Johnson's two studies, 'New Evidence for the Authorship of Walton's Boethius', *Notes and Queries*, n.s. 43 (1996), 19–21, and 'Placing Walton's Boethius', in Lodi Nauta and Maarten J. F. M. Hoenen (eds.), *Boethius in the Middle Ages: Latin and Vernacular Traditions of the 'Consolatio Philosophiae'* (Leiden, 1997), pp. 217–42.

29. John Walton, *Boethius, 'De consolatione philosophiae'*, ed. Mark Science, EETS OS 170 (London, 1927), p. xix.
30. Science knew that 'Here and there copious marginal commentaries are inserted' (p. xxi) in the Copenhagen manuscript, but nevertheless did not consider the possibility that they might be related to the apparatus in the printed edition. However, he was confident that the printed edition was 'taken from a MS. very closely related to the author's original' (p. xlvii).
31. See Brian Donaghey and Irma Taavitsainen, 'Walton's Boethius: From Manuscript to Print', *English Studies*, 80 (1999), 398–407.
32. As I demonstrated in my article 'Aspects of the Medieval French and English Traditions of Boethius' *De Consolatione Philosophiae*', in M. T. Gibson (ed.), *Boethius: His Life, Thought and Influence* (Oxford, 1981), pp. 312–61 (pp. 343–7, 350–1). See further Ian Johnson, 'Walton's Sapient Orpheus', in Alastair Minnis (ed.), *The Medieval Boethius: Studies in the Vernacular Translations of 'De Consolatione Philosophiae'* (Woodbridge, 1987), pp. 139–68.
33. Cf. Hanna, 'Sir Thomas Berkeley' p. 896, and Hanna, 'Ricardian Prose Translation', p. 325.
34. Anne Hudson, 'Lollardy: The English Heresy?', in Hudson, *Lollards and their Books*, pp. 141–63 (p. 150).
35. Cf. Hanna, 'Sir Thomas Berkeley', p. 895.
36. On which see Henry Hargreaves, 'The Marginal Glosses to the Wycliffite New Testament', *Studia Neophilologica*, 33 (1961), 285–300, and Hargreaves, 'Popularising Bible Scholarship: The Role of the Wycliffite *Glossed Gospels*', in W. Lourdaux and D. Verhelst (eds.), *The Bible and Medieval Culture* (Leuven, 1979), pp. 171–89; also Hudson, *Premature Reformation*, pp. 248–59. To this list of major Lollard hermeneutic achievements may be added the glossed Wycliffite Psalter preserved uniquely in Oxford, Bodleian Library, MS Bodley 554, which is being edited by Michael Kuczynski.
37. Arundel's fifth constitution is of particular importance in this regard, since it prohibited elementary schoolmasters from including in their teaching 'anything concerning the exposition of Scripture, except in expounding the text in the manner customary since ancient times'. As Rita Copeland suggests in her excellent discussion of this statute, it aims at 'driving pedagogy and hermeneutics apart', any 'kind of commentative activity that would admit controversy' being banned. *Pedagogy, Intellectuals and Dissent in the Later Middle Ages. Lollardy and Ideas of Learning* (Cambridge, 2001), p. 121. This study subtly explores, *inter alia*, the proposition that Lollardy pedagogy may be seen as 'literacy acquisition for the purpose of attaining exegetical competence' (p. 17).
38. Edited by H. R. Bramley, *The Psalter Translated by Richard Rolle of Hampole* (Oxford, 1884). On yet another English Glossed Psalter, which is derived from a (lost) French original, see R. C. St-Jacques, 'The *Middle English Glossed Prose Psalter* and its French Source', in Beer (ed.), *Medieval Translators and their Craft*, pp. 135–54.

39. On which see Hudson, *Premature Reformation*, pp. 259–64.
40. Hudson, *Premature Reformation*, p. 267. One version has been edited by E. Fridner, *An English Fourteenth Century Apocalypse Version with a Prose Commentary*, Lund Studies in English, 29 (Lund and Copenhagen, 1961); the other by W. Sauer, *Die mittelenglische Übersetzung der Apokalypse mit Kommentar (Version B)* (Heidelberg, 1971). Of unquestionably Lollard origin is the Latin Apocalypse commentary known as the *Opus arduum* (c. 1389–90), discussed by Anne Hudson, 'A Neglected Wycliffite Text', in Hudson, *Lollards and their Books*, pp. 43–66; see also Hudson, *Premature Reformation*, pp. 264–7, and Copeland, *Pedagogy, Intellectuals*, pp. 156–61.
41. Text edited by C. F. Bühler, 'A Lollard Tract: On Translating the Bible into English', *Medium Ævum*, 7 (1938), 167–83. On Ullerston's arguments see Gillespie, 'Vernacular Theology', pp. 412–14 and 415–16, who describes this schoolman as 'groping towards a justification of vernacular theology that anticipates in embryo the arguments used later by Reginald Pecock' (p. 413).
42. See Anne Hudson, 'The Debate on Bible Translation, Oxford 1401', in Hudson, *Lollards and their Books*, pp. 67–84, and Watson, 'Censorship and Cultural Change'.
43. Hudson, 'The English Heresy?', p. 145.
44. Mary Dove's total is c. 253; see her list in *The First English Bible: The Text and Context of the Wycliffite Versions* (Cambridge, 2007), pp. 281–306.
45. Hudson, 'The English Heresy?', p. 149.
46. Cf. Minnis, *Fallible Authors*, esp. pp. 221–31, and Chapter 4 below.
47. Watson, 'Censorship and Cultural Change', 858.
48. Thomas Walsingham, *Historia anglicana*, ed. H. T. Riley, Rolls Series, 28 (London, 1863–4; repr. 1965), II. 215–17.
49. Nigel Saul, *Richard II* (New Haven and London, 1997), pp. 300–3.
50. Bennett, *Richard II and the Revolution of 1399*, p. 88.
51. Bennett, *Richard II and the Revolution of 1399*, p. 69. 'The challenge of heresy, so salient in the 1380s and 1390s, greatly strengthened the bond' between the king and the archbishop, Bennett argues (p. 89); Arundel 'kept on trying to believe in him until the time of his brother's execution and his own exile' (p. 68). A few years later, things had changed utterly. Arundel returned from exile with Henry Bolingbroke in early July 1399, to play a crucial role in the establishment of Lancastrian power.
52. Bennett, *Richard II and the Revolution of 1399*, p. 68.
53. On Lollard attacks on swearing and the uttering of great oaths, see Hudson, *Premature Reformation*, pp. 371–4.
54. G. R. Owst, *The 'Destructorium viciorum' of Alexander Carpenter* (London, 1952), p. 4. Carpenter has been seriously misread, and even Owst (whilst accepting that Carpenter is 'no avowed Wycliffite', p. 6) has problems in recognizing (what I myself regard as) the clear blue sea which separates his views from Lollard doctrine. Carpenter is not protesting about the persecution of Lollards; rather he is complaining that ordinary decent (and impeccably

orthodox) priests, who in attacking Avarice and criticizing immoral
behaviour – particularly within the priesthood – are just trying to do their
job, are accused of being Lollards and threatened with persecution. 'If many
voluptuous priests and prelates... shall have heard any faithful preacher or
any other faithful man barking against their sins, immediately they bark
against such, by slandering him with the teeth of detraction, gnawing him
for errors and heresies, accusing him most falsely, cruelly imprisoning him
and sometimes even persecuting him to death with a mighty malice' (p.
8). Quite unambiguous is Carpenter's assault on the Lollard impulse towards
Donatism; 'dicunt heretici quod pravi sacerdotes non dant vera sacramenta' (p.
7 n. 3). On the problematics of Lollard Donatism see Minnis, *Fallible Authors*,
pp. 19–22, 55–7, 60–7, etc., and pp. 92–3, 206 n. 46 below.

55. Owst, *The 'Destructorium viciorum'*, p. 7. Carpenter seems to associate
Lollardy with social disorder; those who genuinely hold such views are termed
destroyers 'of ecclesiastical liberty', reprovers 'of the honest behaviour and
estate of temporal lords', and disturbers 'of the whole populace'.

56. Owst, *The 'Destructorium viciorum'*, p. 7.

57. Audelay seems to have spent his last days at Haghmond Abbey near Shrews-
bury, a house of Austin Canons. See *The Poems of John Audelay*, ed. Ella
Keats Whiting, EETS OS 184 (London, 1931), pp. xiv–xv. James Simpson has
done much to bring Audelay's achievements as a satirist to our attention. See
especially his *The Oxford English Literary History*, II: *1350–1547. Reform and Cultural Revolution* (Oxford, 2002), pp. 378–80, and 'Saving Satire after Arundel's
Constitutions: John Audelay's "Marcol and Solomon"', in Helen Barr and Ann
M. Hutchinson (eds.), *Text and Controversy from Wyclif to Bale: Essays in
Honour of Anne Hudson*, Medieval Church Studies 4 (Turnhout, 2005),
pp. 387–404.

58. *Poems of Audelay*, ed. Whiting, p. 141.

59.   And ȝif þe secular say a soþ anon þai bene e-schent,
                  And lyen apon þe leud men and sayn hit is lollere;
                  Þus þe pepul and prestis beþ of one asent;
                  Þai dare no noder do,
                  Fore dred of þe clerge
                  Wold dampnen hem vnlaufully
                  To preche apon þe pelere,
                  And bren hem after too.
                           (*Poems of Audelay*, ed. Whiting, p. 34)

60. *Poems of Audelay*, ed. Whiting, p. 15.

61. Thomas Hoccleve, *The Minor Poems*, ed. F. J. Furnivall and I. Gollancz, EETS
ES 61 and 73 (London, repr. 1970), p. 14.

62. The normative affective piety of Love's treatise is brought out well in Ian
Johnson's doctoral dissertation,'The Late-Medieval Theory and Practice of
Translation with Special Reference to Some Middle English Lives of Christ'
(University of Bristol, 1990). Moreover, a version of the *Mirrour* may have
been in circulation before Arundel inspected and approved the treatise in 1410:

see Ian Doyle, 'Reflections on Some Manuscripts of Nicholas Love's *Myrrour of the Blessed Lyf of Jesu Christ*', *Leeds Studies in English*, n.s. 14 (1983), 82–93.

63. The extent to which Love wrote the *Mirrour* as 'an orthodox riposte to the Wycliffite Bible' should therefore not be exaggerated, *pace* Watson, 'Conceptions of the Word', 94. It may be noted that the passage wherein St Cecilia is described as continually performing her sequence of meditations concerning the life of Christ, which Watson regards as 'endlessly repetitive' and spiritually 'crude' (p. 98; cf. 'Censorship and Cultural Change', pp. 853–4), is present in the Latin original. This is not to deny that he may have exploited it for his own ends, to be sure, but here as elsewhere the translation's fidelity to its source makes it harder to argue that Love has re-cast the entire text in an Arundelian mould. An excellent review of the range of current scholarly opinion on the *Mirrour*, along with a highly revealing comparison of the Middle English text with its source, is included in Michelle Karnes's fine article, 'Nicholas Love and Medieval Meditations on Christ', *Speculum*, 82.2 (2007), 380–408, which proposes (*inter alia*) that the *Mirrour*'s spirituality, while being 'far removed from a Lollard one', 'does not exist solely as an antidote' to it (p. 407).

64. However, the attribution is by no means secure, since in only one of the five extant manuscripts is Hilton named as author. Cf. Walter Hilton, *Latin Writings*, ed. John P. H. Clark and Cheryl Taylor, Analecta Cartusiana, 124 (Salzburg, 1987), i. 175–6. On Hilton's views on images and imagery see especially Nicholas Watson, '"Et que est huius ydoli materia? Tuipse": Idols and Images in Walter Hilton', in Jeremy Dimmick, James Simpson, and Nicolette Zeeman (eds.), *Images, Idolatry, and Iconoclasm in Late Medieval England* (Oxford, 2002), pp. 95–111.

65. Walter Hilton, *The Scale of Perfection*, ed. Thomas H. Bestul (Kalamazoo, 2000), p. 39.

66. Walter Hilton, *The Mixed Life*, ed. S. J. Ogilvie-Thomson, Salzburg Studies in English Literature, Elizabethan and Renaissance Studies, 92.15 (Salzburg, 1986), pp. 14–15. In terms which echo *Scale*, i. 9, Hilton explains that pure contemplative life 'longeþ' to men and women who 'maken hem self pore and naked to þe bare nede of þe bodili kynde, and fleen fro souereynte of alle oþere men to þe seruice of God' (pp. 12–13). The nature of Hilton's achievement in this treatise is brought out well in ch. 3 of Nicole Rice's *Lay Piety and Religious Discipline in Middle English Literature* (Cambridge, 2008).

67. Of course, the notion that the preacher or teacher should suit his material to the different needs and capacities of different audiences was a long-standing tradition in Christian rhetoric, one of its concomitants being a policy of 'discrimination' in both senses of that term. The Christian teacher had a duty to be discriminating in bringing the truth, no matter how difficult, to the varied understandings of others (cf. Augustine, *De doctrina christiana*, iv.ix.23). On the other hand one had to discriminate (adopting the modern idiom) against people of limited intellectual ability who could be led into heresy through exposure to theological difficulty. 'Profound investigation of Holy Scripture should be left to spiritual and perfect men, for to others it

is perilous.' Here I quote from my summary of Henry of Ghent's (quite representative) views on the subject; 'Medium and Message: Henry of Ghent on Scriptural Style', in Richard G. Newhauser and John A. Alford (eds.), *Literature and Religion in the Later Middle Ages: Philological Studies in Honor of Siegfried Wenzel* (Binghamton, NY, 1995), pp. 209–35 (p. 225).

68. This passage may be compared with the fuller 'documentary allegories' of the Charters of Christ, on which see pp. 84, 200 n. 56 below.

69. Watson, 'Conceptions of the Word', 107–10. I myself can find nothing here by way of specific empowerment of the vernacular reader or writer; the allegorical discourse which is to be written on the heart is beyond all human language, whether Latin, English, or anything else.

70. Cf. Minnis, *Magister amoris*, pp. 132–3; also Minnis, 'Fifteenth-Century Versions of Literalism: Girolamo Savonarola and Alfonso de Madrigal', in Robert Lerner (ed.), *Neue Richtungen in der hoch- und spätmittelalterlichen Bibelexegese*, Schriften des Historischen Kollegs Kolloquien, 32 (Munich, 1996), pp. 163–80 (pp. 170–5). This is not, of course, to deny the value of allegory as an *affectus*-moving and imaginatively persuasive device; cf. Minnis, *Magister amoris*, pp. 114, 138–40.

71. One of Watson's crucial arguments is that 'anxieties and antipathies' concerning the use of the vernacular 'sometimes paralleled those surrounding the eucharistic image of God's body' ('Conceptions of the Word', 90).

72. Cf. Ralph Hanna's treatment of *The Chastising of God's Children* in 'Ricardian Prose Translation', 330–1, following on from a discussion of Love's *Mirrour*.

73. That certainly is the view of Richard Rex, who, in his brief monograph *The Lollards* (Houndmills, Basingstoke, Hampshire, 2002), has taken literary critics to task for overstating the historical importance of Lollardy in general. In his opinion, 'the Lollards were neither numerically significant in their own time nor of great importance for the course of English history' (p. xv): we have been beguiled by the 'disproportionate survival of Lollard texts' and 'the romantic appeal of the Lollards as a criminalised minority' (p. xv). 'Only a very restricted range of texts circulated' (p. 143), he declares – a claim which hardly sits well with his earlier statement concerning 'disproportionate survival'; one might also pose the question, 'disproportionate' in relation to what? Most controversial is Rex's claim that Lollardy 'was far from uppermost in the minds of clergy or laity in the fifteenth century' (p. 145), and therefore 'devotional literature only rarely alludes to the threat of heresy, and with little passion . . . Polemics against Lollardy . . . do not survive in the sort of quantities which suggest that they were much read' (p. 146). Rex goes so far as to suggest that 'the scattered and sporadic burning of heretics was hardly a reign of terror: it never even approached the scale of the 1530s or the 1550s [in England], let alone that of the Spanish Inquisition under Ferdinand and Isabelle' (pp. 148–9). Not the Spanish Inquisition, then. But cultural significance cannot always be measured by body-count. And it goes without saying that trivialization of the suffering and sacrifice of those criminalized Christians who actually were burned alive should be avoided.

74. Kerby-Fulton, *Books under Suspicion*, pp. 397–401.
75. Kerby-Fulton, *Books under Suspicion*, p. 397.
76. On which see especially Dove, *The First English Bible*, pp. 281–306, and also her account of the problems attendant on such numeration. See further Conrad Lindberg's latest study, *A Manual of the Wyclif Bible, including the Psalms. Dedicated to the Memory of Sven L. Fristedt* (Stockholm, 2007).
77. Cf. Hudson, *Premature Reformation*, pp. 233–4, and the revisionary comments of Hanna, *London Literature, 1300–1380*, pp. 308–13.
78. Cf. Dove, *The First English Bible*, p. 120. Only four of these Prologue manuscripts form part of complete Wycliffite Bibles, and only two come at the beginning of the Bible. There are small portions or fragments of the Prologue in eight more manuscripts (p. 127). Given this very limited circulation, it may be wondered if the Prologue exercised much influence on the readership of the Wycliffite Bible itself. (I am grateful to Dr Dove for valuable discussion of these issues.)
79. *Lollards of Coventry, 1486–1522*, ed. and trans. Shannon McSheffrey and Norman Tanner, Camden Fifth Series, 23 (Cambridge, 2003), p. 42.
80. *Lollards of Coventry*, ed. and trans. McSheffrey and Tanner, p. 31. They speculate further that a 'double standard' may have existed, 'a supposition that those of higher station could be trusted to act appropriately if given direct access to the word of God, while the lower orders might misunderstand the message if it were not interpreted for them' (p. 31). The alternative viewpoint is, of course, that the men and women of Coventry's civic élite were genuinely innocent of Lollardy – or, rather, those specific doctrines which, in the later fifteenth century, were deemed to constitute Lollardy. Further evidence for a 'double standard' may be found in the fate of Reginald Pecock, bishop of Chichester. He does not seem to have been troubled by the *Constitutions* when, in the 1430s, he began creating an extensive corpus of vernacular theology and philosophy – even though his activities were *prima facie* in breach of several of them. But it may be argued that Pecock's situation was exceptional; as a high-ranking churchman whose professed motivation in writing *in vulgari* was to counter Lollard heresy, he was an unlikely candidate for investigation. Indeed, it may be concluded that what brought him down was an excess of anti-Lollard zeal; in seeking to counter their fideistic principles he went to the other extreme, championing the agency of human reason to a degree that his opponents found deeply disturbing. On Pecock's life and trial see especially Wendy Scase, *Reginald Pecock*, English Writers of the Late Middle Ages, vol. 3, no. 8 (Aldershot, 1996), pp. 69–146.
81. *Lollards of Coventry*, ed. and trans. McSheffrey and Tanner, p. 32.
82. Transcribed from Paris, Bibliothèque Nationale de France, MS fr. 22913, fol. iv, in Caroline Boucher's doctoral thesis, 'La mise en scène de la vulgarisation: les traductions d'autorités en langue vulgaire aux XIIIe et XIVe siècles', École Pratique des Hautes Études, 5e section (Paris, 2005), pp. 443, 614–15.
83. *Friars's Prologue*, iii(d), 1272, 1275–6; cf. p. 28 above.

84. In the sense of 'making public'. Cf. the meaning of the Latin term *publicatio*, discussed at the beginning of my introductory chapter.

85. Raoul's prologue is extant in only one manuscript, London, British Library, MS Lansdowne 1175; I quote from the edition included in Samuel Berger, *La Bible française au Moyen Âge* (Paris, 1884), pp. 245–7 (p. 247). As we have it, the translation breaks off at ch. 19 of the Gospel of St Matthew. It is unclear if Raoul ever finished it (his labours may have been cut short by death) or if the final part has been lost.

86. Anne Hudson and H. L. Spencer, 'Old Author, New Work: The Sermons of MS Longleat 4', *Medium Ævum*, 53 (1984), 220–38.

87. The way in which a 'rhetoric of persecution' developed in this period is a fascinating topic. Wyclif himself displayed signs of a persecution complex long before the actual repression began; cf. Michael Wilks, 'Wyclif and the Great Persecution', in Michael Wilks (ed.), *Studies in Church History*, Subsidia 10: Prophecy and Eschatology (Oxford, 1994), pp. 39–63.

88. Cf. Hudson, *Premature Reformation*, pp. 418–21.

89. As Hanna says of the figure of the Lord in Trevisa's dialogues; 'Sir Thomas Berkeley', p. 895.

90. *Dives and Pauper*, ed. P. H. Barnum, EETS OS 275 and 280 (Oxford, 1976–80), I. 82.

91. *Dives and Pauper*, ed. Barnum, II. 108.

92. *Dives and Pauper*, ed. Barnum, II. 169–71.

93. Reginald Pecock, *The Reule of Crysten Religioun*, ed. W. C. Greet, EETS OS 171 (London, 1927), pp. 20–1.

94. Hudson and Spencer, 'Sermons of Longleat 4', 228. In marked contrast, William Langland complained about those great nobles who presume to talk at table of Christ and his powers (*Piers Plowman*, B x. 103–10).

95. The damage which such tools could do in the hands of layfolk is vividly illustrated by the case of Walter Brut, who, in addition to professing many of the more routine Lollard heresies, believed that righteous women could preach and confect the Eucharist. He had a major advantage, however, in being able to argue to great effect in Latin. Cf. Alcuin Blamires (ed.), *Woman Defamed and Woman Defended* (Oxford, 1992), pp. 250–60, and Chapter 4 below. An excellent example of the techniques of academic debate and Biblical hermeneutics being practised in Middle English may be found in the Lollard dramatization of an alleged confrontation between William Thorpe and Thomas Arundel; cf. Anne Hudson's edition in *Two Wycliffite Texts*, EETS OS 301 (Oxford, 1993), pp. 24–93. At one point Thorpe even presumes to lecture Arundel on the correct way to read allegorically the Bible's references to music and minstrelsy: such passages, he claims, are not 'to be taken neiþer vsid after þe letter. But þese instruments wiþ her musyk owen to be interpretid goostly' (p. 65). Earlier in the text Arundel complains that this 'losel' and many others like him 'pike out scharpe sentencis of holy writ and of doctours for to maynteyne her sect and her loore' (p. 51), and later he quizzes Thorpe on the interpretation of one of Chrysostom's homilies (p. 76). See further the

discussion by Copeland, *Pedagogy, Intellectuals*, pp. 191–219, which brings out well how the Thorpe treatise 'imagines connections between a university culture and the community beyond it' (p. 218). On the influence of disputational technique on Lollard strategies of evasion see Copeland, *Pedagogy, Intellectuals*, pp. 175–83.

96. Scase, *Reginald Pecock*, pp. 115, 124.

97. Here I wish to invoke the literary-theoretical principles constitutive of the late medieval 'ethical poetic', described so well by the late Judson B. Allen, *The Ethical Poetic of the Later Middle Ages* (Toronto, 1982).

98. Christine's original and Hoccleve's translation have been edited by T. S. Fenster and M. C. Erler, *Poems of Cupid, God of Love. Christine de Pizan's 'Epistre au dieu d'Amours' and 'Dit de la Rose'; Thomas Hoccleve's 'The Letter of Cupid'* (Leiden and New York, 1990).

99. The term is Gontier Col's, describing the *querelle* as a battlefield; *Le Débat*, ed. Hicks, p. 34.

100. *Livre de éthiques*, ed. Menut, p. 100; cf. *Livre de politiques*, ed. Menut, p. 27.

101. *Livre de politiques*, ed. Menut, p. 44. The Cicero quotation also appears in the preface to Oresme's *Livre de éthiques*.

102. *Chemin de long estude*; quoted by Sherman, *Imaging Aristotle*, p. 7; see also p. 9.

103. 'John Trevisa, *Dialogue* and *Epistle*', in Wogan-Browne *et al.* (eds.), *The Idea of the Vernacular*, pp. 133–4; Chaucer, prologue to *Treatise on the Astrolabe*, in *Riverside Chaucer*, ed. Benson, p. 662. 'God woot that in alle these langages and in many moo' his scientific conclusions have been 'suffisantly lerned and taught', asserts Chaucer, adding that 'diverse pathes leden diverse folk the righte way to Rome'. But subsequent political events in England were inimical to the promotion of such a positive view of the relationship between learning and linguistic diversity.

104. *Prologue to Wycliffite Bible*, ch. 15, Anne Hudson (ed.), *Selections from English Wycliffite Writings* (Cambridge, 1978; repr. Toronto, 1997), pp. 70–1. There are many other examples of similar statements, including the complaint in the *Opus arduum* that, while the divine law is commonly available to all Hebrews, Greeks and Latins, Englishmen are not allowed 'to have the divine law in our vernacular' (cited Hudson, 'Neglected Wycliffite Text', p. 53). See also Bühler, 'A Lollard Tract', p. 173, which may be compared with Ullerston's Latin treatise, as quoted by Hudson, 'Debate on Bible Translation', pp. 71–2. The Wycliffite Bible passage quoted above makes very clear the crucial connection between textual hermeneutics and translation; cf. Ullerston's recognition that, as Hudson puts it, 'whilst interpretation is possible without translation, translation conversely cannot proceed without interpretation': 'Wyclif and the English Language', p. 91. The notion that *translatio* is the exposition of meaning (*expositio sententiae*) through another language was a grammarians' commonplace; cf. Copeland, *Rhetoric, Hermeneutics and Translation*, pp. 88–91, and Minnis, *Magister amoris*, p. 270.

2 LOOKING FOR A SIGN: THE QUEST FOR NOMINALISM IN RICARDIAN POETRY

1. Walter Hilton, *Scale*, II. 3, ed. Bestul, p. 139.

2. For a bibliography of discussions of Chaucer in relation to Nominalism see Richard J. Utz and William H. Watts, 'Nominalist Perspectives on Chaucer's Poetry: A Bibliographical Essay', *Mediaevalia et humanistica*, n.s. 20 (1993), 147–73; see further the essays and references in Richard J. Utz (ed.), *Literary Nominalism and the Theory of Rereading Late Medieval Texts* (Lewiston and Queenston, 1995), and Keiper, Bode, and Utz (eds.), *Nominalism and Literary Discourse*. W. J. Courtenay's essay in the second of these collections, 'The Dialectic of Divine Omnipotence in the Age of Chaucer: A Reconsideration' (pp. 111–21), provides a review of scholarship on the 'two powers' distinction from 1960 through 1994.

3. The scholarly literature on Langland and Nominalism is substantial; I have taken special note of G. H. Russell, 'The Salvation of the Heathen: The Exploration of a Theme in *Piers Plowman*', *Journal of the Warburg and Courtauld Institutes*, 29 (1966), 101–16; Denise Baker, 'From Plowing to Penitence: *Piers Plowman* and Fourteenth-Century Theology', *Speculum*, 55 (1980), 715–25; Janet Coleman, *'Piers Plowman' and the 'Moderni'* (Rome, 1981); Gordon Whatley, *'Piers Plowman* B 12.277–94: Notes on Language, Text, and Theology', *Modern Philology*, 82 (1984), 1–12; Pamela Gradon, *'Trajanus Redivivus*: Another Look at Trajan in *Piers Plowman*', in Douglas Gray and E. G. Stanley (eds.), *Middle English Studies Presented to Norman Davis* (Oxford, 1983), pp. 95–114; Robert Adams, 'Piers's Pardon and Langland's Semi-Pelagianism', *Traditio*, 39 (1983), 367–418, also his later review, 'Langland's Theology', in John A. Alford (ed.), *A Companion to 'Piers Plowman'* (Berkeley and Los Angeles, 1988), pp. 87–114 (especially pp. 107–9); and of course Grady, *Representing Righteous Heathens*.

4. W. J. Courtenay, *Schools and Scholars in Fourteenth-Century England* (Princeton, 1987), p. 173 n. 205.

5. Cf. Minnis, *Fallible Authors*, ch. 3.

6. W. J. Courtenay, *'Antiqui* and *Moderni* in Late-Medieval Thought', *Journal of the History of Ideas*, 48 (1987), 3–10 (p. 6).

7. Russell Peck, 'Chaucer and the Nominalist Questions', *Speculum*, 53 (1978), 745–60.

8. Courtenay, *Schools and Scholars*, p. 213; here the debt of Ockham to Duns Scotus in particular is emphasized.

9. R. A. Pratt, 'Some Latin Sources of the Nonnes Preest on Dreams', *Speculum*, 52 (1977), 538–70. Behind this study lies the pioneering work of K. O. Petersen, the first person to postulate Holcot's influence: *Sources of the Nonnes Preestes Tale*, Radcliffe College Monographs, 10 (Boston, 1896).

10. See further the fuller account of Holcot's doctrine on pp. 49, 51 below.

11. On this distinction see Alastair Minnis, 'From Medieval to Renaissance? Chaucer's Position on Past Gentility', *Proceedings of the British Academy*, 72 (1986), 205–46.

12. On Chaucer and Bersuire see Meg Twycross, *The Medieval Anadyomene: A Study in Chaucer's Mythography*, Medium Ævum Monographs, n.s. 1 (Oxford, 1972); Alastair Minnis, *Chaucer and Pagan Antiquity* (Cambridge, 1982), pp. 20–1, 109–14 *passim*, 116–18, also Minnis, *Oxford Guides to Chaucer: The Shorter Poems*, pp. 99, 192–3, 195–6, 199, 203.

13. Thomas Bradwardine, *De causa Dei*, 1.1, coroll. 32; ed. Henry Savile (London, 1618), pp. 29–37.

14. Furthermore, as Edith Wilks Dolnikowski has recently emphasized, Bradwardine 'actually shared' with Ockham 'many common assumptions about natural philosophy and theology', which she points out in her study *Thomas Bradwardine: A View of Time and a Vision of Eternity in Fourteenth-Century Thought* (Leiden, 1995), quotation on p. 13. This also contains a useful account of past and present approaches to Bradwardine.

15. On these commentaries see Beryl Smalley, *English Friars and Antiquity in the Early Fourteenth Century* (Oxford, 1960), pp. 58–65, 88–100, 299.

16. See W. A. Pantin, 'John of Wales and Medieval Humanism', in *Medieval Studies Presented to Aubrey Gwynn* (Dublin, 1961), pp. 297–319 (p. 309); cf. Minnis, 'From Medieval to Renaissance?', 213–14.

17. That said, it is perfectly reasonable to claim that, given the well-established 'vernacular virtuous heathen scene', an ascent 'was generally a good thing. Troilus's ultimate destination may be mysterious, his ascent ambiguous – but given the context it's not *that* ambiguous.' Grady, *Representing Righteous Heathens*, pp. 107–8. Here, as elsewhere, Chaucer subtly ensures his good pagans are placed in the best possible light, whilst occluding his own position behind rhetorical professions of ignorance or lack of expertise.

18. Giovanni Boccaccio, *Teseida*, book 10, stanzas 95 and 99; trans. B. McCoy (New York, 1974), p. 279. In his self-commentary Boccaccio describes Elysium as the dwelling-place of 'the souls of those who had been valiant and good men, who had not, however, deserved to become gods' (trans. McCoy, p. 286).

19. On this genre see especially Barbara Nolan, *Chaucer and the Tradition of the 'Roman Antique'* (Cambridge, 1992), wherein the issue of pagan virtue is discussed extensively. See further the essays edited by Danielle Buschinger, *Le roman antique au Moyen Âge: Actes du Colloque du Centre d'études médiévales de l'Université de Picardie, Amiens, 14–15 Janvier 1989* (Göppingen, 1992). On the genre's origins and continuing popularity see Jean Bessière and Daniel-Henri Pageaux (eds.), *Formes et imaginaire du roman: perspectives sur le roman antique, médiéval, classique, moderne et contemporain* (Paris, 1998).

20. *Eneas. Roman du XIIe siècle*, ed. J.-J. Salverda de Grave (Paris, 1925–9), 1. 66; trans. John A. Yunck, *Eneas: A Twelfth-Century French Romance* (New York, 1974), p. 99.

21. For recent discussion see Alastair Minnis (ed.), *Chaucer's 'Boece' and the Medieval Tradition of Boethius* (Woodbridge, 1993).

22. See Minnis, 'Aspects of the Medieval French and English Traditions of the *De Consolatione Philosophiae*', p. 342; Minnis, *Chaucer and Pagan Antiquity*, p. 100.

23. *Responsiones ad argumenta Radulfi Strode*, in John Wyclif, *Opera minora*, ed. J. Loserth (London, 1913), p. 181.

24. On the problem of reconciling necessity and future contingency in Bradwardine's theology, see especially Dolnikowski, *Bradwardine: A View of Time*, pp. 165–207. The intellectual context in which he worked is brought to life in Katherine H. Tachau's magisterial *Vision and Certitude in the Age of Ockham: Optics, Epistemology, and the Foundations of Semantics, 1250–1345* (Leiden and New York, 1988). See further Paul A. Streveler and Katherine H. Tachau (eds.), *Robert Holcot: Seeing the Future Clearly. Questions on Future Contingents* (Toronto, 1995), esp. pp. 47–55. On the attempt made by fellow-Mertonian Thomas Buckingham (d. 1349) to refute the arguments of *De causa Dei*, see Bartholomew R. De la Torre, *Thomas Buckingham and the Contingency of Futures: The Possibility of Human Freedom* (Notre Dame, IN, 1987), esp. pp. 91–140.

25. See for example Wyclif's use of the idea in *De potestate pape*, ed. J. Loserth (London, 1907), p. 313, and Thomas Netter's critique of his alleged necessitarianism, *Doctrinale*, III, col. 372. For a substantial and sympathetic attempt to deduce what Wyclif really did think (which emphasizes the measure of contingency that Wyclif's theory allows), see Ian Christopher Levy, 'Wyclif and the Christian Life', in Levy (ed.), *Companion to Wyclif*, pp. 293–363 (esp. p. 356).

26. As Nicholas Watson says; 'Visions of Inclusion', 151. The fullest account of this bizarre text and its reception is by Iain Macleod Higgins, *Writing East: The 'Travels' of Sir John Mandeville* (Philadelphia, 1997). A discussion was also included in T. G. Hahn's groundbreaking thesis – which, because it was never formally published, has not enjoyed the influence it deserves: 'God's Friends: Virtuous Heathen in Later Medieval Thought and English Literature' (Ph.D. diss., University of California at Los Angeles, 1974).

27. Discussed and quoted by Benson, *Public 'Piers Plowman'*, p. 148.

28. G. H. Russell has argued that there are major differences between Langland's treatment of the 'salvation of the heathen' theme in the B- and C-texts; in the later text he finds a 'quite different line of thought', a 'projection of what seems to be a new attitude to one of the notoriously difficult problems confronting medieval Christian thinking'. 'Some Aspects of the Process of Revision in *Piers Plowman*', in S. S. Hussey (ed.), *Piers Plowman: Critical Approaches* (London, 1969), pp. 27–49 (p. 46); this builds on his earlier study 'The Salvation of the Heathen: The Exploration of a Theme in *Piers Plowman*'. However, I myself do not believe that the revisions add up to such a significant change. In the C-text St Gregory retains his crucial role (as described below) in effecting Trajan's salvation.

29. Here 'Sarasen' (meaning 'Muslim') is of course being used as a synonym for 'heathen' or 'pagan'.

30. Coleman, *'Piers Plowman' and the 'Moderni'*, pp. 133–4.
31. Adams, 'Piers's Pardon', 392.
32. The clause 'and that is ferme bileve' has been taken as a gloss on 'fullyng' by 'fir', the idea being that here is an allusion to the relationship between steadfast faith and *baptismus flaminis* (cf. the ways in which Aquinas and Bonaventure explain this, cited on pp. 47 and 48 below). On the other hand, 'and that is ferme bileve' may be understood as a statement concerning the entire doctrine of the three kinds of baptism as explained in this passage; i.e. *all* of what has been said here constitutes a 'ferme bileve' of Christianity. This suggestion is lent support by the C-text reading, 'and al is ferme bileue' (Pearsall, xiv. 208).
33. Book iv, dist. iv, cap. 4; in Peter Lombard, *Sententiae in IV Libris Distinctae*, 3rd edn (Grottaferrata, 1971–81), ii. 255–9.
34. Aquinas, *Summa theologiae*, 3a 66, ii, responsio, lvii. 48–9. By rendering *baptismus flaminis* as 'baptism by fire' I am following Langland's translation; alternatively it may be rendered 'baptism of the wind' or 'blowing' or indeed 'of the spirit'; cf. the note by James Cunningham, Aquinas, *Summa theologiae*, lvii. 48. The conflation of *flamma* ('fire') and *flamen* ('a blowing') is understandable in view of the account of Pentecost in Acts 2:2–4, 'And suddenly there came a sound from leaven, as of a mighty wind coming . . . And there appeared to them parted tongues, as it were of fire . . . And they were all filled with the Holy Ghost.'
35. *In IV Sent.*, dist. iv, qu. 3, art. 3, questiunc. 2; *Aquinatis opera*, vii. 520.
36. However, as has often been noted (see for example Adams, 'Langland's Theology', p. 98) Trajan was born well after the beginning of the Christian era, and hence his historical circumstances were highly favourable. As Adams notes ('Langland's Theology', p. 98), 'the standard opinion was that such persons could enter heaven only through baptism', given that the Christian belief-system was on offer to them. However, vernacular writers often blurred together pagans from various historical periods into a single vague category. Hence Chaucer is not interested in stating that his 'Tartre Cambyuskan' was born after the advent of Christ (if we may assume that Chaucer had in mind an historical character such as Genghis Khan or Kublai Khan). Besides, none of the scholastic applications of the Trajan story which I have read specifically raise this issue in considering his salvation. And such a questioning of the emperor's acumen is, as one would expect, quite absent from 'classicizing' accounts of Trajan, such as John of Salisbury's, wherein he is presented as 'the epitome not only of benignly just and successful rulership, of government based on rational virtue and natural wisdom, but also of personal morality and justice' (as Gordon Whatley puts it; 'The Uses of Hagiography: The Legend of Pope Gregory and the Emperor Trajan in the Middle Ages', *Viator*, 15 (1984), 25–63 (p. 33)).
37. *In IV Sent*, dist. iv, p. 2, qu.1, art. 1; *Bonaventurae opera*, iv.106–7.
38. Jacobus de Voragine (Jacopo da Varazze), *The Golden Legend*, trans. W. G. Ryan (Princeton, NJ, 1993), i. 179; for the Latin text see *Legenda aurea. Vulgo historia Lombardica dicta*, ed. T. Graesse, 3rd edn (1890; repr. Osnabrück,

1969), pp. 196–7. The first of these theories loosely follows Aquinas's *Sentences* commentary, while the second is a verbatim quotation from it. John the Deacon's ninth-century *Vita sancti Gregorii* (printed in Migne, *PL* 75, 59–242) takes the line that Gregory merely wept for Trajan, whose degree of suffering in hell was thereby lessened: the emperor was not actually released from his place of torment. Cf. Whatley, 'Uses of Hagiography', 28–30.

39. Paolo Molteni, *Roberto Holcot O.P., Dottrina della grazia e della giustificazione, con due questioni quodlibetali inedite* (Pinerolo, 1967), pp. 174–204.

40. For late medieval thought on God's absolute and ordained powers see H. A. Oberman, *The Harvest of Medieval Theology. Gabriel Biel and Late Medieval Nominalism*, rev. edn (Grand Rapids, MI, 1967), pp. 30–56; Marilyn McCord Adams, *William Ockham* (Notre Dame, IN, 1987), II. 1186–207; Eugenio Randi, *Il sovrano e l'orologiaio. Due immagini di Dio nel dibattito sulla 'potentia absoluta' fra XIII e XIV secolo* (Florence, 1987); W. J. Courtenay, *Covenant and Causality in Medieval Thought* (London, 1984), and *Capacity and Volition: A History of the Distinction of Absolute and Ordained Power* (Bergamo, 1990); Stephen F. Brown, 'Abelard and the Medieval Origins of the Distinction between God's Absolute and Ordained Power', in M. D. Jordan and K. Emery Jr (eds.), *Ad Litteram. Authoritative Texts and their Medieval Readers* (Notre Dame, IN, and London, 1992), pp. 199–215; Lawrence Moonan, *Divine Power: The Medieval Power Distinction up to its Adoption by Albert, Bonaventure, and Aquinas* (Oxford, 1994); and of course Wood, 'Ockham's Repudiation of Pelagianism'.

41. 'Argumentum suum eque procedit absque illa condicione sicut cum illa': A. Pelzer, 'Les 51 articles de Guillaume Occam censurés en Avignon en 1326', *Revue d'histoire ecclésiastique*, 18 (1922), 240–71 (p. 252); cf. Gordon Leff, *Bradwardine and the Pelagians* (Cambridge, 1957), p. 191.

42. William of Ockham, *Philosophical Writings*, ed. and trans. P. Boehner (London, 1957), pp. xix–xx, xlviii–xlix.

43. Courtenay, 'The Dialectic of Divine Omnipotence in the Age of Chaucer: A Reconsideration', pp. 114, 116–17.

44. For these, and other, examples see William of Ockham, *Quodlibetal Questions*, trans. A. J. Freddoso and F. E. Kelley (New Haven and London, 1991), pp. 42, 120, 290, 304, 324, 376, 587–8, and 500–2. The theologians who sought to ridicule Walter Brut's claim that women can, in certain circumstances at least, confect the Eucharist, came up with even more bizarre examples; see pp. 96–7 below.

45. Cf. Leff, *Bradwardine and the Pelagians*, pp. 74–9.

46. Oberman, *Harvest of Medieval Theology*, pp. 471–2; cf. Gordon Leff, *William of Ockham: The Metamorphosis of Scholastic Discourse* (Manchester, 1975), pp. 494–5.

47. 'Pelagius held that grace is not in fact required in order to have eternal life, but that an act elicited in a purely natural state merits eternal life condignly. I, on the other hand, claim that such an act is meritorious only through God's absolute power accepting it [as such].' *Quodlibet VI*, qu. 1, art. 1, in

William of Ockham: Quodlibetal Questions, trans. Freddoso and Kelley, p. 493.
On Ockham's insistence on the freedom of God see further H. R. Klocker,
'Ockham and the Divine Freedom', *Franciscan Studies*, 45 (1985), 245–61; also
Adams, *William Ockham*, ii. 1257–347.

48. Ockham, *In IV Sent.*, quaestiones 10–11, solutio dubiorum; *Quaestiones in
Librum Quartum Sententiarum (Reportatio)*, ed. Riga Wood and Gedeon Gál,
Opera theologica 7 (St Bonaventure, NY, 1984), p. 233. Quoted and discussed
by Leff, *Bradwardine and the Pelagians*, p. 205n.

49. Cf. Oberman, *Harvest of Medieval Theology*, pp. 235–48.

50. Cf. the even more cautious statement of Scripture at в x. 344–55, that mere
baptism (apparently *baptismus fluminis*) may suffice *in extremis* for the salvation
of 'Sarsens and Jewis', but more is required of 'Cristene men'.

51. Coleman, *'Piers Plowman' and the 'Moderni'*, p. 141.

52. Here I cite W. W. Skeat's edition of the c-text ((Oxford, 1886), i. 461), which
at this point I prefer to Pearsall's reading (= xvii. 123–4; p. 283). Hereafter
(and as before) all citations of the c-text are from Pearsall's edition.

53. Adams, 'Piers's Pardon', 392.

54. Coleman, *'Piers Plowman' and the 'Moderni'*, pp. 126, 134, 146, 195.

55. Moreover, quite extraordinary opinions were sometimes expressed in the
form of *dubitationes* ('doubtful statements'); thus the scholastic method could
license the expressions of radical, even bizarre, thoughts, ultimately controlling
them within the framework of the disputation.

56. The term 'boone' may be Englishing the Latin term *petitio* as used in Jacobus's
report of what was said by the voice of God: 'I have granted your petition.'
Cf. *Legenda aurea*, ed. Graesse, p. 196.

57. As is well brought out in Whatley's excellent article, 'Uses of Hagiography'.

58. My argument concerning the significance of Gregory's tears has been antici-
pated by Gradon ('*Trajanus Redivivus*', p. 104), who however takes the text's
rejection of masses as possible evidence of Langland's concern 'to point out that
Trajan was saved by his own merits'. But this rejection may be explained, at
least in part, by the argument that masses are being seen as an aspect of clergial
learning, which here is being opposed not only to specific achievement but also
to spiritual 'affection' in general, as I suggest below. Even more importantly,
the rejection of masses certainly does not constitute a rejection of Gregory's
role altogether. See further Whatley ('Uses of Hagiography', 53), who, whilst
noting the influence of 'the old hagiographical tradition established by John
the Deacon' that 'Gregory did not actually pray for Trajan but only wept for
him', nevertheless regards Gregory in Langland's text as a sort of functionless
fossil, an aspect of the legend which 'was impossible to dislodge . . . entirely'; in
Whatley's view it rather gets in the way of what Langland was really interested
in, the fact that 'Trajan was outside the Church's sacramental system when
he was saved'. I would allow Gregory more significance than that. Moreover,
Whatley argues that the rejection of the pope's prayer 'seems to contradict
ll. 146–9, which describe Gregory's intercessory tears *and prayers*' (p. 53, my
emphasis). In fact, ll. 146–9 do not mention prayers at all, simply the pope's
desire or 'will' that the emperor should be saved, which wish was expressed

(in Langland's version) through tears rather than prayers. It may be added, however, that tears could perform an intercessory function similar to that performed by prayers, according to the medieval theology of compunction, on which see Sandra J. McEntire, *The Doctrine of Compunction in Medieval England: Holy Tears* (Lewiston, 1990). McEntire documents the belief that tears may benefit not only one's own spiritual situation but also that of another (pp. 29–30, 64–5, 104, 145, 153, 155, 157, 159, 174–5).

59. *Summa aurea*, lib. IV, tract. xviii, cap. 4, qu. I, in William of Auvergne, *Summa aurea*, ed. Jean Ribaillier (Paris and Grottaferrata, 1980–5), IV. 536.

60. Aquinas, *De veritate*, qu. 6, art. 6; trans. Robert W. Mulligan, James V. McGlynn, and Robert W. Schmidt, *Truth: St Thomas Aquinas* (Chicago, 1952–4), I. 286.

61. *De veritate*, qu. 14, art. II; trans. Mulligan, McGlynn, and Schmidt, II. 262. Here Aquinas is rather more optimistic about the spiritual development of one brought up in a 'wilde wildernesse' full of 'wilde beestes' than was Langland (cf. p. 52 above).

62. As the *Legenda aurea* puts it; trans. Ryan, I. 178.

63. On this line see especially Whatley, '*Piers Plowman* B 12.277–94', pp. 5–6.

64. As when, according to Ockham, *de potentia dei absoluta* He saved certain people in antiquity without *any* kind of baptism, whether by water, blood or fire. See Ockham's *Tractatus contra Benedictum*, III. 3, in *Opera politica*, III, ed. H. S. Offler (Manchester, 1956), p. 233.

65. *Pace* A. V. C. Schmidt (*Piers Plowman: A New Translation* (Oxford, 1992), p. 307n) there is no reason to take such statements as *Quia voluit* ('Because his will was it should be!', B XII. 216) as referring to *potentia absoluta*. Absolute power is not needed for the activities of God's helping hand as described here.

66. *De veritate*, qu. 14, art. II; trans. Mulligan, McGlynn, and Schmidt, II. 263.

67. Alexander of Hales, *Summa theologica* (Quaracchi, 1924–48), III. 331.

68. See especially Robert Holcot, *Sapientiae Regis Salamonis praelectiones* (Basel, 1586), pp. 103, 348, 521–3; cf. Holcot's *Sentences* commentary, *In I Sent.*, qu. iv, art. 3, Q (Lyon, 1497), unfol. See further the discussion in Minnis, *Chaucer and Pagan Antiquity*, pp. 56–9.

69. I retain my view of the quite positive role played by Ymaginatif, as argued in my article, 'Langland's Ymaginatif and Late-Medieval Theories of Imagination', *Comparative Criticism*, 3 (1981), 71–103; subsequently this approach was reinforced by Ernest Kaulbach, *Imaginative Prophecy in the B-text of 'Piers Plowman'* (Cambridge, 1993). Such a view, however, is quite compatible with the one expressed here, namely that Langland chose not to put the opinions in question in the mouth of an authority-figure whose status was unequivocally of the highest order.

70. Wyclif, *Tractatus de ecclesia*, ed. Loserth, p. 531.

71. *Tractatus de ecclesia*, ed. Loserth, pp. 533–4.

72. Netter, *Doctrinale*, v. 96–7 (II. 563–75; cf. II. 611–15). Netter is responding to Wyclif, *Trialogus*, ed. G. V. Lechler (Oxford, 1869), pp. 281–92. See further the discussion in Hudson, *Premature Reformation*, pp. 290–4.

73. 'One of the soldiers with a spear opened his side: and immediately there came out blood and water'. See further John 5:6 and 8.
74. *Responsiones ad argumenta Radulfi Strode*, in Wyclif, *Opera minora*, ed. Loserth, pp. 176–8.
75. Wyclif then proceeds to apply the same principle to the priesthood, coming close to saying that the 'true sons of God' are best equipped to perform the priestly office, even though they may not have been consecrated by a bishop, and lack the priestly tonsure and the *character* which formal ordination imposes.
76. Netter, *Doctrinale*, II. 573–5.
77. Netter, *Doctrinale*, II. 575–6. Wyclif's sacramental theology was, of course, rather more complicated than this, as is well brought out by Hudson, *Premature Reformation*, pp. 281–301, and Stephen Penn, 'Sacraments', in Levy (ed.), *Companion to John Wyclif*, pp. 241–91.
78. Wyclif, *Opera minora*, ed. Loserth, p. 178.
79. Netter, *Doctrinale*, III. 342.
80. *Registrum Johannis Trefnant*, ed. Capes, p. 243.
81. See Hudson, *Premature Reformation*, p. 141.
82. See Minnis, *Chaucer: The Shorter Poems*, pp. 20, 26.
83. Thomas Walsingham, *Historia anglicana*, ed. Riley, II. 253; John Trokelowe, Henry Blaneforde *et al.*, *Chronica et annales* (London, 1866), p. 348.
84. Thomas Walsingham, *Historia anglicana*, ed. Riley, II. 253; Trokelowe, Blaneforde *et al.*, *Chronica et annales*, p. 348.
85. K. B. McFarlane, *Lancastrian Kings and Lollard Knights* (Oxford, 1972), p. 212.
86. Cf. Hudson, *Premature Reformation*, p. 114.
87. At best, James Palmer was in minor orders; see Lucy Freeman Sandler, *Omne bonum: A Fourteenth-Century Encyclopedia of Universal Knowledge* (London, 1996), I. 26. Cf. Penn R. Szittya, *The Antifraternal Tradition in Medieval Literature* (Princeton, 1986), pp. 67–81; also my discussion in Chapter 4 below. Furthermore, there is the fact that, in early fourteenth-century England, schoolmen produced books which achieved a popularity beyond the schools, such as Holcot's Wisdom commentary, Thomas Ringstead's Proverbs commentary, Bradwardine's *De causa Dei*, and Richard Fitzralph's *Summa in questionibus Armenorum*. Such works helped prepare the ground for the vernacular theology which is a feature of the second half of the century – and perhaps even for Wyclif's appeal to secular textual communities.
88. David Aers, 'Christianity for Courtly Subjects: Reflections on the *Gawain*-Poet', in Derek Brewer and Jonathan Gibson (eds.), *A Companion to the 'Gawain'-Poet* (Woodbridge, 1997), pp. 91–101 (pp. 99, 101). One of the many fascinating issues raised in this stimulating paper is the possibility that Gawain's so-called 'confession' of his fault to Bertilak near the end of the poem can be read as a reflex of the doctrine that 'in an emergency "if no priest is available, one can gain God's forgiveness if one desires it and confesses one's crime to one's [lay] companion"'. This was a perfectly orthodox doctrine, but one

which, in the late fourteenth century, could bespeak Lollard sympathy, given the Wycliffite belief that 'absolution can only be licit if it is declarative of God's prior and quite independent forgiveness' (p. 98). To which may be added the point that some Wycliffites declared it was far better to confess to a virtuous layman than to a corrupt priest. However, a crucial part of the orthodox doctrine, as expressed in Peter Lombard's *Libri sententiarum*, Book IV, dist. xvii (and elaborated in a long tradition of commentary on this *distinctio*), was that 'the sinner' is not 'truly humble and penitent if he does not desire and seek the judgment of the priest'. If one confesses to a companion, that action is given value only by the evidence it affords of one's 'desire for a priest' – and a priest should be sought subsequently. In other words, confession to a (non-ordained) companion is efficacious only if the sinner is unable to seek, or prevented from seeking (for example, by death), a priest following his initial confession. Lombard, *Lib. sent.*, IV, dist. xvii, capi. 3, 8; 4, 1; 4, 8 (*Sententiae in IV libris distinctae*, II. 350, 351, 353); cf. E. F. Rogers, *Peter Lombard and the Sacramental System* (New York, 1976), pp. 180–6. Returning to *Sir Gawain*: while we do not see Gawain seeking a priest after his encounter with Bertilak, there is nothing to suggest that he has rejected that course of action – a statement to that effect *would* be quite suspicious.

89. As I argue in '*I speke of folk in seculer estaat*: Vernacularity and Secularity in the Age of Chaucer', *SAC*, 27 (2005), 25–58.

90. Nicholas Watson, 'The *Gawain*-Poet as a Vernacular Theologian', in Brewer and Gibson (eds.), *A Companion to the 'Gawain'-Poet*, pp. 293–313 (p. 296). Watson seems to be offering a more moderate version of the Aers approach when he remarks, 'Nowhere does a clerical author refashion his role as homilist to the point where his writing is so fully taken over – on a moral, social, and aesthetic level – by the mores of his [aristocratic] audience' (p. 313). However, whereas Aers punishes the *Gawain*-poet for not being Langland, Watson reacts against his 'indifference to interiority' – in other words, he wishes the anonymous author was more like Julian of Norwich. Cf. Watson, 'The *Gawain*-Poet as a Vernacular Theologian', p. 296, and Hugh White's relevant comments in his review of the Brewer and Gibson anthology, in *The Review of English Studies*, 49.195 (1998), 345–7 (p. 346). The house of late medieval Christianity had, I would like to believe, many mansions, some more ornately decorated than others.

91. I.e. into the vineyard of Christian life. Some scholars have, however, detected traces of Pelagianism elsewhere in the poem; cf. the discussion in my introductory chapter. I remain unconvinced.

92. To some extent this story derives from the version of the Trajan legend in which the virtuous pagan is briefly restored to life in order to receive baptism; on this see Whatley, 'Uses of Hagiography', pp. 37–9. This specific precedent is not considered by Clifford Peterson in the introduction to his edition of *Saint Erkenwald* (Philadelphia, 1977), where the poet is credited with having brought together 'the incorrupt body theme and the Trajan-Gregory legend' (p. 42).

93. As Eamon Duffy puts it, 'The emotional and theological dilemmas of the poem are acutely felt, but are resolved not by stretching theological categories, but by an artistic *coup* – the convergence of human pity, moral bafflement, and the demands of theological orthodoxy, in the sacramental efficacy of the bishop's words and tears. The priestly character of the saint is heavily emphasized throughout the poem, and the saint himself delivers a stinging rebuke to the human curiosity and rationalist presumption which might seek a solution to the problem of human salvation outside the orthodox framework of grace and revelation.' 'St Erkenwald: London's Cathedral Saint and his Legend', in Janet Backhouse (ed.), *The Medieval English Cathedral: Papers in Honour of Pamela Tudor-Craig* (Donington, Lincolnshire, 2003), pp. 150–67 (pp. 158–9). A similar reading of *St Erkenwald* was offered previously by Gordon Whatley, who regards the poem as 'a conservative and defensive response' to what he describes as 'the markedly secular character of the Gregory/Trajan story in the late medieval period', a narrative pattern which, he believes, influenced Langland's treatment of Trajan; 'Heathens and Saints: *St Erkenwald* in its Legendary Context', *Speculum*, 61.2 (1986), 330–63. My own reading of the Trajan episode narrows the distance here postulated between *Piers Plowman* and *St Erkenwald*.

94. *St Erkenwald*, ed. Ruth Morse (Cambridge, 1975), p. 64.

95. The careful conservatism of these two poems is particularly significant in light of the condemned opinions of Uthred of Boldon OSB (*c.* 1320–97), Oxford theologian and one-time opponent of Wyclif, who was accused of believing that baptism was unnecessary for the salvation of pagans, Jews, and unbaptized infants. For instance, the eighth proposition condemned in 1368 stated that 'the sacrament of baptism . . . is not requisite to the salvation of any dying infant'. Uthred claimed that his ideas had been grossly oversimplified, and (proceeding from the traditional doctrine of the three types of baptism) offered an argument which affords great importance to *baptismus flaminis*. While certainly not saying anything derogatory about *baptismus fluminis*, Uthred holds that *baptismus flaminis* is all that is necessary for the salvation of either an infant or an adult. In marked contrast, *Pearl* and *St Erkenwald* unequivocally affirm the importance of *baptismus fluminis*. On Uthred's views see M. E. Marcett, *Uthred de Boldon, Friar William Jordan and Piers Plowman* (New York, 1938); M. D. Knowles, 'The Censured Opinions of Uthred of Boldon', *Proceedings of the British Academy*, 37 (1951), 306–42; Kerby-Fulton, *Books under Suspicion*, pp. 360–74. Following Marcett's identification of a possible allusion to Uthred's opponent Friar William Jordan in *Piers Plowman*, various speculations concerning Langland's attitudes to Uthred have been offered; see especially Russell, 'The Salvation of the Heathen'; Kerby-Fulton, *Books under Suspicion*, pp. 375–83, and Ralph Hanna III, *William Langland* (Aldershot, 1993), p. 13. In my own view, if Langland did indeed allude to Jordan (at B XIII. 84, 'I schal iangle to this jurdan', with a pun on 'jordan' = 'chamber pot'; cf. p. 156 below) he was an incidental rather than a primary target of Langland's satire, which concerns conscience-free academic learning in general.

96. Therefore I cannot accept Kerby-Fulton's suggestion (*Books under Suspicion*, p. 375, cf. p. 495n) that Langland 'held the A text back from circulation for so long' because of fears raised by the 1368 condemnation of Uthred of Boldon's views on exceptional salvations, on which see the previous note. 'Langland was no fool about sensitive or dangerous issues', as Kerby-Fulton says (p. 377); hence the care and discretion he applied in treating of the virtuous heathen. So there was no need to withhold the text.

97. Thomas Walsingham, *Historia anglicana*, ed. Riley, II. 253; Trokelowe, Blaneforde *et al.*, *Chronica et annales*, p. 348; cf. McFarlane, *Lancastrian Kings*, p. 212, and Hudson, *Premature Reformation*, p. 114.

98. In this regard it should be noted that in the C-text Langland places extreme predestinarian views in the mouth of the figure Recklessness; see C XI. 196–311.

99. With this statement regarding Lollardy, cf. Hudson, *Premature Reformation*, p. 403. Of course, this is not to question the occasional resemblances and parallels between certain passages of *Piers* and aspects of Lollard thought, on which see Hudson's full discussion, pp. 400–8; also her article '*Piers Plowman* and the Peasants' Revolt: A Problem Revisited', *The Yearbook of Langland Studies*, 8 (1994), 85–106 (pp. 85–6).

100. As evidenced by, for example, Wyclif's attacks on 'worshippers of signs' (*cultores signorum*) and 'doctors of signs' (*doctores signorum*), possibly to be identified as Nominalists. On such remarks see Penn, 'Sacraments', pp. 248, 265–7.

101. Grady, *Representing Righteous Heathens*, pp. 6, 7. Cf. pp. 5 above and 167 n. 26 below, where Nicholas Watson's argument for the existence of a vernacular theology of universal salvation is also discussed.

102. David Benson has argued that 'the poet, and even more important, his readers, need not have been advanced theologians to be familiar' with 'non-standard' ideas concerning virtuous heathen; *Public 'Piers Plowman'*, p. 148. Similarly, Ralph Hanna III has reacted against what he describes as 'the recent tendency to bring high medieval learnedness to bear upon Ymaginatif' by locating some of Langland's materials among 'sub-learned' grammar school discourse and 'the oddments parish priests routinely collected and jotted down in their working books'; 'Langland's Ymaginatif: Images and the Limits of Poetry', in Dimmick, Simpson, and Zeeman (eds.), *Images, Idolatry, and Iconoclasm*, pp. 81–94 (p. 89). These points are well made, and I myself am keen to emphasize Langland's debt to populist religious belief and practice. But the nature of Langland's interest in unconventional salvations seems to put at least parts of Passus XII well within the parameters of 'a "scholastic" or "theological" discourse' (to appropriate Hanna's phrasing, p. 87).

103. On which see n. 95 above.

104. Cf. W. J. Courtenay, 'Theology and Theologians from Ockham to Wyclif', in J. Catto and R. Evans (eds.), *History of the University of Oxford*, II: *Late Medieval* (Oxford, 1992), pp. 1–34 (pp. 33–4); also Kerby-Fulton, *Books under Suspicion*, pp. 373, 377, 392–3.

105. Ralph Higden, *Polychronicon Radulphi Higden*, ed. C. Babington and J. R. Lumby (London, 1865–6), V. 7.

106. And not just in Middle English, of course. Above I quoted the French *Roman d'Aneas*; there are several other ambitious romances of antiquity in that vernacular, including the *Roman de Thebes* and Benoît de Sainte-Maure's *Roman de Troie*, both known to Chaucer. Special mention should be made of the *Willehalm* on which Wolfram von Eschenbach worked during the second decade of the thirteenth century. Here the Saracen knights who are Guillaume d'Orange's foes are lavishly described in all their colourful glory and exemplary chivalry, and the hero's beloved, Queen Giburc, is a converted pagan. She defends the besieged town of Orange in Willehalm's absence, refusing to relinquish her new faith in the face of threats (together with a lively *reductio ad absurdum* of Christian doctrine) from her own father, who is leading the Saracen forces. Subsequently, in an extraordinary speech, Giburc declares that the first man God created was a pagan, as were Elijah and Enoch; 'Noah, too, who was saved in the Ark, . . . and Job was certainly also one, but God did not cast him down on that account.' 'Heathens are not all condemned to perdition', she exclaims; 'after all, we were all of us heathens once.' Willehalm also believes that pagans are God's creatures, and therefore their indiscriminate slaughter is sinful; it grieves him to think 'that their god Tervigant may have destined them for hell'. Wolfram von Eschenbach, *Willehalm*, trans. Marion E. Gibbs and Sidney M. Johnson (London, 1984), pp. 155–6, 218, 26.

3 PIERS'S PROTEAN PARDON: LANGLAND ON THE LETTER AND SPIRIT OF INDULGENCES

1. Letter T278/G357, probably to Bartolomea di Domenico; *Lettere di S. Caterina da Siena*, ed. N. Tommasèo and P. Misciattelli (Florence, 1939–47), IV. 188; trans. Suzanne Noffke, *The Letters of Catherine of Siena* (Tempe, AZ, 2000–7), II. 353.
2. *Extravagantium communium*, v: de simonia, tit. IX, cap. 2; *Corpus iuris canonici*, ed. E. A. Friedberg and E. L. Richter (Leipzig, 1879–81), II. 1304. The power of the keys is discussed below.
3. As Eamon Duffy says, the process may be likened to a 'transfer of credit to an over-drawn current account from an abundant deposit account'; *Stripping of the Altars*, p. 288. See further Shaffern, *The Penitents' Treasury*, pp. 79–88, and his article, 'Images, Jurisdiction, and the Treasury of Merit', *Journal of Medieval History*, 22.3 (1996), 237–47. An indulgence was concerned solely with the satisfaction due for the requisite penitential punishment. It alleviated the 'temporal' punishments (on which more below) that the sinner would have to undergo whether in this life or in the next, i.e. in purgatory; its power certainly did not extend to the eternal punishments of hell. A plenary indulgence remitted all of the *pena*, whereas a partial indulgence remitted part of it (the exact amount being specified in the bull which authorized and announced the issue of the pardons in question). Sometimes one and the same pardon could offer different amounts of remission to different categories of people, a point of some importance for our ensuing discussion.

4. '*Quaestor*' was the normal Latin term for a Pardoner – designating one who 'sought out' alms from sundry folk. Cf. the anonymous *Memoriale presbitero-rum*, III. 43: 'Questores dicitur a querendo, eo quod mittuntur ad querendum elemosinas fidelium'. Cambridge, Corpus Christi College, 148, fol. 77r. The *Memoriale* goes on to explain that the alms collected in this way are used in the service of hospitals and the sick people therein, and for the repair of churches, together with bridges and roads (to ensure easy access to hospitals and churches). This treatise dates from the mid-fourteenth century, and has a connection with Norwich Cathedral Priory. On the problems of licensing and controlling those who preached for alms (*pro questu*) see Forrest, *Detection of Heresy*, pp. 60–3.

5. John Heywood, *The Plays*, ed. Richard Axton and Peter Happé (Cambridge, 1991), p. 114.

6. *In IV Sent.*, dist. XX, E, art. 17, sed contra, 3, in *Alberti opera*, XXIX. 850. Cf. the *Summa* of Alexander of Hales (which was completed by Alexander's pupils after his death), pars IV, qu. 83, mem. 1, art. 1; *Summa theologica: pars quarta* (s.l., 1516), fol. 130v.

7. *In IV Sent.*, dist. XX, qu. 1, art. 3, sed contra and sol. 1; *Aquinatis opera*, VII.2. 843–4.

8. As Langland puts it in Passus VII. 183ff, where Matthew 16:19 is cited once again, Piers – who by now has morphed into St Peter – was authorized by Christ to 'assoile of alle manere synnes'. The ending of the Pardon Passus may also be compared with the use made of Matthew 16:19 in *The Pricke of Conscience*, IV. 3798–951, where it features within an orthodox defence of indulgences, 'þe tresur of haly kirke', and the 'playn power' of the pope (as 'Godes vicar') to 'Louse and bynde at his wille': *The Pricke of Conscience*, ed. Richard Morris (Berlin, 1863), pp. 103–8.

9. 'Indulgentiae autem facere pertinet ad clavem iurisdictionis, non autem ad clavem ordinis', to quote William Lyndwood's *Provinciale*, lib. v, tit. 16; *Provinciale seu constitutiones angliae* (Oxford, 1679; repr. Farnborough, Hants., 1968), p. 336. There was considerable controversy over whether bishops could act autonomously in the granting of indulgences.

10. To make matters even more complicated, *both* of these actions could be, and often were, characterized as *absolutio* from sin; cf. the two senses of this term, as discussed below.

11. Membership of confraternities, as run (for instance) by the various orders of friars, offered many spiritual advantages, including participation in what may be called a 'group indulgence' (cf. p. 75 below), together with the right to choose one's own confessor, and burial with all the ecclesiastical trimmings. See R. N. Swanson, 'Letters of Confraternity and Indulgence in Late Medieval England', *Archives: The Journal of the British Records Association*, 25.102 (2000), 40–57.

12. Cf. R. N. Swanson, 'Treasuring Merit/Craving Indulgence: Accounting for Salvation in Pre-Reformation England', inaugural lecture, University of Birmingham (Birmingham, 2003), p. 6. The Lollard William Swinderby ridiculed trust in material indulgences on the grounds that they could easily 'be lost,

drenchede, or brende, or a rat myghte eten hem'. *Registrum Johannis Trefnant*, ed. Capes, pp. 247–8.

13. *Pricke of Conscience*, ed. Morris, p. 104.

14. *Pricke of Conscience*, ed. Morris, p. 106.

15. There were, to be sure, other requirements for valid pardoning. As Thomas Aquinas explains, in addition to the recipient being in possession of charity, there had to be a good cause for the issuing of the indulgence and the person who issued it had to have the authority to do so. Cf. *In IV Sent.*, dist. xx, qu. 1, art. 3, quaestiunc. 2, sol.; *Aquinatis opera*, vii.2. 844–5.

16. Lyndwood, *Provinciale*, lib. iii, tit. 23 (pp. 231–2). A brief discussion of this passage may be found in Margaret Harvey, *England, Rome and the Papacy 1417–1464* (Manchester and New York, 1993), p. 237.

17. An unusual variation on this theme may be found in the *vita* of Catherine of Genoa (1447–1510), who was so concerned to subject herself to divine justice, and be 'thoroughly chastised', that 'she refrained from using indulgences, and also from recommending herself to the intercession of others, so as ever to be subject to every punishment and condemned as she deserved'. We are assured that Catherine does indeed hold 'plenary indulgences' in 'great reverence and devotion', and considers 'them to be most useful and of great value'. The point is rather that 'her own self-seeking part' should, she believes, be 'chastised and punished' as it deserves. See Catherine of Genoa, *Life and Sayings*, ed. and trans. Paul Garvin (New York, 1964), p. 104.

18. *Provinciale*, lib. iii, tit. 23 (p. 231).

19. Alliterating phrases about 'purchasing pardon' sometimes occur in Middle English, but they should not automatically be understood to mean 'buying' with money or some other form of collateral: the *MED* attests the sense of 'acquiring' or 'obtaining' – or indeed 'earning'. Turning to the theology of indulgences, it should be recognized that not all acquisitions of indulgences involved money changing hands, and even when money *was* involved, this was not enough to acquire the total benefit of an indulgence. In order to have any hope of that, the sinner had to be cleansed of *culpa*, as already noted. See further Alastair Minnis, 'Purchasing Pardon: Material and Spiritual Economies on the Canterbury Pilgrimage', in Lawrence Besserman (ed.), *Sacred and Secular in Medieval and Early Modern Cultures* (Houndmills, 2006), pp. 63–82.

20. By contrast, the legal right to issue indulgences derived from possession of a quite separate basis of authority, the 'key' of jurisdiction, as explained above.

21. For discussion see Minnis, *Fallible Authors*, pp. 109–10, 163, 391n, 392–3n, 432n.

22. 'Non potest dare indulgentiam a pena et a culpa, quia culpa est materia repugnans indulgentie; non enim remittitur nisi per contritionem et confessionem . . .'; 'in foro iudiciali non potest absolvere a culpa, sed tantum in penitentiali'. Francis proceeds to defend the papal curia against the charge that it has issued indulgences *a pena et a culpa*. *In IV Sent.*, dist. xix, qu. 3; Francis of Meyronnes, *Commentarius in libros sententiarum*, etc. (Venice, 1520; repr. Frankfurt, 1966), fol. 207r.

23. For these citations, and further discussion of the issue, see Nikolaus Paulus, 'Die Anfänge des sogenannten Ablasses von Schuld und Strafe', *Zeitschrift für katholische Theologie*, 36 (1912), 67–96 (especially pp. 93, 94); and also Shaffern, *The Penitents' Treasury*, pp. 157–9.
24. Thomas Walsingham, *Historia anglicana*, ed. Riley, II. 79–80.
25. Henry Knighton, *Chronicon*, ed. J. R. Lumby (London, 1895; repr. 1965), II. 199.
26. *Select English Works of John Wyclif*, ed. Thomas Arnold (Oxford, 1871), I. 210. For Wyclif's own criticisms of indulgences, and their development by his supporters, see especially Anne Hudson, 'Dangerous Fictions: Indulgences in the Thought of Wyclif and his Followers', in R. N. Swanson (ed.), *Promissory Notes on the Treasury of Merits: Indulgences in Late Medieval Europe* (Leiden and Boston, 2006), pp. 197–214. In his famous *quaestio de indulgentiis* (1412), John Hus follows verbatim Wyclif's arguments in *Tractatus de ecclesia* (ed. Loserth, pp. 549–87). See further the essay by Eva Doležalová, Jan Hrdina, František Šmahel, and Zdeněk Uhlíř, 'The Reception and Criticism of Indulgences in the Late Medieval Czech Lands', also in Swanson (ed.), *Promissory Notes*, pp. 101–41 (esp. pp. 120–41).
27. James Simpson, *Piers Plowman: An Introduction to the B-Text* (London and New York, 1990), p. 72. Simpson goes on to remark that Langland's strategy is 'to use certain penitential practices, like pilgrimage, or the distributing of pardons, as the basis of his narrative, before he suddenly confronts the reader with the inadequacy of such practices' (p. 75). True, but Langland never comes close to condemning the practice of issuing indulgences *per se* – any more than does Chaucer in his *Pardoner's Prologue and Tale*, or Heywood in his two plays which satirize unscrupulous pardoners, *The Foure PP* and *The Pardoner and the Frere*.
28. On the *toties-quoties* indulgences obtainable *c.* 1450 in the Roman churches of Sts Peter and Paul see John Capgrave's eyewitness account: *Ye Solace of Pilgrimes. A Description of Rome circa A.D. 1450*, ed. C. A. Mills (Oxford, 1911), pp. 62–63, 67. This type of indulgence is discussed well by Sumption, *Pilgrimage*, pp. 294–5. A full account of the Capgrave treatise has been provided by Peter J. Lucas, 'An Englishman in Rome: Capgrave's 1450-Jubilee Guide, *The Solace of Pilgrimes*', in Anne Marie D'Arcy and Alan J. Fletcher (eds.), *Studies in Late Medieval and Early Renaissance Texts in Honour of John Scattergood* (Dublin, 2005), pp. 201–17.
29. *Aquinatis opera*, VII.2. 845.
30. However, it may be noted that Boniface IX (1389–1404) finally bowed to pressure and revoked all indulgences which contained misleading statements about remission *a pena et culpa* (clear evidence that many such misleading documents were in circulation). So, at least one set of indulgences was terminated on that occasion. Cf. Henry Charles Lea, *A History of Auricular Confession and Indulgences in the Latin Church* (1896; repr. New York, 1968), III. 66–7.
31. But those children would have to reach the age of discretion before indulgences were of any value to them. This issue is addressed in the first theological

handbook on indulgences, which was written by the Dominican John of Dambach (1288–1372), and is entitled *De virtute indulgenciarum*. (The only surviving fourteenth-century manuscript of this treatise is in the possession of the Austrian Cistercian monastery of Heiligenkreuz, MS 208.) John says that indulgences do not benefit small children, because baptism has removed the punishment owing to original sin, and because they are not old enough to sin intentionally; that is to say, they have no debt of sin. This discussion, which was brought to my attention by Robert Shaffern, may be found on fol. 91r–v of the Heiligenkreuz manuscript.

32. On this major development see Swanson, 'Treasuring Merit/Craving Indulgence', 6.

33. Thus the collective indulgence would offer release from temporal punishment or *pena*, as per usual, while the chosen confessor would absolve from guilt or *culpa*. On such practice see Swanson, 'Letters of Confraternity and Indulgence'.

34. The Pardoner described at B Prol. 68–75 seems to be peddling fraternity membership; each client is tapped on the head with his 'brevet' (bull) as a sign that he or she has been admitted.

35. See for example Thomas Aquinas's discussion of 'the custom of the Church', which assigns 'now a greater, now a lesser indulgence, for the same cause'. The pope may grant 'now a year's indulgence, now one of only forty days' to people visiting one and the same church on different occasions. Or he may specify that an indulgence of five years may be granted 'to those who come from across the seas', but only one of three years 'to those who come from across the mountains'. *In IV Sent.*, dist. xx, qu. 1, art. 3, quaestiunc. 2, sol.; *Aquinatis opera*, VII.2. 844–5.

36. *Pricke of Conscience*, ed. Morris, p. 104.

37. *Quodl.* 2, qu. 8, art. 2, resp.; St Thomas Aquinas, *Quaestiones quodlibetales*, ed. R. Spiazzi, 8th edn (Turin and Rome, 1949), p. 37; trans. S. Edwards, *St. Thomas Aquinas: Quodlibetal Questions 1 and 2* (Toronto, 1983), p. 113. See further R. Cessario, 'St. Thomas Aquinas on Satisfaction, Indulgences, and Crusades', *Medieval Philosophy and Theology*, 2 (1992), 74–96.

38. *In Sent. IV*, dist. xx, pars 2, art. un., qu. 4, ad ob. 4; *Bonaventurae opera*, IV. 537.

39. And Thomas Aquinas notes the fact that 'sometimes the same indulgence is granted to those who preach a crusade as to those who take part in it': *In IV Sent.*, dist. xx, qu. 1, art. 3, sol., ad 2um; *Aquinatis opera*, VII.2. 843.

40. Cf. Diana Webb, *Pilgrims and Pilgrimage in the Medieval West* (London and New York, 1999), pp. 65–8, and Sumption, *Pilgrimage*, p. 241. See further Debra J. Birch, *Pilgrimage to Rome in the Middle Ages: Continuity and Change* (Woodbridge, 1998), pp. 142–3, 179–81, 194–6. Here, as in so many areas relating to indulgences, the rich and powerful inevitably received special treatment. See also B. Matray's statistics concerning the indulgence grants made by two popes to aristocrats and high-ranking churchmen; 'Les indulgences au XIVe siècle: étude des lettres de Jean XXII (1316–1334) et d'Urbain V (1363–1370)', *Cahiers d'histoire*, 33.2 (1988), 135–51.

41. Cf. Webb, *Pilgrims and Pilgrimage*, pp. 66, 77–8; Sumption, *Pilgrimage*, p. 240; and Diana Wood, *Clement VI: The Pontificate and Ideas of an Avignon Pope* (Cambridge, 1989), pp. 32–3.
42. Wyclif, *English Works*, ed. Thomas Arnold, I. 137.
43. Here I quote from a fuller account of the same allegation, in *English Works*, ed. Arnold, II. 302.
44. Sumption, *Pilgrimage*, p. 292.
45. This text therefore differs from the ones cited above, inasmuch as it presents the Pardoner as ready to hand 'at home' with safe and painless remedies (cf. the readiness of Chaucer's Pardoner to give the Canterbury pilgrims 'pardoun' and 'assoile' them as they 'wende'; VI(C) 925–7, 931–4), these being offered in place of the benefits which one would obtain at those many and various pilgrimage sites.

> . . . yf there were a thousand soules on a hepe,
> I wolde brynge them all to hevene as good chepe
> As ye have brought your selfe of pylgrimage
> In the leste quarter of your vyage . . .
> (*The Foure PP*, 139–42)

In contrast, the texts previously quoted are concerned with the practice of getting the reward for a given pilgrimage without actually going on it.
46. This explanation is, I believe, more convincing than the suggestion that Langland may be alluding to the Statutes of Labourers at VII. 5 (which would mean the intrusion of a new idea at that point – and an idea which hardly fits in with what immediately follows, since 'kynges and knyghtes', 'Bysshopes' and 'Merchaunts' (9, 13, 18) were certainly not the target of that legislation). My reading enables the first eight lines of the Passus to be read as a consistent deployment of discourses relating to literal/historical indulgences, which Langland has taken as the basis of his allegorical pardon.
47. Cf. Judson B. Allen, 'Langland's Reading and Writing: *Detractor* and the Pardon Passus', *Speculum*, 59 (1984), 342–62.
48. These lines constitute an extract from the Athanasian Creed, where they are preceded by the statement that Christ 'shall come to judge the living and the dead. At whose coming all men shall rise again with their bodies and shall give account for their own works.' As an expression of orthodoxy, Langland's extract commands respect – but that does not make it a pardon, in the sense of 'a remission of a just penalty addressed to the man who transgresses the law', to borrow a phrase from Denise Baker, 'The Pardons of *Piers Plowman*', *Neuphilologische Mitteilungen*, 85 (1984), 462–72 (p. 470 n. 16). However, an allegorical reading of Piers's document in terms of the Atonement (on which see below) *does* turn it into such a pardon.
49. Cf. William Lyndwood's use of this passage, noted on p. 71 above.
50. These conflicting authorities are brought together in St Bonaventure's *Sentences* commentary, in the course of discussing whether one person can render satisfaction for another; see Bonaventure, *In IV Sent.*, dist. XX, pars 2, art. un., qu. 1; *Bonaventurae opera*, IV. 530–1. An identical account may be found in Alexander of Hales's *Summa*, pars IV, qu. 83, mem. 1, art. 2 (fol. 131r).

51. *In IV Sent.*, dist. xx, pars 2, art. un., qu. 1; *Bonaventurae opera*, iv. 530–1.
52. This does not mean that Bonaventure is unaware of the force of the opposing arguments, as intimated by 2 Cor. 5:10 and Ps. 61:13 – far from it. He resolves the apparent conflict through a crucial distinction between the punitive and the medicinal aspects of penance. Indulgences relate only to the former. If, however, we talk in terms of medicinal healing of the soul, then it must be said that the penitent must shoulder his or her own burden. The punishment of damnation or spiritual death is not sustained on another's behalf. Thomas Aquinas also believed that an indulgence 'does not take the place of satisfaction as medicinal'; see *Quodl.* 2, qu. 8, art. 2, resp., ad 3um (ed. Spiazzi, p. 37; trans. Edwards, p. 113).
53. That context is Langland's discussion of the vexed issue of the salvation of righteous heathen (cf. Chapter 2 above). Having discussed his own situation, Trajan holds forth on matters which are not exclusive to virtuous pagans (see especially ll. 196–210). God could have made us all rich, had He wished, but He chose to distinguish between rich and poor. However, all of us are, as it were, blood-relations – Christ's creatures together, mutually enriched out of his treasury. Thanks to the resurrection, when Christ bought us back from the devil, we – 'bothe riche and povere' alike – are his brothers and sisters. Therefore we should love one another, as affectionate children do. And anyone who has more than he needs should use it to benefit others; indeed, 'every' man 'should 'helpe oother' – for we are all faced with death. *Alter alterius onera portate* (Galatians 5:2). Here, then, is Trajan's moving application of the principle that we should bear one another's burdens – quite consonant with St Bonaventure's, as summarized above.
54. This reading has a long and distinguished pedigree, going back to Nevill Coghill's 1945 paper 'The Pardon of *Piers Plowman*', repr. in Robert J. Blanch (ed.), *Style and Symbolism in 'Piers Plowman'* (Knoxville, 1969), pp. 40–86 (see esp. pp. 52, 66).
55. This passage has proved controversial in Chaucer criticism, the key issue being whether it indicates the existence of some modicum of grace in the Pardoner, a degree of remorseful self-awareness of his dire spiritual condition. For a recent discussion see Minns, *Fallible Authors*, pp. 167, 418–19n.
56. See for example the Vernon *Testamentum Christi*, in *The Minor Poems of the Vernon Manuscript, Part II*, ed. F. J. Furnivall, EETS OS 117 (London, 1901), pp. 637–57. See further the discussions by Mary Caroline Spalding, *The Middle English Charters of Christ* (Bryn Mawr, PA, 1914); Rosemary Woolf, *The English Religious Lyric in the Middle Ages* (Oxford, 1968), pp. 211–14; and Emily Steiner, 'Langland's Documents', *Yearbook of Langland Studies*, 14 (2000), 95–107 (esp. pp. 99–100), together with her monograph, *Documentary Culture and the Making of Medieval English Literature* (Cambridge, 2003), ch. 3. To reduce Piers himself to the pardon would do violence to the shifting, cumulative nature of Langland's allegorical technique, and identify him with Christ long before the poem does so; in any case, there is no attempt whatever by Langland to merge the figure of the plowman with the document he tears up.

57. The notion of the 'confection' or priestly 'making' of the Eucharist will be discussed in the following chapter.

58. William of Auvergne, who taught first arts and then theology at the University of Paris and became bishop of Paris in 1228, explains that 'the keys have been given to the Church and their office and power to priests for the purpose of dispensing the riches of God's mercy', that they might make them open to those who knock, and lead in those who wish to enter. *De sacramento poenitentiae*, IV, in William of Auvergne, *Opera omnia* (Paris, 1674), I. 462.

59. *In IV Sent.*, dist. XVIII, qu. I, art. I, sol. I, ad Ium; *Aquinatis opera*, VII.2. 809. Cf. *Summa theologiae*, Suppl. qu. 17, art. I, ad Ium; *Aquinatis opera*, IV. 466.

60. Traugott Lawler, 'The Pardon Formula in *Piers Plowman*: Its Ubiquity, Its Binary Shape, Its Silent Middle Term', *The Yearbook of Langland Studies*, 14 (2000), 117–52 (p. 130). 'To do evil but to repent is to do well, and in practice is the only way to do well since everyone sins' (p. 118). Of course, this is not spelled out in Langland's text, and Lawler's objective is to explain why not. 'The most probable explanation for the brief binary form of the pardon', he suggests, 'is that it copies the form of numerous brief binary formulations of Jesus's mission by John the Baptist and by Jesus himself' (p. 137). I cannot share his confidence that 'the more capacious versions elsewhere' (i.e. in other sources) 'fill in' Langland's 'cryptic expression . . . amply, and leave no room to doubt its status as an expression of the redemptive mercy of Christ'. In my view, there is considerable 'room' left for 'doubt', and such answers as may be found come later in the poem. Hence I favour a 'developmental' reading of the Pardon in particular and the poem in general, to borrow a term from Lawler's statement of opposition to James Simpson's approach ('The Pardon Formula', 136 n. 14).

61. Lawler, 'The Pardon Formula', 136–7.

62. Robert W. Frank, *'Piers Plowman' and the Scheme of Salvation* (New Haven, 1957), p. 28.

63. It is, of course, theologically incorrect to speak in terms of 'buying' indulgences; supererogatory merit was not for sale. Cf. n. 19 above. The comments of Frank and McLeod here quoted illustrate a (quite typical) lack of understanding of, or sympathy with, medieval theology of indulgences.

64. Susan H. McLeod, 'The Tearing of the Pardon in *Piers Plowman*', *Philological Quarterly*, 56 (1977), 14–26 (pp. 22–3).

65. Desiderius Erasmus, *Opera omnia*, I. 3 (Amsterdam, 1972), pp. 147–50; trans. C. R. Thompson, *Collected Works of Erasmus: Colloquies*, XXXIX (Toronto, 1997), pp. 36–9.

66. *De utilitate colloquiorum*, in *Opera omnia*, I. 3, p. 743; trans. Thompson, p. 1100.

67. Cf. the justifications by Albert the Great and Thomas Aquinas quoted on p. 69 above. Indeed, the question 'whether indulgences really have the value with which they are credited' was a standard one in *Sentences* commentaries. And the failsafe answer was that one can have confidence in indulgences because one has confidence in the pope who has the authority to issue them (whether this is done directly, or by means of delegation to others). Luther,

attacking an 'assertion of the seven sacraments' which the young Henry VIII had written during his time as *fidei defensor*, mockingly reduced this defence to the shallow principle, 'indulgences are not impostures because [the pope who issued them] is a good man'. Writing in support of his king, Thomas More spelled out the shocking consequences of Luther's doctrine. He would tumble 'down to hell in a common damnation' people 'deceased now for so many ages, together with the bishops and clergy'; thus both the dispensers and the recipients of indulgences would be degraded together. Thomas More, *Complete Works*, ed. R. Sylvester, C. H. Miller *et al.* (New Haven and London, 1976–97), I. 326–31.

68. Cf. my explanation of this epithet for Langland on p. 5 above.

69. For example, Erasmus's *Pilgrimage for Religion's Sake* (on which see below, pp. 132–3) was soon pressed into the service of Protestant apologetics. To the work's first English translation is added a preface (composed between October 1536 and February 1537) which declares that Erasmus has revealed here 'the supersticyouse worshipe and false honor gyuyn to bones, heddes, iawes, armes, stockes, stones, shyrtes, smokes, cotes, cappes, hattes, shoes, mytres, slyppers, saddels, rynges, bedes, gyrdles, bolles, belles, bokes, gloues, ropes, taperes, candelles, bootes, spoores with many other soche dampanable allusyones to the duuylle to use them as goddes contrary to the immaculate scripture of gode'. Desiderius Erasmus, *The Earliest English Translations of Erasmus's Colloquia*, ed. Henry de Vocht (Leuven, 1928), pp. 104–5.

4 MAKING BODIES: CONFECTION AND CONCEPTION IN WALTER BRUT'S VERNACULAR THEOLOGY

1. 'Look at Walter Brut – who they pursue busily, for he spoke the truth to them. And yet, sir, furthermore, they may harm him no more. But it is said that he is a heretic and believes what is evil, and preaches it from the pulpit to blind the people. They want to curse that creature for his good deeds, and so they chew up charity just like dogs chew chaff.' *The Piers Plowman Tradition*, ed. Helen Barr (London, 1993), p. 89.

2. *Registrum Johannis Trefnant*, ed. Capes, p. 364, no. 30; cf. Margaret Aston, 'Lollard Women Priests?', in her *Lollards and Reformers. Images and Literacy in Late Medieval Religion* (London, 1984), pp. 49–70 (p. 52).

3. On the trial and its implications see the summary account by K. B. McFarlane, *John Wycliffe and the Beginnings of English Nonconformity* (London, 1952), pp. 135–8, and especially Aston, 'Lollard Women Priests?', pp. 49–70; also Hudson, *Premature Reformation*, pp. 47–8, 281–2, 284n, 291, 295, 298–9, 326–7, 368, etc., together with her article '"Laicus litteratus": The Paradox of Lollardy', in Peter Biller and Anne Hudson (eds.), *Heresy and Literacy, 1000–1530* (Cambridge, 1994), pp. 222–36.

4. *Registrum Johannis Trefnant*, ed. Capes, p. 285.

5. *Registrum Johannis Trefnant*, ed. Capes, p. 279.

6. *Registrum Johannis Trefnant*, ed. Capes, p. 278.

7. *Registrum Johannis Trefnant*, ed. Capes, pp. 359–60.
8. Lollard *cedulae*, or *rollis* as they were called in English, seem to have been ephemeral documents; for discussion see Anne Hudson, 'Some Aspects of Lollard Book Production', repr. in Hudson, *Lollards and their Books*, pp. 181–91 (pp. 183–4).
9. *Registrum Johannis Trefnant*, ed. Capes, pp. 368–94. Capes (following the manuscript's apparent error) erroneously labels this section as a response to William Swinderby, whose trial is also recorded in Trefnant's register. Cf. Aston, 'Lollard Women Priests?', p. 54 n. 21, and especially Anne Hudson, 'The Problems of Scribes: The Trial Records of William Swinderby and Walter Brut', *Nottingham Medieval Studies*, 49 (2005), 80–104 (p. 92). Hudson's discussion brings out well the 'deeply perplexing' nature of the materials as recorded in the register; 'not all of them' are 'fully understood or placed in the correct position by the scribe', and there are significant gaps (pp. 80, 103).
10. Even Arundel's *Constitutions* recognized the academic needs of scholastic disputation, in the very act of warning against philosophical formulation of Christian truths in curious terms and words, and banning debate which might undermine the authority of canon law. Cf. John Foxe, *The Acts and Monuments*, 4th edn, ed. Josiah Pratt (London, 1877), III. 246.
11. See the edition by A. Blamires and C. W. Marx, 'Woman Not to Preach: A Disputation in British Library MS Harley 31', *Journal of Medieval Latin*, 3 (1993), 34–63, and the partial translation in Blamires (ed.), *Woman Defamed and Woman Defended*, pp. 251–5.
12. See p. 113 below, and also the relevant discussion in Minnis, *Fallible Authors*, ch. 3.
13. London, British Library, MS Harley 31, fols. 196v–205r.
14. MS Harley 31, fols. 218r–23r.
15. On the significance of 1 Peter 2:9 in Wyclif's own (brief and inchoate) treatment of women priests in *De potestate pape* see Minnis, *Fallible Authors*, p. 219. It seems clear that Brut's opponent was well aware of Wyclif's treatment.
16. Named after the fourth-century bishop of Carthage, Aelius Donatus the Great. The issue of whether, and/or to what extent, Wyclif himself fell into this heresy is a matter of some scholarly controversy. See Ian Christopher Levy, 'Was John Wyclif's Theology of the Eucharist Donatistic?', *Scottish Journal of Theology*, 53 (2000), 137–53, and my own discussion in *Fallible Authors*, pp. 19–22, 55–67, 135–7, 142–3, 231–6, 241, etc.
17. Brut's opponent is, of course, putting this forward just for the argument's sake. The orthodox position, as explained succinctly by John Duns Scotus, was that, if some bishop attempted to ordain a woman, even though he said the correct words no valid ordination could take place. The bishop is merely an instrumental agent acting under God as the principal and superior agent. His powers are limited to those allowed him by the principal agent, and since God does not permit the ordination of women the bishop is unable to

bestow the priestly *character* on any female. Duns Scotus, *In IV Sent.*, dist. xxv, qu. 2 (*Utrum sexus muliebris, vel aetas puerilis, impediat susceptionem ordinum*); *Opera omnia* (Lyon, 1639; repr. Hildesheim, 1969), xi.2. 785.

18. There is much truth in this proposition, though of course Brut's opponent cannot see it or accept it. Up until the end of twelfth century 'ordination' was quite interchangeable with words like 'consecration' and 'blessing' (or 'veiling', in the case of nuns). Abbesses, deaconesses, and nuns were routinely spoken of as having been ordained, every bit as much as monks and priests – and, indeed, as emperors, empresses, kings, and queens, for the discourse could apply to secular as well as sacred ceremonials. Subsequently, however, its range of possible applications was severely curtailed. Ecclesiastical 'ordination' came to be confined to the all-male institutions of priesthood and the deaconate, and women were, so to speak, 'defined out of ordination'. That is to say, in relation to church ritual the semantic range of the term narrowed to cover only a small range of duties (administering the sacraments and preaching being the most important), duties which women were judged to lack the capacity, and the institutional authority, to perform. Such is the thesis of Gary Macy's provocative study, *The Hidden History of Women's Ordination: Female Clergy in the Medieval West* (New York, 2007).

19. MS Harley 31, fol. 197r.

20. See for example (in respect of baptism) *Lib. sent.* iv, dist. v, cap. 1; Peter Lombard, *Sententiae in IV libris distinctae*, ii. 263–6. On the problems posed by fornicator priests see *Lib. sent.* iv, dist. xiii, cap. 1, 1–3 (ii. 311–12); and concerning heretics and excommunicates, see *Lib. Sent.* iv, dist. xiii, cap. 1, 4–6 (ii. 312–13).

21. MS Harley 31, fol. 201v.

22. On the Lollard emphasis on the importance of preaching see Chapter 5.

23. Cf. the simpler formulation in one of Brut's own statements, as recorded in *Registrum Johannis Trefnant*, ed. Capes, p. 345; quoted and discussed on pp. 114–15 below.

24. This alludes to Luke 11:27–8; cf. Chapter 5 below.

25. A fuller treatment of the above excursus is provided on pp. 115–16 below.

26. MS Harley 31, fols. 218r–223r.

27. MS Harley 31, fol. 219v.

28. Philip Lyndon Reynolds, *Food and the Body: Some Peculiar Questions in High Medieval Theology* (Leiden, 1999), p. 1.

29. Reynolds, *Food and the Body*, p. 9. Hence, as Bynum puts it, 'the new life that is born into flesh comes from the mother's blood; her blood literally continues in – *is* – the child's body. And the blood in that body is its life'. *Wonderful Blood*, p. 161. See further her discussion of 'Woman as Body and as Food' in *Holy Feast and Holy Fast: The Religious Significance of Food to Medieval Women* (Berkeley and Los Angeles, 1987), pp. 260–76.

30. MS Harley 31, fol. 220v.

31. Cf. the discussion and references in Chapter 2 above.

32. Women could, of course, be allowed the gift of prophecy – if certain strict conditions were met, and if the putative prophetess could satisfy her male interlocutors that she met all the criteria laid down by the established system of *discretio spirituum*, on which see especially Rosalynn Voaden, *God's Words, Women's Voices. The Discernment of Spirits in the Writings of Late-Medieval Women Visionaries* (Woodbridge, 1999). To become an approved prophetess meant proving extraordinary purity of personal life – whereas the personal purity of ordained priests was not a requisite for the successful performance of their sacred duties. (Cf. the relevant argument in *Fallible Authors*, ch. 3.) Brut and many other Lollards found this contrast both irrational and unacceptable. But it was one of the very foundation stones of late medieval theology, both pastoral and speculative, and hence impossible to shift.

33. MS Harley 31, fol. 220v.

34. MS Harley 31, fol. 221r.

35. Here I refer to the Lollard obsession with *scriptura sola*, on which see M. Hurley, '*Scriptura sola*: Wyclif and his Critics', *Traditio*, 16 (1960), 275–352. On the *reductio ad absurdum* of such beliefs by Wyclif's opponents William Woodford OFM and Reginald Pecock see Minnis, *Fallible Authors*, pp. 259–60.

36. MS Harley 31, fol. 221v.

37. *Alberti opera*, XXXVII. 87.

38. *Alberti opera*, XXXVII. 86.

39. Here I draw on the final part of Albert's general answer to *quaestiones* 36–43; *Alberti opera*, XXXVII. 84–7.

40. Caroline Walker Bynum, *Fragmentation and Redemption: Essays on Gender and the Human Body in Medieval Religion* (New York, 1992), p. 212. Cf. her *Holy Feast and Holy Fast*, pp. 268–9.

41. Bynum, *Fragmentation*, p. 212. Furthermore, in the Presentation in the Temple Mary 'offered the Christchild to God', an action which was sometimes presented as analogous to priestly confection (p. 219; caption to a fifteenth-century French panel painting depicting 'The Priesthood of the Virgin').

42. Albert puts an impressive spin on this exclusion by asserting that the Blessed Virgin was not ordained 'because of her humble conformity to other women, who are excluded from this sacrament' of holy orders 'on account of the unworthiness of their sex, of their greater weakness regarding sin, and due to what follows from these factors – the incongruity of their holding office'.

43. *Alberti opera*, XXXVII. 79.

44. Netter, *Doctrinale*, III. 371.

45. For a full discussion see Alastair Minnis, 'John Wyclif – All Women's Friend?', in Bonnie Wheeler (ed.), *Mindful Spirit in Late Medieval Literature: Essays in Honor of Elizabeth D. Kirk* (Houndmills, 2006), pp. 121–33; also Minnis, *Fallible Authors*, pp. 211–21.

46. On which see especially Hudson, *Premature Reformation*, pp. 4–5, 98, 315, 359–62, etc.; Jesse M. Gellrich, *Discourse and Dominion in the Fourteenth Century: Oral Contexts of Writing in Philosophy, Politics, and Poetry* (Princeton, 1995), pp. 97–106; Michael Wilks, 'Predestination, Property, and Power: Wyclif's Theory of Dominion and Grace', in Wilks, *Wyclif: Political Ideas and Practice*, ed. Anne Hudson (Oxford, 2000), pp. 16–32; and Stephen E. Lahey, *Philosophy and Politics in the Thought of John Wyclif* (Cambridge, 2003). *Dominium* theory and Donatism (cf. n. 16 above) are, to be sure, formally separate areas of thought and should not be blurred together: but surely there is some consonance between the idea that personal righteousness is requisite for the proper holding of any sovereign position (*dominium* theory) and the idea that a priest lacking in personal righteousness cannot properly administer the sacraments, the powers conferred at ordination having been problematized or indeed nullified by his personal iniquity (Donatism).

47. McFarlane, *Wycliffe*, p. 136.

48. Compare *Registrum Johannis Trefnant*, ed. Capes, pp. 345–7, with Foxe, *Acts and Monuments*, ed. Pratt, III. 179.

49. The sophistication of his eucharistic thought has been demonstrated ably by David Aers, *Sanctifying Signs: Making Christian Tradition in Late Medieval England* (Notre Dame, IN, 2004), pp. 67–82; cf. his article, 'Walter Brut's Theology of the Sacrament of the Altar', in F. Somerset, J. C. Havens, and D. G. Pitard (eds.), *Lollards and their Influence in Late-Medieval England* (Woodbridge, 2003), pp. 115–26. Brut also comes across as an effective polemicist; one can easily imagine him as a superb preacher.

50. Indeed, Swinderby may have converted Brut. Trefnant's register presents the Welshman as a follower, citing a list of propositions previously condemned at Swinderby's trial which, it asserts, Brut continued to hold.

51. We know a little about the contents of this work, thanks to Thomas Netter's attack on it in his *Doctrinale*, wherein he claims that he owns a copy which was taken from Purvey in prison. Cf. Anne Hudson, 'John Purvey: A Reconsideration of the Evidence for his Life and Writings', in her *Lollards and their Books*, pp. 85–110 (p. 94). See further Maureen Jurkowski, 'New Light on John Purvey', *English Historical Review*, 110 (1995), 1180–90 (esp. p. 1186).

52. McFarlane seems to be following a remark by Foxe (unsubstantiated by the Latin documents in Trefnant's register) that the bishop, finding Brut's first excursus 'too short and obscure', 'required him to write upon the same again more plainly and more at large': Foxe, *Acts and Monuments*, ed. Pratt, III. 139. I can discern no change of style in the second excursus.

53. In this regard he was not atypical. For instance: no anti-Wycliffite writer I know brings together doctrines of the sacraments as 'empty signs' and of the priesthood of all members of the *vera ecclesia*, to confront the idea that 'priesthood' is, within Lollard theology, of greatly diminished status, since such ministers are presiding over 'sacraments' of a radically revalued – or devalued, as orthodox schoolmen would have said – kind. The defenders of the *status quo* insist on treating their opponents as if they were trying to gain access to

administering the sacraments on their own (orthodox) understanding of the term and the procedures.

54. As quoted at the very beginning of this book.

55. Indeed, if Roger Wright's controversial but fascinating hypothesis is accepted, the boundary between Medieval Latin and the Romance vernaculars was even more permeable than is usually allowed. Attacking the 'two norm' theory (i.e. that during the period *c.* 400–850 the educated clerics spoke Latin while everyone else spoke whatever vernacular was current in their community), Wright has argued that *c.* 800 Carolingian scholars drove a wedge between Latin and vernacular, as they imposed an archaizing system of pronunciation on spoken (Church) Latin, in an attempt to stabilize performance of the liturgy. Otherwise the spoken word was simply the local vernacular, Old French, Spanish, etc. In short, the Romance languages emerged from different manners of speaking Latin; later spoken Latin *was* early Romance. See Wright's two major studies, *Late Latin and Early Romance in Spain and Carolingian France* (Liverpool, 1982), and *A Sociophilological Study of Late Latin*, Utrecht Studies in Medieval Literacy, 10 (Turnhout, 2002).

56. In Elisabeth's case there is the issue of the extent to which her brother served as an amanuensis, but her knowledge of Latin is not in doubt, and we have many testimonies to the Latinity of holy women who had their revelations recorded by men. The interpretive problem is well addressed in the collection of essays edited by Catherine M. Mooney, *Gendered Voices: Medieval Saints and their Interpreters* (Philadelphia, 1999). Cf. the account of how Juliana of Mont-Cornillon (d. 1258) learned to read Latin fluently; as a child she knew the Psalter by heart, and in later life committed to memory more than twenty sermons from the last part of St Bernard's commentary on the Song of Songs. *The Life of Juliana of Mont-Cornillon*, trans. Barbara Newman (Toronto, 1999), pp. 16, 30, 33. Sometimes divine inspiration is claimed for a breakthrough in language comprehension, as in the curious case of St Catherine of Siena: cf. Raymond of Capua, *Vita Catharinae Serensis*, 1.xi.113, ed. Jörg Jungmayr (Berlin, 2004), 1.154–7; trans. Conleth Kearns, Dominican Publications, Dublin, 1 (Wilmington, DE, 1980), pp. 104–5.

57. For such reasons I must take issue with Walter Ong's extraordinary statement, 'No longer a mother tongue, Learned Latin left all its users free of the rich, emotional, unconscious, but often confusingly subjective involvements of a language learned orally from infancy'; 'Orality, Literacy, and Medieval Textualization', *New Literary History*, 16 (1984–5), pp. 1–12 (p. 9). To which Melissa Furrow has responded: 'But Latin was the language of Mother Church, and its use was both more practically necessary and more emotion-laden than the phrase "learned Latin" suggests' ('Unscholarly Latinity and Margery Kempe', p. 241).

58. Most of the thirteen surviving copies are of Hussite origin. Cf. Hudson, 'A Neglected Wycliffite Text'; see also Hudson, *Premature Reformation*, pp. 264–7, and Copeland, *Pedagogy, Intellectuals*, pp. 156–61.

59. See Maurice Keen, 'Wyclif, the Bible, and Transubstantiation', in Anthony Kenny (ed.), *Wyclif in his Times* (Oxford, 1986), pp. 1–16. See further J. I. Catto, 'John Wyclif and the Cult of the Eucharist', in K. Walsh and D. Wood (eds.), *The Bible in the Medieval World: Essays in Memory of Beryl Smalley* (Oxford, 1985), pp. 269–86.

60. See especially Hudson, 'The Debate on Bible Translation, Oxford 1401', and Watson, 'Censorship and Cultural Change', esp. pp. 842–3. On the arguments against English – that it is barbarous, grammatically very different from Latin, and lacks crucial equivalent terms – see also Hudson, 'Lollardy: The English Heresy?' pp. 153–4.

61. Wogan-Browne *et al.* (eds.), *The Idea of the Vernacular*, is an intriguing case in point. While impressively demonstrating the range and sophistication of literary theory in Middle English, this comprehensive and admirably edited anthology occasionally lapses into unfortunate remarks concerning what certain languages can and cannot do in respect of their supposed capacities and resources. To imply that Latin (in this case the Latin of Dante's *De vulgari eloquentia*) is deficient in 'drama, idiom, situated language, wit, irony' (in opposition to John Trevisa's English *Dialogue* on translation, which is supposed to be rich in such qualities) takes one uncomfortably close to (for instance) Thomas Palmer's argument against an English Bible on account of the alleged inadequacies of the vernacular. In *The Idea of the Vernacular* it is the alleged inadequacies of Latin which are put in the dock, on equally dubious grounds. And, a few pages later, George Ashby's *Active Policy of a Prince* is quoted to illustrate how the Middle English theoretical term *entent* can signify meaning which comes from human agency rather than some 'transcendent source', in contrast with the corresponding Latin term, *intentio*, which is presented as a narrow and formal means of affirming authority – the implication being that this term can function in no other way. Here no recognition is allowed of the wide range of meanings which *intentio* can bear within Latin literary theory. Cf. *The Idea of the Vernacular*, pp. 324, 328–9; also Margaret Deanesly, *The Lollard Bible and Other Medieval Versions* (Cambridge, 1920), pp. 426–8.

62. Nicholas Watson's research has been quite crucial in this regard. To take but one example of his timely polemic: in 'Visions of Inclusion' he challenges the assumptions that 'ideas expressed' by vernacular writers are 'merely simplified versions of ideas developed in Latin by clerics, and that vernacular culture was characterized by feeling, not thought, and by practical rather than speculative approaches to truth'. In this article and elsewhere, Watson has powerfully highlighted the limitations of such attitudes, and conclusively demonstrated that 'Not only do vernacular texts derive material from an array of Latin systems of thought, they generate their own systems.' Hence Watson's promotion of the term 'vernacular theology', which stems from an acute sensitivity to the rich 'internal resources of vernacular culture' in general. Cf. 'Visions of Inclusion', 145–6.

63. Such an attitude may be found in McFarlane's account of Walter Brut, as quoted above; furthermore, he remarks that Swinderby did much to make Wyclif's 'doctrines intelligible to the unlearned, while adding much of his own simplicity as well': *Wycliffe*, p. 135.

64. Assuming for the moment that Hilton was indeed the author of this treatise; cf. p. 178 n. 64 below. Of course, my point holds good irrespective of whoever wrote it.

65. *'The Cloud of Unknowing' and Related Treatises*, ed. Phyllis Hodgson, Analecta Cartusiana 3 (Salzburg, 1982), p. 1.

66. On the 'louyng miȝt' as the highest cognitive power in the *Cloud* (in line with Thomas Gallus's doctrine of *principalis affectio*) see Alastair Minnis, 'Affection and Imagination in *The Cloud of Unknowing* and Walter Hilton's *Scale of Perfection*', *Traditio*, 39 (1983), 323–66 (p. 338).

67. The status of the *Mirrour* as a primer for popular/populist piety should be appreciated. Its significance as anti-Lollard propaganda need not occlude its appeal to readers both clerical and lay, male and female, who were seeking instruction in how best to draw nearer to their God through 'devout imagination', on which see the discussion included in Johnson's thesis, 'The Late-Medieval Theory and Practice of Translation with Special Reference to some Middle English Lives of Christ', and also the relevant comments in Chapter 1 above.

68. The bibliography on 'affective piety' is vast. I have found particularly helpful R. W. Southern, *The Making of the Middle Ages* (London and New York, 1953), pp. 232–40 (with the following plates); Woolf, *The English Religious Lyric in the Middle Ages*, pp. 5–15, 19–66; Douglas Gray, *Themes and Images in the Medieval English Religious Lyric* (London, 1972), pp. 18–30; and Caroline Walker Bynum, *Jesus as Mother: Studies in the Spirituality of the High Middle Ages* (Berkeley and Los Angeles, 1982), pp. 3–21, 77–81, 105–9, 129–35, etc.

69. *Cloud*, ch. 5; ed. Hodgson, pp. 13–14. Cf. ch. 9, where it is explained that spontaneous thinking of any good and spiritual thing is a hindrance rather than a help to contemplation: surely the person who 'sekiþ God parfitely' will not settle for the recollection of any angel or saint that is in heaven (p. 19).

70. In ch. 65 of the *Cloud* it is conceded that the disobedience of the imagination can be controlled through frequent meditation on one's own wretchedness, the passion and kindness of our Lord, and so forth. But here our anonymous author has in mind people who have newly turned 'fro þe woreld vnto deuocion'. Similarly, in the *Book of Privy Counselling* he admits that 'faire meditacions' are the best way for the beginner to commence his 'goostly felyng of himself & of God' (ed. Hodgson, p. 90). Walter Hilton showed himself far more aware of the needs and capabilities of his lesser brethren; his *Scale of Perfection* affords each and every Christian his or her rung on the ladder. The way in which the second book of the *Scale* places the *Cloud*'s doctrine within a larger and more comprehensive vision is a remarkable achievement. Given that the *Scale* takes account of Richard Rolle's devotional fervour as well,

it may be regarded as a veritable *Summa theologica anglicana.* Cf. Nicholas Watson's discussion of Hilton, 'Middle English Mystics', pp. 555–7.

71. As he tells us himself at the beginning of *The Book of Privy Counselling*, ed. Hodgson, p. 76.

72. *Pace* Watson, 'Middle English Mystics', p. 554. And I see no evidence whatever for the claims that chapters 57–61 of the *Cloud* are addressed specifically to *vernacular* readers who tend 'to treat as literal what is meant to be taken spiritually' (p. 552 n. 45) and that the work's anonymous author believes 'his vernacular readers are *better* able to strip themselves naked for the naked encounter with God than the learned' (p. 553). Rather he seems to be addressing *all* users of language (whatever their specific language or languages); this universalizing approach is quite in line with Pseudo-Dionysian literary theory, on which see Minnis, Scott, and Wallace (eds.), *Medieval Literary Theory and Criticism*, pp. 165–96. Language in general is regarded as a 'bodely werk' or corporeal encumbrance by the *Cloud*-author. As humans we have to use it in discussing spiritual things (there being no alternative), but such discourse – whatever specific linguistic form it may take – must be interpreted spiritually and not corporeally; i.e. we should avoid the trap of supposing that divine beings are actually like those earthly analogues or images which language uses to figure them. Remarks about the uninitiated or uneducated being unaware of the right way to read such imagery (as marking the differences between earth and heaven rather than any spurious and deceptive similarities) are a commonplace of the Dionysian tradition.

73. Cf. Sandler, *Omne bonum*, I. 26.

74. London, British Library, MS Royal 6.E.VII, fols. 114r–117v. Cf. Sandler, *Omne bonum*, I. 115–18.

75. I have attempted to do this in my *Fallible Authors*; see especially the introductory chapter.

76. *Tractatus de regibus*, I, *Selections from English Wycliffite Writings*, ed. Hudson, p. 127.

77. Rudolf Beddensieg, *John Wiclif, Patriot and Reformer: Life and Writings* (London, 1884), p. 51.

78. 'That he ever wrote anything in the vernacular is open to question', comments McFarlane (*Wycliffe*, p. 118); cf. Hudson's statement that 'None of the English texts can certainly be ascribed to Wyclif himself' (*Selections from English Wycliffite Writings*, p. 10). Of course, Wyclif preached publicly *in vulgari*, in accordance with the normal practice of the time, and 'very occasionally . . . speaks as having set out his views on a topic in Latin and also in English': Hudson, 'Wyclif and the English Language', p. 89. Margaret Aston has argued that Wyclif played an active role in promoting his eucharistic doctrine in English, which may have included the writing and dissemination of key documents: 'Wycliffe and the Vernacular', in her *Faith and Fire: Popular and Unpopular Religion, 1350–1600* (London and Rio Grande, 1993), pp. 27–72. But none of these documents have survived – at least, not evidently – and so Aston's suggestion must remain as speculation (though plausible speculation).

79. Dove, *The First English Bible*; Deanesly, *The Lollard Bible*.

80. Hudson, 'Wyclif and the English Language', p. 90; cf. the relevant discussion in my introductory chapter.

81. Mary Dove, 'Wyclif and the English Bible', in Levy (ed.), *Companion to Wyclif*, pp. 365–406 (p. 395).

82. Dove, 'Wyclif and the English Bible', p. 397.

83. Dove, 'Wyclif and the English Bible', p. 395.

84. John Wyclif, *De veritate sacrae scripturae*, 1.6, ed. R. Buddensieg (London, 1904), II. 107–11; partially trans. Ian Christopher Levy, *On the Truth of Holy Scripture* (Kalamazoo, 2001), pp. 97–8. See further Alastair Minnis, '"Authorial Intention" and "Literal Sense" in the Exegetical Theories of Richard FitzRalph and John Wyclif', *Proceedings of the Royal Irish Academy*, 75, section C, no. 1 (Dublin, 1975), 13–16.

85. Cf. Beryl Smalley, 'The Bible and Eternity: John Wyclif's Dilemma', *Journal of the Warburg and Courtauld Institutes*, 27 (1964), 73–89. See further Ian Christopher Levy, 'John Wyclif's Neoplatonic View of Scripture in its Christological Context', *Medieval Philosophy and Theology*, 11 (2003), 227–40.

86. Lyre, second prologue to the *Postilla litteralis*, trans. Minnis, Scott and Wallace, *Medieval Literary Theory*, p. 269.

87. *De veritate*, ed. Buddensieg, 1. 114; trans. Levy, *On the Truth of Holy Scripture*, p. 102.

88. Dove, 'Wyclif and the English Bible', p. 375. Cf. *De veritate*, ed. Buddensieg, 1. 238; trans. Levy, *On the Truth of Holy Scripture*, p. 159.

89. *De veritate*, ed. Buddensieg, 1. 111; trans. Levy, *On the Truth of Holy Scripture*, p. 99.

90. *De veritate*, ed. Buddensieg, 1. 114; trans. Levy, *On the Truth of Holy Scripture*, p. 102.

91. Kantik Ghosh, *The Wycliffite Heresy: Authority and the Interpretation of Texts* (Cambridge, 2002), p. 56.

92. *The Holy Bible, Containing the Old and New Testaments, in the Earliest English Versions, Made from the Latin Vulgate by John Wycliffe and his Followers*, ed. Josiah Forshall and Frederic Madden (Oxford, 1850), I. 49.

93. Wyclif, *Trialogus*, ed. Lechler, p. 240. See further Hudson, 'Lollardy: The English Heresy?', pp. 144–5, who here draws on Michael Wilks, 'Misleading Manuscripts: Wyclif and the Non-Wycliffite Bible', *Studies in Church History*, 11 (1975), 147–61 (pp. 154–5).

94. Dove, 'Wyclif and the English Bible', p. 375.

95. Dove, 'Wyclif and the English Bible', p. 376. Another attempt to mitigate the apparent harshness of Wyclif's words about Scripture understood in the fifth and lowest sense has been made by Ian Levy. Emphasizing the Christological basis of the truth of sacred Scripture in Wyclif's thought, Levy takes the line that 'Scripture is true because Christ is true.' Both perform their salvific function through material forms, Scripture being 'the immutable truth revealed in the flesh of the sensible parchment, proclaiming the highest level of saving

gospel. The parchment and ink present the Word to the senses much as the flesh and blood of Christ present the Second Person of the Trinity.' 'John Wyclif's Neoplatonic View of Scripture', 239–40. Here, then, is an eloquent and persuasive means of attributing value to the parchment and ink. However, the gap between the Bible as the Book of Life and as a material object seems, in light of Wyclif's own robust and dismissive language, to be more vast and irreconcilable than the distance between the divine and human natures of Christ. I would suggest further that there is an impulse towards Monophysitism in some of Wyclif's statements, which would repay further investigation.

96. For a contrasting view see Gellrich, *Discourse and Dominion*, p. 93, where it is argued that 'Wyclif is not denaturing voice and writing, nor is he valuing only their ideal, transcendent counterparts.'

97. Here I draw on idioms from the General Prologue, ch. 15; *The Holy Bible*, ed. Forshall and Madden, I. 57.

98. Cf. Minnis, Scott, and Wallace (eds.), *Medieval Literary Theory*, pp. 266–8.

99. *Quaestiones disputatae*, I: *De veritate*, ed. R. Spiazzi, 8th edn (Turin and Rome, 1949), pp. 127–9.

100. *Wyclif and the Oxford Schools* (Cambridge, 1966), p. 146.

101. Hudson, 'Wyclif and the English Language', pp. 90–1

102. *Registrum Johannis Trefnant*, ed. Capes, pp. 293–4. Brut concludes that 'the Britons, amongst other nations, have been, as it were by the special election of God, called and converted to the faith'. Cf. Geoffrey of Monmouth, *Historia regum Britanniae*, IV. 19. The story is also told in Bede's *Historia ecclesiastica*, I. 4.

103. *Registrum Johannis Trefnant*, ed. Capes, p. 360.

104. However, it is important to note that the very act of insisting upon English as the medium for theological discussion could be a gesture of religious dissent, a way of affirming one's refusal to conform to the norms of conventional belief and established practice. To take but one example, William Sawtry 'was evidently quite capable in Latin' yet chose to speak English at his trial before Archbishop Arundel: cf. Aston, 'Wycliffe and the Vernacular', p. 48. The crucial role which English came to play in Lollard proselytizing is well described by Hudson, 'Lollardy: The English Heresy?'.

105. In modern English translation, of course, given that English has become the new Latin.

106. Quoted by Hudson from a tract in Cambridge, University Library, MS Ii.6.26, fol. 4v, in 'Lollardy: The English Heresy?', p. 158. The Lollard's point is that, in comparison, English books are not so bad after all. Cf. the similar statement in a Lollard tract in defence of Bible translation: 'wyte wele þat we fynden in Latyne mo heretikes þan of all oþer langagis': Curt F. Bühler, 'A Lollard Tract: On Translating the Bible into English', *Medium Ævum*, 7 (1938), 167–83 (p. 176).

5 SPIRITUALIZING MARRIAGE: MARGERY KEMPE'S ALLEGORIES OF FEMALE AUTHORITY

* My title is indebted to the title and discourse of Maureen Quilligan's monograph, *The Allegory of Female Authority: Christine de Pizan's 'Cité des dames'*
(Ithaca, 1991).

1. '... viuas sicut cetere mulieres. Accipias uirum, et procrea filios ad humani
generis augmentum. Quod si desideras Deo placere, numquid non et sancte
nupserunt? Saram considera, Rebecham pariter et Rachelem. Ut quid hanc
singularem uitam accepisti, in qua nullo modo ualebis perseuerare?' Raymond
of Capua, *Vita Catharinae*, 1.xi.105, ed. Jungmayr, 1.144; trans. Kearns, p. 98.
Giving up on this tactic, the devil proceeds to try a more blatantly sexual
approach, conjuring up 'pictures of men and women of licentious conduct
(*ymagines mulierum et hominum turpissime*) who seemed to posture lasciviously
before her, filling her eyes with obscene sights and her ears with filthy language
(*fedos et uerba inhonestissima*), and calling on her with frenzied cries to join
in their orgies (*turpia*)' (*Vita Catharinae*, 1.xi.106, ed. Jungmayr, 1.146; trans.
Kearns, p. 99. There is an interesting parallel here with an episode in *BMK*
(1.59/282) wherein the devil causes Margery Kempe to experience a vision
'of mennys membrys, and swech other abhominacyons'). Earlier in his *vita*
Raymond recounts how the devil 'lodged in the mind' of Catherine's 'parents
and relatives the fixed idea that willy-nilly they would marry her off, using her
as a puppet to ally themselves with some family of distinction'. Hence, after the
death (in childbirth) of Catherine's sister Buonaventura, they redouble 'their
efforts to find a husband' for her. But Catherine 'soon realized what they were
at and, enlightened by God, saw through the wiles of the old Enemy' (*Vita
Catharinae*, 1.iv.46, ed. Jungmayr, 1.66; trans. Kearns, pp. 44–5).

2. *BMK* 1.52/253. For more on Margery's stirring, 'ghostly' and 'fruitful' *comownycacyon* see *BMK* 1.16/111–12 and 1.69/314–15. Within Margery's devotional lexi-
con *dalyawns* (see for example 1.16/111) sometimes functions as a synonym for
comownycacyon.

3. Aquinas, *Summa theologiae*, 2a 2ae, qu. 177, art. 2 (XLV. 132–5).

4. *Summa quaestionum ordinariarum* (Paris, 1520; repr. Leuven and Paderborn,
1953), fols. 77v–78r. This question has been reprinted as an appendix to the
study and edition by Blamires and Marx of one of the anti-Brut *quaestiones*,
'Woman Not to Preach' (pp. 50–5). It forms part of the prologue to Henry of
Ghent's *Summa quaestionum ordinariarum*, first written *c.* 1275–6 and edited
towards the end of his career, in 1289. A full account of the views of Aquinas
and Henry of Ghent is included in my *Fallible Authors*, ch. 3.

5. Here *in silentio* designates 'private', 'domestic', and 'non-public' speech rather
than the absence of speech (the spoken word being necessary in the teaching
situation here envisaged!), though the connection with St Paul's statement
(1 Tim. 2:12) that a woman should not teach but 'be in silence' (*esse in silentio*)
is evident and no doubt intended. The Latin term *silentium* covers a range of
meanings including 'stillness, quiet, tranquillity, obscurity'.

6. Netter, *Doctrinale*, 1.638. There is an interesting connection (albeit an indirect one) between Thomas Netter and Margery Kempe: at one point (in his capacity as 'the Provincyal of the White Frerys') Netter forbade Alan of Lynn O. Carm., a major supporter who put great value on Margery's 'communicacyon', to speak with her and instruct her in Scripture; *BMK* 1.69/314–15. Subsequently this prohibition was lifted: at *BMK* 1.70/317 we hear that Alan 'had leve of hys sovereyn [presumably Netter] to spekyn with the sayd creatur'. Kerby-Fulton speculates interestingly about 'what changed Netter's mind about Margery' (*Books under Suspicion*, pp. 259–60), but it is risky to presume he was personally aware of her to the extent which Kerby-Fulton's treatment implies.

7. Cf. pp. 102 above and 206 n. 51 below.

8. Cf. Jerome, *Epist.* LIII: *Ad Paulinum, de studio scriptuarum*, 6 and 7; in Migne, *PL* 22, 544.

9. Netter, *Doctrinale*, 1. 639.

10. On the many understandings of Mary Magdalene in the later Middle Ages, including her controversial role as *praedicatrix*, see now Katherine L. Jansen, *The Making of the Magdalen: Preaching and Popular Devotion in the Later Middle Ages* (Princeton, 2000), especially pp. 52–99.

11. On scholastic doctrine concerning the *magisterium* of preacher and teacher, see Jean Leclercq, 'Le magistère du prédicateur au XIIIe siècle', *Archives d'histoire doctrinale et littéraire du moyen âge*, 21 (1946), 105–47. See further Minnis, *Fallible Authors*, pp. 36–54.

12. Cf. the cogent discussion by John H. Arnold, 'Margery's Trials: Heresy, Lollardy and Dissent', in John H. Arnold and Katherine J. Lewis (eds.), *A Companion to 'The Book of Margery Kempe'* (Woodbridge, 2004), pp. 75–93 (p. 91).

13. A good example of what the authorities could have deemed private, 'amicable', and 'familiar' conversational teaching is afforded when Margery tells Archbishop Bowet and his associates the 'good tale' of the priest and the pear tree; they are quite impressed, despite their initial suspicions: *BMK* 1.52/93–4. Other passages in her *Book* confirm that Margery had a gift for such moral tale-telling.

14. The 'lowde voys' is Margery's rendering of the Vulgate *extollens vocem*, translated as 'lifting up her voice' in the Douay Bible. Did Margery identify with her in some way, I wonder? Cf. n. 25 below.

15. *BMK* 1.52/251–2.

16. Karma Lochrie, *Margery Kempe and Translations of the Flesh* (Philadelphia, 1991), p. 111.

17. *Registrum Johannis Trefnant*, ed. Capes, p. 345.

18. As discussed in the previous chapter.

19. This may seem like a quite shocking diminution of the role of the Virgin Mary; Brut's opponent may be deploying the idea tactically, to bring out the horrors of Lollardy. And, of course, Brut himself had given him a good opening, to judge from his views as recorded in Trefnant's register (cf. pp. 114–15 above).

20. See for example Augustine, *Enarrationes in psalmos, In Ps. 44*, 23 and *In Ps. 113*, 1 (Migne, *PL* 36, 508–9 and *PL* 37, 1479); Augustine, *Contra Epistolam Parmeniani*, ii.xi.23 (Migne, *PL* 43, 66–7); Bede, *Explanatio in quintum librum Mosis*, 25 (Migne, *PL* 91, 393B–C); Hraban Maur, *De Universo*, 3 (Migne, *PL* iii, 187D–188A); Peter Abelard, *Sermones ad Virgines Paraclitenses in oratorio ejus constitutas*, 7 (Migne, *PL* 178, 431D–432A); Peter Lombard, *In Ep. I ad Cor.*, 4 (Migne, *PL* 191, 1569D–1570A); *Glossa ordinaria in I Cor. 4* (*Biblia glossata*, vi. 229–30).

21. Of course, the point of the entire excursus, within the context of the question *Utrum mulieres sunt ministri ydonei ad conficiendum eukaristie sacramentum*, is to make the case that women can indeed confect – before proceeding to demolish it. Cf. Chapter 4 above.

22. *De officio pastorali*, in *The English Works of Wyclif, Hitherto Unprinted*, ed. F. D. Matthew, 2nd rev. edn, EETS OS 74 (Oxford, 1902), p. 441. Cf. Hudson, *Premature Reformation*, pp. 353–7, who comments that 'preaching was, in Lollard eyes, the only *raison d'être* of the clergy' (p. 355).

23. On Margery Kempe as one among many holy women who spoke out against the sins of the clergy see Janette Dillon, 'Holy Women and their Confessors or Confessors and their Holy Women? Margery Kempe and the Continental Tradition', in Rosalynn Voaden (ed.), *Prophets Abroad: The Reception of Continental Holy Women in Late-Medieval England* (Woodbridge, 1998), pp. 115–40. Edward Craun has argued that underlying such criticism is a well-established, and hence legitimating, tradition of spiritual correction; '*Fama* and Pastoral Constraints on Rebuking Sinners: *The Book of Margery Kempe*', in T. Fenster and D. L. Small (eds.), *Fama: The Politics of Talk and Reputation in Medieval Europe* (Ithaca, NY, 2003), pp. 187–209.

24. Even more tactless was Margery's bold rebuking of many of Archbishop Thomas Arundel's 'clerkys and other rekles men . . . which sworyn many gret othis and spokyn many rekles wordys' (1.16/109). Suspicious minds could easily have taken it as evidence of Lollardy, given the heretics' particular aversion to the uttering of oaths, on which see Hudson, *Premature Reformation*, pp. 371–4. Furthermore, speaking 'with reverence' to the archbishop himself, she advises him either to correct or to dismiss those foul-mouthed familiars. However, far from taking offence, Arundel 'ful benyngly and mekely' asks Margery to speak her mind and then gives her a 'fayr answer'. Indeed, their conversation continued until 'sterrys apperyd in the fyrmament' – an almost idyllic portrait of holy woman and archbishop united in their love for 'owyr alders Lord, almyty God' (p. 111). Whatever the truth of this encounter, no doubt Margery's amanuensis was happy to present such a reassuring account of his subject's relaxed encounter with the church's arch-persecutor of heretics. It stands in sharp contrast to the more aggressive interaction between Margery and Archbishop Henry Bowet.

25. This 'woman from the crowd' (*mulier de turba*) is interpreted as a woman *of* the crowd, in the postil on the whole Bible which Hugh of St Cher and his team of Dominicans compiled at Paris between 1230 and 1235. 'Neither rich

nor noble but of the common people', she signifies the simpler and lesser folk (*simplices et minores*) who, while the important and literate are blaspheming, praise the Lord. Christ 'speaks therefore in praise of simple layfolk who, in the midst of blaspheming clerics, praise God'. Hugh of St Cher, *Postilla domini Hugonis Cardinalis* (Basel, 1504), v.186r. Nicholas of Lyre identifies the woman as Marcella, a servant of Martha, the sister of Lazarus; *Biblia glossata*, VI. 845–6. Whether Margery was aware of such exegesis is, of course, impossible to gauge; suffice it to say that she would have found it germane.

26. *Biblia glossata*, v. 845.

27. *Biblia glossata*, v. 845–6. Indeed, Augustine went so far as to say that 'Mary's kinship as mother would have been of no benefit to her' had she not also borne Christ in her heart. 'Mary was more blessed by her grasp of faith in Christ than by conceiving Christ in the flesh.' *De sancta virginitate*, 3, in Augustine, '*De bono coniugali*' and '*De sancta virginitate*', ed. P. G. Walsh (Oxford, 2001), pp. 68–9.

28. *Biblia glossata*, v. 845.

29. *English Works of Wyclif*, ed. Matthew, p. 441.

30. It should be added that orthodox allegorical commentary on Luke 11:27–8 was eminently capable of transforming the female prerogatives of childbearing and suckling into male priestly activities. For example, Hugh of St Cher interprets the *ubera que sixisti* as preachers who suckle the very young in the Church with the milk of simple doctrine; *Postilla Hugonis Cardinalis*, v.186r. Here is another route that Margery did not wish to go down.

31. *BMK* 1.51/244. This emphasis is broadly in line with traditional allegorical commentary on Genesis 1:28. Both the interlinear and marginal components of the *Glossa* quote Jerome's dictum, 'Marriage replenishes the earth, virginity fills paradise', the point being that God is not enjoining marriage and corporeal procreation on everyone: *Biblia glossata*, I. 35–6; cf. Jerome, *Adversus Jovinianum*, 1.16 (Migne, *PL* 23, 235C). Furthermore, Augustine is quoted as having reported the view that 'increase and multiply' refers not to carnal fecundity but to that of the soul, as is indicated by the comparable phrasing of Psalm 137:3, 'Thou shalt multiply strength in my soul' (*De civitate dei*, XIV.21). St Cyprian of Carthage emphasizes the superiority of those who are capable of continence, and make themselves eunuchs for the kingdom of heaven (cf. Matthew 19:12): *Biblia glossata*, I. 35, citing Cyprian's *Liber de habitu virginum*, 33 (Migne, *PL* 4, 463A). Hugh of St Cher reads the passage *moraliter*, glossing *crescite* with 'in gratia' and *multiplicami* with 'in bonis operibus'; filling the earth becomes filling the Church with doctrine and good examples. *Biblia cum postillis Hugonis de Sancto Charo* (Basel, 1498–1502), I, unfol.

32. Cf. the definitions in Gerald J. Schiffhorst's introduction to his edited collection of essays, *The Triumph of Patience: Medieval and Renaissance Studies* (Orlando, FL, 1978), pp. 1–31, and also in Ralph Hanna III's contribution, 'Some Commonplaces of Late Medieval Patience Discussions: An Introduction', on pp. 65–87. Hanna notes that Gregory the Great made a major contribution to the tradition – as befits the author of the *Moralia in Iob*. Examples

of the prodigious feats of patience performed by holy women are included in ch. 3 ('Patience') of Richard Kieckhefer's *Unquiet Souls: Fourteenth-Century Saints and their Religious Milieu* (Chicago and London, 1984).

33. I am grateful to Richard Kieckhefer for his help here.

34. *Dialogi*, I.ii.8, in Migne, *PL* 77, 161B; Francis Clark, *The Pseudo-Gregorian Dialogues* (Leiden, 1987), p. 301. The issue of authorship is discussed extensively by Clark.

35. *Dialogi*, I.ii.8, I.ii.12, in Migne, *PL* 77, 161B, 164A; Clark, *The Pseudo-Gregorian Dialogues*, pp. 301–2. It should be noted, however, that the notion of teaching by example, of implementing holy precepts *in opere* (cf. pp. 116–17 above), was – in contexts far removed from the monastic milieu presupposed by the *Dialogues* – frequently deployed by male clerics as a means of keeping holy women in their place. For example, in an epilogue which appears in some manuscripts of the visions of Angela of Foligno (*c.* 1248–1309), Angela – yet another married holy woman – is described as a 'teacher (*doctrix*) in the discipline of God', but it is made quite clear that her mission consisted in teaching by action and observance rather than by public address. Angela's *observantia* has, so to speak, done the teaching, i.e. she recuperated the Franciscan Rule which was 'buried under by strong men and their worldly speculations'. *Il libro della Beata Angela da Foligno*, ed. L. Thier and A. Calufetti, Spicilegium Bonaventurianum 25 (Grottaferrata, 1985), p. 742; trans. Paul Lachance, *Angela of Foligno: Complete Works* (New York, 1993), pp. 317–18.

36. Alcuin Blamires, 'The Wife of Bath and Lollardy', *Medium Ævum*, 58 (1989), 224–42 (p. 233).

37. *Selections from English Wycliffite Writings*, ed. Hudson, p. 28.

38. Roger Dymmok, *Liber contra XII errores et hereses Lollardorum*, ed. H. S. Cronin (London, 1921), p. 275. Dymmok addressed his work to King Richard II, and offered many reasons why Lollards should be seen as 'enemies of the Crown as well as the Church'; cf. Patricia Eberle, 'The Politics of Courtly Style at the Court of Richard II', in Glyn Burgess and Robert A. Taylor (eds.), *The Spirit of the Court: Selected Proceedings of the Fourth Congress of the International Courtly Literature Society* (Cambridge, 1985), pp. 168–78 (pp. 173–8).

39. *Heresy Trials in the Diocese of Norwich, 1428–31*, ed. Norman P. Tanner, Camden Fourth Series, 20 (London, 1977), p. 57. Similar views are attributed to Isabella Davy (p. 64), William Bate de Sythyng (pp. 158, 160), and Richard Clerk (p. 192).

40. *Norwich Heresy Trials*, ed. Tanner, p. 166.

41. Wyclif, *Trialogus*, ed. Lechler, p. 322. See further Minnis, *Fallible Authors*, pp. 264–6, 273–5, 279–81, 444n, 450n, and Penn, 'Sacraments', pp. 281–2.

42. On which see Shannon McSheffrey, *Gender and Heresy: Women and Men in Lollard Communities, 1420–1530* (Philadelphia, 1995), pp. 82–7, and Dyan Elliott, 'Lollardy and the Integrity of Marriage and the Family', in Sherry Roush and Cristelle L. Baskins (eds.), *The Medieval Marriage Scene: Prudence, Passion, Policy* (Tempe, AZ, 2005), pp. 37–54.

43. Netter, *Doctrinale*, III. 411–24, 940, 943.

44. J. A. F. Thomson, *The Later Lollards, 1414–1520* (London, 1965), p. 122.

45. On White's peregrinations, see Hudson, *Premature Reformation*, pp. 139, 141–2. His importance within the Norwich group of Lollards is emphasized by Thomson, *Later Lollards*, pp. 127, 130, 131, and Margaret Aston, 'William White's Lollard Followers', in her *Lollards and Reformers*, pp. 71–99.

46. Hudson, *Premature Reformation*, p. 358. On the other hand, clerks travelled, and (generally speaking) the greater the clerk the more opportunities for travel he had.

47. *Of Weddid Men and Wifis and of Here Children Also*, ed. Eve Salisbury, in *The Trials and Joys of Marriage* (Kalamazoo, 2002), pp. 191–210 (p. 192).

48. The bibliography on this topic is vast, but see especially the relevant material in James A. Brundage *Law, Sex and Christian Society in Medieval Europe* (Chicago, 1987) and *Sex, Law and Marriage in the Middle Ages*, Collected Studies Series (Aldershot, Hampshire, and Brookfield, VT, 1993); also Pierre J. Payer, *The Bridling of Desire: Views of Sex in the Later Middle Ages* (Toronto and London, 1993), and Vern L. Bullough and James A. Brundage (eds.), *Handbook of Medieval Sexuality* (New York and London, 1996).

49. Marcia L. Colish, *Peter Lombard* (Leiden, 1994), p. 628.

50. *Of Weddid Men*, ed. Salisbury, p. 192.

51. Malcolm Lambert, *Medieval Heresy: Popular Movements from the Gregorian Reform to the Reformation*, 3rd edn (Oxford, 2002), p. 117. Margery Kempe abstained from meat (see especially the divine command to that effect, recorded at *BMK* 1.5/71, and the two versions of a 'maner of proverbe' which circulated about her, expressive of a suspicion that her food abstentions were hypocritical, as discussed – a fishy tale indeed – at 11.9/415–16). However, Margery was relatively untroubled by issues of diet, having been instructed by Christ that fasting 'is good for yong begynnars' – she herself having gone far beyond that stage – and been assured that He does not require her to wear a hair shirt or fast on bread and water (1.35 and 36/195). The *BMK* is full of references to shared meals and invitations to dine. Margery seems a far distance away from those holy anorexics and blessed bulimics described by Rudolph M. Bell, *Holy Anorexia* (Chicago and London, 1985), and Bynum, *Holy Feast and Holy Fast*.

52. *Selections from Wycliffite Writings*, ed. Hudson, p. 25. Luxurious diet had its dangers for women too, according to the eleventh of the *Twelve Conclusions*. Certain widows who are 'deliciousliche fed' insist on taking the mantle and ring (as tokens of their vow of chastity), but it is far better for them to re-marry, otherwise their lusts will lead them into 'priue synnis'. *Selections*, ed. Hudson, p. 28. Margery Kempe wishes to take the mantle and ring (*BMK* I.15/106–7) – a major problem being that she is not a widow. Cf. pp. 124 and 220 n. 60 below.

53. *Of Weddid Men*, ed. Salisbury, p. 192.

54. *Of Weddid Men*, ed. Salisbury, p. 193.

55. Neither is there any trace of that other shocking view occasionally attributed to Lollards, belief in the communality of wives. See for example *Norwich Heresy Trials*, ed. Tanner, p. 91, and Dymmok, *Liber contra XII errores*,

ed. Cronin, p. 275. Late medieval scholasticism derived its information on the subject largely from the *Politics* II.2–4, where Aristotle had attacked Plato's recommendation that in the ideal republic wives should be held in common.

56. For a rare (twelfth-century) invasion, see Peter Biller, 'William of Newburgh and the Cathar Mission to England', in D. Wood (ed.), *Life and Thought in the Northern Church c. 1100–c. 1700: Essays in Honour of Claire Cross*, Studies in Church History, Subsidia, 12 (Woodbridge, 1999), pp. 11–30; see further his later article, 'The Earliest Heretical Englishwomen', in Jocelyn Wogan-Browne *et al.* (eds.), *Medieval Women: Texts and Contexts in Late Medieval Britain. Essays for Felicity Riddy*, Medieval Women: Texts and Contexts 3 (Turnhout, 2000), pp. 363–76.

57. MS Harley 31, fol. 198v. See further Minnis, *Fallible Authors*, pp. 240–2, 437n, which is responding to a comment by C. W. Marx in Blamires (ed.), *Woman Defamed and Woman Defended*, p. 257. Pythagoras was credited with doctrines relating to the immortality, pre-existence, and transmigration of souls; see for example Augustine, *De trinitate*, XV.24, and *Contra academicos*, III.xvii, 37; cf. Isidore of Seville, *Etymologiae*, VIII.5: *de haeresibus Christianorum*, 69. Tertullian was particularly vocal on the subject of metempsychosis; see his *Apologeticus adversus gentes pro christianis*, 48 (Migne, *PL* 1, 521A–527B), *Ad nationes*, 1.19 (Migne, *PL* 1, 585B), and *De anima*, 28 (Migne, *PL* 2, 697A–698C).

58. Cf. Alan of Lille, *De fide catholica*, 1.xi: 'asseruit animam hominis merito peccati post mortem intrare in corpus alterius hominis vel bruti animalis' (Migne, *PL* 210, 317B–C). Also Bernard Gui, *Manuel de l'Inquisiteur*, ed. G. Mollat (Paris, 1926), p. 18, and Moneta of Cremona, *Adversus Catharos et Valdenses libri quinque*, 1.iv.5; ed. T. Ricchini (Rome, 1743; repr. Ridgewood, NJ, 1964), pp. 61–2. A general discussion has been provided by Roland Poupin, *Les Cathares, l'Âme et la Réincarnation* (Portet-sur-Garonne, 2000).

59. The extent of Margery's knowledge of the *Revelations* of St Bridget of Sweden (who is widely recognized as having exercised considerable influence on Margery's piety) is unclear, but she just might have known Bridget's vehement attack on the horrifying possibility that clerical marriage would be permitted by some foolish pontiff. If a pope were rash enough to concede to priests 'a license to contract carnal marriage', Bridget asserts, God would condemn him to the most extreme of spiritual punishments, culminating in his soul being 'tormented eternally in hell', serving as 'the food of demons everlastingly and without end' (*Revelations*, VII.10.16–17). Bridget sought to ensure that priests who consecrate the 'precious sacrament' of the Eucharist 'should by no means live in the easily contaminated, carnal delight of marriage', her zeal kindled by a desire to defend the 'holy' and 'worthy' office of priesthood (*Revelations*, VII.10.13). *Den Heliga Birgittas Revelaciones Bok VII*, ed. Birger Bergh (Uppsala, 1967), pp. 172–3; trans. A. R. Kezel, *Birgitta of Sweden: Life and Selected Revelations* (New York, 1990), pp. 172–73. On Margery's interest in Bridget see especially *BMK* 1.20/129–30, 1.39/202–4, and 1.58/280. See further Julia B. Holloway, 'Bride, Margery, Julian, and Alice: Bridget of

Sweden's Textual Community in Medieval England', in Sandra J. McEntire (ed.), *Margery Kempe: A Book of Essays*, Garland Medieval Casebooks, 4 (New York, 1992), pp. 203–22 (p. 203).

60. Repington had been one of Wyclif's closest followers at Oxford, but had recanted in 1382. This abjuration does not seem to have harmed his subsequent career. His problematic past may, however, help to explain why he was such a stickler for procedure in the case of Margery's request – though to be fair to Repington, it was normally widows who asked to make vows of chastity before him.

61. See *BMK* 1.15/106–8. The standard work on spiritual (= chaste) marriage is by Dyan Elliott, *Spiritual Marriage: Sexual Abstinence in Medieval Wedlock* (Princeton, 1993). For the special problems presented by Margery's request, see Michael Vandussen, 'Betokening Chastity: Margery Kempe's Sartorial Crisis', *Forum for Modern Language Studies*, 41.3 (2005), 275–88.

62. *BMK* 1.21/132. Christ, whose words the *BMK* quotes here, goes on to reassure Margery that Jesus loves her 'as wel as any mayden in the world'. On the extraordinary scene in which Margery, 'portrayed as a coy young bride', experiences a mystical marriage with God the Father, see especially Isabel Davis, 'Men and Margery: Negotiating Medieval Patriarchy', in Arnold and Lewis (eds.), *Companion to 'The Book of Margery Kempe'*, pp. 35–54 (pp. 40–1).

63. Lambert, *Medieval Heresy*, pp. 205–6, 418.

64. Lambert, *Medieval Heresy*, p. 205.

65. Robert E. Lerner, *The Heresy of the Free Spirit in the Later Middle Ages* (Berkeley and Los Angeles, 1972), pp. 5–6.

66. Anne Hudson, 'A Lollard Mass', in her *Lollards and their Books*, pp. 111–23 (p. 114); followed by Kerby-Fulton, *Books under Suspicion*, pp. 247–9, who assumes that William Ramsbury's Free Spirit credentials (on which see below) are unquestionable.

67. *'The Chastising of God's Children' and 'The Treatise of Perfection of the Sons of God'*, ed. J. Bazire and E. Colledge (Oxford, 1957), pp. 138–44. Here I follow the interpretation of Kerby-Fulton, *Books under Suspicion*, pp. 264–5.

68. Hilton, *Eight Chapters of Perfection*, in *English Mystics of the Middle Ages*, ed. Barry Windeatt (Cambridge, 1994), p. 141. The discourse in both these texts is consonant with that found in Marguerite Porete's *Mirouer des simples ames* (generally taken as the fullest extant statement of allegedly Free Spirit heresies) as translated into English by 'M.N.'; cf. *English Mystics*, ed. Windeatt, pp. 237–47, and the extensive discussion in Kerby-Fulton, *Books under Suspicion*, pp. 272–96.

69. To be more exact, the *Chastising* author's source seems to be a Latin translation by Gerhard Grote of Ruysbroeck's *Die Geestelike Boulocht*; cf. Kerby-Fulton, *Books under Suspicion*, pp. 263–4. The *Chastising*, which may be of Carthusian origin (though the evidence is inconclusive), has been unjustly neglected. A reappraisal has been urged by Annie Sutherland, who believes that 'of all the late medieval devotional texts' this is 'arguably' the one 'that bears the most cogent witness to the difficulties faced by a theological orthodox writer in

attempting to negotiate a correct relationship between the traditional Latinity of the church and the vernacular discourse which could render basic theology accessible to a significant proportion of the population'. '*The Chastising of God's Children*: A Neglected Text', in Helen Barr and Ann M. Hutchinson (eds.), *Text and Controversy from Wyclif to Bale: Essays in Honour of Anne Hudson*, Medieval Church Studies 4 (Turnhout, 2005), pp. 353–73 (p. 354).

70. *English Mystics*, ed. Windeatt, p. 137. On Cambridge's reaction against continental heresies see J. P. H. Clark, 'Walter Hilton and "Liberty of Spirit"', *The Downside Review*, 96 (1978), 61–78, and 'Late Fourteenth-Century Cambridge Theology and the English Contemplative Tradition', in Marion Glasscoe (ed.), *The Medieval Mystical Tradition in England*, v (Cambridge 1992), pp. 1–16.

71. As Hudson says; 'A Lollard Mass', p. 114. I fully support this claim, while believing that the case for Ramsbury's advocacy of Free Spirit ideas is at best marginal.

72. *Pace* Blamires, who (influenced by remarks in Lambert's *Medieval Heresy*) is inclined to dismiss it on the grounds that the 'sect' was too 'shadowy'; 'Wife of Bath and Lollardy', 232–3. 'Suspicions about Lollardy' could instead 'have been the basis' for the 'test question put to Margery Kempe', continues Blamires. The same point is made by Windeatt in his edition of *BMK*, p. 243. I agree that this is the more likely place to look, while wishing to argue the merits of another solution to the problem (as offered below).

73. As expressed in her article entitled 'A Lollard Mass', originally published in 1972. The summary account included in her 1988 *Premature Reformation* adds some analogous material from other Lollard trials (but describes Ramsbury's advocacy of divorcing infertile wives as 'unique'), while retaining the suggestion that there are some similarities here with 'the views of the Brethren of the Free Spirit' (pp. 292 n. 81, 385).

74. Hudson, 'A Lollard Mass', p. 113.

75. Hudson, 'A Lollard Mass', p. 121.

76. Netter, *Doctrinale*, II. 759–84 (esp. cols. 759–65); cf. Wyclif, *Trialogus*, ed. Lechler, pp. 315–17. Netter seizes on Phronesis's remark, 'it seems to me a probable opinion (*probabile*), that those who cannot procreate carnally are, in a certain way, joined together unlawfully'. Cf. the view expressed in Wyclif's earlier *De mandatis divinis* that (in Stephen Penn's words) 'only for as long as sexual intercourse is practised as a means of procreation may it be regarded as a legitimate act. Wyclif therefore regards any other form of sexual activity sinful, and as a breach of the law of marriage.' Penn, 'Sacraments', p. 280; *De mandatis divinis*, ed. J. Loserth and F. D. Matthew (London, 1922), pp. 347–8.

77. On the long-running controversy concerning the nature of the marital relationship between Mary and Joseph, see especially Colish, *Peter Lombard*, pp. 630, 631, 633–4, 635, 639–40, 642–4, 648–9, 651–2, 655–6; and Irven M. Resnick, 'Marriage in Medieval Culture: Consent Theory and the Case of Mary and Joseph', *Church History*, 69.2 (2000), 350–71. In fact, elsewhere Wyclif specifically defends the perfection of the marriage of Mary and Joseph. Cf. *Opus evangelicum*, ed. J. Loserth and F. D. Matthew (London, 1895–6),

1.169, with which may be compared *Lollard Sermons*, ed. Gloria Cigman, EETS 294 (Oxford, 1989), p. 57. However, Wyclif's failure to address this issue in the *Trialogus* discussion gave Netter an opening which he promptly took.

78. Heterodox views on marriage were of long duration in Kent, to judge by the records of trials conducted by Archbishop Warham of Canterbury between April 1511 and June 1512 – though these do not include, however, anything relating to the necessity of procreation for marriage. What we have are abjurations of claims that 'the sacrament of matrimony is of noon effecte' (p. 22), 'solennisation of matrymony is not necessary nor profitable for the wele of mannys soule' (pp. 27, 29, 30, 37, 39, 41, 77; cf. the Latin version on pp. 2, 9, 17, 44, 51), and 'whan a man and a woman be contracted togider, it is not necessary to solemnize it in the churche' (p. 20). All these page references are to *Kent Heresy Proceedings 1511–12*, ed. Norman Tanner (Maidstone, Kent, 1997).

79. As Netter contemptuously called him; *Doctrinale*, III. 630.

80. To borrow another phrase from Hudson, 'A Lollard Mass', p. 113. Neither do I believe it is necessary to postulate Free Spirit influence for the view of Thomas Palmer, a Stamford friar, that 'a Religious Man may flesshly medele and comune with a womman and not synne deedly'. Palmer revoked this erroneous opinion in 1424. Cf. *The Register of Henry Chichele, Archbishop of Canterbury, 1414–1443*, III, ed. E. F. Jacob, Canterbury and York Series, 46 (Oxford, 1945), p. 99; brought to our attention by Hudson, 'A Lollard Mass', p. 114. Perhaps, once again, an explanation can be found in Lollard thought of the kind I am reconstructing above – though it must be admitted that no other Wycliffite opinion is attributed to Palmer in Chichele's Register. As the present chapter has indicated (and cf. Minnis, *Fallible Authors*, pp. 265–8, 282, 287–90, 444n, 445n) a remarkable number of Lollard statements encouraging religious people, both male and female, to break their vows of chastity, are extant, though they certainly do not advocate or encourage promiscuous sex. It seems reasonable to compare Palmer's opinion with them. But, could we simply be dealing with a bad chat-up line? Probably not: the fact that Palmer preached his opinion in a public sermon (*in vulgari*) may indicate that some intellectual conviction (however febrile) was involved, rather than a simple wish to justify philandering.

81. An alternative argument would be that certain extreme Lollard views on marriage were highly receptive to Free Spirit infiltration – functioning as a magnetic force (so to speak) which attracted them.

82. To use Anne Hudson's term again; cf. p. 66 above.

83. Besides, anti-Lollard polemic 'rarely ran' to accusations of 'sexual immorality', perhaps because this 'proto-puritanical' sect gave its opponents little reason or excuse for such outrage. Cf. Dyan Elliott, 'Response to Alfred Thomas's "*The Wycliffite Woman*: Reading Women in Fifteenth-Century Bohemia"', in Linda Olson and Kathryn Kerby-Fulton (eds.), *Voices in Dialogue: Reading Women in the Middle Ages* (Notre Dame, IN, 2005), pp. 302–5. Therefore

Dymmok's accusation is unusual, and may smack of desperation. But see n. 87 below.

84. *BMK* 1.53/258.
85. *BMK* 1.54/265.
86. Cf. the argument made by David Aers, *Community, Gender, and Individual Identity: English Writing, 1360–1430* (London and New York, 1988), p. 102, and also Shklar, 'Chobham's Daughter', 294–5.
87. It should be noted, however, that 'Friar Daw' taunts Lollards with the charge that they draw away men's wives 'and maken hem scolers of þe newe scole' (ll. 100–4). *Jack Upland, Friar Daw's Reply and Upland's Rejoinder*, ed. P. L. Heyworth (London and New York, 1968), p. 76. There may be an implication of sexual exploitation in that remark.
88. *BMK* 1.48/236.
89. In the case of Lollardy I have in mind Dymmok's accusation, as quoted above.
90. *BMK* 1.86/375. The fact that John Kempe was alive and in good health could have presented a major impediment to Margery's spiritual aspirations, in contrast with the cases of (for example) Bridget of Sweden and Angela of Foligno, whose husbands had died, thereby leaving them utterly free to follow their spiritual callings. Margery gives her husband considerable personal credit for supporting her at *BMK* 1.15/103–4, but elsewhere she is less complimentary.
91. *BMK* 1.51/244.
92. Eustace's text is edited by Leclercq, 'Le magistère', 119–20. For discussion see especially Alcuin Blamires, 'Women and Preaching in Medieval Orthodoxy, Heresy, and Saints' Lives', *Viator*, 26 (1995), 135–52 (pp. 142, 147–9).
93. An informed guess may be ventured as to what Eustace might have done. The exceptional nature of St Bridget's case would have been emphasized, many and marvellous reasons given why she functioned above and beyond the 'common state of women'. This is exactly what happens in an anonymous sermon composed in the first half of the fifteenth century at Vadstena Abbey, wherein we are assured that the Pauline prohibition of female teaching (at 1 Tim. 2) does not apply to St Bridget, since 'she was privileged (*privilegiata erat*) by Christ' and 'the privileges of a few do not constitute common law'. That is to say, Bridget's special treatment by Christ has no major implications for the female sex in general; ordinary women remain just as they are, stay where they were. On this and related texts see Claire L. Sahlin, *Birgitta of Sweden and the Voice of Prophecy* (Woodbridge, 2001), pp. 212–20, and her article 'The Prophetess as Preacher: Birgitta of Sweden and the Voice of Prophecy', *Medieval Sermon Studies*, 40 (1997), 29–44 (especially pp. 32–3).
94. That said, it must be admitted that in certain fifteenth-century cases and contexts the boundary between heresy and orthodoxy appears ill-defined and even porous. This has been illustrated superlatively well in Robert Lutton's recent study, which focuses on a single large parish (Tenterden in Kent), albeit within a time-frame (*c.* 1480 to *c.* 1530) later than the one covered in this chapter: *Lollardy and Orthodox Religion in Pre-Reformation England: Reconstructing Piety* (Woodbridge, 2006).

95. *BMK* 1.52/249. Furthermore, there is no reason to suppose that the mysterious 'thyng in conscyens' which Margery wanted to confess at the time of her first child's birth (when she was close to death) was a youthful association with Lollardy, perhaps due to the preaching of William Sawtry, *pace* C. S. Stokes, 'Margery Kempe: Her Life and the Early History of her Book', *Mystics Quarterly*, 25 (1999), 9–68 (p. 25), and Stephen Medcalf, 'Inner and Outer', in Medcalf (ed.), *The Context of English Literature: The Later Middle Ages* (London, 1981), pp. 108–71 (pp. 116–17). Supporting evidence is simply lacking, and many other possibilities for the 'defawt' may be proposed. Neither is it helpful to say, with N. F. Partner, that Margery's 'style was Lollard', particularly in view of the many parallels which may be drawn between Margery's attitudes and activities and those of continental holy women; cf. Partner's article 'Reading *The Book of Margery Kempe*', *Exemplaria*, 3 (1991), 29–66 (p. 33).

6 CHAUCER AND THE RELICS OF VERNACULAR RELIGION

1. Monica McAlpine, 'The Pardoner's Homosexuality and How it Matters', *Publications of the Modern Language Association of America*, 95 (1980), 8–22 (p. 8).
2. 'The Pardoner's Homosexuality', 17.
3. Steven Kruger, 'Claiming the Pardoner: Toward a Gay Reading of Chaucer's Pardoner's Tale', *Exemplaria*, 6 (1994), 115–39. What Kruger regards as the 'angry' language of the passage quoted above is said to participate 'in the physical debasement of the Pardoner's false relics and queer body even as it rejects these'.
4. All *Roman de la Rose* references are to the edition by Félix Lecoy (Paris, 1965–70). On the *ad placitum* theory of language see my discussion in *Magister Amoris*, pp. 140–58.
5. Gurevich, *Medieval Popular Culture*, pp. ix, xiv.
6. Cf. once again Hugutio of Pisa's derivation of *vulgo* from *volo* ('I wish/want'), the *vulgo* being perceived as a multitude of people who do whatever they want. *Derivationes*, ed. Cecchini *et al.*, II. 1292–3 (U 46).
7. Desiderius Erasmus, *Peregrinatio religionis ergo*, in *Opera omnia*, I. 3, pp. 487–8; *Collected Works of Erasmus: Colloquies*, trans. C. R. Thompson, XL (Toronto, 1997), pp. 642–3. Erasmus explained later that in this account he sought to draw attention 'to those who exhibit doubtful relics for authentic ones, who attribute to them more than is proper, and basely make money by them'; *De utilitate colloquiorum*, in *Opera omnia*, I. 3, p. 743; *Collected Works of Erasmus: Colloquies*, trans. Thompson, XL, p. 1104. In contrast, the authenticity and valence of the relics which await Chaucer's fictional pilgrims at Canterbury are never called in question; there is no suggestion whatever that the spiritual treasures of Becket's shrine are in any way 'doubtful' or have more attributed to them than is proper.

8. I.e. the circular band of white wool which archbishops wore on their shoulders; cf. *Collected Works of Erasmus: Colloquies*, trans. Thompson, XL, p. 668 (n. 153).

9. Thomson declares that the *sudarium* (face-cloth or napkin) here mentioned 'was undoubtedly the archbishop's amice, worn around the neck under the liturgical garments to protect them from sweat and the wearing from chafing'; *Collected Works of Erasmus: Colloquies*, XL, p. 668 (n. 154).

10. *Peregrinatio*, p. 488; trans. Thompson, p. 642.

11. *Peregrinatio*, p. 491; trans. Thompson, p. 647. Erasmus is certainly writing satirically, but his views are rather more complicated than those posited by Daniel Knapp, 'The Relyk of a Seint: A Gloss on Chaucer's Pilgrimage', *English Literary History*, 39.1 (1972), 1–26. Cf. the discussion of pilgrimage and pardoning in Chapter 3 above.

12. *Peregrinatio*, p. 490; trans. Thompson, p. 645.

13. *Peregrinatio*, p. 487; trans. Thompson, p. 642.

14. Pieces of clothing once worn by a saint, or other objects s/he had come into contact with, were also revered as relics. On this belief see, for example, Caroline Walker Bynum, 'Bleeding Hosts and their Contact Relics in Late Medieval Northern Germany', *Medieval History Journal*, 7.2 (2004), 227–41, and also her *Wonderful Blood*, pp. 40, 77–9, 96–8, etc. The practice has survived in the present-day Catholic Church. Small pieces of Pope John Paul II's white cassock – veritable contact relics – were offered (via the website of the Holy Diocese of Rome) as part of the campaign to beatify him. However, fears of public misunderstanding led the Vatican to warn that buying relics is sacrilege. Cf. the BBC website http://news.bbc.co.uk/2/hi/europe/7012421.stm, and also http://news.bbc.co.uk/2/hi/europe/4543501.stm, both accessed on 26 Sept. 2007. In 2006 a group calling itself 'The International Crusade for Holy Relics' started lobbying to 'block the online sale of objects purported to contain the remains of Christian saints'. 'The sale of so-called "first-class relics" – bone, flesh, hair, nails and fragments of other body parts – remains a murky subculture, one that's increasingly shifting from the back rooms of dealers' shops to the Web's worldwide mall.' Brian Murphy, 'Religious Relics Selling on eBay', *Desert News* (Salt Lake City), 9 Dec. 2006; consulted online on 26 Sept. 2007 at http://findarticles.com/p/articles/mi_qn4188/is_20061209/ai_n16900213.

15. *Peregrinatio*, p. 487; trans. Thompson, p. 642.

16. Ed. John M. Bowers in *The Canterbury Tales: Fifteenth-Century Continuations and Additions* (Kalamazoo, 1992), p. 64.

17. Robyn Malo, 'The Pardoner's Relics (and Why They Matter the Most)', *ChR*, 43.1 (2008), 83–103; a fuller account is provided in her thesis, 'Saints' Relics in Medieval Literature' (Ph.D. diss., Ohio State University, Columbus, OH, 2007). Cf. Ben Nilson, *Cathedral Shrines of Medieval England* (Woodbridge, 1998), who describes tall shrine bases which inhibited close access to shrines; for example, one for William of York, built in 1472, was eleven feet high. Nilson remarks that an eight-foot tall shrine base was probably 'the practical maximum, being the highest a man could reach to lift the reliquary on and off,

lock the cover, or do other necessary tasks around the feretrum without the aid of a ladder . . . Anything lower [would have been] less impressive and too accessible to light-fingered pilgrims' (p. 48). An excellent summary account of late medieval developments in shrine architecture, with special reference to the Becket shrine, has been provided by Tim Tatton-Brown, 'Canterbury and the Architecture of Pilgrimage Shrines in England', in Colin Morris and Peter Roberts (eds.), *Pilgrimage: The English Experience from Becket to Bunyan* (Cambridge, 2002), pp. 90–107.

18. The containers themselves were often objects of great beauty, adorned with precious metals and stones. See the magnificent examples in Henk van Os, *The Way to Heaven: Relic Veneration in the Middle Ages* (Baarn, 2000), pp. 34, 118, 146, 149, 151, 152, 154–5, 161, and 179. Most of the reliquaries pictured on these pages retain their relics. More usually nowadays they are viewed as *objets d'art* in modern museums, having been emptied of contents which are offensive to modern taste – an experience quite different from whatever was common in the Middle Ages. Furthermore, many reliquaries had hinged doors and/or removable panels which allowed their contents to be viewed on special occasions and by special visitors. Excellent examples are afforded by the elaborately enamelled reliquary (1338) and the marble taberna-cle (finished around 1363) made for the relics associated with a miracle which occurred at Bolsena (near Orvieto, in Umbria) in 1264, when a consecrated host bled on to a corporal, i.e. the square white linen cloth upon which the host is placed during the celebration of mass. They were placed in the specially constructed Chapel of the Corporal in Orvieto Cathedral, where they may still be viewed today. Cf. Catherine D. Harding, *Guide to the Cappella del Corporale of Orvieto Cathedral* (Perugia, 2004), esp. pp. 21–45, 48–50. The relationship between relic cults and eucharistic devotion has been analysed by G. J. C. Snoek, *Medieval Piety from Relics to the Eucharist: A Process of Mutual Interaction* (Leiden and New York, 1995).

19. Sumption, *Pilgrimage*, pp. 82–3. On the 'almost insatiable demand for water in which the relics of saints or other sanctified objects had been diluted, powdered or immersed' see Carole Rawcliffe, 'Curing Bodies and Healing Souls: Pilgrimage and the Sick in Medieval East Anglia', in Morris and Roberts (eds.), *Pilgrimage*, pp. 108–40 (pp. 121–2).

20. Sumption, *Pilgrimage*, p. 83.

21. Sumption, *Pilgrimage*, p. 83.

22. On the *ampullae* and their representation in Canterbury stained glass of the late twelfth and early thirteenth centuries, see Sarah Blick, 'Comparing Pilgrim Souvenirs and Trinity Chapel Windows at Canterbury Cathedral', *Mirator* (September 2001), 1–27.

23. Sumption, *Pilgrimage*, p. 83.

24. *The Life of Saint Douceline, Beguine of Provence*, trans. Kathleen Garay and Madeline Jeay (Cambridge, 2001), pp. 105–8. On another occasion, the lady Laura of Hyères puts 'a finger of the holy virgin' in her mouth, in order to cure the swelling in her head, neck and face; trans. Garay and Jeay, pp. 104–5.

25. To return to Steven Kruger's comment, as quoted at the beginning of this chapter.

26. Cf. the account in the Laud MS of the *South-English Legendary*

> . . . next is flesche þe here was : with knottes mani on,
> Þat deope in is flesche seten : some riȝt to þe bon;
> Þar-of he hadde schurte and brech : luytel aise he miȝte i-fele . . .
> Ful of wormes was is flesch : to al oþur wo,
> In none creature, ich onderstonde : neuere ne weren i-seie mo . . .
>
> (2207–14)

Oxford, Bodleian Library, MS Laud 108, *The Early South-English Legendary or Lives of Saints*, ed. Carl Horstmann, EETS OS 87 (London, 1887), p. 170.

27. *Collected Works of Erasmus: Colloquies*, trans. Thompson, XL, p. 667 (n. 142).

28. Knapp, 'The Relyk of a Seint'. However, I disagree with Knapp's view that, on the strength of Chaucer's attack on fake relics, we may infer that he considered absurd the kissing of relics in general, and, by extension, the entire pilgrimage to Canterbury – that being (on Knapp's argument) why Chaucer planned to bring the pilgrims back to Southwark, since the arrival at Canterbury could not serve as a fitting climax. In my own view, the Pardoner's dirty breeches, as a mock-relic created in the Host's imagination, may certainly be seen as the parodic equivalent of Becket's hair-breeches at Canterbury – but this need not mean that Chaucer lacked respect for the genuine relic. *Pace* John V. Fleming, I see no evidence of 'a dissenter's scorn' in 'the several overt and covert references to the shrine of Becket in Chaucer's poem': 'Chaucer and Erasmus on the Pilgrimage to Canterbury: An Iconographical Speculation', in Thomas J. Heffernan (ed.), *The Popular Literature of Medieval England* (Knoxville, 1985), pp. 148–66 (p. 153).

29. Richard Firth Green, 'The Pardoner's Pants (and Why They Matter)', *SAC*, 15 (1993), 131–45.

30. Green, 'The Pardoner's Pants', 136–9.

31. In *Recueil de farces (1450–1550)*, ed. A. Tissier (Geneva, 1986–), VI. 185–261.

32. Green, 'The Pardoner's Pants', 140.

33. As Malcolm Jones puts it; *The Secret Middle Ages: Discovering the Real Medieval World* (Trupp, Stroud, Gloucestershire, 2002), p. 31.

34. Duffy, *Stripping of the Altars*, pp. 200–5. Duffy notes that St Walstan was 'a figure of some consequence in the popular religious imagination in Norfolk between the late thirteenth and the early sixteenth century' (p. 200). Cf. M. R. James, 'Lives of St Walstan', *Norfolk Archaeology*, 19 (1917), 238–67.

35. Duffy, *Stripping of the Altars*, p. 204. Generally speaking, 'the presence of a saint or his or her relics in a given place or region could stimulate the productive forces of nature', as Vauchez says; *Sainthood*, p. 463.

36. Duffy, *Stripping of the Altars*, p. 204; cf. F. Blomefield and C. Parkin, *An Essay towards a Topographical History of the County of Norfolk* (London, 1805–10), II. 389.

37. For an account of the various ways in which the Pardoner could have been considered a 'eunuch' in Chaucer's day see my *Fallible Authors*, pp. 147–61, 168, 181.

38. On the other hand, Thomas à Becket might well have performed the same service. See pp. 144–5 below.

39. More, *Dialogue concerning Heresies*, I. 17, ed. Lawler, Marc'Hadour, and Marius, in *The Yale Edition of the Complete Works of St. Thomas More*, executive ed. Sylvester, VI, pt I, p. 98.

40. The Messenger proceeds to complain about the way in which the head of one and the same saint can be shown in three places, and sometimes a whole saint's body in several countries, if 'we byleue the lyes of the people'. 'And in bothe the places is the one body worshypped where the one or the other is false / and one body mystaken for another / an euyll man happely for a good.' Yet priests in both places take offerings, in which case either you must say that the miracles of the one place are false and feigned or that miracles neither make your matter good nor prove your pilgrimages true.

41. This point is preserved in John Heywood's amplification of this passage in his play, *The Pardoner and the Frere*, ll. 105–21; Heywood, *Plays*, ed. Axton and Happé, pp. 96–7. It is intriguing that Chaucer, followed by Heywood, does not suggest that the *human* procreative powers of the 'good-man' will be increased by drinking this holy water; the point is rather that, if he takes his medicine, his beasts and his possessions shall increase and multiply – possibly a *reductio ad absurdum*, given the apparent disjunction between the different species (man and 'beestes') and between animate and inanimate things (man and 'stoor'). Does this chime with one of the interpretations suggested at the end of this chapter, that, considered as a *relyk*, the Pardoner's *coillons* are the biggest fake of all, of no help to anyone who might wish to enhance his sexual potency by kissing them?

42. More, *Dialogue concerning Heresies*, II.9, ed. Lawler *et al.*, p. 217.

43. More, *Dialogue concerning Heresies*, II.9, ed. Lawler *et al.*, p. 221.

44. More, *Dialogue concerning Heresies*, II.9, ed. Lawler *et al.*, p. 223.

45. More, *Dialogue concerning Heresies*, II.10, ed. Lawler *et al.*, p. 226.

46. Cf. David Farmer, *The Oxford Dictionary of Saints*, 4th edn (Oxford, 1997), pp. 160–1.

47. Cf. Farmer, *Oxford Dictionary of Saints*, pp. 238–9.

48. Cf. Farmer, *Oxford Dictionary of Saints*, p. 27.

49. Cf. Farmer, *Oxford Dictionary of Saints*, pp. 525–6.

50. Cf. Farmer, *Oxford Dictionary of Saints*, pp. 430–1.

51. Cf. Farmer, *Oxford Dictionary of Saints*, pp. 506–7. Oats were also offered at the shrine of a mysterious 'Maiden Cutbrogh', according to a report made to Thomas Cromwell, Henry VIII's chief minister, by Dr John London (Warden of New College, Oxford, and an infamous despoiler of monasteries). Under the feet of this image 'was a trough of wood descending under the altar which was hollow. Thither resorted such as were troubled with the headache, or had any sluttish widows' locks, viz. hair growing together in a tuft. There they must put into the trough a peck of oats, and when they were once slid under

the altar, the Cross Friars should behind the altar privily steal them out, and the sick person must give to the friar a penny for a pint of these cutbrogh oats, and then their heads should ache no more until the next time.' London may be describing Thelsford, a Trinitarian friary in Warwickshire. *Letters to Cromwell*, ed. Cook, pp. 209–10.

52. Cf. More, *Dialogue concerning Heresies*, II.II, ed. Lawler *et al.*, p. 234.

53. Cf. *MED*, s.v. *ston* (n), 13(a), 'A calculus or stone in the bladder, kidney, etc.; a kidney stone'; *maladie (siknesse) of the ston* is defined as 'an acute kidney stone attack or similar ailment'.

54. More, *Dialogue concerning Heresies*, II.10, ed. Lawler *et al.*, p. 228. We shall address the evidence of 'mennes gere & womens gere' made in metal later.

55. Cf. Duffy, *Stripping of the Altars*, pp. 197, 199. In 1443 Margaret Paston's mother promised to Our Lady of Walsingham an image of Margaret's husband John, who had been sick – this seems to have been a life-sized effigy, given that it is described as being of John's own weight. In the *vita* of Douceline of Digne a young noblewoman from Marseilles prays concerning her serious eye ailment to the 'saint', promising to bring to her tomb 'as an offering a pound of wax in the shape of eyes'; *Life of Douceline*, trans. Garay and Jeay, pp. 103–4. And one of the post-mortem miracles of Bridget of Sweden involved the resuscitation of an apparently dead baby, whereupon the grateful mother kept her vow to visit Bridget's tomb with a wax image (presumably a life-sized effigy of the child). Cf. Susan Signe Morrison, *Women Pilgrims in Late-Medieval England: Private Piety and Public Performance* (London, 2000), pp. 18, 22. On the care and healing of children by saints see especially Ronald C. Finucane, *The Rescue of the Innocents: Endangered Children in Medieval Miracles* (New York, 1997). On the practice of making vows to saints see Vauchez, *Sainthood*, pp. 454–63.

56. Cf. Duffy, *Stripping of the Altars*, pp. 197–8.

57. A small golden model of a baby boy was one of the gifts sent to the shrine of St Gilles in Provence by Władysław Herman, king of Poland, who was anxious to beget an heir. Cf. Sumption, *Pilgrimage*, p. 81.

58. Duffy, *Stripping of the Altars*, p. 199.

59. More, *Dialogue concerning Heresies*, II.10, ed. Lawler *et al.*, pp. 228–9.

60. More, *Dialogue concerning Heresies*, II.II, ed. Lawler *et al.*, p. 234.

61. More, *Dialogue concerning Heresies*, II.II, ed. Lawler *et al.*, pp. 234–5. Given that this is an English situation, More feels that he can comment on it. A few lines earlier he remarks that he himself has often seen ('I haue my selfe sene yt often tymes') bread and ale being offered to St 'Germyn'. And there is nothing much amiss here. He has never seen a priest or clerk drinking the offered wine; rather it is given to children or to poor folk to pray for a sick child. And it wouldn't be any kind of offence to offer up a whole ox and distribute it among poor people! (p. 234).

62. 'Somwhat is it in dede that ye say'; More, *Dialogue concerning Heresies*, II.II, ed. Lawler *et al.*, p. 232.

63. More, *Dialogue concerning Heresies*, II.II, ed. Lawler *et al.*, p. 235.

64. More, *Dialogue concerning Heresies*, II.II, ed. Lawler *et al.*, p. 236.

65. More, *Dialogue concerning Heresies*, II.II, ed. Lawler *et al.*, p. 237.
66. More, *Dialogue concerning Heresies*, II.II, ed. Lawler *et al.*, p. 232.
67. Cf. Farmer, *Oxford Dictionary of Saints*, p. 117.
68. More, *Dialogue concerning Heresies*, II.II, ed. Lawler *et al.*, p. 233. Cf. Farmer, *Oxford Dictionary of Saints*, p. 140.
69. Cf. p. 1 above.
70. Cf. Catherine Randall Coats, *Subverting the System: Agrippa d'Aubigné and Calvinism*, Sixteenth Century Essays and Studies, 14 (Kirksville, MO, 1990), p. 102.
71. *Confession du Sieur de Sancy*, II.2, in Agrippa d'Aubigné, *Œuvres*, ed. H. Weber, J. Bailbé, and M. Soulié (Paris, 1969), p. 633.
72. Cf. Chaucer's euphemistic reference to the Wife of Bath's genitalia as her *bele chose* ('pretty thing'); *Wife of Bath's Prologue*, III(D), 447, 510. Cf. *MED*, s.v. *chose* and also s.v. *thing*, 13a(b).
73. An (even more distorted) version of this kind of story may be found in Reginald Scot's *Discoverie of Witchcraft* (1584), where a woman named 'Katharine Loe', 'having a husband not so readilie disposed that waie as she wished him to be', is said to have 'made a waxen image to the liknes of hir husbands bewitched member, and offered it up at S. *Anthonies* altar; so as, through holiness of the masse it might be sanctified, to be more couragious, and of better disposition and abilitie, etc.'. This may be read as a garbled version of the practice of offering wax votives. *Discoverie of Witchcraft, Published with an Introduction by M. Summers* (New York, 1972), pp. 247–8 (IV. 6: 'Certeine popish and magicall cures, for them that are bewitched in their privities'). The 'St Antony' in question is Anthony of Padua, OFM (1195–1231), on whom see below, p. 146.
74. *Apologie pour Hérodite*, in Henri Estienne, *Œuvres*, ed. P. Ristelhuber (Paris, 1879), II. 321–3.
75. Cf. Jones, *Secret Middle Ages*, p. 31.
76. *Tableau des differens de la religion*, bk 1, pt. 5, cap. 10, in Philippe de Marnix, *Œuvres*, ed. E. Quenet (Brussels; 1857, repr. Geneva, 1971), ii.387.
77. The latter is St Judoc (Josse); cf. Farmer, *Oxford Dictionary of Saints*, p. 278. Marnix also mentions St Guerlichou and the St Foutin (here called 'Faustin') in Perigreux who is known as 'Saint Chose' by the women of the region; a fuller version of the Perigreux tale is found in Agrippa d'Aubigné's *Confession de Sancy*, as quoted above.
78. William of Canterbury, *Miracula sancti Thomae Cantuariensis*, in J. C. Robertson (ed.), *Materials for the History of Thomas Becket*, I, Rolls Series 67.1 (London, 1875), pp. 156–8.
79. Benedict of Peterborough, *Miracula sancti Thomae Cantuariensis*, in J. C. Robertson (ed.), *Materials for the History of Thomas Becket*, II, Rolls Series 67.2 (London, 1876), pp. 173–82. On the lives of Becket see especially Jennifer M. Lee, 'Searching for Signs: Pilgrims' Identity and Experience made Visible in the *Miracula Sancti Thomae Cantuariensis*', in Sarah Blick and Rita Tekippe (eds.), *Art and Architecture of Late Medieval Pilgrimage in Northern Europe and the British Isles* (Leiden, 2005), pp. 473–91.

80. Trinity Chapel Ambulatory, n. III (old number 5), 18, 19, 16 (probably created soon after the return of the monks to Canterbury in 1213). For a recent account, with good illustrations, see M. A. Michael, *Stained Glass of Canterbury Cathedral* (London, 2004), pp. 124, 134–7.

81. Christopher Norton, *St William of York* (York and Woodbridge, 2006), p. 201.

82. Norton, *St William of York*, p. 170.

83. See Paul Hyams, 'The Strange Case of Thomas of Elderfield', *History Today*, 36.6 (1986), 9–15.

84. To quote a common *ampulla* inscription; cf. Blick, 'Comparing Pilgrim Souvenirs', 10.

85. Gurevich, *Medieval Popular Culture*, pp. xv, xvi; Le Goff, *Time, Work and Culture*, pp. 156–8.

86. Pierre Sanchis, 'The Portuguese "romarias"', in Stephen Wilson (ed.), *Saints and their Cults: Studies in Religious Sociology, Folklore and History* (Cambridge, 1983), pp. 261–89 (p. 271). This material is made into talismans which, the women believe, will help them conceive.

87. Sanchis, 'The Portuguese "romarias"', p. 271.

88. Sanchis, 'The Portuguese "romarias"', p. 285 n. 43.

89. Sanchis, 'The Portuguese "romarias"', p. 271.

90. Mary Lee Nolan and Sidney Nolan, *Christian Pilgrimage in Modern Western Europe* (Chapel Hill and London, 1989), p. 151, and B. Blackburn and L. Holford-Strevens (eds.), *The Oxford Companion to the Year* (Oxford, 1999), pp. 247–8 (re 13 June).

91. Jones, *Secret Middle Ages*, p. 32.

92. *Lais féeriques des XIIe et XIIIe siècles*, ed. A. Micha (Paris, 1992), p. 106. On the perceived relationship between barrenness and divine displeasure see Sumption, *Pilgrimage*, p. 81. Rather later in Provence, a noble baron named Raynaud and his wife promised Douceline of Digne 'that if she wished to give them a son, they would offer the child's weight in wax' at her tomb; 'before long they had a fine son'. Cf. *Life of Douceline*, trans. Garay and Jeay, p. 102.

93. Morrison, *Women Pilgrims*, p. 73. Morrison makes an excellent case that 'Gender-specific illnesses, mainly having to do with fertility and childbirth, are fundamental to understanding women's relationship to pilgrimage' (p. 3). 'Women went on pilgrimage, vowed to go on pilgrimage, or had someone else go on pilgrimage in order: to get pregnant, to have a safe delivery, to help an apparently damaged or sick foetus, to avoid childbirth pain' (p. 19). See further Rawcliffe's discussion of women's needs: 'Pilgrimage and the Sick', pp. 133–8. We are now in need of research on paranatural methods of healing in relation to medieval constructions of masculinity. Catherine Rider's book *Magic and Impotence in the Middle Ages* (Oxford, 2006) has achieved much, but much remains to be done, especially in respect of healing saints and their shrines.

94. These details follow Erasmus's account in *Peregrinatio religionis ergo* (*Peregrinatio*, p. 487; trans. Thompson, pp. 632–3), where he is giving a sceptical account of this relic and its transmission to England. A little earlier he has Mary complain about prayers which women make to her: 'sometimes they ask of a Virgin what a modest youth would hardly dare ask of a bawd – things I'm ashamed to put in writing'. The petitions 'she' does manage to put in writing include: 'An unmarried girl cries, "Mary, give me a rich and handsome bridegroom". A married one, "Give me fine children". A pregnant woman, "Give me an easy delivery"' (*Peregrinatio*, p. 473; trans. Thompson, p. 625). Here once again we see an intellectual's scorn for the attractions and comforts of 'popular' religion. No doubt things looked very different to women fearing death in childbirth. Little wonder that during labour they wished to be, for example, wrapped in the clothes of Marie d'Oignies (1177–1213), which held out freedom 'from the danger of death' and the joy of 'a happy birth'; *The Anonymous History of the Church of Oignies*, trans. Hugh Feiss, in *Two Lives of Marie d'Oignies*, trans. Margot King and Hugh Feiss (Toronto, 1993), p. 268. According to Dr John London, Monk Ferleigh in Wiltshire possessed 'The Vincula of S. Petrus' (i.e. the fetters or girdle of St Peter) 'which women put about them at the time of their delivery'; *Letters to Cromwell*, ed. Cook, p. 38. On relics which helped women to travel safely see Dr Richard Layton's account on p. 40.

95. Morrison, *Women Pilgrims*, pp. 23–4. On medieval cults of Marian relics see further P. V. Bétérous, 'A propos d'une des légendes mariales les plus répandues: le "Lait de la Vierge"', *Bulletin de l'Association Guillaume Budé*, 4 (1975), 403–11; Vincent, *The Holy Blood*, pp. 41–2. Mary's milk may be deemed a blood-relic, given the common medieval belief that breast milk was transmuted blood; the cessation of a woman's menstrual blood during breast-feeding was taken as evidence that it was being transformed into milk. Cf. Bynum, *Jesus as Mother*, pp. 132–3; Bynum, *Holy Feast and Holy Fast*, pp. 178–9. On earlier Christian tradition, together with Hippocrates's opinion that milk is blood, see Elizabeth S. Bolman, 'The Enigmatic Coptic Galaktotrophousa and the Cult of the Virgin Mary in Egypt', in Maria Vassilaki (ed.), *Images of the Mother of God: Perceptions of the Theotokos in Byzantium* (Aldershot, Hants., 2005), pp. 13–22 (esp. p. 17).

96. Susan Starr Sered, 'Rachel's Tomb and the Milk Grotto of the Virgin Mary: Two Women's Shrines in Bethlehem', *Journal of Feminist Studies in Religion*, 2.2 (1986), 7–22. Legend has it that the grotto's black walls miraculously turned white when the Virgin, as she was nursing the baby Jesus, dropped a little milk.

97. Nolan and Nolan, *Christian Pilgrimage*, pp. 71–3. See further Stephen Wilson's account of votive offerings in Paris churches, based on field-work undertaken in 1978; 'Cults of Saints in the Churches of Central Paris', in Wilson (ed.), *Saints and their Cults*, pp. 233–60. On some of the relics serving as primary objects of veneration today see Nolan, *Christian Pilgrimage*, pp. 172–9.

98. Duffy notes that the objects clustered around the tomb of Richard Scrope in York Minster included four breasts; *Stripping of the Altars*, p. 197. See further V. M. Radford, 'The Wax Images Found in Exeter Cathedral', *Antiquaries Journal*, 29 (1949), 164–8.

99. That desperation is well illustrated by the scenes following the death of the Provençal holy woman Douceline of Digne. Crowds came in search of relics, cutting up 'all her clothing, and the friars could do nothing to prevent it. One of the friars almost lost his arm trying to protect her from them.' During the burial procession, three tunics are put on the corpse but each is 'cut to pieces one after the other'. 'The guards, who were protecting her with swords and clubs, were barely able to keep the people from tearing the body apart in their great devotion.' *Life of Douceline*, trans. Garay and Jeay, pp. 92–3. Following the death of St Francis of Assisi, his followers hid his body (so well that they had difficulty in recovering it later), no doubt to protect it from the excesses of 'popular' devotion. Patrick Geary has remarked that 'the danger of someone murdering an aging holy man in order to acquire his relics, or at least stealing his remains as soon as he was dead was ever present': 'Sacred Commodities: The Circulation of Medieval Relics', in A. Appadurai (ed.), *The Social Life of Things: Commodities in Cultural Perspective* (Cambridge, 1986), pp. 169–90 (p. 177).

100. Duffy, *Stripping of the Altars*, pp. 198–9; see also Ronald C. Finucane, *Miracles and Pilgrims: Popular Beliefs in Medieval England* (London, 1977), pp. 97–9.

101. Boccaccio, *Decameron*, Conclusione dell'autore, ed. Branca, p. 718.

102. Cf. p. 142 above.

103. A. M. Koldeweij, 'Lifting the Veil on Pilgrim Badges', in J. Stopford (ed.), *Pilgrimage Explored* (Woodbridge, 1999), pp. 161–88 (p. 187).

104. Cited and discussed by Finucane, *Miracles and Pilgrims*, p. 95.

105. John Shinners (ed.), *Medieval Popular Religion* (Peterborough, Ont., 1997), p. 171.

106. To quote from the account by Jean Seguin, *Saints guérisseurs, saints imaginaires, dévotions populaires*, 2nd edn (Paris, 1943), pp. 12–13. The first edition was published in 1929. I am grateful to Richard Firth Green for drawing my attention to a copy of the second edition in the library of the Ohio State University in Columbus.

107. Koldeweij, 'Lifting the Veil on Pilgrim Badges', p. 185. As Ruth Mellinkoff says, to judge from the numbers which have survived they must have been manufactured in hundred of thousands; *Averting Demons: The Protective Power of Medieval Visual Motifs and Themes* (Los Angeles, 2004), i. 51. More expensive versions, in silver or gold, were produced for the wealthy, but few of these have survived.

108. The first significant discussion of the Seine badges was included in the pioneering study of Thomas Wright, 'The Worship of the Generative Powers during the Middle Ages of Western Europe', published as the second part of R. P. Knight and T. Wright, *Discourse on the Worship of Priapus, and its Connection with the Nuptic Theology of the Ancients, to Which Is Added*

an Essay on the Worship of the Generative Powers during the Middle Ages of Western Europe (London, 1865). The Dutch materials have recently been catalogued: H. J. E. Van Beuningen and A. M. Koldeweij (eds.), *Heilig en Profann. 1000 Laat-middeleeuwse insignes uit de collectie H. J. E. Van Beuningen* (Cothen, 1993), and H. J. E. Van Beuningen, A. M. Koldeweij, and D. Kicken (eds.), *Heilig en Profann 2. 1200 Laat-middeleeuwse insignes uit openbare en particuliere collecties* (Cothen, 2001).

109. Nicola McDonald makes this point in the introduction to her edited collection, *Medieval Obscenities* (York and Woodbridge, 2006), pp. 1–16 (pp. 8–9); cf. Brian Spencer, *Pilgrim Souvenirs and Secular Badges: Medieval Finds from Excavations in London* (London, 1998), pp. 317–18.

110. Birch, *Pilgrimage to Rome*, p. 78. See further the comprehensive review by M. Mitchener, *Medieval Pilgrim and Secular Badges* (London, 1986).

111. Cf. Birch, *Pilgrimage to Rome*, p. 76. On the notion of such badges as *signa peregrinationis* see E. Cohen, '*In Haec Signa*: Pilgrim Badge Trade in Southern France', *Journal of Medieval History*, 2 (1976), 193–214.

112. *The Canterbury Tales: Fifteenth-Century Continuations*, ed. Bowers, p. 64.

113. They could have bought pilgrim badges representing the head reliquary of Becket, his shrine, the sword that killed him (which could pull out of its tiny scabbard), 'Canterbury bells' with his name on them, and sundry good luck/Becket charms, such as the four-leaf clover with the initial 'T' for Thomas in the middle. (I am grateful to Sarah Blick for her help here.) Souvenirs had been sold at Canterbury for over 300 years, from 1171 until the 1530s. 'No other shrine in England or Europe matched Canterbury's production of pilgrim souvenirs, in terms of variety, quantity, and quality'; Blick, 'Comparing Pilgrim Souvenirs', 23 n. 38. See further Blick, 'Reconstructing the Shrine of St. Thomas Becket, Canterbury Cathedral', in Blick and Tekippe (eds.), *Art and Architecture of Late Medieval Pilgrimage*, pp. 405–41 (pp. 419–23).

114. For medieval examples of winged phallus badges see Van Beuningen and Koldeweij (eds.), *Heilig en Profann*, afb. 634–40, 646–8, and Van Beuningen, Koldeweij and Kicken (eds.), *Heilig en Profann 2*, afb. 1757–9, 1761. See further Spencer, *Pilgrim Souvenirs and Secular Badges*, pp. 317–18, and the convenient list of references in A. M. Koldeweij, 'A Barefaced *Roman de la Rose* (Paris, B.N., ms. Fr. 25526) and Some Late Medieval Mass-Produced Badges of a Sexual Nature', in M. Smeyers and B. Cardon (eds.), *Flanders in a European Perspective* (Leuven, 1995), pp. 499–516 (p. 500).

115. For examples see the relevant drawings in Wright, 'Worship of the Generative Powers', and the photographs in Mellinkoff, *Averting Demons*, II. 282–3 (figs. VI.87–8). On the next page is an interesting variant – a woman riding a phallus with legs which has a bell tied around its tip, this being a French artifact now preserved in the Musée de Cluny, Paris (p. 284; fig. VI.89).

116. Koldeweij, 'Lifting the Veil on Pilgrim Badges', p. 185.

117. A. M. Koldeweij, '"Shameless and Naked Images": Obscene Badges as Parodies of Popular Devotion', in Blick and Tekippe (eds.), *Art and Architecture of Late Medieval Pilgrimage*, pp. 493–510 (pp. 499–500).

118. Jones, *Secret Middle Ages*, p. 253.
119. Van Beuningen, Koldeweij and Kicken (eds.), *Heilig en Profann 2*, afb. 1752.
120. This badge survives in various forms; for examples see Jones, *Secret Middle Ages*, p. 256 (fig. 12.3) and Mellinkoff, *Averting Demons*, ii. 291 (fig. vi.97), both dated *c.* 1375–1425 and both in the Van Beuningen Collection. Imagery of this kind is best known to students of literature from the end of Jean de Meun's continuation of the *Roman de la Rose*, where the lover's members are thinly allegorized as a pilgrim's staff and scrip, and the Rose's genitalia are described as relics; cf. p. 131 above. For a recent discussion of the Host's response to the Pardoner in light of the *Rose*, see Marijane Osborn, 'Transgressive Word and Image in Chaucer's Enshrined *coillons* Passage', *ChR*, 37.4 (2003), 365–84. The illustrations in one manuscript of the *Rose*, Paris, Bibliothèque Nationale de France, MS fr. 25526, have sexual iconography similar to that found on the genital badges: see Koldeweij, 'A Barefaced *Roman de la Rose*'.
121. Jones, *Secret Middle Ages*, p. 267 (fig. 12.8); Mellinkoff, *Averting Demons*, ii. 286 (fig. vi.91); discussed by Spencer, *Pilgrim Souvenirs and Secular Badges*, pp. 315–16. Cf. the similar badge featuring a purse with a central protruding bar that suggests a penis, four copies of which were found at Butlers Wharf; illustrated and discussed by Spencer, *Pilgrim Souvenirs and Secular Badges*, pp. 314 (fig. 314b), 317–18. The purse image is particularly appropriate for this kind of badge because 'purse' was a common medieval metaphor for the scrotum; cf. the *MED*, s.v. *purs(e)*, 4. When, following the end of his tale, Chaucer's Pardoner urges the Host to 'unbokele' his 'purs' to make an offering to his relics (943–5), Harry may see a sexual innuendo there (whether the Pardoner had intended it or not) and perhaps that is what triggers his interest in the Pardoner's own *coillons*.
122. The difficulties involved in interpreting sexual imagery are well exemplified by the recently discovered mural which adorns a thirteenth-century fountain at Massa Marittima in Tuscany; this features a 'penis tree' (phalluses being 'distributed fairly evenly through all the branches') and a group of women in 'before and after' scenes, the first scene being peaceful and the second expressive of some sort of discord (recent restoration has revealed two of these women fighting over a large phallus). The fifteenth-century *Malleus maleficarum* claims that witches 'sometimes collect male organs in great numbers, and put them in a bird's nest, . . . where they move themselves like living members'; could this be a clue to the meaning of the mural? George Ferzoco thinks so, and further proposes a political message: the women may be witches, 'engaged not simply in an occult ritual but in a political activity, linked to Ghibellinism, working against the common and natural good of the city republic'. In other words: when the Ghibellines come into power, things fall apart; women become witches, sexual norms are violated, social and natural order break down completely. Cf. George Ferzoco, *Il murale di Massa Marittima / The Massa Marittima Mural*, Toscana Studies, 1 (Florence, 2004), pp. 71–92 (pp. 73, 80–1).

123. Peter Burke, 'Editorial preface' to Gurevich, *Medieval Popular Culture*, p. ix; cf. the relevant discussion in my introductory chapter.
124. Jones, *Secret Middle Ages*, p. 248. He suggests origins in antiquity, citing Plutarch's statement (*Quaestiones conviviales*, v.7.3) that 'the Romans believed that indecent or ridiculous images drew the eyes of ill-disposed spirits and men to themselves and thus averted the malevolent gaze of the Evil Eye from the vulnerable, distracted it, "fascinated" it, indeed' (p. 253). Mellinkoff supports the apotropaic thesis, arguing that the 'entire conglomeration of motifs and themes' included in her study have one and the same purpose – the avoidance of evil. The 'basic reason' for the long-standing 'use of amulets and talismans' is fear, 'Fear of unknown and potential dangers such as physical injuries, bodily ailments, loss of fertility (of land, people, or animals): fear of death; fear of the loss of one's soul.' These motifs and themes, then, 'were chiefly intended for an audience of demons – not of clerics, not for lay viewers, and not for patrons. They were meant to dispel the armies of demons that in those times virtually everyone believed to lurk everywhere, awaiting opportunities to do every manner of harm' (*Averting Demons*, I. 42). Mellinkoff incautiously dissolves the category of 'secular' badges in her discussion, all the relevant items she illustrates being deemed 'pilgrim badges'.
125. Jones, *Secret Middle Ages*, p. 249.
126. Cf. the Messenger's criticisms of pilgrimage malpractices in More's *Dialogue concerning Heresies*, quoted on p. 138 above.
127. Cited by both Jones, *Secret Middle Ages*, p. 256, and Koldeweij, '"Shameless and Naked Images"', p. 494, in support of their arguments in favour of a satiric and parodic function for the badges.
128. Jones, *Secret Middle Ages*, p. 256.
129. Jones, *Secret Middle Ages*, p. 255 (fig. 12.2), also in Mellinkoff, *Averting Demons*, II. 289 (fig. VI.94).
130. Jones, *Secret Middle Ages*, p. 29 (fig. 2.8); Mellinkoff, *Averting Demons*, II. 287 (fig. VI.92).
131. Cit. Jones, *Secret Middle Ages*, p. 28.
132. Jones, *Secret Middle Ages*, p. 29.
133. As suggested by Koldeweij in his article '"Shameless and Naked Images"', esp. pp. 506–10.
134. Indeed, laughter and pleasurable experiences were believed to have a 'hygienic' value, function as a guard against melancholy. See Glending Olson, *Literature as Recreation in the Middle Ages* (Ithaca, NY, 1982).
135. It is interesting to note that production of the Canterbury pilgrim badges was not under the control of the church in Canterbury; cf. Blick, 'Comparing Pilgrim Souvenirs', 23 n. 44.
136. Sanchis, 'The Portuguese "romarias"', p. 285 n. 43.
137. Cf. Minnis, *Fallible Authors*, pp. 384n, 387–8n, and the discussion of these matters in the introductory chapter to the present book.

138. As argued by Leo Steinberg, *The Sexuality of Christ in Renaissance Art and in Modern Oblivion*, 2nd edn (Chicago and London, 1996). Many of Steinberg's fundamental points, I believe, have survived the controversy which followed the original publication of this book in 1983, though Caroline Walker Bynum has rightly drawn attention to the fact that 'Christ's flesh was sometimes seen as female, as lactating and giving birth'; 'The Body of Christ in the Later Middle Ages: A Reply to Leo Steinberg', repr. in her *Fragmentation and Redemption*, pp. 79–117.

139. Thomas of Chobham, *Summa de arte praedicandi*, ed. Morenzoni, p. 110; cf. Vincent, *The Holy Blood*, p. 85. This treatise was written probably in the 1220s.

140. *De missarum mysteriis*, Migne, *PL* 217, 876–7; discussed and translated by Vincent, *The Holy Blood*, p. 86. Charlemagne enjoyed a substantial reputation as a recoverer of relics. For example, in the French Romance *Fierabras* (translated into Middle English perhaps *c.* 1377) he receives the crown of thorns and the nails which pierced Christ at the crucifixion, which were preserved by the eponymous hero of the romance, a Saracen who converts to Christianity. Cf. *Sir Ferumbras*, ed. S. J. Herrtage, EETS ES 34 (London, 1879), esp. pp. 183–9.

141. Thomas of Chobham, *Summa de arte praedicandi*, ed. Morenzoni, p. 110; trans. Vincent, *The Holy Blood*, p. 85. On pp. 82–117 Vincent provides an excellent discussion of the scholastic debate on blood relics and the holy foreskin, with extensive bibliography. See further Bynum, *Wonderful Blood*, pp. 37–40, 50, 98, 101, 106, 122, 128, 130, 144, 178, 295n, etc.

142. Gervase of Tilbury, *Otia imperialia*, III. 24, ed. and trans. S. E. Banks and J. W. Binns (Oxford, 2002), pp. 598–601. Gervase's source is probably John the Deacon, a twelfth-century canon of the Lateran. The belief that the holy foreskin was preserved in the Lateran sanctuary is also included in Pope Innocent III's account.

143. Agnes Blannbekin, *Life and Revelations*, translated from the Latin with Introduction, Notes, and Interpretive Essay, by Ulrike Wiethaus (Cambridge, 2002), p. 35.

144. Here I draw on Bynum's discussion of Catherine of Siena, which in some measure can also be applied to Agnes, who cried 'over the blood Christ deigned to shed so early at the beginning of His childhood' (trans. Wiethaus, p. 35), seeing in it a foreshadowing of the greater blood-sacrifice of the crucifixion. I extrapolate Bynum's words from *Holy Feast*, pp. 175, 178, 246, 376–7 n. 135.

145. Bynum, *Holy Feast*, pp. 377 n. 136, 175.

146. Which is, of course, troubling, and raises the possibility of two different saints being involved here, that being the point of the Pardoner's wordplay. But perhaps this is to be over-cautious. H. Marshall Leicester, Jr, has argued that 'if the pun is not present when Harry Bailly first uses the oath, it comes into being when the Pardoner repeats it'; *The Disenchanted Self: Representing the Subject in the Canterbury Tales* (Berkeley, 1990), p. 173.

147. Frederick Tupper, 'The Quarrels of the Canterbury Pilgrims', *Journal of English and Germanic Philology*, 14 (1915), 256–70 (p. 258n); reiterated in his later article 'Chaucer's Sinners and Sins', *Journal of English and Germanic Philology*, 15 (1916), 56–106 (pp. 66–7).
148. Adolf Tobier and Erhard Lommatzsch (eds.), *Altfranzösisches Wörterbuch* (Berlin and Wiesbaden, 1925–2002), s.v. *rein, roin* (VIII, cols. 654–6). Cf. L. W. Stone, W. Rothwell *et al.* (eds.), *Anglo-Norman Dictionary* (London, 1977), s.v. *reins, rains, reinz*; *re(i)nes, roynez*; *rens* (p. 619).
149. Tobier and Lommatzsch (eds.), *Altfranzösisches Wörterbuch*, s.v. *reignon, roignon* (VIII, col. 652). It may be added that the early French *reignons*, which philologically evolved into *roignons*, is also an Anglo-Norman variant, defined in the *Anglo-Norman Dictionary* as meaning both kidneys and loins; s.v. *reinon, -oun; re(i)gnon, rengon* (p. 619).
150. Cf. the Middle English *reine*, defined in the *MED* as (in the plural) designating the kidneys and the loins and, following the Biblical use, (a) the seat of the passions and (b) the male generative organ. Note especially the citations which describe 'lecherie' as 'outragieous loue and ydel ordeyned in lykyng of reyns or in delyt of fleschely lustes' (*Book of Virtues and Vices*, earliest MS c. 1400) and locate the dwelling of Venus 'in the reynys' (Lydgate, translation of *Pilgrimage of the Life of Man*). Cf. *MED*, s.v. *urine*, 'Urine is als myche to say in Englyssh as "on the reynis"'. The word 'kidneys', of obscure formation, has its first recorded instance in the *Tretiz* which, in the late thirteenth century, Walter de Bibbesworth wrote to provide anglophone landowners with French vocabulary appertaining to the management of their estates (English not having yet been established as a language of record). Here 'kidenere' is used to gloss 'reynoun' – of special interest to us given our interest in 'Seint Ronyan/Ronyon'. Walter de Bibbesworth, *Le Tretiz*, ed. William Rothwell, Anglo-Norman Text Society, Plain Texts Series 6 (London, 1990), consulted online, http://www.anglo-norman.net/texts/bibbes-contents.html. The *Oxford English Dictionary*, s.v. *kidney* (c.pl.) provides sixteenth-century citations which prove that *reynes, kydneis/kydneys* and the French *rognons* were understood as synonyms.
151. Tobier and Lommatzsch (eds.), *Altfranzösisches Wörterbuch*, s.v. *reignon, roignon* (VIII, col. 652).
152. Norton, *St William of York*, p. 156.
153. *MED*, s.v. *jordan* (b). I believe that in l. 305 the term is functioning as a synonym, or near-synonym, of 'urynal'; cf. *MED*, s.v. *urinal*.
154. *Riverside Chaucer*, p. 904.
155. John Mennis and James Smith, *Facetiae: Musarum deliciae* (London, 1817), I. 85–6.
156. Cf. also the Anglo-Norman *roigne*, defined in the *Anglo-Norman Dictionary* as 'mange', 'scab' (p. 661).
157. For an excellent discussion of this poem, which includes the point about Chaucer, see David O. Franz, *Festum voluptatis: A Study of Renaissance Erotica* (Columbus, OH, 1989), pp. 188–98.

158. Thomas Nashe, *Works*, ed. Ronald B. McKerrow with F. P. Wilson (Oxford, 1958), III. 413, 414, 263. An attempt has been made (unconvincingly, in my view) to link this account of the 'Eunuke dilldo' to Chaucer's Pardoner, interpreted as a eunuch, by Robert C. Evans, 'Nashe's "Choise" and Chaucer's Pardoner', *American Notes and Queries*, 9.4 (1996), 21–4. There is no clear evidence that Nashe read the Pardoner in that way.

159. Nashe, *Works*, ed. McKerrow, p. 413. This, I believe, is a more satisfactory explanation than the editor's attempt to connect the saint's name with Shakespeare's *runnion/ronyon*; Nashe, *Works*, ed. McKerrow, p. 482, note on III. 413. Franz, *Festum voluptatis*, rejects McKerrow's suggestion and draws attention to Chaucer's 'Seint Ronyan', understood as designating the male organ; 'that, of course, would be a most appropriate saint for Frances to swear by' (p. 197).

160. Geoffrey Fenton, *Certain Tragical Discourses*, v, ed. R. L. Douglas, Tudor Translations, 19 and 20 (Edinburgh, 1898), I. 232. This work is based on the *Novelle* of Matteo Bandello, but has many additions, including the passage quoted.

161. Cf. the note in Heywood, *Plays*, ed. Axton and Happé, p. 249 (which refers to Malcolm Jones).

162. Sir Thomas Elyot, *Pasquil the Playne* (London, 1533), p. 14, as consulted via Early English Books Online, http://ets.umdl.umich.edu/cgi/t/text/.

163. *The Playe Called the Foure PP*, l. 31, in Heywood, *Plays*, ed. Axton and Happé, p. 112. Here I follow the editors' dating.

164. *Respublica: An Interlude for Christmas 1553, attributed to Nicholas Udall*, ed. W. W. Greg, EETS OS 226 (London, 1952), p. 58.

165. As proposed by Ann S. Haskell, *Essays on Chaucer's Saints* (The Hague and Paris, 1976), pp. 17–25. See further Farmer, *Oxford Dictionary of Saints*, p. 368, and Nicholas Roscarrock, *Lives of the Saints: Cornwall and Devon*, ed. Nicholas Orme, Devon and Cornwall Record Society, n.s. 35 (Exeter, 1992), pp. 167–8.

166. As proposed by James Sledd, 'Canterbury Tales, C 310, 320: "By Seint Ronyan"', *Mediaeval Studies*, 13 (1951), 226–33. Cf. Farmer, *Oxford Dictionary of Saints*, p. 433.

167. If this wordplay is not acceptable then another should be sought; this, I believe, is where a solution is is to be found, rather than in the identification of some actual saint with supposedly appropriate characteristics. A pun on *rogne* ('scab'; cf. *rogneux*, 'a scurvy fellow') remains a tantalizing possibility (cf. Sledd, 'Canterbury Tales', 229). On this interpretation, the Pardoner appropriately invokes Saint Ronyan/Ronyan as he prepares to launch into his scurvy 'myrthe or japes' (following Harry Bailly's invocation and instruction); however the 'gentils' see that 'ribaudye' is coming and redirect the Pardoner to tell 'som moral thyng' (318–25). The irony is that the Pardoner will prove himself a *rogneux*, or, following Shakespeare's usage, a *runnion/ronyon* – a character who is 'mangy' in morals as well as in appearance. Finally, a wild card: the *MED* has picked up the mysterious word *runian* (with two citations

from the mid-fifteenth century), which seems to have been an affectionate way of referring to a favoured person of low station, such as a farm labourer (*MED*, s.v. *runian*). Chaucer's joke, whatever its nature, was an obscure one – as is borne out by the variations on the name in the manuscript tradition; cf. John M. Manly and Edith Rickert, *The Text of the Canterbury Tales* (Chicago, 1940), VII. 37–8. Many of Chaucer's scribes just didn't get it. Whatever 'it' may have been.

168. *Epilogue to the Nun's Priest's Tale*, VII. 3448–51. Here the Host fulsomely explains that he is not accusing this priest of immorality; his point is rather that, if this cocky character were a layman (*seculer*), then he would require many hens ('Ya, moo than seven tymes seventene') to meet his sexual needs. On *ston* as meaning 'kidney stone' and also as 'a testicle of a man or an animal' cf. *MED*, s.v. *ston*, 13 and 14 (a).

169. As McAlpine claims; 'The Pardoner's Homosexuality', 17.

170. 'The ultimate issue is not perfection in the physical order but holiness in the spiritual order', McAlpine declares ('The Pardoner's Homosexuality', 17). But, within the late medieval economy of enshrinement (which Harry is here mimicking), 'perfection in the physical order' is directly linked to that 'holiness in the spiritual order' which ensures that whoever venerates a powerful relic will receive physical cures for physical problems.

171. Why would the Pardoner need help in carrying this object? Because of the wondrous size of the disembodied *coillons*? If so, bathos soon follows as the Host proposes that they should be 'shryned in an hogges toord'. Alternatively, the Host is so (mock-)zealous to see the Pardoner's testicles cut off and turned into a prize relic that he will help him carry them, no matter how light or heavy the resulting portable shrine may be – in which case, size doesn't matter.

172. On castration as a punishment for sodomy see especially Klaus van Eickels, 'Gendered Violence: Castration and Blinding as Punishment for Treason in Normandy and Anglo-Norman England', *Gender and History*, 16.3 (2004), 588–602. This refers mainly to practices inaugurated by the so-called 'Laws of William the Conqueror', and Lee Patterson is quite right to point out that 'in later medieval England castration as a punishment for any crime is very rare, if not in fact entirely absent'; 'Chaucer's Pardoner on the Couch: Psyche and Clio in Medieval Literary Studies', *Speculum*, 76 (2001), 638–80 (pp. 659–60). But folk memories of the Norman regime no doubt persisted, and miracle stories concerning men like Ailward of Western, Ralph of York, and Thomas of Eldersfield (who had been punished by castration and blinding) would have kept the idea alive, even if the outmoded law was no longer being implemented.

173. Cf. my discussion in *Fallible Authors*, pp. 159–61.

174. See the relevant discussion in Chapter 4 above, and in my *Fallible Authors*, pp. 266–7.

175. Quoted from *William of Nassyngton, Speculum vitae*, compiled by Christine Robinson, consulted via the Oxford Text Archive, on http://ota.ahds.ac.uk. Reproduced with Dr Robinson's permission. The punctuation in this and the following quotation is my own.

176. The affinities are even closer in another play of Heywood's, *The Pardoner and the Frere*; see ll. 97–128, 175–80, etc.

177. Which Heywood had included in his list of risible relics in *The Pardoner and the Frere*; cf. n. 41 above.

178. Heywood, *Plays*, ed. Axton and Happé, p. 124.

179. Heywood, *Plays*, ed. Axton and Happé, p. 125.

180. Here Chaucer moves from human excrement – the Pardoner's stained breeches – to pigshit. The Pardoner's familiarity with this creature is indicated by the fact that one of his relics is nothing other than 'pigges bones', treated with (mock-)reverence by being protected in a 'glas' container (cf. General Prologue, I(A), 700). So, the enshrining substance recommended by the Host for the Pardoner's *relyk* should hardly come as a surprise.

Bibliography

PRIMARY SOURCES

Agnes Blannbekin, *Life and Revelations*, translated from the Latin with Introduction, Notes, and Interpretive Essay, by Ulrike Wiethaus (Cambridge, 2002).

Agrippa d'Aubigné, *Œuvres*, ed. H. Weber, J. Bailbé, and M. Soulié (Paris, 1969).

Alexander of Hales, *Summa theologica* (Quaracchi, 1924–48).

Summa theologica: pars quarta (s.l., 1516).

Angela of Foligno, *Il libro della Beata Angela da Foligno*, ed. L. Thier and A. Calufetti, Spicilegium Bonaventurianum 25 (Grottaferrata, 1985); trans. Paul Lachance, *Angela of Foligno: Complete Works* (New York, 1993).

The Anonymous History of the Church of Oignies, trans. Hugh Feiss, in *Two Lives of Marie d'Oignies*, trans. Margot King and Hugh Feiss (Toronto, 1993).

Apocalypse versions, *An English Fourteenth Century Apocalypse Version with a Prose Commentary*, ed. E. Fridner, Lund Studies in English, 29 (Lund and Copenhagen, 1961); *Die mittelenglische Übersetzung der Apokalypse mit Kommentar* (Version B), ed. W. Sauer (Heidelberg, 1971).

Aquinas, St Thomas, *The Disputed Questions on Truth*, trans. S. Edwards (Toronto, 1983).

Quaestiones disputatae, I: *De veritate*, ed. R. Spiazzi, 8th edn (Turin, 1949).

Quaestiones quodlibetales, ed. R. Spiazzi, 8th edn (Turin and Rome, 1949); trans. S. Edwards, *St. Thomas Aquinas Quodlibetal Questions 1 and 2* (Toronto, 1983).

De veritate, trans. Robert W. Mulligan, James V. McGlynn, and Robert W. Schmidt, *Truth: St Thomas Aquinas* (Chicago, 1952–4).

Audelay, John, *The Poems of John Audelay*, ed. Ella Keats Whiting, EETS OS 184 (London, 1931).

Augustine, *'De bono coniugali' and 'De sancta virginitate'*, ed. P. G. Walsh (Oxford, 2001).

Benedict of Peterborough, *Miracula sancti Thomae Cantuariensis*, in J. C. Robertson (ed.), *Materials for the History of Thomas Becket*, II, Rolls Series 67.2 (London, 1876).

Boccaccio, Giovanni, *Decameron*, ed. Vittore Branca (Florence, 1976).

Teseida, trans. B. McCoy (New York, 1974).

Bradwardine, Thomas, *De causa Dei*, ed. Henry Savile (London, 1618).

Bridget of Sweden, *Den Heliga Birgittas Revelaciones Bok VII*, ed. Birger Bergh (Uppsala, 1967); trans. A. R. Kezel, *Birgitta of Sweden: Life and Selected Revelations* (New York, 1990).

Brut, Walter, *Quaestiones* apparently written against Brut, in London, British Library, MS Harley 31.

   Utrum liceat mulieribus docere viros publice congregatos (MS Harley 31, fols. 194v–196r), ed. A. Blamires and C. W. Marx, 'Woman Not to Preach: A Disputation in British Library MS Harley 31', *Journal of Medieval Latin*, 3 (1993), 34–63.

   Utrum mulieres conficiunt vel conficere possunt (MS Harley 31, fols. 218r–223r)

   Utrum mulieres sunt ministri ydonei ad conficiendum eukaristie sacramentum (MS Harley 31, fols. 196v–205r).

   Utrum quilibet laicus iustus sit sacerdos noue legis (MS Harley 31, fols. 216r–218r).

The Canterbury Tales: Fifteenth-Century Continuations and Additions, ed. John M. Bowers (Kalamazoo, 1992).

Capgrave, John, *Ye Solace of Pilgrimes. A Description of Rome circa A.D. 1450*, ed. C. A. Mills (Oxford, 1911).

Catherine of Genoa, St, *Life and Sayings*, ed. and trans. Paul Garvin (New York, 1964).

Catherine of Siena, *Lettere di S. Caterina da Siena*, ed. N. Tommasèo and P. Misciattelli (Florence, 1939–47); trans. Suzanne Noffke, *The Letters of Catherine of Siena* (Tempe, AZ, 2000–7).

'*The Chastising of God's Children*' and '*The Treatise of Perfection of the Sons of God*', ed. J. Bazire and E. Colledge (Oxford, 1957).

Christine de Pizan, *Livre des fais et bonnes meurs du sage roy Charles V*, ed. S. Solente (Paris, 1936).

'*The Cloud of Unknowing*' and *Related Treatises*, ed. Phyllis Hodgson, Analecta Cartusiana 3 (Salzburg, 1982).

Corpus iuris canonici, ed. E. A. Friedberg and E. L. Richter (Leipzig, 1879–81).

The Court of Sapience, ed. Ruth Harvey (Toronto, 1984).

The Court of Sapience: Spät-mittelenglisches allegorisch-didaktisches Visionsgedicht, ed. Robert Spindler, Beiträge zur englischen Philologie, 6 (Leipzig, 1927).

Dabydeen, David, *Slave Song* (Mundelstrup, 1984).

Dante Alighieri, *Il convivio*, ed. Cesare Vasoli and Domenico de Robertis, in *Dante Alighieri Opere minori*, 1.2 (Milan and Naples, 1979–88); trans. Christopher Ryan, *Dante: The Banquet*, Stanford French and Italian Studies, 61 (Saratoga, CA, 1989).

   Vita nuova, ed. Domenico de Robertis (Milan and Naples, 1980); trans. Barbara Reynolds (Harmondsworth, 1969).

   De vulgari eloquentia, ed. and trans. Steven Botterill (Cambridge, 1996).

Dives and Pauper, ed. P. H. Barnum, EETS OS 275 and 280 (Oxford, 1976–80).

Douceline, 'Saint', *The Life of Saint Douceline, Beguine of Provence*, trans. Kathleen Garay and Madeline Jeay (Cambridge, 2001).

Douglas, Gavin, *Virgil's Aeneid Translated into Scottish Verse*, ed. David F. C. Coldwell, Scottish Text Society (Edinburgh and London, 1957–64).

Duns Scotus, John, *Opera omnia* (Lyon, 1639; repr. Hildesheim, 1969).

Dymmok, Roger, *Liber contra XII errores et hereses Lollardorum*, ed. H. S. Cronin (London, 1921).

The Early South-English Legendary or Lives of Saints, ed. Carl Horstmann, EETS OS 87 (London, 1887).

Elyot, Sir Thomas, *Pasquil the Playne* (London, 1533).

Eneas. Roman du XIIe siècle, ed. J.-J. Salverda de Grave (Paris, 1925–9); trans. John A. Yunck, *Eneas: A Twelfth-Century French Romance* (New York, 1974).

English Mystics of the Middle Ages, ed. Barry Windeatt (Cambridge, 1994).

The English Works of Wyclif, Hitherto Unprinted, ed. F. D. Matthew, 2nd rev. edn, EETS OS 74 (Oxford, 1902).

Erasmus, Desiderius, *Collected Works*, trans. R. A. B. Mynors, C. R. Thompson *et al.* (Toronto, 1974–).

    The Earliest English Translations of Erasmus's Colloquia, ed. Henry de Vocht (Leuven, 1928).

    Opera omnia (Amsterdam, 1969–).

Estienne, Henri, *Œuvres*, ed. P. Ristelhuber (Paris, 1879).

Evrart de Conty, *Le livre des eschez amoureux moralisés*, ed. Françoise Guichard-Tesson and Bruno Roy, Bibliothèque du moyen français, 2 (Montreal, 1993).

Fenton, Geoffrey, *Certain Tragical Discourses*, v, ed. R. L. Douglas, Tudor Translations, 19 and 20 (Edinburgh, 1898).

Firmin Le Ver, *Dictionarius: dictionnaire latin-français de Firmin Le Ver*, ed. Brian Merrilees and William Edwards, CCCM, Lexica Latina Medii Ævi, 1 (Turnhout, 1994).

Foxe, John, *The Acts and Monuments*, 4th edn, ed. Josiah Pratt (London, 1877).

Francis of Meyronnes, *Commentarius in libros sententiarum*, etc. (Venice, 1520; repr. Frankfurt, 1966).

Gervase of Tilbury, *Otia imperialia*, ed. and trans. S. E. Banks and J. W. Binns (Oxford, 2002).

Giovanni de'Balbi, *Catholicon* (Mainz, 1460; repr. 1971).

Gui, Bernard, *Manuel de l'Inquisiteur*, ed. G. Mollat (Paris, 1926).

Henry of Ghent, *Summa quaestionum ordinariarum* (Paris, 1520; repr. Leuven and Paderborn, 1953).

Heresy Trials in the Diocese of Norwich, 1428–31, ed. Norman P. Tanner, Camden Fourth Series, 20 (London, 1977).

Heywood, John, *The Plays*, ed. Richard Axton and Peter Happé (Cambridge, 1991).

Higden, Ralph, *Polychronicon*, ed. C. Babington and J. R. Lumby (London, 1865–86).

Hilton, Walter, *Latin Writings*, ed. John P. H. Clark and Cheryl Taylor, Analecta Cartusiana, 124 (Salzburg, 1987).

    The Mixed Life, ed. S. J. Ogilvie-Thomson, Salzburg Studies in English Literature, Elizabethan and Renaissance Studies, 92.15 (Salzburg, 1986).

    The Scale of Perfection, ed. Thomas H. Bestul (Kalamazoo, 2000).

Hoccleve, Thomas, *'Complaint' and 'Dialogue'*, ed. J. A. Burrow, EETS OS 313 (Oxford, 1999).

The Minor Poems, ed. F. J. Furnivall and I. Gollancz, EETS ES 61 and 73 (London, repr. 1970).

Holcot, Robert, *In Quatuor libros sententiarum quaestiones* (Lyon, 1497).

Sapientiae Regis Salamonis praelectiones (Basel, 1586).

The Holy Bible, Containing the Old and New Testaments, in the Earliest English Versions, Made from the Latin Vulgate by John Wycliffe and his Followers, ed. Josiah Forshall and Frederic Madden (Oxford, 1850).

Hugh of St Cher, *Biblia cum postillis Hugonis de Sancto Charo* (Basel, 1498–1502).

Postilla domini Hugonis Cardinalis (Basel, 1504).

Hugutio of Pisa, *Derivationes*, ed. Enzo Cecchini *et al.* (Florence, 2004).

Jack Upland, Friar Daw's Reply and Upland's Rejoinder, ed. P. L. Heyworth (London and New York, 1968).

Jacobus de Voragine (Jacopo da Varazze), *Legenda aurea. Vulgo historia Lombardica dicta*, ed. T. Graesse, 3rd edn (1890; repr. Osnabrück, 1969); trans. W. G. Ryan, *The Golden Legend* (Princeton, 1993).

Jean le Danois, *Summa grammatica*, ed. Alfred Otto, Corpus philosophorum Danicorum Medii Ævi (Copenhagen, 1955).

John the Deacon, *Vita sancti Gregorii*, in Migne, *PL* 75, 59–242.

Le jubilé de Saint Thomas Becket du XIIIe au XVe siècle (1220–1470): études et documents, ed. Raymonde Foreville (Paris, 1958).

Juliana of Mont-Cornillon, *Life*, trans. Barbara Newman (Toronto, 1999).

Kent Heresy Proceedings 1511–12, ed. Norman Tanner (Maidstone, Kent, 1997).

Knighton, Henry, *Chronicon*, ed. J. R. Lumby (London, 1895; repr. 1965).

Lais féeriques des XIIe et XIIIe siècles, ed. A. Micha (Paris, 1992).

Letters to Cromwell on the Suppression of the Monasteries, ed. G. H. Cook (London, 1965).

Lollard Sermons, ed. Gloria Cigman, EETS 294 (Oxford, 1989).

Lollards of Coventry, 1486–1522, ed. and trans. Shannon McSheffrey and Norman Tanner, Camden Fifth Series, 23 (Cambridge, 2003).

Lombard, Peter, *Sententiae in IV Libris Distinctae*, 3rd edn (Grottaferrata, 1971–81).

Lydgate, John, *Reason and Sensuality*, ed. E. Sieper, EETS ES 84 (London, 1901).

Lyndwood, William, *Provinciale seu constitutiones angliae* (Oxford, 1679, repr. Farnborough, Hants., 1968).

Memoriale presbiterorum, in Cambridge, Corpus Christi College, 148.

Mennis, John, and James Smith, *Facetiae: Musarum deliciae* (London, 1817).

Moneta of Cremona, *Adversus Catharos et Valdenses libri quinque*, ed. T. Ricchini (Rome, 1743, repr. Ridgewood, NJ, 1964).

More, Thomas, *The Yale Edition of the Complete Works of St. Thomas More*, executive ed. R. S. Sylvester (New Haven and London, 1963–97).

Nashe, Thomas, *Works*, ed. Ronald B. McKerrow with F. P. Wilson (Oxford, 1958).

Of Weddid Men and Wifis and of Here Children Also, ed. Eve Salisbury, in *The Trials and Joys of Marriage* (Kalamazoo, 2002).

Oresme, Nicole, *Le livre de éthiques d'Aristote*, ed. A. D. Menut (New York, 1940).

Le livre de politiques d'Aristote, ed. A. D. Menut, Transactions of the American Philosophical Society, n.s. 60, pt 6 (Philadelphia, 1970).

Pecock, Reginald, *The Reule of Crysten Religioun*, ed. W. C. Greet, EETS OS 171 (London, 1927).

Philippe de Marnix, *Œuvres*, ed. E. Quenet (Brussels, 1857; repr. Geneva, 1971).

Piers Plowman: A New Translation, by A. V. C. Schmidt (Oxford, 1992).

The Piers Plowman Tradition, ed. Helen Barr (London, 1993).

Poems of Cupid, God of Love. Christine de Pizan's 'Epistre au dieu d'Amours' and 'Dit de la Rose'; Thomas Hoccleve's 'The Letter of Cupid', ed. T. S. Fenster and M. C. Erler (Leiden and New York, 1990).

The Pricke of Conscience, ed. Richard Morris (Berlin, 1863).

Querelle de la Rose documents, ed. Eric Hicks, *Le débat sur le Roman de la Rose* (Paris, 1977).

Raymond of Capua, *Vita Catharinae Serensis*, ed. Jörg Jungmayr (Berlin, 2004), trans. Conleth Kearns, Dominican Publications, Dublin, 1 (Wilmington, DE, 1980).

Recueil de farces (1450–1550), ed. A. Tissier (Geneva, 1986–).

The Register of Henry Chichele, Archbishop of Canterbury, 1414–1443, III, ed. E. F. Jacob, Canterbury and York Series, 46 (Oxford, 1945).

Respublica: An Interlude for Christmas 1553, attributed to Nicholas Udall, ed. W. W. Greg, EETS OS 226 (London, 1952).

Rolle, Richard, *The Psalter Translated by Richard Rolle of Hampole*, ed. H. R. Bramley (Oxford, 1884).

Roman de la Rose, ed. Félix Lecoy (Paris, 1965–70).

Roscarrock, Nicholas, *Lives of the Saints: Cornwall and Devon*, ed. Nicholas Orme, Devon and Cornwall Record Society, n.s. 35 (Exeter, 1992).

Saint Erkenwald, ed. Clifford Peterson (Philadelphia, 1977).

St Erkenwald, ed. Ruth Morse (Cambridge, 1975).

Scot, Reginald, *Discoverie of Witchcraft, Published with an Introduction by M. Summers* (New York, 1972).

Select English Works of John Wyclif, ed. Thomas Arnold (Oxford, 1871).

Selections from English Wycliffite Writings, ed. Anne Hudson (Cambridge, 1978; repr. Toronto, 1997).

Simon of Cremona, *Disputationes de indulgentiis*, ed. F. Stegmüller, *Annali della biblioteca governatica et libreria civica di Cremona*, Monumenta Cremonensia, 2 (Cremona, 1955), pp. 1–17, and D. Trapp, 'The Portiuncula Discussion of Cremona (ca. 1380)', *Recherches de théologie ancienne et médiévale*, 22 (1955), 79–94.

Sir Ferumbras, ed. S. J. Herrtage, EETS ES 34 (London, 1879).

Thomas of Chobham, *Summa de arte praedicandi*, ed. F. Morenzoni, CCCM 82 (Turnhout, 1988).

Trokelowe, John, Henry Blaneforde *et al.*, *Chronica et annales*, ed. H. T. Riley, Rolls Series, 28.3 (London, 1866).

Two Wycliffite Texts, ed. Anne Hudson, EETS OS 301 (Oxford, 1993).

The Vernon *Testamentum Christi*, in *The Minor Poems of the Vernon Manuscript, Part II*, ed. F. J. Furnivall, EETS OS 117 (London, 1901), pp. 637–57.

Walsingham, Thomas, *Historia anglicana*, ed. H. T. Riley, Rolls Series, 28.1 (London, 1863–4; repr. 1965).

Walter de Bibbesworth, *Le Tretiz*, ed. William Rothwell, Anglo-Norman Text Society, Plain Texts Series 6 (London, 1990); consulted online, http://www.anglo-norman.net/texts/bibbes-contents.html.

Walton, John, *Boethius, 'De consolatione philosophiae'*, ed. Mark Science, EETS OS 170 (London, 1927).

William of Auvergne, *Opera omnia* (Paris, 1674).

    Summa aurea, ed. Jean Ribaillier (Paris and Grottaferrata, 1980–5).

William of Canterbury, *Miracula sancti Thomae Cantuariensis*, in J. C. Robertson (ed.), *Materials for the History of Thomas Becket*, 1, Rolls Series, 67.1 (London, 1875).

William of Nassyngton, *Speculum vitae*, compiled by Christine Robinson, consulted via the Oxford Text Archive, on http://ota.ahds.ac.uk.

William of Ockham, *Opera politica*, III, ed. H. S. Offler (Manchester, 1956).

    Philosophical Writings, ed. and trans. P. Boehner (London, 1957).

    Quaestiones in Librum Quartum Sententiarum (Reportatio), ed. Riga Wood and Gedeon Gál, Opera theologica, 7 (St Bonaventure, NY, 1984).

    Quodlibetal Questions, trans. A. J. Freddoso and F. E. Kelley (New Haven and London, 1991).

Wolfram von Eschenbach, *Willehalm*, trans. Marion E. Gibbs and Sidney M. Johnson (London, 1984).

Wyclif, John, *De mandatis divinis*, ed. J. Loserth and F. D. Matthew (London, 1922).

    Opera minora, ed. J. Loserth (London, 1913).

    Opus evangelicum, ed. J. Loserth and F. D. Matthew (London, 1895–6).

    De potestate pape, ed. J. Loserth (London, 1907).

    Tractatus de ecclesia, ed. J. Loserth (London, 1886).

    Trialogus, ed. G. V. Lechler (Oxford, 1869).

    De veritate sacrae scripturae, ed. R. Buddensieg (London, 1904); partially trans. Ian Christopher Levy, *On the Truth of Holy Scripture* (Kalamazoo, 2001).

SECONDARY SOURCES

Adams, Marilyn McCord, *William Ockham* (Notre Dame, IN, 1987).

Adams, Robert, 'Langland's Theology', in John A. Alford (ed.), *A Companion to 'Piers Plowman'* (Berkeley and Los Angeles, 1988), pp. 87–114.

    'Piers's Pardon and Langland's Semi-Pelagianism', *Traditio*, 39 (1983), 367–418.

Aers, David, 'Christianity for Courtly Subjects: Reflections on the *Gawain*-Poet', in Brewer and Gibson (eds.), *Companion to the 'Gawain'-Poet*, pp. 91–101.

    Community, Gender, and Individual Identity: English Writing, 1360–1430 (London and New York, 1988).

    Faith, Ethics and Church: Writing in England, 1360–1409 (Cambridge, 2000).

    Sanctifying Signs: Making Christian Tradition in Late-Medieval England (Notre Dame, IN, 2004).

'Walter Brut's Theology of the Sacrament of the Altar', in F. Somerset, J. C. Havens, and D. G. Pitard (eds.), *Lollards and their Influence in Late-Medieval England* (Woodbridge, 2003), pp. 115–26.

Aers, David, and Lynn Staley, *The Powers of the Holy: Religion, Politics, and Gender in Late-Medieval English Culture* (University Park, PA, 1996).

Allen, Judson B., *The Ethical Poetic of the Later Middle Ages* (Toronto, 1982).
'Langland's Reading and Writing: *Detractor* and the Pardon Passus', *Speculum*, 59 (1984), 342–62.

Arnold, John H., 'Margery's Trials: Heresy, Lollardy and Dissent', in Arnold and Lewis (eds.), *Companion to 'The Book of Margery Kempe'*, pp. 75–93.

Arnold, John H., and Katherine J. Lewis (eds.), *A Companion to 'The Book of Margery Kempe'* (Woodbridge, 2004).

Aston, Margaret, 'Lollard Women Priests?', in Aston, *Lollards and Reformers*, pp. 49–70.
Lollards and Reformers. Images and Literacy in Late Medieval Religion (London, 1984).
'William White's Lollard Followers', in Aston, *Lollards and Reformers*, pp. 71–99.
'Wycliffe and the Vernacular', in Aston, *Faith and Fire: Popular and Unpopular Religion, 1350–1600* (London and Rio Grande, 1993), pp. 27–72.

Autrand, Françoise, *Charles V: le sage* (Paris, 1994).

Baker, Denise, 'From Plowing to Penitence: *Piers Plowman* and Fourteenth-Century Theology', *Speculum*, 55 (1980), 715–25.
'The Pardons of *Piers Plowman*', *Neuphilologische Mitteilungen*, 85 (1984), 462–72.

Barański, Zygmunt G., 'Dante Alighieri: Experimentation and (Self-) Exegesis', in *CHLCMA*, pp. 561–82.

Beaston, Lawrence, 'The *Pearl* Poet and the Pelagians', *Religion and Literature*, 36 (2004), 15–38.

Beer, Jeanette (ed.), *Medieval Translators and their Craft* (Kalamazoo, 1989).
'Patronage and the Translator: Raoul de Presles's *La Cité de Dieu* and Calvin's *Institutio religionis Christianae*', in Jeanette Beer and K. Lloyd-Jones (eds.), *Translation and the Transmission of Culture between 1300 and 1600* (Kalamazoo, 1995), pp. 91–141.

Bell, Rudolph M., *Holy Anorexia* (Chicago and London, 1985).

Bennett, Michael, *Richard II and the Revolution of 1399* (Thrupp, Stroud, 1999).

Benson, David, *Public 'Piers Plowman': Modern Scholarship and Late Medieval English Culture* (Pennsylvania, 2004).

Berger, Samuel, *La Bible française au Moyen Âge* (Paris, 1884).

Bessière, Jean, and Daniel-Henri Pageaux (eds.), *Formes et imaginaire du roman: perspectives sur le roman antique, médiéval, classique, moderne et contemporain* (Paris, 1998).

Bétérous, P. V., 'A propos d'une des légendes mariales les plus répandues: le "Lait de la Vierge"', *Bulletin de l'Association Guillaume Budé*, 4 (1975), 403–11.

Biller, Peter, 'The Earliest Heretical Englishwomen', in Jocelyn Wogan-Browne *et al.* (eds.), *Medieval Women: Texts and Contexts in Late Medieval Britain. Essays for Felicity Riddy*, Medieval Women: Texts and Contexts 3 (Turnhout, 2000), pp. 363–76.

'William of Newburgh and the Cathar Mission to England', in D. Wood (ed.), *Life and Thought in the Northern Church c. 1100–c. 1700: Essays in Honour of Claire Cross*, Studies in Church History, Subsidia, 12 (Woodbridge, 1999), pp. 11–30.

Birch, Debra J., *Pilgrimage to Rome in the Middle Ages: Continuity and Change* (Woodbridge, 1998).

Blackburn, B., and L. Holford-Strevens (eds.), *The Oxford Companion to the Year* (Oxford, 1999).

Blamires, Alcuin, 'The Wife of Bath and Lollardy', *Medium Ævum*, 58 (1989), 224–42.

'Women and Preaching in Medieval Orthodoxy, Heresy, and Saints' Lives', *Viator*, 26 (1995), 135–52.

Blamires, Alcuin (ed.), *Woman Defamed and Woman Defended* (Oxford, 1992).

Blick, Sarah, 'Comparing Pilgrim Souvenirs and Trinity Chapel Windows at Canterbury Cathedral', *Mirator* (September 2001), 1–27.

'Reconstructing the Shrine of St. Thomas Becket, Canterbury Cathedral', in Blick and Tekippe (eds.), *Art and Architecture of Late Medieval Pilgrimage*, pp. 405–41.

Blick, Sarah, and Rita Tekippe (eds.), *Art and Architecture of Late Medieval Pilgrimage in Northern Europe and the British Isles* (Leiden, 2005).

Blomefield, F., and C. Parkin, *An Essay towards a Topographical History of the County of Norfolk* (London, 1805–10).

Bolman, Elizabeth S., 'The Enigmatic Coptic Galaktotrophousa and the Cult of the Virgin Mary in Egypt', in Maria Vassilaki (ed.), *Images of the Mother of God: Perceptions of the Theotokos in Byzantium* (Aldershot, Hants., 2005), pp. 13–22.

Boucher, Caroline, 'La mise en scène de la vulgarisation: les traductions d'autorités en langue vulgaire aux XIIIe et XIVe siècles', École Pratique des Hautes Études, 5e section (Paris, 2005).

'Des problèmes pour exercer l'entendement des lecteurs: Évrart de Conty, Nicole Oresme et la recherche de la nouveauté', in Pieter De Leemans and Michèle Goyens (eds.), *Aristotle's 'Problemata' in Different Times and Tongues* (Leuven, 2006), pp. 175–97.

Brewer, Derek, and Jonathan Gibson (eds.), *A Companion to the 'Gawain'-Poet* (Woodbridge, 1997).

Brown, Stephen F., 'Abelard and the Medieval Origins of the Distinction between God's Absolute and Ordained Power', in M. D. Jordan and K. Emery Jr (eds.), *Ad Litteram. Authoritative Texts and their Medieval Readers* (Notre Dame, IN, and London, 1992), pp. 199–215.

Brown-Grant, Rosalind, *Christine de Pizan and the Moral Defence of Women* (Cambridge, 1999).

Brundage, James A., *Law, Sex and Christian Society in Medieval Europe* (Chicago, 1987).

Sex, Law and Marriage in the Middle Ages, Collected Studies Series (Aldershot, Hampshire, and Brookfield, VT, 1993).

Buddensieg, Rudolf, *John Wiclif, Patriot and Reformer: Life and Writings* (London, 1884).

Bühler, Curt F., 'A Lollard Tract: On Translating the Bible into English', *Medium Ævum*, 7 (1938), 167–83.

The Sources of 'The Court of Sapience', Beiträge zur englischen Philologie, 23 (Leipzig, 1932).

Bullough, Vern L., and James A. Brundage (eds.), *Handbook of Medieval Sexuality* (New York and London, 1996).

Buschinger, Danielle (ed.), *Le roman antique au Moyen Âge: Actes du Colloque du Centre d'études médiévales de l'Université de Picardie, Amiens, 14–15 Janvier 1989* (Göppingen, 1992).

Bynum, Caroline Walker, 'Bleeding Hosts and their Contact Relics in Late Medieval Northern Germany', *Medieval History Journal*, 7.2 (2004), 227–41.

Fragmentation and Redemption: Essays on Gender and the Human Body in Medieval Religion (New York, 1992).

Holy Feast and Holy Fast: The Religious Significance of Food to Medieval Women (Berkeley and Los Angeles, 1987).

Jesus as Mother: Studies in the Spirituality of the High Middle Ages (Berkeley and Los Angeles, 1982).

Cadden, Joan, '"Nothing Natural Is Shameful": Vestiges of a Debate about Sex and Science in a Group of Late-Medieval Manuscripts', *Speculum*, 76 (2001), 66–89.

Catto, J. I., 'John Wyclif and the Cult of the Eucharist', in K. Walsh and D. Wood (eds.), *The Bible in the Medieval World: Essays in Memory of Beryl Smalley* (Oxford, 1985), pp. 269–86.

Cessario, R., 'St. Thomas Aquinas on Satisfaction, Indulgences, and Crusades', *Medieval Philosophy and Theology*, 2 (1992), 74–96.

Clark, Francis, *The Pseudo-Gregorian Dialogues* (Leiden, 1987).

Clark, J. P. H., 'Late Fourteenth-Century Cambridge Theology and the English Contemplative Tradition', in Marion Glasscoe (ed.), *The Medieval Mystical Tradition in England*, v (Cambridge 1992), pp. 1–16.

'Walter Hilton and "Liberty of Spirit"', *The Downside Review*, 96 (1978), 61–78.

Clopper, Lawrence M., 'The God of the *Gawain*-Poet', *Modern Philology*, 94.1 (1996), 1–18.

Coats, Catherine Randall, *Subverting the System: Agrippa d'Aubigné and Calvinism*, Sixteenth Century Essays and Studies, 14 (Kirksville, MO, 1990).

Coghill, Nevill, 'The Pardon of *Piers Plowman*', repr. in Robert J. Blanch (ed.), *Style and Symbolism in 'Piers Plowman'* (Knoxville, 1969), pp. 40–86.

Cohen, E., '*In Haec Signa*: Pilgrim Badge Trade in Southern France', *Journal of Medieval History*, 2 (1976), 193–214.

Coleman, Janet, *'Piers Plowman' and the 'Moderni'* (Rome, 1981).

Colish, Marcia L., *Peter Lombard* (Leiden, 1994).

Copeland, Rita, *Pedagogy, Intellectuals and Dissent in the Later Middle Ages. Lollardy and Ideas of Learning* (Cambridge, 2001).

Rhetoric, Hermeneutics and Translation in the Middle Ages: Academic Traditions and Vernacular Texts (Cambridge, 1991).

Courtenay, W. J., '*Antiqui* and *Moderni* in Late-Medieval Thought', *Journal of the History of Ideas*, 48 (1987), 3–10.

Capacity and Volition: A History of the Distinction of Absolute and Ordained Power (Bergamo, 1990).

Covenant and Causality in Medieval Thought (London, 1984).

'The Dialectic of Divine Omnipotence in the Age of Chaucer: A Reconsideration', in Keiper, Bode, and Utz (eds.), *Nominalism and Literary Discourse*, pp. 111–21.

Schools and Scholars in Fourteenth-Century England (Princeton, 1987).

'Theology and Theologians from Ockham to Wyclif', in J. Catto and R. Evans (eds.), *History of the University of Oxford*, ii: *Late Medieval* (Oxford, 1992), pp. 1–34.

Craun, Edward, '*Fama* and Pastoral Constraints on Rebuking Sinners: *The Book of Margery Kempe*', in T. Fenster and D. L. Small (eds.), *Fama: The Politics of Talk and Reputation in Medieval Europe* (Ithaca, NY, 2003), pp. 187–209.

Davis, Isabel, 'Men and Margery: Negotiating Medieval Patriarchy', in Arnold and Lewis (eds.), *Companion to 'The Book of Margery Kempe'*, pp. 35–54.

De la Torre, Bartholomew R., *Thomas Buckingham and the Contingency of Futures: The Possibility of Human Freedom* (Notre Dame, IN, 1987).

Deanesly, Margaret, *The Lollard Bible and Other Medieval Versions* (Cambridge, 1920).

Delany, Sheila, *Chaucer's 'House of Fame': The Poetics of Skeptical Fideism* (Chicago, 1972).

Dembowski, Peter, 'Scientific Translation and Translators' Glossing in Four Medieval French Translators', in Jeanette Beer (ed.), *Translation Theory and Practice in the Middle Ages* (Kalamazoo, 1997), pp. 113–34.

Dictionnaire latin–français des auteurs chrétiens, ed. Albert Blaise (Turnhout, 1954–67).

Dillon, Janette, 'Holy Women and their Confessors or Confessors and their Holy Women? Margery Kempe and the Continental Tradition', in Rosalynn Voaden (ed.), *Prophets Abroad: The Reception of Continental Holy Women in Late-Medieval England* (Woodbridge, 1998), pp. 115–40.

Dimmick, Jeremy, James Simpson, and Nicolette Zeeman (eds.), *Images, Idolatry, and Iconoclasm in Late Medieval England* (Oxford, 2002).

Doležalová, Eva, Jan Hrdina, František Šmahel, and Zdeněk Uhlíř, 'The Reception and Criticism of Indulgences in the Late Medieval Czech Lands', in Swanson (ed.), *Promissory Notes*, pp. 101–41.

Dolnikowski, Edith Wilks, *Thomas Bradwardine: A View of Time and a Vision of Eternity in Fourteenth-Century Thought* (Leiden, 1995).

Donaghey, Brian, and Irma Taavitsainen, 'Walton's Boethius: From Manuscript to Print', *English Studies*, 80 (1999), 398–407.

Dove, Mary, *The First English Bible: The Text and Context of the Wycliffite Versions* (Cambridge, 2007).

    'Wyclif and the English Bible', in Levy (ed.), *Companion to Wyclif*, pp. 365–406.

Doyle, Ian, 'Reflections on Some Manuscripts of Nicholas Love's *Myrrour of the Blessed Lyf of Jesu Christ*', *Leeds Studies in English*, n.s. 14 (1983), 82–93.

Duffy, Eamon, 'St Erkenwald: London's Cathedral Saint and his Legend', in Janet Backhouse (ed.), *The Medieval English Cathedral: Papers in Honour of Pamela Tudor-Craig* (Donington, Lincolnshire, 2003), pp. 150–67.

    The Stripping of the Altars: Traditional Religion in England, 1400–1580 (New Haven, 1994).

Eberle, Patricia, 'The Politics of Courtly Style at the Court of Richard II', in Glyn Burgess and Robert A. Taylor (eds.), *The Spirit of the Court: Selected Proceedings of the Fourth Congress of the International Courtly Literature Society* (Cambridge, 1985), pp. 168–78.

Echard, Siân, 'Glossing Gower: In English, in Latin, and *in absentia*: The Case of Bodleian Ashmole 35', in R. F. Yeager (ed.), *John Gower: Recent Readings* (Asheville, NC, 1998), pp. 237–56.

Elliott, Dyan, 'Lollardy and the Integrity of Marriage and the Family', in Sherry Roush and Cristelle L. Baskins (eds.), *The Medieval Marriage Scene: Prudence, Passion, Policy* (Tempe, AZ, 2005), pp. 37–54.

    'Response to Alfred Thomas's "*The Wycliffite Woman*: Reading Women in Fifteenth-Century Bohemia"', in Linda Olson and Kathryn Kerby-Fulton (eds.), *Voices in Dialogue: Reading Women in the Middle Ages* (Notre Dame, IN, 2005), pp. 302–5.

    Spiritual Marriage: Sexual Abstinence in Medieval Wedlock (Princeton, 1993).

Evans, Robert C., 'Nashe's "Choise" and Chaucer's Pardoner', *American Notes and Queries*, 9.4 (1996), 21–4.

Farmer, David, *The Oxford Dictionary of Saints*, 4th edn (Oxford, 1997).

Ferzoco, George, *Il murale di Massa Marittima / The Massa Marittima Mural*, Toscana Studies, 1 (Florence, 2004).

Finucane, Ronald C., *Miracles and Pilgrims: Popular Beliefs in Medieval England* (London, 1977).

    The Rescue of the Innocents: Endangered Children in Medieval Miracles (New York, 1997).

Fleming, John V., 'Chaucer and Erasmus on the Pilgrimage to Canterbury: An Iconographical Speculation', in Thomas J. Heffernan (ed.), *The Popular Literature of Medieval England* (Knoxville, 1985), pp. 148–66.

Forrest, Ian, *The Detection of Heresy in Late Medieval England* (Oxford, 2005).

Frank, Robert W., *'Piers Plowman' and the Scheme of Salvation* (New Haven, 1957).

Franz, David O., *Festum voluptatis: A Study of Renaissance Erotica* (Columbus, OH, 1989).

Fredborg, F. M., 'Universal Grammar according to Some Twelfth-Century Grammarians', in K. Koerner, H.-J. Niederehe, and R. H. Robins (eds.), *Studies
in Medieval Linguistic Thought Dedicated to G. L. Bursill-Hall* (Amsterdam,
1980), pp. 69–84.

Furrow, Melissa, 'Unscholarly Latinity and Margery Kempe', in M. J. Toswell and
E. M. Tyler (eds.), *Studies in English Language and Literature. 'Doubt Wisely'.
Papers in Honour of E. G. Stanley* (London and New York, 1996), pp. 240–51.

Geary, Patrick, *Furta sacra: Thefts of Relics in the Central Middle Ages*, rev. edn
(Princeton, 1990).

'Sacred Commodities: The Circulation of Medieval Relics', in A. Appadurai
(ed.), *The Social Life of Things: Commodities in Cultural Perspective* (Cambridge, 1986), pp. 169–90.

Gellrich, Jesse M., *Discourse and Dominion in the Fourteenth Century: Oral Contexts
of Writing in Philosophy, Politics, and Poetry* (Princeton, 1995).

Ghosh, Kantik, *The Wycliffite Heresy: Authority and the Interpretation of Texts*
(Cambridge, 2002).

Gill, Katherine, '*Scandalia*: Controversies concerning *clausura* and Women's Religious Communities in Late Medieval Italy', in S. L. Waugh and Peter D. Diehl
(eds.), *Christendom and its Discontents: Exclusion, Persecution, and Rebellion*
(Cambridge, 1996), pp. 177–203.

Gillespie, Vincent, 'Vernacular Theology', in Paul Strohm (ed.), *Middle English*,
Oxford Twenty-First Century Approaches to Literature (Oxford, 2007),
pp. 401–20.

Gradon, Pamela, '*Trajanus Redivivus*: Another Look at Trajan in *Piers Plowman*',
in Douglas Gray and E. G. Stanley (eds.), *Middle English Studies Presented to
Norman Davis* (Oxford, 1983), pp. 95–114.

Grady, Frank, *Representing Righteous Heathens in Late Medieval England* (New
York, 2005).

Grant, Kevin (ed.), *The Art of David Dabydeen* (Leeds, 1997).

Gravelle, Sarah Stever, 'The Latin-Vernacular Question and Humanist Theory of
Language and Culture', *Journal of the History of Ideas*, 49.3 (1988), 367–86.

Gray, Douglas, *Themes and Images in the Medieval English Religious Lyric* (London,
1972).

Green, Richard Firth, 'The Pardoner's Pants (and Why They Matter)', *SAC*, 15
(1993), 131–45.

Grendler, Paul F., *Schooling in Renaissance Italy* (Baltimore, 1989).

Guichard-Tesson, F., 'Evrart de Conty, auteur de la *Glose des Echecs amoureux*', *Le
moyen français*, 8–9 (1981), 111–48.

'Le métier de traducteur et de commentateur au XIVe siècle d'après Evrart de
Conty', *Le moyen français*, 24–5 (1990), 131–67.

Gurevich, Aron, *Medieval Popular Culture: Problems of Belief and Perception*, trans.
János M. Bak and Paul A. Hollingsworth (Cambridge, 1988; repr. 1997).

Hahn, T. G., 'God's Friends: Virtuous Heathen in Later Medieval Thought and
English Literature' (Ph.D. diss., University of California at Los Angeles,
1974).

Hanna, Ralph, III, 'The Difficulty of Ricardian Prose Translation: The Case of the Lollards', *Modern Language Quarterly*, 51 (1990), 319–40.

'Langland's Ymaginatif: Images and the Limits of Poetry', in Dimmick, Simpson, and Zeeman (eds.), *Images, Idolatry, and Iconoclasm*, pp. 81–94.

London Literature, 1300–1380 (Cambridge, 2005).

'Sir Thomas Berkeley and his Patronage', *Speculum*, 64 (1989), 878–916.

'Some Commonplaces of Late Medieval Patience Discussions: An Introduction', in Schiffhorst (ed.), *The Triumph of Patience*, pp. 65–87.

William Langland (Aldershot, 1993).

Harding, Catherine D., *Guide to the Cappella del Corporale of Orvieto Cathedral* (Perugia, 2004).

Hargreaves, Henry, 'The Marginal Glosses to the Wycliffite New Testament', *Studia Neophilologica*, 33 (1961), 285–300.

'Popularising Bible Scholarship: The Role of the Wycliffite *Glossed Gospels*', in W. Lourdaux and D. Verhelst (eds.), *The Bible and Medieval Culture* (Leuven, 1979), pp. 171–89.

Harvey, Margaret, *England, Rome and the Papacy 1417–1464* (Manchester and New York, 1993).

Haskell, Ann S., *Essays on Chaucer's Saints* (The Hague and Paris, 1976).

Hexter, Ralph J., *Ovid and Medieval Schooling. Studies in Medieval School Commentaries on Ovid's 'Ars Amatoria', Epistulae ex Ponto', and 'Epistulae Heroidum'* (Munich, 1986).

Higgins, Iain Macleod, *Writing East: The 'Travels' of Sir John Mandeville* (Philadelphia, 1997).

Hollander, Robert, 'Dante and his Commentators', in Rachel Jacoff (ed.), *The Cambridge Companion to Dante* (Cambridge, 1993), pp. 226–36.

Holloway, Julia B., 'Bride, Margery, Julian, and Alice: Bridget of Sweden's Textual Community in Medieval England', in Sandra J. McEntire (ed.), *Margery Kempe: A Book of Essays*, Garland Medieval Casebooks, 4 (New York, 1992), pp. 203–22.

Hudson, Anne, 'Dangerous Fictions: Indulgences in the Thought of Wyclif and his Followers', in Swanson (ed.), *Promissory Notes*, pp. 197–214.

'The Debate on Bible Translation, Oxford 1401', in Hudson, *Lollards and their Books*, pp. 67–84.

'John Purvey: A Reconsideration of the Evidence for his Life and Writings', in Hudson, *Lollards and their Books*, pp. 85–110.

'"Laicus litteratus": The Paradox of Lollardy', in Peter Biller and Anne Hudson (eds.), *Heresy and Literacy, 1000–1530* (Cambridge, 1994), pp. 222–36.

'A Lollard Mass', in Hudson, *Lollards and their Books*, pp. 111–23.

'Lollardy: The English Heresy?', in Hudson, *Lollards and their Books*, pp. 141–63.

'A Neglected Wycliffite Text', in Hudson, *Lollards and their Books*, pp. 43–66.

'*Piers Plowman* and the Peasants' Revolt: A Problem Revisited', *The Yearbook of Langland Studies*, 8 (1994), 85–106.

'The Problems of Scribes: The Trial Records of William Swinderby and Walter Brut', *Nottingham Medieval Studies*, 49 (2005), 80–104.

'Some Aspects of Lollard Book Production', repr. in Hudson, *Lollards and their Books*, pp. 181–91.

'Wyclif and the English Language', in Anthony Kenny (ed.), *Wyclif in his Times* (Oxford, 1986), pp. 85–103.

Hudson, Anne, and H. L. Spencer, 'Old Author, New Work: The Sermons of MS Longleat 4', *Medium Ævum*, 53 (1984), 220–38.

Hurley, M., '*Scriptura sola*: Wyclif and his Critics', *Traditio*, 16 (1960), 275–352.

Hyams, Paul, 'The Strange Case of Thomas of Elderfield', *History Today*, 36.6 (1986), 9–15.

James, M. R., 'Lives of St Walstan', *Norfolk Archaeology*, 19 (1917), 238–67.

Jansen, Katherine L., *The Making of the Magdalen: Preaching and Popular Devotion in the Later Middle Ages* (Princeton, 2000).

Javitch, Daniel, *Proclaiming a Classic: The Canonization of 'Orlando Furioso'* (Princeton, NJ, 1991).

Johnson, Ian, 'The Late-Medieval Theory and Practice of Translation with Special Reference to Some Middle English Lives of Christ' (Ph.D. thesis, University of Bristol, 1990).

'New Evidence for the Authorship of Walton's Boethius', *Notes and Queries*, n.s. 43 (1996), 19–21.

'Placing Walton's Boethius', in Lodi Nauta and Maarten J. F. M. Hoenen (eds.), *Boethius in the Middle Ages: Latin and Vernacular Traditions of the 'Consolatio Philosophiae'* (Leiden, 1997), pp. 217–42.

'Walton's Sapient Orpheus', in Alastair Minnis (ed.), *The Medieval Boethius: Studies in the Vernacular Translations of 'De Consolatione Philosophiae'* (Woodbridge, 1987), pp. 139–68.

Jones, Malcolm, *The Secret Middle Ages: Discovering the Real Medieval World* (Trupp, Stroud, Gloucestershire, 2002).

Jurkowski, Maureen, 'New Light on John Purvey', *English Historical Review*, 110 (1995), 1180–90.

Karnes, Michelle, 'Nicholas Love and Medieval Meditations on Christ', *Speculum*, 82.2 (2007), 380–408.

Kaulbach, Ernest, *Imaginative Prophecy in the b-text of 'Piers Plowman'* (Cambridge, 1993).

Keen, Maurice, 'Wyclif, the Bible, and Transubstantiation', in Anthony Kenny (ed.), *Wyclif in his Times* (Oxford, 1986), pp. 1–16.

Keightley, Ronald G., 'Alfonso de Madrigal and the *Cronici canones* of Eusebius', *Journal of Medieval and Renaissance Studies*, 7 (1977), 225–48.

Keiper, Hugo, Christoph Bode, and Richard J. Utz (eds.), *Nominalism and Literary Discourse: New Perspectives* (Amsterdam and Atlanta, GA, 1997).

Kennedy, William J., *Authorizing Petrarch* (Ithaca and London, 1994).

Kieckhefer, Richard, *Unquiet Souls: Fourteenth-Century Saints and their Religious Milieu* (Chicago and London, 1984).

Klocker, H. R., 'Ockham and the Divine Freedom', *Franciscan Studies*, 45 (1985), 245–61.

Knapp, Daniel, 'The Relyk of a Seint: A Gloss on Chaucer's Pilgrimage', *English Literary History*, 39.1 (1972), 1–26.

Knowles, M. D., 'The Censured Opinions of Uthred of Boldon', *Proceedings of the British Academy*, 37 (1951), 306–42.

Koldeweij, A. M., 'A Barefaced *Roman de la Rose* (Paris, B.N., ms. Fr. 25526) and Some Late Medieval Mass-Produced Badges of a Sexual Nature', in M. Smeyers and B. Cardon (eds.), *Flanders in a European Perspective* (Leuven, 1995), pp. 499–516.

'Lifting the Veil on Pilgrim Badges', in J. Stopford (ed.), *Pilgrimage Explored* (Woodbridge, 1999), pp. 161–88.

'"Shameless and Naked Images": Obscene Badges as Parodies of Popular Devotion', in Blick and Tekippe (eds.), *Art and Architecture of Late Medieval Pilgrimage*, pp. 493–510.

Kruger, Steven, 'Claiming the Pardoner: Toward a Gay Reading of Chaucer's Pardoner's Tale', *Exemplaria*, 6 (1994), 115–39.

Lahey, Stephen E., *Philosophy and Politics in the Thought of John Wyclif* (Cambridge, 2003).

Lambert, Malcolm, *Medieval Heresy: Popular Movements from the Gregorian Reform to the Reformation*, 3rd edn (Oxford, 2002).

Lawler, Traugott, 'The Pardon Formula in *Piers Plowman*: Its Ubiquity, Its Binary Shape, Its Silent Middle Term', *The Yearbook of Langland Studies*, 14 (2000), 117–52.

Le Goff, Jacques, *The Birth of Purgatory*, trans. Arthur Goldhammer (London, 1984).

Time, Work and Culture in the Middle Ages, trans. Arthur Goldhammer (Chicago, 1986).

Lea, Henry Charles, *A History of Auricular Confession and Indulgences in the Latin Church* (1896; repr. New York, 1968).

Leclercq, Jean, 'Le magistère du prédicateur au XIIIe siècle', *Archives d'histoire doctrinale et littéraire du Moyen Âge*, 21 (1946), 105–47.

Lee, Jennifer M., 'Searching for Signs: Pilgrims' Identity and Experience made Visible in the *Miracula Sancti Thomae Cantuariensis*', in Blick and Tekippe (eds.), *Art and Architecture of Late Medieval Pilgrimage*, pp. 473–91.

Leff, Gordon, *Bradwardine and the Pelagians* (Cambridge, 1957).

William of Ockham: The Metamorphosis of Scholastic Discourse (Manchester, 1975).

Leicester, H. Marshall, Jr, *The Disenchanted Self: Representing the Subject in the Canterbury Tales* (Berkeley, 1990).

Lerner, Robert E., *The Heresy of the Free Spirit in the Later Middle Ages* (Berkeley and Los Angeles, 1972).

Levy, Ian Christopher, 'John Wyclif's Neoplatonic View of Scripture in its Christological Context', *Medieval Philosophy and Theology*, 11 (2003), 227–240.

'Was John Wyclif's Theology of the Eucharist Donatistic?', *Scottish Journal of Theology*, 53 (2000), 137–53.

'Wyclif and the Christian Life', in Levy (ed.), *Companion to Wyclif*, pp. 293–363.

Lewis, C. T., and C. Short (eds.), *A Latin Dictionary* (Oxford, impression of 1975).

Lindberg, Conrad, *A Manual of the Wyclif Bible, including the Psalms. Dedicated to the Memory of Sven L. Fristedt* (Stockholm, 2007).

Lochrie, Karma, *Margery Kempe and Translations of the Flesh* (Philadelphia, 1991).

Lucas, Peter J., 'An Englishman in Rome: Capgrave's 1450-Jubilee Guide, *The Solace of Pilgrimes*', in Anne Marie D'Arcy and Alan J. Fletcher (eds.), *Studies in Late Medieval and Early Renaissance Texts in Honour of John Scattergood* (Dublin, 2005), pp. 201–17.

Lutton, Robert, *Lollardy and Orthodox Religion in Pre-Reformation England: Reconstructing Piety* (Woodbridge, 2006).

McAlpine, Monica, 'The Pardoner's Homosexuality and How it Matters', *Publications of the Modern Language Association of America*, 95 (1980), 8–22.

McDonald, Nicola (ed.), *Medieval Obscenities* (York and Woodbridge, 2006).

McEntire, Sandra J., *The Doctrine of Compunction in Medieval England: Holy Tears* (Lewiston, 1990).

McFarlane, K. B., *John Wycliffe and the Beginnings of English Nonconformity* (London, 1952).

Lancastrian Kings and Lollard Knights (Oxford, 1972).

McGinn, Bernard, 'Meister Eckhart and the Beguines in the Context of Vernacular Theology', in McGinn (ed.), *Meister Eckhart and the Beguine Mystics: Hadewijch of Brabant, Mechthild of Magdeburg, and Marguerite Porete* (New York, 1994), pp. 4–14.

McLeod, Susan H., 'The Tearing of the Pardon in *Piers Plowman*', *Philological Quarterly*, 56 (1977), 14–26.

McSheffrey, Shannon, *Gender and Heresy: Women and Men in Lollard Communities, 1420–1530* (Philadelphia, 1995).

Macy, Gary, *The Hidden History of Women's Ordination: Female Clergy in the Medieval West* (New York, 2007).

Malo, Robyn, 'The Pardoner's Relics (and Why They Matter the Most)', *ChR*, 43.1 (2008), 83–103.

'Saints' Relics in Medieval Literature' (Ph.D. diss., Ohio State University, Columbus, OH, 2007).

Manierù, Alfonso, 'The Philosophy of Language', in Giulio Lepschy (ed.), *History of Linguistics, II: Classical and Medieval Linguistics* (London and New York, 1994), pp. 272–315.

Manly, John M., and Edith Rickert, *The Text of the Canterbury Tales* (Chicago, 1940).

Marcett, M. E., *Uthred de Boldon, Friar William Jordan and Piers Plowman* (New York, 1938).

Matray, B., 'Les indulgences au XIVe siècle: étude des lettres de Jean XXII (1316–1334) et d'Urbain V (1363–1370)', *Cahiers d'histoire*, 33.2 (1988), 135–51.

Mazzocco, Angelo, *Linguistic Theories in Dante and the Humanists: Studies of Language and Intellectual History in Late Medieval and Early Renaissance Italy* (Leiden, 1993).

Medcalf, Stephen, 'Inner and Outer', in Medcalf (ed.), *The Context of English Literature: The Later Middle Ages* (London, 1981), pp. 108–71.

Mellinkoff, Ruth, *Averting Demons: The Protective Power of Medieval Visual Motifs and Themes* (Los Angeles, 2004).

Michael, M. A., *Stained Glass of Canterbury Cathedral* (London, 2004).

Minnis, Alastair, 'Affection and Imagination in *The Cloud of Unknowing* and Walter Hilton's *Scale of Perfection*', *Traditio*, 39 (1983), 323–66.

'*Amor* and *Auctoritas* in the Self-Commentary of Dante and Francesco da Barberino', *Poetica* [Tokyo], 32 (1990), 25–42.

'Aspects of the Medieval French and English Traditions of Boethius' *De Consolatione Philosophiae*', in M. T. Gibson (ed.), *Boethius: His Life, Thought and Influence* (Oxford, 1981), pp. 312–61.

'"Authorial Intention" and "Literal Sense" in the Exegetical Theories of Richard FitzRalph and John Wyclif', *Proceedings of the Royal Irish Academy*, 75, section c, no. 1 (Dublin, 1975).

Chaucer and Pagan Antiquity (Cambridge, 1982).

'Fifteenth-Century Versions of Literalism: Girolamo Savonarola and Alfonso de Madrigal', in Robert Lerner (ed.), *Neue Richtungen in der hoch- und spätmittelalterlichen Bibelexegese*, Schriften des Historischen Kollegs Kolloquien, 32 (Munich, 1996), pp. 163–80.

'John Wyclif – All Women's Friend?', in Bonnie Wheeler (ed.), *Mindful Spirit in Late Medieval Literature: Essays in Honor of Elizabeth D. Kirk* (Houndmills, 2006), pp. 121–33.

'Langland's Ymaginatif and Late-Medieval Theories of Imagination', *Comparative Criticism*, 3 (1981), 71–103.

Magister amoris: The 'Roman de la Rose' and Vernacular Hermeneutics (Oxford, 2001).

'From Medieval to Renaissance? Chaucer's Position on Past Gentility', *Proceedings of the British Academy*, 72 (1986), 205–46.

Medieval Theory of Authorship: Scholastic Literary Attitudes in the Later Middle Ages, 2nd edn (Aldershot, 1988).

'Medium and Message: Henry of Ghent on Scriptural Style', in Richard Newhauser and John A. Alford (eds.), *Literature and Religion in the Later Middle Ages: Philological Studies in Honor of Siegfried Wenzel* (Binghamton, NY, 1995), pp. 209–35.

Oxford Guides to Chaucer: The Shorter Poems (Oxford, 1995).

'Purchasing Pardon: Material and Spiritual Economies on the Canterbury Pilgrimage', in Lawrence Besserman (ed.), *Sacred and Secular in Medieval and Early Modern Cultures* (Houndmills, 2006), pp. 63–82.

'*Respondet Walterus Bryth*... Walter Brut in Debate on Women Priests', in Helen Barr and Ann M. Hutchinson (eds.), *Text and Controversy from Wyclif to Bale: Essays in Honour of Anne Hudson*, Medieval Church Studies, 4 (Turnhout, 2005), pp. 229–49.

'*I speke of folk in seculer estaat*: Vernacularity and Secularity in the Age of Chaucer', *SAC*, 27 (2005), 25–58.

Minnis, Alastair (ed.), *Chaucer's 'Boece' and the Medieval Tradition of Boethius* (Woodbridge, 1993).

Minnis, Alastair, and A. B. Scott with David Wallace (eds.), *Medieval Literary Theory and Criticism, c. 1100–c. 1375: The Commentary Tradition.* rev. edn (Oxford, 1991; repr. 2001).

Mitchener, M., *Medieval Pilgrim and Secular Badges* (London, 1986).

Molteni, Paolo, *Roberto Holcot O.P., Dottrina della grazia e della giustificazione, con due questioni quodlibetali inedite* (Pinerolo, 1967).

Moonan, Lawrence, *Divine Power: The Medieval Power Distinction up to its Adoption by Albert, Bonaventure, and Aquinas* (Oxford, 1994).

Mooney, Catherine M. (ed.), *Gendered Voices: Medieval Saints and their Interpreters* (Philadelphia, 1999).

Morris, Colin, and Peter Roberts (eds.), *Pilgrimage: The English Experience from Becket to Bunyan* (Cambridge, 2002).

Morrison, Susan Signe, *Women Pilgrims in Late-Medieval England: Private Piety and Public Performance* (London, 2000).

Nilson, Ben, *Cathedral Shrines of Medieval England* (Woodbridge, 1998).

Nolan, Barbara, *Chaucer and the Tradition of the 'Roman Antique'* (Cambridge, 1992).

Nolan, Mary Lee, and Sidney Nolan, *Christian Pilgrimage in Modern Western Europe* (Chapel Hill and London, 1989).

Norton, Christopher, *St William of York* (York and Woodbridge, 2006).

Oberman, H. A., *The Harvest of Medieval Theology. Gabriel Biel and Late Medieval Nominalism*, rev. edn (Grand Rapids, MI, 1967).

Olson, Glending, *Literature as Recreation in the Middle Ages* (Ithaca, NY, 1982).

O'Mara, Philip F., 'Robert Holcot's "Ecumenism" and the Green Knight', *ChR*, 26.4 (1992), 329–42, and 'Holcot and the *Pearl*-Poet', *ChR*, 27.1 (1992), 97–106.

Ong, Walter, 'Orality, Literacy, and Medieval Textualization', *New Literary History*, 16 (1984–5), 1–12.

Osborn, Marijane, 'Transgressive Word and Image in Chaucer's Enshrined *coillons* Passage', *ChR*, 37.4 (2003), 365–84.

Ouy, Gilbert, 'Humanism and Nationalism in France at the Turn of the Fifteenth Century', in B. P. McGuire (ed.), *The Birth of Identities: Denmark and Europe in the Middle Ages* (Copenhagen, 1996), pp. 107–25.

Owst, G. R., *The 'Destructorium viciorum' of Alexander Carpenter* (London, 1952).

Pantin, W. A., 'John of Wales and Medieval Humanism', in *Medieval Studies Presented to Aubrey Gwynn* (Dublin, 1961), pp. 297–319.

Partner, N. F., 'Reading *The Book of Margery Kempe*', *Exemplaria*, 3 (1991), 29–66.

Partridge, Stephen, 'Glosses in the Manuscripts of Chaucer's *Canterbury Tales*: An Edition and Commentary' (Ph.D. diss., Harvard University, 1992).

Patterson, Lee, 'Chaucer's Pardoner on the Couch: Psyche and Clio in Medieval Literary Studies', *Speculum*, 76 (2001), 638–80.

Paulus, Nikolaus, 'Die Anfänge des sogenannten Ablasses von Schuld und Strafe', *Zeitschrift für katholische Theologie*, 36 (1912), 67–96.

Payer, Pierre J., *The Bridling of Desire: Views of Sex in the Later Middle Ages* (Toronto and London, 1993).

Pearsall, Derek, 'Gower's Latin in the *Confessio amantis*', in Alastair Minnis (ed.), *Latin and Vernacular: Studies in Late-Medieval Texts and Manuscripts* (Cambridge, 1989), pp. 13–25.

Peck, Russell, 'Chaucer and the Nominalist Questions', *Speculum*, 53 (1978), 745–60.

Pelzer, A., 'Les 51 articles de Guillaume Occam censurés en Avignon en 1326', *Revue d'histoire ecclésiastique*, 18 (1922), 240–71.

Penn, Stephen, 'Sacraments', in Levy (ed.), *Companion to John Wyclif*, pp. 241–91.

Petersen, K. O., *Sources of the Nonnes Preestes Tale*, Radcliffe College Monographs, 10 (Boston, 1896).

Poupin, Roland, *Les Cathares, l'Âme et la Réincarnation* (Portet-sur-Garonne, 2000).

Pratt, R. A., 'Some Latin Sources of the Nonnes Preest on Dreams', *Speculum*, 52 (1977), 538–70.

Quilligan, Maureen, *The Allegory of Female Authority: Christine de Pizan's 'Cité des dames'* (Ithaca, 1991).

Radford, V. M., 'The Wax Images Found in Exeter Cathedral', *Antiquaries Journal*, 29 (1949), 164–8.

Randi, Eugenio, *Il sovrano e l'orologiaio. Due immagini di Dio nel dibattito sulla 'potentia absoluta' fra XIII e XIV secolo* (Florence, 1987).

Rawcliffe, Carole, 'Curing Bodies and Healing Souls: Pilgrimage and the Sick in Medieval East Anglia', in Morris and Roberts (eds.), *Pilgrimage*, pp. 108–40.

Resnick, Irven M., 'Marriage in Medieval Culture: Consent Theory and the Case of Mary and Joseph', *Church History*, 69.2 (2000), 350–71.

Rex, Richard, *The Lollards* (Houndmills, Basingstoke, Hampshire, 2002).

Reynolds, Philip Lyndon, *Food and the Body: Some Peculiar Questions in High Medieval Theology* (Leiden, 1999).

Rhodes, Jim, *Poetry Does Theology: Chaucer, Grosseteste, and the 'Pearl'-Poet* (Notre Dame, IN, 2001).

Rice, Nicole, *Lay Piety and Religious Discipline in Middle English Literature* (Cambridge, 2008).

Riddy, Felicity, 'Publication before Print: The Case of Julian of Norwich', in Julia Crick and Alexandra Walsham (eds.), *The Uses of Script and Print, 1300–1700* (Cambridge, 2003), pp. 29–49.

'"Women Talking about the Things of God": A Late Medieval Sub-Culture', in Carol M. Meale (ed.) *Women and Literature in Britain, 1150–1500* (Cambridge, 1993), pp. 104–27.

Rider, Catherine, *Magic and Impotence in the Middle Ages* (Oxford, 2006).

Rigg, George, *A History of Anglo-Latin Literature 1066–1422* (Cambridge, 1992).

Robson, J. A., *Wyclif and the Oxford Schools* (Cambridge, 1966).

Rogers, E. F., *Peter Lombard and the Sacramental System* (New York, 1976).

Russell, G. H., 'The Salvation of the Heathen: The Exploration of a Theme in *Piers Plowman*', *Journal of the Warburg and Courtauld Institutes*, 29 (1966), 101–16.

'Some Aspects of the Process of Revision in *Piers Plowman*', in S. S. Hussey (ed.), *Piers Plowman: Critical Approaches* (London, 1969), pp. 27–49.

Sahlin, Claire L., *Birgitta of Sweden and the Voice of Prophecy* (Woodbridge, 2001).

'The Prophetess as Preacher: Birgitta of Sweden and the Voice of Prophecy', *Medieval Sermon Studies*, 40 (1997), 29–44.

St-Jacques, R. C., 'The *Middle English Glossed Prose Psalter* and its French Source', in Beer (ed.), *Medieval Translators and their Craft*, pp. 135–54.

Sanchis, Pierre, 'The Portuguese "romarias"', in Wilson (ed.), *Saints and their Cults*, pp. 261–89.

Sandler, Lucy Freeman, *Omne bonum: A Fourteenth-Century Encyclopedia of Universal Knowledge* (London, 1996).

Saul, Nigel, *Richard II* (New Haven and London, 1997).

Scase, Wendy, *Reginald Pecock*, English Writers of the Late Middle Ages, vol. 3, no. 8 (Aldershot, 1996).

Schiffhorst, Gerald J. (ed.), *The Triumph of Patience: Medieval and Renaissance Studies* (Orlando, FL, 1978).

Schmidt, J.-C., '"Religion populaire" et culture folklorique', *Annales ESC*, 31 (1976), 141–53.

Seguin, Jean, *Saints guérisseurs, saints imaginaires, dévotions populaires*, 2nd edn (Paris, 1943).

Sered, Susan Starr, 'Rachel's Tomb and the Milk Grotto of the Virgin Mary: Two Women's Shrines in Bethlehem', *Journal of Feminist Studies in Religion*, 2.2 (1986), 7–22.

Shaffern, Robert W., 'Images, Jurisdiction, and the Treasury of Merit', *Journal of Medieval History*, 22.3 (1996), 237–47.

'A New Canonistic Text on Indulgences: *De quantitate indulgenciarum* of John of Dambach O.P. (1288–1372)', *Bulletin of Medieval Canon Law*, n.s. 21 (1991), 25–45.

The Penitents' Treasury: Indulgences in Latin Christendom, 1175–1375 (Scranton, PA, and London, 2007).

Sherman, C. R., *Imaging Aristotle: Verbal and Visual Representation in Fourteenth-Century France* (Berkeley and Los Angeles, 1995).

'Les thèmes humanistes dans le programme de traduction de Charles V: compilation des textes et illustrations', in Monique Ornato and Nicole Pons (eds.), *Pratiques de la culture écrite en France au XVe siècle: Actes du Colloque International du CNRS, Paris, 16–18 mai 1992*, Textes et études du Moyen Âge, 2 (Louvain-La-Neuve, 1995), pp. 527–37.

Shinners, John (ed.), *Medieval Popular Religion* (Peterborough, Ont., 1997).

Shklar, Ruth, 'Chobham's Daughter: *The Book of Margery Kempe* and the Power of Heterodox Thinking', *Modern Language Quarterly*, 56.3 (1995), 277–304.

Simpson, James, *The Oxford English Literary History*, II: *1350–1547. Reform and Cultural Revolution* (Oxford, 2002).

Piers Plowman: An Introduction to the B-Text (London and New York, 1990).

'Saving Satire after Arundel's *Constitutions*: John Audelay's "Marcol and Solomon"', in Barr and Hutchinson (eds.), *Text and Controversy*, pp. 387–404.

Sledd, James, 'Canterbury Tales, C 310, 320: "By Seint Ronyan"', *Mediaeval Studies*, 13 (1951), 226–33.

Smalley, Beryl, 'The Bible and Eternity: John Wyclif's Dilemma', *Journal of the Warburg and Courtauld Institutes*, 27 (1964), 73–89.

English Friars and Antiquity in the Early Fourteenth Century (Oxford, 1960).

Snoek, G. J. C., *Medieval Piety from Relics to the Eucharist: A Process of Mutual Interaction* (Leiden and New York, 1995).

Somerset, Fiona, '*Eciam mulier*: Women in Lollardy and the Problem of Sources', in Linda Olson and Kathryn Kerby-Fulton (eds.), *Voices in Dialogue: Reading Women in the Middle Ages* (Notre Dame, IN, 2005), pp. 245–60.

Southern, R. W., *The Making of the Middle Ages* (London and New York, 1953).

Spalding, Mary Caroline, *The Middle English Charters of Christ* (Bryn Mawr, PA, 1914).

Spencer, Brian, *Pilgrim Souvenirs and Secular Badges: Medieval Finds from Excavations in London* (London, 1998).

Steinberg, Leo, *The Sexuality of Christ in Renaissance Art and in Modern Oblivion*, 2nd edn (Chicago and London, 1996).

Steiner, Emily, *Documentary Culture and the Making of Medieval English Literature* (Cambridge, 2003).

'Langland's Documents', *Yearbook of Langland Studies*, 14 (2000), 95–107.

Stokes, C. S., 'Margery Kempe: Her Life and the Early History of her Book', *Mystics Quarterly*, 25 (1999), 9–68.

Stone, L. W., W. Rothwell *et al.* (eds.), *Anglo-Norman Dictionary* (London, 1977).

Streveler, Paul A., and Katherine H. Tachau (eds.), *Robert Holcot: Seeing the Future Clearly. Questions on Future Contingents* (Toronto, 1995).

Sumption, Jonathan, *Pilgrimage: An Image of Medieval Religion* (Totowa, NJ, 1976).

Sutherland, Annie, '*The Chastising of God's Children*: A Neglected Text', in Barr and Hutchinson (eds.), *Text and Controversy*, pp. 353–73.

Swanson, R. N., 'Letters of Confraternity and Indulgence in Late Medieval England', *Archives: The Journal of the British Records Association*, 25.102 (2000), 40–57.

'Treasuring Merit/Craving Indulgence: Accounting for Salvation in Pre-Reformation England', inaugural lecture, University of Birmingham (Birmingham, 2003).

Swanson, R. N. (ed.), *Promissory Notes on the Treasury of Merits: Indulgences in Late Medieval Europe* (Leiden and Boston, 2006).

Szittya, Penn R., *The Antifraternal Tradition in Medieval Literature* (Princeton, NJ, 1986).

Tachau, Katherine H., *Vision and Certitude in the Age of Ockham: Optics, Epistemology, and the Foundations of Semantics, 1250–1345* (Leiden and New York, 1988).

Tatton-Brown, Tim, 'Canterbury and the Architecture of Pilgrimage Shrines in England', in Morris and Roberts (eds.), *Pilgrimage*, pp. 90–107.

Thomson, J. A. F., *The Later Lollards, 1414–1520* (London, 1965).

Tobier, Adolf, and Erhard Lommatzsch (eds.), *Altfranzösisches Wörterbuch* (Berlin and Wiesbaden, 1925–2002).

Tupper, Frederick, 'Chaucer's Sinners and Sins', *Journal of English and Germanic Philology*, 15 (1916), 56–106.

'The Quarrels of the Canterbury Pilgrims', *Journal of English and Germanic Philology*, 14 (1915), 256–70.

Twycross, Meg, *The Medieval Anadyomene: A Study in Chaucer's Mythography*, Medium Ævum Monographs, n.s. 1 (Oxford, 1972).

Utz, Richard J. (ed.), *Literary Nominalism and the Theory of Rereading Late Medieval Texts* (Lewiston and Queenston, 1995).

Utz, Richard J., and William H. Watts, 'Nominalist Perspectives on Chaucer's Poetry: A Bibliographical Essay', *Mediaevalia et humanistica*, n.s. 20 (1993), 147–73.

Van Beuningen, H. J. E., and A. M. Koldeweij (eds.), *Heilig en Profann. 1000 Laat-middeleeuwse insignes uit de collectie H. J. E. Van Beuningen* (Cothen, 1993).

Van Beuningen, H. J. E., A. M. Koldeweij, and D. Kicken (eds.), *Heilig en Profann 2. 1200 Laat-middeleeuwse insignes uit openbare en particuliere collecties* (Cothen, 2001).

Van Eickels, Klaus, 'Gendered Violence: Castration and Blinding as Punishment for Treason in Normandy and Anglo-Norman England', *Gender and History*, 16.3 (2004), 588–602.

Van Os, Henk, *The Way to Heaven: Relic Veneration in the Middle Ages* (Baarn, 2000).

Vandussen, Michael, 'Betokening Chastity: Margery Kempe's Sartorial Crisis', *Forum for Modern Language Studies*, 41.3 (2005), 275–88.

Vauchez, André, *Sainthood in the Later Middle Ages*, trans. Jane Birrell (Cambridge, 1997).

Vincent, Nicholas, *The Holy Blood: King Henry III and the Westminster Blood Relic* (Cambridge, 2001).

Voaden, Rosalynn, *God's Words, Women's Voices. The Discernment of Spirits in the Writings of Late-Medieval Women Visionaries* (Woodbridge, 1999).

Wallace, David, '*Cleanness* and the Terms of Terror', in R. J. Blanch, M. Miller and J. Wasserman (eds.), *Text and Matter: New Critical Perspectives of the 'Pearl'-Poet* (Troy, NY, 1991), pp. 93–104.

Watson, Nicholas, 'Censorship and Cultural Change in Late Medieval England: Vernacular Theology, the Oxford Translation Debate and Arundel's *Constitutions* of 1409', *Speculum*, 70 (1996), 822–64.

'Conceptions of the Word: The Mother Tongue and the Incarnation of God', *New Medieval Literatures*, 1 (1997), 85–124.

'"Et que est huius ydoli materia? Tuipse": Idols and Images in Walter Hilton', in Dimmick, Simpson, and Zeeman (eds.), *Images, Idolatry, and Iconoclasm*, pp. 95–111.

'The *Gawain*-Poet as a Vernacular Theologian', in Brewer and Gibson (eds.), *A Companion to the 'Gawain'-Poet*, pp. 293–313.

'The Middle English Mystics', in David Wallace (ed.), *The Cambridge History of Medieval English Literature* (Cambridge, 1999), pp. 539–65.

'Visions of Inclusion: Universal Salvation and Vernacular Theology in Pre-Reformation England', *Journal of Medieval and Early Modern Studies*, 27.2 (1997), 145–87.

Webb, Diana, *Pilgrims and Pilgrimage in the Medieval West* (London and New York, 1999).

Weiss, Julian, *The Poet's Art: Literary Theory in Castile, c. 1400–60*, Medium Ævum Monographs, n.s. 14 (1990).

Whatley, Gordon, 'Heathens and Saints: *St Erkenwald* in its Legendary Context', *Speculum*, 61.2 (1986), 330–63.

'*Piers Plowman* B 12.277–94: Notes on Language, Text, and Theology', *Modern Philology*, 82 (1984), 1–12.

'The Uses of Hagiography: The Legend of Pope Gregory and the Emperor Trajan in the Middle Ages', *Viator*, 15 (1984), 25–63.

Wilks, Michael, 'Misleading Manuscripts: Wyclif and the Non-Wycliffite Bible', *Studies in Church History*, 11 (1975), 147–61.

'Predestination, Property, and Power: Wyclif's Theory of Dominion and Grace', in Wilks, *Wyclif: Political Ideas and Practice*, ed. Anne Hudson (Oxford, 2000), pp. 16–32.

'Wyclif and the Great Persecution', in Michael Wilks (ed.), *Studies in Church History*, Subsidia 10: Prophecy and Eschatology (Oxford, 1994), pp. 39–63.

Willard, C. C., 'Raoul de Presles's Translation of Saint Augustine's *De civitate Dei*', in Beer (ed.), *Medieval Translators and their Craft*, pp. 329–46.

Wilson, Stephen, 'Cults of Saints in the Churches of Central Paris', in Wilson (ed.), *Saints and their Cults*, pp. 233–60.

Wilson, Stephen (ed.), *Saints and their Cults: Studies in Religious Sociology, Folklore and History* (Cambridge, 1983).

Wogan-Browne, Jocelyn, Nicholas Watson, Andrew Taylor, and Ruth Evans (eds.), *The Idea of the Vernacular: An Anthology of Middle English Literary Theory, 1280–1520* (University Park, PA, 1999).

Wood, Diana, *Clement VI: The Pontificate and Ideas of an Avignon Pope* (Cambridge, 1989).

Wood, Rega, 'Ockham's Repudiation of Pelagianism', in P. V. Spade (ed.), *The Cambridge Companion to Ockham* (Cambridge, 1999), pp. 350–73.

Woolf, Rosemary, *The English Religious Lyric in the Middle Ages* (Oxford, 1968).

Wright, Roger, *Late Latin and Early Romance in Spain and Carolingian France* (Liverpool, 1982).

A Sociophilological Study of Late Latin, Utrecht Studies in Medieval Literacy, 10 (Turnhout, 2002).

Wright, Thomas, 'The Worship of the Generative Powers during the Middle Ages of Western Europe', published as the second part of R. P. Knight and T. Wright, *Discourse on the Worship of Priapus, and its Connection with the*

Nuptic Theology of the Ancients, to Which Is Added an Essay on the Worship of the Generative Powers during the Middle Ages of Western Europe (London, 1865).

Yeager, R. F., 'English, Latin, and the Text as "Other": The Page as Sign in the Work of John Gower', *Text*, 3 (1987), 251–67.

— '"Oure englisshe" and Everyone's Latin: The *Fasciculus morum* and Gower's *Confessio amantis*', *South Atlantic Review*, 46 (1981), 41–53.

Index

266